Introduction to Sport Marketing

Now in a fully revised and updated third edition, *Introduction to Sport Marketing* is a clear, straightforward, and concise introduction to the theory and practice of sport marketing, and the only sport marketing textbook you will ever need.

Built around a step-by-step framework for developing effective sport marketing plans, and full of real-world, international cases, data, and examples, the text helps students to develop the essential skills and subject knowledge required to thrive in today's fast-paced sport industry. It covers sport marketing at all levels, from grassroots and community sport to international mega-events, and across all sectors from professional sport to public and not-for-profit organisations. Leading the reader through the marketing process, from analysis and setting a strategy to planning the marketing mix, implementation, and evaluation, the text introduces the products, services, distribution channels, and stakeholders that generate value, including brands, merchandise and licensed products, players and athletes, leagues and franchises, and events. This new edition includes expanded coverage of cutting-edge topics, including social media, digital sport marketing, esports, the social impact of sport, 'sportwashing' and soft power, innovation and fast prototyping, consumer psychology, and diversity and equity. It includes useful features throughout, from review questions to guides to further resources.

This is an essential textbook for any sport marketing course taken as a part of a degree programme in sport management, sport marketing, sport business, sport development, or business, management, and marketing.

Aaron C.T. Smith is Professor and Director of the University of Canberra Research Institute for Sport and Exercise (UC-RISE) in Australia, and Professor in the Institute for Sport Business at Loughborough University London, UK. Aaron works at the intersections of money and meaning, and brains and brands to explain sport performance, business innovation, fan psychology, and digital engagement.

Constantino Stavros is Professor of Marketing at RMIT University, Australia, and Deputy Dean (Learning & Teaching) in its School of Economics, Finance & Marketing. He possesses a global understanding of contemporary marketing practice, particularly in the application of strategic concepts in communication and the development and function of marketing both through, and of, sport.

James Skinner is Dean of Newcastle Business School in NSW, Australia. Prior to this appointment, he was the Director of the Institute for Sport Business, and Professor of Sport Business at Loughborough University London, UK. His research transverses both the commercial and socio-cultural contributions and challenges of sport. His current research centres on the global political economy of sport and role of sport in shaping and reshaping a nation's identity and building its brand.

Andrea N. Geurin is Professor in Sport Business at Loughborough University London, UK, where she also serves as the Director of the Institute for Sport Business. Her research focuses primarily on athletes' and sport organisations' use of social and digital media as a marketing communication tool. In 2023, she was honoured with the North American Society for Sport Management's (NASSM) inaugural Distinguished Research Award, recognising her outstanding contributions to the field of sport management. She currently serves as an Associate Editor for *European Sport Management Quarterly* and *Managing Sport and Leisure*.

Lauren M. Burch is Senior Lecturer in the Institute for Sport Business at Loughborough University London, UK. She also serves as the Programme Director for MSc in Sport Analytics and Technologies. Her current research interests focus on the examination of discourse and sentiment within content on social media, specifically focusing on online abuse from a racial or gendered perspective in sport.

Sport Management Series

Series Editor: Russell Hoye, La Trobe University, Australia

This **Sport Management Series** has been providing a range of texts for core subjects in undergraduate sport business and management courses around the world for more than 10 years. These textbooks are considered essential resources for academics, students and managers seeking an international perspective on the management of the complex world of sport.

Many millions of people around the globe are employed in sport organisations in areas as diverse as event management, broadcasting, venue management, marketing, professional sport, community and collegiate sport, and coaching as well as in allied industries such as sporting equipment manufacturing, sporting footwear and apparel, and retail.

At the elite level, sport has moved from being an amateur pastime to one of the world's most significant industries. The growth and professionalisation of sport has driven changes in the consumption and production of sport and in the management of sporting organisations at all levels.

Managing sport organisations at the start of the 21st century involves the application of techniques and strategies evident in leading business, government and nonprofit organisations. This series explains these concepts and applies them to the diverse global sport industry.

To support their use by academics, each text is supported by current case studies, targeted study questions, further reading lists, links to relevant web-based resources, and supplementary online materials such as case study questions and classroom presentation aids.

Available in this series:

Sport and the Media
Managing the Nexus (Second edition)
Matthew Nicholson, Anthony Kerr and Merryn Sherwood

Sport Management
Principles and Applications (Fifth edition)
Russell Hoye, Aaron C.T. Smith, Matthew Nicholson and Bob Stewart

Sport Management
Principles and Applications (Sixth edition)
Russell Hoye, Katie Misener, Michael Naraine and Catherine Ordway

Introduction to Sport Marketing (Third edition)
Aaron C.T. Smith, Constantino Stavros, James Skinner, Andrea N. Geurin and Lauren M. Burch

For more information about this series, please visit: https://www.routledge.com/Sport-Management-Series/book-series/SMS

Introduction to Sport Marketing

THIRD EDITION

Aaron C.T. Smith, Constantino Stavros, James Skinner, Andrea N. Geurin, and Lauren M. Burch

Routledge
Taylor & Francis Group
LONDON AND NEW YORK

Designed cover images: zeljkosantrac, FG Trade, Bet_Noire, Vladimir Vladimirov and Ryan McVay/Getty Images

Third edition published 2024
by Routledge
4 Park Square, Milton Park, Abingdon, Oxon, OX14 4RN

and by Routledge
605 Third Avenue, New York, NY 10158

Routledge is an imprint of the Taylor & Francis Group, an informa business

First edition published by Routledge 2012
Second edition published by Routledge 2015

British Library Cataloguing-in-Publication Data
A catalogue record for this book is available from the British Library

Library of Congress Cataloging-in-Publication Data
Names: Smith, Aaron, 1972- author. | Stavros, Constantino, author. | Skinner, James, author. | Geurin, Andrea N., author. | Burch, Lauren M., author.
Title: Introduction to sport marketing / Aaron C.T. Smith, Constantino Stavros, James Skinner, Andrea N. Geurin and Lauren M. Burch.
Description: Third edition | Abingdon, Oxon ; New York, NY : Routledge, 2024. | Series: Sport management series | Includes bibliographical references and index. | Identifiers: LCCN 2023047627 | ISBN 9781032489001 (hardback) | ISBN 9781032488943 (paperback) | ISBN 9781003391319 (ebook)
Classification: LCC GV716 .S56 2024 | DDC 796.0688--dc23/eng/20231023
LC record available at https://lccn.loc.gov/2023047627

ISBN: 978-1-032-48900-1 (hbk)
ISBN: 978-1-032-48894-3 (pbk)
ISBN: 978-1-003-39131-9 (ebk)

DOI: 10.4324/9781003391319

Typeset in Berling
by KnowledgeWorks Global Ltd.

Access the Support Material: www.routledge.com/9781003391319

Contents

1 Sport marketing introduction 1

2 Sport markets 33

3 Sport consumers 57

4 Sport marketing opportunities 78

5 Sport marketing strategy 110

6 Sport products and branding 136

7 Sport pricing 171

8 Sport distribution 204

9 Sport promotion 226

10 Sport sponsorship 255

11 Sport services 293

12 Sport digital marketing and social media 320

13 Sport marketing implementation and control 353

Appendix *385*

Index *399*

CHAPTER 1

Sport marketing introduction

LEARNING OUTCOMES

At the end of this chapter, readers should be able to:

- appreciate the context in which sport marketing occurs, including the growth of the sport industry.
- consider the evolution of sport's commercialisation and how it underpins the need for a specialised form of sport marketing.
- conceptualise the stakeholders in the sport industry and the structure of the industry.
- explain what the terms 'marketing' and 'sport marketing' mean.
- reflect on the history of sport marketing and its emergence as a specialised approach to marketing.
- describe how sport marketing can be represented by a philosophy, a process, a set of principles, and a suite of tools.
- understand the relationship between the philosophy, processes, principles, and tools of sport marketing.
- identify the two different 'angles' of sport marketing.
- consider how sport marketing has unique aspects that demand specialised responses.
- explain the difference between selling and marketing.
- identify the components of the Sport Marketing Framework.

OVERVIEW

A sound knowledge of sport marketing enables sport professionals to successfully position their sport, association, league, team, players, venue, or event so that it can secure a competitive edge. This text offers a comprehensive exploration of sport marketing, delving into its fundamental concepts and strategies for effectively promoting various aspects of the sports industry. The chapters sequentially introduce the concept of sport marketing, discuss the structure of sport markets, analyse consumer motivations and communication

DOI: 10.4324/9781003391319-1

strategies, detail the identification and exploitation of marketing opportunities through a Sport Marketing Framework, elucidate the development of strategic marketing direction and positioning, examine product strategies and branding, explore pricing processes, delve into distribution channels and ticket distribution, explain the role and tools of promotion, describe sponsorship's significance in sport marketing, highlight principles of delivering quality sport services and establishing customer relationships, address digital marketing and social media's impact, and conclude with guidance on implementing and controlling sport marketing strategies. This comprehensive coverage equips readers with a holistic understanding of sport marketing's intricacies, making it an indispensable resource for navigating the dynamic landscape of sport marketing. Throughout the text, case studies from a diverse variety of sports and geographies help to reveal how sport marketing works in practice. Readers will find a case study summary in Appendix 1.

This chapter begins by discussing the context in which sport marketing occurs – the 'sport business marketplace' – leading to a brief introduction to the structure and stakeholders that comprise the sport industry. It next considers the growth of the sport industry, which stimulated the need for specific approaches to the marketing of sport, predominantly driven by commercialisation. In consequence of this growth, this chapter explains how sport marketing has emerged as a significant specialisation within marketing that responds to some unique properties and characteristics inherent in sport products and services. With the background to sport marketing laid out, this chapter elaborates on the concept of sport marketing, before explaining how its principles and tools can be applied to the marketing of sport organisations both professional and amateur. That is, sport leagues, governing bodies, players/athletes, sporting equipment and merchandise suppliers, and anyone running sport events. It also makes the distinction between two types of sport marketing. The first type involves the marketing of sport itself, while the second involves the use of sport to market some other, sometimes non-sport, products. It also introduces the basic marketing concepts and outlines the 'Sport Marketing Framework' that will be used to guide the structure and content of the remaining chapters.

THE SPORT BUSINESS CONTEXT

While neither this text nor this chapter aims to provide a detailed history of sport or its transformation into a business demanding professional and specialised sport marketers, it is instructive to briefly summarise some of the major developments that have shaped the industry's marketing needs. A better understanding of the context in which sport marketing has emerged can yield insight concerning what makes sport marketing a task requiring dedicated texts like this one. Let us begin by introducing some historical developments noteworthy in the emergence of sport as a business and industry.

Much of sport's modern impetus can be traced back as far as the early history of civilisation when sport provided training for the martial skills needed in war, now packaged as entertainment and competition. No account of sport can begin without acknowledging the Ancient Greeks who conducted the Olympic Games, first in 776 BCE, and which regularly attracted spectators from across the Greek empire. At this time, there was no organised business structure as such, with events organised by local authorities, but mostly undertaken spontaneously and with leisure or skills training as goals for local communities or by individuals. Yet, sport was taken seriously, and for some, involved regular training, prize money, gambling, and spectators.

Skipping ahead to the late 19th century, the emergence of sport as a business and the early signs of professionalism marked an inflection point. In sports such as baseball, cricket, rugby, football (soccer), and boxing, players began to receive payments for their performances, chiefly because sports leagues had started to organise competitions into standardised structures. For example, in the United States, the formation of the National League of Professional Baseball Clubs in 1876, and the establishment of the first professional (American) football league in 1920, laid some foundations for modern sports business in North America. Meanwhile, in England, the FA (Football Association) Cup had been operating since 1871–1872. These leagues proved to be a formula worth duplicating for a mass of new leagues in over 200 sports to follow over the next century.

Until the early 20th century, most people could only experience competitive sport by being a spectator at an event. However, the first versions of mass media stimulated a prodigious transformation in the way sport could be viewed, and set up what was to become one the foundational features of the sport business landscape. Television broadcasts of major sporting events, such as the Olympic Games and the World Cup (of Football – soccer), transported sport to a global audience, and in so doing also delivered a lucrative new revenue stream for sport broadcasters and organisations through advertising and sponsorship. The first live television broadcast of a sport event was the 1936 Berlin Olympics, transmitted to 41 countries.

On the back of mass media coverage of sport, corporate sponsorship emerged as a major component of sport business in the 1960s and 1970s. Companies were starting to recognise the value of sponsoring sport events, leagues, teams, and athletes in reaching a large audience and to promote their brands through favourable associations. The first major corporate sponsorship deal was signed in 1960 between Coca-Cola and the International Olympic Committee (IOC).

With sponsorship arrived money from larger, ambitious companies, which were increasingly concerned with expanding their markets beyond local and national geographical borders. Their efforts propelled the globalisation of sport in the late 20th and early 21st centuries, especially as broadcasting and television access had spread almost everywhere in the world. Correspondingly, international competitions like the World Cup, the Summer and Winter Olympic Games, the Tour de France, the Cricket World Cup, the (American football) Super Bowl, the World Series (of baseball), the Wimbledon (tennis open), Formula 1 (motor racing), and heavyweight boxing underwent spectacular growth. With the growth came even more money, commercial opportunities, and the need for marketing to promote the events to a wide range of diverse geographic markets. At the same time, the expansion of sport franchises into new markets, such as the establishment of Major League Baseball (MLB) in Japan and the National Basketball Association in China, created new revenue streams for sport in places that a few decades earlier had never been contemplated.

With the 21st century well underway, digital technology and the exponential expansion of the internet brought another turning point in sport's business scale. With it arrived the centrality of social media and streaming services along with new ways for content providers, packagers, broadcasters, technology platforms, and sport organisations to invent innovative sport-related products and services, reach audiences anywhere and anytime, and, of course, create revenue streams. It also heralded questions about what can be included as sport since an inclusive view of the sporting industry might be seen to encompass any product or service in any way related or reliant on sport or physical competition. Perhaps even more important is the question of who watches all the different varieties of sport and why?

CASE 1.1

World Wrestling Entertainment (WWE)

WWE has accumulated an immense, global fan base, with millions of people watching – through network television, pay-per-view, streaming replay services, and social media – their favourite (and most despised) wrestlers compete in scripted matches. But why do some many people become WWE fans? Why do they love wrestling even though it is known to be orchestrated theatre? What draws them to this unique form of so-called sport entertainment.

Although we might guess that most WWE fans are (pre)adolescent boys, in fact the age range of most fans falls between 18 and 49. According to a recent report released by the WWE, the fan base is relatively diverse in terms of ethnicity, race, gender, and socioeconomic status. They also reside in different geographic locations, with fans from more than 100 countries tuning in to watch various kinds of WWE programming. The report further revealed that WWE fans are 70% men and 30% women, with 54% under the age of 35. In terms of education, 62% of WWE fans have completed some kind of post high school qualification, while 25% have a college/university degree. Finally, fans have an average annual household income of US$75,000 or less.

Common demographic characteristics of fans can be helpful in signposting why they follow certain forms of sport viewing or participation. However, sport marketers try to dig deeper when seeking to understand the fan motivations that lurk below the surface of stereotypes or assumptions. They use the term 'psychographics' to capture these deeper motivations, which might comprise fans' interests, activities, opinions, attitudes, and goals, but can be summarised as their driving motivation. Not all fans share the same psychographic motivations. For example, some WWE fans report that they enjoy the storytelling aspect of wrestling, while others appreciate the athleticism and physical feats that the wrestlers perform, including for others still, a bit of 'harmless' violence. Then, for some fans, wrestling is an escape from reality, and they enjoy immersing themselves in the alternative world of WWE where they can for a brief period live vicariously through the experiences of their favourite wrestlers. Further psychographic categories might suggest that some fans enjoy the community aspect of being a wrestling fan, attending live events, and connecting with other fans online. In short, there are numerous different reasons why fans love WWE, including the athleticism and skill required to perform, the storylines and drama that unfold, the escape from everyday life, and the opportunity for social bonding.

Non-WWE fans might find it hard to understand the motivations described previously and may suggest that WWE wrestling is 'fake'. While it is true that the matches are orchestrated, WWE fans counter-claim that the physical feats the wrestlers perform are real and that the injuries they sustain are also genuine, even if they were not caused intentionally. Curiously, most WWE fans recognise that the matches are predetermined, and that the drama is for spectacle, but accept this as part of the entertainment value of wrestling. In fact, fans might argue that the choreographed nature of wrestling also allows for complex storylines and character development that fans can follow and invest in. Fans enjoy watching their favourite wrestlers evolve and grow, and they become emotionally invested in the storylines that unfold on screen. In this respect, WWE has reinvented theatre through the collision of hyperbolic, larger than life heroes and villains, dramatic contests, breath-taking athleticism, and radical plots, all packaged into a stunning pageant of broadcasting commercialisation.

QUESTIONS

1. Start by reviewing the WWE website (www.wwe.com). Does it provide some insight into the motivations of WWE viewers and fans? Explain why.
2. There are nearly 30 million followers on the WWE Instagram page (www.instagram.com/wwe). Examine the content posted and discuss what common attributes and features it focuses on.
3. Choose a demographic segment (e.g., boys between 10 and 14 or women over 50) and describe what you think might be the primary motivations for being WWE fans.

THE COMMERCIALISATION OF SPORT AS A BUSINESS

Distinct from many traditional businesses, sport business is often deeply intertwined with the culture and identity of its fans and supporters. As a result, sport creates a unique emotional attachment and loyalty that can drive significant revenue and growth for sport organisations and the diverse mass of other enterprises which seek to offer products and services associated with, or around, sport. The loyalty and passion of sports fans also cultivate a sense of community, which lay at the heart of the remarkable engagement, brand loyalty, and even social change that sport organisations and its players and athletes can command. At the same time, sport business faces some challenges that are not conventionally found in other forms of business. For example, sport events often have a finite lifespan, which means that sport organisations need to continually create new events, products, and services to maintain fan attention and, in a business context, ensure consistent and ongoing revenue streams. Another challenge is that sport organisations frequently must manage the complex relationships with stakeholders, such as athletes, fans, media, and sponsors, and balance their sometimes contradictory expectations and demands. Yet, sport business can also be seen as a form of entertainment. Many people view sport as a leisure activity, and sport events are often marketed as entertainment experiences, designed to create a spectacle, with music, lights, and special effects, and an almost theatrical promotion of players' anticipated performances.

The metamorphosis into 'sport-as-business' begins with sport as a recreational and cultural practice where sport organisations are rudimentary, their revenue streams are modest, sport is played mainly for fun, and activities are organised and managed by volunteer officials or schoolteachers. This model is sometimes described as a kitchen-table approach to sport's management and marketing since the game is administered by few officials making key decisions from a member's home. It has some strengths since it not only ensures the involvement of grassroots players, members, or students, and provides a strong local community club focus but it also nurtures a strong set of values that centre on playing the game for its own sake and the associated ideal of amateurism. At the same time, it perpetuates a primitive system of management driven by an administrative committee – or in the case of some parts of the world like North America – school or college officials.

The second phase of commercialisation is characterised by a nascent professional model, where more revenue streams are exploited, and both staff and players are paid for their services. Whereas the kitchen-table model depends upon member subscriptions, player registration fees, school support, and social activities for their financial viability, the commercialised sport model uses sport's commercial value to attract corporate and other sponsors. In this phase, sports that have the capacity to draw large crowds also seek to increase an awareness in their 'products', secure a special and exclusive sales channel, or obtain access to a market segment that will be receptive to their product. Sport is still a recreational and cultural practice, where the sport's overall development is the primary goal, but there is also an emerging or secondary strategy that focuses on elite development and the building of pathways by which players can move to a more elite level in college or in a professionalised league or competition.

The third phase is bureaucratisation, where the structures of sport organisations become more complex, administrative controls are established, and functional specialisation increases. This phase is heavily dependent upon the preceding phase since an effective bureaucracy requires additional resources. In this phase, club, league, association, or school structures are transformed to include a board of directors or independent governance specialists, whose prime responsibility is to set the strategic direction and ensure compliance with regulation. The transfer of governance authority establishes an organisational divide between the steerers (the board) and the rowers (the chief executive officer and operational staff), who are expected to implement the board's plans and policies. In addition, a business-like set of functions and processes are created, which are built around administrative support, marketing, finance, game development, coaching and player development, and human resources. In this phase, less management space is given to the sport-as-recreation-and-cultural-practice model, and more to the sport-as-business model.

The fourth and final phase is corporatisation, where sport fully embraces the business model by valuing brand management as much as it does player and fan relations. Revenue streams are increasingly dominated by sponsorships and broadcast rights fees, merchandise sales are deepened, and managers adopt a more professional outlook where the need to secure a competitive edge overrules the desire to hold on to old traditions. This is the phase in which players become full-time employees, player associations are established to protect their interests, and the sport's governing bodies take on the role of employers. A formal industrial relations system is created that leads to detailed contractual arrangements, collective bargaining agreements, and codes of conduct. The marketing process also becomes increasingly sophisticated as the sport enterprise becomes a brand, members and fans become customers, sponsors become corporate partners, and the brand name and image are used to strengthen its corporate partnership arrangements and build up a merchandising arm. This phase also features a hearty move towards managerialism, whereby sport becomes more accountable to its stakeholders for its performance and use of resources. One area managerialism is particularly evident may be seen in sport's relationship with government, where government funding becomes increasingly contingent upon sport meeting certain specific and agreed upon outcomes.

Managerialism also leads to greater transparency through an emphasis in performance measurement. It is no longer appropriate to only measure player performance but also internal processes and efficiency, financial performance, market performance, employer, and, in particular, player behaviour, social responsibility, and, of course, marketing outcomes. Finally, sport becomes more regulated, with some being defined by government-framed parameters and legislation and others being internal to sports, leagues, or the competitive structures in which college teams participate. The more government-bound controls involve venue safety, anti-discrimination programmes, and crowd control policies, for example. Internal regulation is highly visible within professional sport leagues and competitions, where player recruitment is governed by drafting rules, player behaviour is constrained by a combination of collective agreements and codes of conduct, salaries are often set within a total wage ceiling, revenues are redistributed from the wealthiest to the neediest clubs and associations, and games are scheduled to ensure the lowest cost and greatest revenue. While corporate regulation can be problematic because of its heavy emphasis on bureaucratic control and detailed performance measurement, it also creates a common discipline, which can improve the overall viability of a sport competition by creating a guiding purpose, setting a clear strategic direction, and harnessing the marketing and branding power of the collective.

Sport's corporatisation demands an emphasis on leadership and strategy, revenue growth and value creation, building and sharing profits, product quality and innovation, building brand equity, converting fans and customers into core business pillars, and, finally, establishing a global market. While the cultural dimensions of sport, which focus on its capacity to provide meaning, identity, and sociability, are still relevant, an increasing amount of resources are allocated to sport's commercial imperatives, which in the corporate phase is essentially about entertainment, attracting fans, selling merchandise, securing sponsors, getting the best broadcast rights deal, establishing new revenue sources, and generally building the brand. In other words, cultural and community values are subordinated to business and commercial values, where it unambiguously pursues consumer capitalism.

A pre-condition for the transition from the kitchen-table model to the sport-as-business model is a productive economy where most people are educated to higher level secondary school, a majority of the workforce is employed in the service sector, and a minority in agriculture. As a result, society becomes highly urbanised, new technology increases productivity, leisure time expands, and the desire to engage in sports and games, as either players or spectators, becomes increasingly strong. These conditions not only produce high disposable incomes that can be spent on sport activities but also provide the capital base for the building of sport infrastructure, the development of educational pathways including elite sport, the establishment of professional sport leagues, and the staging of mega-sport events.

From the early days of competition and entertainment to the rise of professionalism, the expansion of media, the growth of corporate sponsorship, globalisation, and digital technology, sport has developed into a substantial global enterprise driven by an equally extensive marketing demand. In fact, sport has become an immense and complex ecosystem of stakeholders, all with customised marketing needs.

THE SPORT INDUSTRY

The global sport industry is a vast network of stakeholders such as athletes, teams, leagues, media outlets, sponsors, and fans. Sport marketing plays a critical role in this industry, as it seeks to build brand values and generate revenue for these stakeholders. By way of brief introduction, some major stakeholders in the structure of the global sport industry are highlighted next, along with their relevance to sport marketing.

First, athletes, clubs, and teams are the heart of the sport industry, as they provide the value that drives fan engagement and therefore revenue. Sport marketing strategies for athletes and teams focus on building a strong brand identity and maximising exposure through sponsorships, endorsements, and media coverage. This can involve developing a personal brand for individual athletes, creating a unique team culture, and leveraging social media and other digital platforms to engage with fans. High-profile examples include the Manchester United Football Club in the English Premier League, the New York Yankees in MLB, and the Los Angeles Lakers in the National Basketball Association.

Second, fans and consumers provide the demand for sport content and drive revenue through ticket sales, merchandise, and other consumer products. Sport marketing strategies for fans and consumers focus on enhancing the fan experience and building long-term loyalty by creating unique fan experiences, developing loyalty programmes, and leveraging technology like social media platforms and 'apps' to improve the fan experience both in-stadium and online.

Third, leagues and governing bodies play a central role in regulating and promoting sport's competitive environment. Sport marketing strategies for leagues and governing bodies focus on enhancing the fan experience and generating revenue streams such as broadcasting rights, ticket sales, and merchandising. Increasingly, leagues and governing bodies dedicate resources to creating new and innovative formats or rules, expanding into new markets, and developing strategic partnerships with sponsors, media outlets, technology providers, and venues. Examples include the National Football League (NFL) in the United States, the IOC, and the Union of European Football Associations (UEFA).

Fourth, sport broadcasting and media outlets such as television networks, streaming services, and social media platforms are key players in the sport industry, as they provide the channels for fans to watch and engage with sport content. Sport marketing strategies for media outlets focus on distributing content, increasing fan engagement, and monetising content through extra features, advertising, and subscriptions. This can involve creating unique and engaging content, leveraging data and analytics to improve the targeting of new fan groups, personalising the product offering to them, and developing strategic partnerships with leagues, teams, and sponsors. Examples include ESPN in the United States, Sky Sports in the United Kingdom, and beIN Sports in the Middle East.

Fifth, sponsors and advertisers deliver critical revenue sources for the sport industry, as they provide financial support in exchange for exposure and an association with the sport and its athletes. Sport marketing strategies for sponsors and advertisers focus on creating brand exposure through partnerships with athletes, teams, and leagues. It can also involve data and analytics to target specific demographics, creating engaging events, and developing long-term relationships with key stakeholders whereby sponsoring companies become firmly associated with the sponsored sport property. Examples include Coca-Cola's sponsorship of the Olympics, Nike's endorsement deals with top athletes such as footballer Cristiano Ronaldo and UK track star Dina Asher-Smith, and Red Bull's support of extreme sports events or the Formula 1 Motor Racing Team.

Sixth, sport facilities and infrastructure provide the venues instrumental for sport events to take place. Examples include Wembley Stadium in London, the Staples Center in Los Angeles, and the Birds Nest in Beijing.

Seventh, sport equipment and apparel companies manufacture the tools, materials, and gear used by athletes to play, as well as the means for fans to show support of their favourite teams and athletes. Examples include adidas, Wilson, Umbro, and Under Armour.

Eighth, major events give fans motivation to travel to different locations to attend major sporting events and participate in sport-related activities. They also provide content for broadcasters and media. Examples include Wimbledon, the Rugby League World Cup, and the Super Bowl.

The sport industry comprises a dynamic and constantly evolving network of participants, which means that the previous list is far from exhaustive depending on where the boundaries of the sport industry are drawn. In addition to these eight major categories of sport industry stakeholders, there is a steady series of new entrants into the sport marketplace who seek to take advantage of various niches, new technologies, and demographic or social shifts. Examples include the astonishing rise of esports, leisure and recreational 'apps' designed to support or add value to athletic experiences including wearable devices, dedicated social media platforms, sport tourism operators, sport documentary makers, and sport marketing and branding specialist companies. New products and services emerge almost daily, some of which operate at the periphery of sport like cryptocurrencies and non-fungible tokens. Others offer entirely new sport experiences.

CASE 1.2

Drone Racing League

The Drone Racing League (DRL) is a professional drone racing league that was founded in 2015 and provides an illustrative case of an entirely new sport and its premier competition, which has successfully transformed a hobby into an entertainment arena. The league has quickly become a popular spectator sport, attracting viewers – mainly online – but also in-venue. One interesting aspect to the DRL's success is the role of what sport marketers call a 'brand strategy', which has helped to establish the league as a leader in the world of drone racing by focusing on specific features of their product and experience that are distinctive and resonant with fans and sponsors. Like many brand-new sports and competitions, the DRL's brand strategy is centred around innovation and technology. As a result, the league's marketing materials and events showcase the cutting-edge technology that goes into drone racing, highlighting the speed, agility, and precision of the drones. To emphasise these features, the league also uses bold colours and futuristic designs to give spectators the sense of a dynamic and exciting entertainment experience.

In terms of its actual entertainment product, the DRL produces intense and action-packed events designed to underscore the excitement and drama of drone racing. To further accentuate the product attributes, the events are held in unique locations, such as abandoned buildings, sports arenas, and even in the middle of forests, which means that they incorporate innovative course designs, with twists, turns, and obstacles that challenge the pilots, demonstrate the speed and agility of the drones, and encourage spectacular incidents.

Since the mainstay of DRL's audience are younger males conversant with smart, mobile technology, the league focuses its marketing through a strong social media presence, with intense activity on platforms like X (formerly Twitter), Facebook, Instagram, and YouTube. For example, it shares updates on upcoming races and events, as well as behind-the-scenes content, drone technology, and drone racing tips. Partnerships with major brands such as Allianz, Swatch, and BMW have also helped promote the league to new audience segments, including middle-aged men and younger women.

With access to a dedicated audience, the DRL has been well placed to grow further by injecting more resources into the competition through the revenue growth delivered by sponsorship deals. They have secured several high-profile sponsorships to help fund its operations and promote the league. In addition to the partnerships mentioned earlier, the DRL has also signed up with companies such as FORTO Coffee Shots, the US Air Force, and the US Army. These partnerships not only bring in revenue but also help to position the DRL as a leader in the new sport.

The DRL case reveals the arrival of a new sport and league that has raced to become a legitimate and growing presence in the world of competitive sport. It has attracted a large and passionate fan base possessing significant expertise in the technology behind the sport, with viewers tuning in from around the world to watch races live and through streaming options. To underpin its drive towards a greater footprint, the league has also secured significant sponsorship deals and is enjoying some attention in major media outlets like ESPN, Forbes, and The New York Times.

QUESTIONS

1 Go to the DRL website (www.thedroneracingleague.com). What is your impression of the sport and competition based on the experience of navigating the site?
2 Visit the DRL drone racing simulator arcade (https://www.drl.io) and visit to the app store, download it, and play! Based on the experience, describe the attributes of drone racing as a sport and explain why it might be so appealing to its participants and audience.
3 What current sports or leagues is the DRL comparable to? What advantages or disadvantages does the DRL possess in relation to these?
4 In terms of viewing experience, what does the DRL have that is unique and distinguishes it from other, mainstream leagues or events?

WHAT IS MARKETING?

Marketing as a business concept is quite young. There were a few references to the marketing of household products in the late 19th century, but it did not really emerge as a serious business issue until the early part of the 20th century. It all started with the initiatives of Frederick Winslow Taylor, who later became known as the father of scientific management as the result of his now famous publication *Principles of Scientific Management* in 1911. Taylor was the first industrialist to examine the production of material goods from a scientific perspective using tools such as time and motion studies. One of Taylor's most cited studies involved the shovelling of coal, where he determined the most efficient way of undertaking physical labour and manual tasks. His maxim that the principal object of management should be to secure the maximum prosperity for the employer, coupled with the maximum prosperity for each employee, provided a catalyst for other business theorists and practitioners to move further down the production and distribution chain, and see how salesmanship and retailing could also become better organised and more efficient. W. Hoyt, in his 1913 publication, *Scientific Sales Management*, explained how sales management could be made more productive, and most of the ideas he outlined revolved around the 'Taylorist' principle of standardisation. This involved breaking down sales jobs into their component parts and discovering 'new tools' to secure more customers and consequently increase sales volume. Sales management techniques could, for example, be made more effective if sales territories and travel routes were rationalised, and the salesperson's 'sales talk' could be placed within a standardised framework. Advertising was also made subject to standardisation.

The major philosophical shift in the idea of selling came when industrial societies became more affluent, more competitive, and more geographically spread out during the 1940s and 1950s. This forced business to develop closer relations with buyers and clients, which in turn made business realise that it was not enough to produce a quality product at a reasonable price. In fact, it was equally essential to deliver products that customers wanted. Henry Ford may have gotten away with producing his best-selling T-model Ford in one colour only (black) in 1908, but in modern societies this was no longer possible. The modernisation of society led to a marketing revolution that destroyed the view that production, and the accompanying salesmanship, would create its own demand. Customers, and the desire to meet their diverse and often complex needs, became the focal point of business.

Today the term 'marketing' has universal currency, although it still tends to be used in a variety of ways. Some think of marketing as the use of advertising, publicity, and personal selling techniques to make others aware of a product or to attract more consumers to buy it. That is, it's all about making a sale. However, marketing is now far more comprehensive than this narrow and mechanistic interpretation. Put simply, and in the most general of ways, marketing is all about satisfying the needs of customers and consumers. In the case of sport marketing, it is about meeting the needs of sport customers and sport consumers. These customers and consumers include people who play sport, but it goes much further than this. It also includes people who watch or listen to sport programmes, buy merchandise, collect memorabilia, purchase sports goods such as clothing and shoes, and additionally 'surf' sport-related websites to find out the latest gossip surrounding their favourite team, player, or event.

Readers may have already noted that the terms 'consumer' and 'customer' have been used to describe those people who buy sports products. A sport consumer is someone who generally uses sport products or services. A sport customer is someone who pays for the use of a specific product or service. In the light of the very slight difference in meaning, it is legitimate to use the terms interchangeably to refer to those people who use and pay for sport products and services.

> *Chapter principle 1.1*: Marketing is more than promotion, advertising, personal selling, or sales gimmicks.

Satisfying the needs of consumers obviously involves more than just putting together a slick advertisement or offering a temporary discount. For example, marketing involves making decisions about what different groups of consumers may need or want: the most effective way of selling a product or service, the best way of making the product or service available, the idea behind a product or service, the unique features of a product or service, and, ultimately, its price. Marketing demands a process where a range of issues are considered in order to maximise the likelihood that a customer will first of all be attracted to the product; will, second, make the decision to buy it; and, third, be satisfied by the product or service once it has been consumed and used. These processes can then be combined in order to construct a workable definition of marketing.

The marketing process

Marketing is generally described as the process of planning and implementing activities that are designed to meet the needs or desires of customers. Marketing pays attention to the development of a product, its pricing, promotion, and distribution. It aims to create an exchange, where the customer gives up something (usually money), for a product or service they believe is of equal or greater value. Although the term 'product' directly refers to tangible items, it is quite common to use it to represent the entire offering to consumers including services. Thus, it is conventional to speak of the 'sport product' in a global sense as a representative term for all offerings associated with sport, whether in physical form, such as sport equipment, or as a service, such as entertainment. Marketing aims to not only entice people to try products or services but also keep them as long-term customers.

> *Chapter principle 1.2*: Marketing aims to create an exchange where the customer gives up something for a product or service.

What is sport marketing?

Sport marketing is a relatively new phenomenon. In the 1940s and 1950s, most sport was not heavily commercialised and was thus seen as an activity people just 'did'. Sport was taken for granted, and the attitudes young people had about sport were usually shaped by tradition, family values, and peer-group influence. Tennis, for instance, was for the most part a middle-class activity that attracted both males and females. It had no body contact and thus was not a sport most working-class males got excited about. These highly energised young people wanted a bit more rough-and-tumble in their leisure time practices, and hence football was their preferred pursuit. On the other hand, tennis had a strong connection to women who wanted something athletic and moderately vigorous but not heavily masculinised. There was, if you like, a type of natural selection operating, where people gravitated to the sport based on its structure, stereotypical image, and aesthetics. No marketing or heavy sales pitch was needed to motivate people to join tennis clubs. It just happened. The proximity of clubs also played a part in driving demand. Tennis clubs were everywhere in Australia; they had a relatively strong presence in New Zealand but were far more dispersed in Britain and the United States. The game's social status also had a role to play in shaping demand. In Britain and the United States, it had a slightly snobbish image, and it was played mostly within the confines of private clubs. In Australia, on the other hand, tennis clubs were spread across the nation, and every small country town had its own public tennis courts. It came as no surprise to find that not only was tennis one of Australia's most popular sports, but also that Australia produced most of the world's most successful players at this time.

Today things are completely different. National governing bodies for tennis operate in most nations around the world and in every case are fighting for the hearts and minds of every young person with an interest in sport. What is more, they are competing against scores of national governing bodies from a range of other sports. Every national governing body for sport now has a modified games unit, schools support unit, a player development unit, a promotions unit, a marketing unit, a media unit, and a partnership and sponsorship unit. Each unit is expected to use appropriate marketing strategies to attract more junior players, get more parents involved as volunteers, keep everyone in the game for longer, build up the public image of the game, attract more spectators to the big events, get a lucrative sponsorship deal, and, in a best case scenario, secure a massive broadcast rights agreement. Every sporting body around the world now recognises that its 'product' can only grow if it is underpinned by a professionally run marketing campaign. To better understand the nature of sport marketing and the need to cultivate specialist marketing skills and expertise, it is useful to appreciate some of the major inflection points that shaped the emergence of sport marketing.

CASE 1.3

Major League Eating

Nathan's Hot Dog Eating Contest is the marquee event in Major League Eating (MLE), the governing body for the professional sport of competitive eating. It might come as a surprise that competitive eating is a sport, let alone that it has an elite, professional, and international league. Yet, MLE includes the sport's global governing body, the International Federation of Competitive Eating, and operates around 70 events annually. The most famous of these events is the Nathan's Famous Fourth of July Hot Dog Eating Contest held in Coney Island, NY, named for its hot dog manufacturer sponsor, and first held in 1916. Like Nathan's, and more so than most sports, MLE attracts a large involvement from sponsors unambiguously associated with the event itself, as the contest typically revolves around who can eat the most of the sponsor's food in the fastest time. According to the MLE, their other sponsors include Hostess, Hooters, Heinz Ketchup, Pizza Hut, Old Navy, Bass Pro Shops, 7-Eleven, ESPN, Taco Bell, Jimmy John's, Pepto Bismol, Wingstop, Harrah's Entertainment, Isle of Capri Casinos, and Roy Rogers. In addition, MLE stages contests at events known for food, such as the New Orleans Oyster Festival, the National Buffalo Wing Festival, Norfolk Harbor Fest, and the Wisconsin State Fair.

Even if you have never heard of competitive eating or the MLE, it would be premature to conclude that it is parochial and transient. The sport has expanded immensely over recent years, particularly with the rise of social media and the curiosity factor associated with sharing remarkable eating achievements. Amongst such achievements is the now legendary performance by Joey Chestnut – the world's number one ranked eater – in setting the world Nathan's record of 76 hot dogs and buns in 10 minutes in 2021. Accompanying the sport's more mainstream exposure has been the attention of sport marketers, broadcasters, sponsors, and social media influencers.

To enhance the spectacle for Nathan's viewers, the contest employs professional commentators to provide play-by-play (dog-by-dog) analysis and uses music, lights, and statistics to create a lively atmosphere. The organisers also strive to create a sense of community and identity amongst fans. For example, Nathan's offers merchandise such as T-shirts, hats, and mugs featuring the contest's logo and other branding. Of course, the company encourages fans to sample their products, as well as share photos and videos of themselves participating in extreme eating challenges for posting on social media. Like many sports and events, Nathan's recruit celebrity guests to promote the contest, including high-profile athletes and entertainers. Finally, the event's marketers liaise with their broadcasting partner ESPN to curate documentary-style features about the contest and its participants, increasing the profile and appeal of extreme eating as a sport and lionising the eaters as heroic athletes.

According to MLE's figures, the Nathan's contest generates over 300 million consumer impressions on domestic television and hundreds of million more in traditional and digital media. In addition, the ESPN telecast has been viewed by at least 1–1.5 million live viewers for more for 15 consecutive years and is covered by thousands of network television affiliates.

QUESTIONS

1. Do you think competitive eating and the MLE use the same kind of sport marketing strategies that more mainstream sports employ? What would these constitute?
2. Why do you think that competitive eating and MLE have grown so much recently, and do you foresee its viewing audience continuing to grow rapidly? Explain why.
3. Visit the MLE website and the YouTube channel of an MLE social media star like Matt Stonie (www.majorleagueeating.com; https://www.youtube.com/@mattstonie). What is the appeal of the sport and to whom?

The emergence of sport marketing

This section begins with some brief observations about the historical context in which sport marketing developed. This section goes further in pinpointing some pivotal moments and influential people in sport marketing with the aim of providing a more granular context to understand how and why the field emerged.

Sponsorship offers a compelling starting point as it is one of the oldest and most important forms of sport marketing. The first major sponsorship deal was recorded in the 1920s when a chewing gum company paid baseballer Babe Ruth to endorse their product. Of course, sponsorship has since become a major revenue stream for sports teams, leagues, and athletes, especially once propelled by the introduction of television in the 1950s.

Mark McCormack could in some ways be considered a founder of sport sponsorship and marketing. He established the company International Management Group (IMG) in 1960, which became the first sport marketing agency. McCormack signed some of the biggest names in sport at the time, including golfers Arnold Palmer, Jack Nicklaus, and tennis player Bjorn Borg. While McCormack codified sport marketing, Evel Knievel – a daredevil and motorcycle stunt performer who gained fame in the 1960s and 1970s – was busy inventing new levels of self-athlete promotion and branding. Noted for his high-flying stunts, which often ended in spectacular crashes, Knievel captivated audiences and made himself into a cultural icon. Knievel was a master of self-promotion, taking personal athlete branding to the extreme, often reinforced using extravagant costumes and daring feats. He also sold merchandise such as T-shirts, posters, and toys, the most famous being his own action figure.

Around the same time, in 1964, Bill Bowerman and Phil Knight set up Nike, which went on to become one of the most successful sport brands in history, its success largely attributable to its innovative marketing campaigns featuring sponsored athletes. Nike was one of the first companies to use celebrity endorsements. Most famously, Nike is associated with Michael Jordan, one of the most successful athletes in history, and in-sport marketing. Jordan's partnership with Nike, which began in 1984 with the release of the first Air Jordan sneakers, revolutionised the sporting apparel industry. It is no exaggeration to say that Jordan's endorsement deals, which also included Gatorade and Hanes, introduced a new era of athlete branding and product marketing. Nike also pioneered the use of product placement in film and television, such as placing its shoes in the movie *Back to the Future*.

Television allowed fans to watch live games and events from their own homes. In so doing, it created opportunities for those seeking to market sport because it vastly increased exposure for teams and athletes and the ability to sell advertising time during broadcasts. Roone Arledge might be the most important figure in the history of sport broadcasting, serving as the president of the US television network ABC Sports, where he led the coverage of major events such as the Olympics, Monday Night Football, and the Super Bowl. Arledge introduced instant replay, slow motion, and other innovations that transformed how sports were broadcast on television. Arledge also pioneered the use of graphics, music, and storytelling to make sport broadcasting more entertaining for viewers. Television advertisements during sport have become amongst the most valuable commercial marketing, thanks in good amount to Arledge's work in making football so attractive to watch.

With greater exposure via broadcasting came the idea of branding. By the 1960s and 1970s, teams and leagues were harnessing the power of developing their brand 'identities' – the visible elements representing the sporting entity including colour, design, and logos that collectively distinguish it to fans as unique and instantly recognisable. In turn, the collective of logos, team colours, and slogans have become a foundational platform in sport's marketing, helping to build a team's fan base and generate revenue through merchandise sales.

In the 1980s and 1990s, sports apparel and merchandise became a significant revenue stream for sports teams and leagues, driven by the increasing popularity of professional sports, as well as the invention of new fabrics and manufacturing techniques delivering more durable and stylish sports apparel.

Digital marketing arrived on the scene in the 1990s and 2000s accompanying the internet. It now incorporates social media marketing, email marketing, and online advertising and has by far eclipsed traditional print media in its capacity for sports teams and athletes to reach fans, promote events, and generate revenue.

In terms of competitions, MLB in the United States is one of the oldest and most successful sport leagues in the world, and it has been at the forefront of many sport marketing innovations, including its transition to the digital economy. In the 1990s, MLB was one of the first big leagues to launch a heavily branded and commercially oriented website, part of which offered the live streaming of games. The league demonstrated how to build a global fan base, with teams playing games in Japan, Mexico, and the United Kingdom. MLB was quick to embrace social media and digital marketing and used platforms such as X (formerly Twitter) and Instagram to engage with fans and promote the league with an agility that most big leagues sought to emulate. Much more recently, the energy drink manufacturer Red Bull has used sport as a key platform in building a distinctive brand identity by associating extreme sports featuring dramatic events with their energy drink products. It sponsors athletes and hosts events such as the Red Bull Air Race and the Red Bull Flugtag (www.redbull.com/au-en/event-series/red-bull-flugtag) in addition to a high-profile Formula 1 racing team. To augment its brand identity, Red Bull also created a content marketing strategy, producing videos and other digital materials that showcase extreme sports and the Red Bull 'lifestyle' where energy and excitement are front and centre. The company's marketing campaigns are founded on sport sponsorship leveraged through identity-driven digital marketing.

Thanks in part to the democratisation of sport through social media and other digital platforms, women's sports have experienced a massive surge in popularity, with more coverage, sponsorship, and marketing opportunities than ever before. The success of female athletes such as Serena Williams, Megan Rapinoe, and Simone Biles has helped to shatter gender stereotypes and create new opportunities for women in sport marketing. One of the pioneers pivotal to the marketing of women's sport, players, and athletes is Billie Jean King, a former professional tennis player. She founded the Women's Tennis Association and helped to secure equal pay for women at the US Open and Wimbledon. King has also been an advocate for LGBTQ+ rights and social justice issues and paved the way for the most successful female tennis player ever who is also one of the most prominent sponsored athletes of the generation, Serena Williams. Not only has Williams accumulated 23 Grand Slam singles titles and 14 Grand Slam doubles titles but she has also been a trailblazer for women in sport marketing, with endorsements from major brands such as Nike, Gatorade, and JPMorgan Chase. Williams has used her platform to advocate for issues such as equal pay, gender equality, and racial justice.

Although mainly known in the United States, another example is Danica Patrick, the former professional race car driver and one of the most successful female drivers in history. Patrick was the first woman to win a pole position in the NASCAR Cup Series and the first woman to lead the Indianapolis 500. Patrick has been a brand ambassador for several companies, including GoDaddy and Coca-Cola. Given her success, Patrick was able to break down barriers and challenge traditional gender roles in a sport that is predominantly male dominated. This made her a powerful figure in the marketing world, as companies sought to align themselves with her brand and appeal to a wider audience.

Another exemplar in women's sport shattering the male-dominated conventions has been the FIFA Women's World Cup, a global football/soccer tournament that has immensely inflated in popularity in recent years, with record-breaking viewership and sponsorship deals. The 2019 Women's World Cup, held in France, and the subsequent event in 2023 held in Australia and New Zealand were both broadcast in over 200 countries and substantially raised the profile of women's sport along with creating new opportunities for female athletes in sport marketing. For example, Mia Hamm, the former professional soccer player and one of the most successful female athletes in history, became a highly valuable 'brand' and a trailblazer for the marketing of women in sport. Hamm won two World Cup titles and two Olympic gold medals with the US women's national team. She has been an ambassador for several brands, including Nike and Gatorade, and has used her visibility and influence to promote women's sport and especially soccer and encourage young girls to pursue their athletic ambitions.

While innumerable other developments might be considered significant in the development of contemporary sport marketing, the rise of esports has been unprecedented. Esports, or competitive video gaming, has become a rapidly growing industry. Esports events, such as the League of Legends World Championship, attract millions of viewers and generate millions of dollars in revenue. Esports sponsors, such as Red Bull and Intel, have found success by targeting a young, tech-savvy audience through digital marketing and social media. It also presents new opportunities for sport marketers to create innovative and immersive experiences for fans, such as by employing streaming, virtual reality, and augmented reality technologies. Sport marketing is only becoming more complex and specialised as a result.

CASE 1.4

Serena Williams

Serena Williams is one of the greatest athletes of all time, and her impact on sport marketing has been unique in inspiring a generational shift for women athletes. Even as a rising player, and along with her similarly remarkable sister Venus, Serena was recognised as a media and branding superstar. Characterised by a powerful serve, lightning reflexes, and an unrelenting competitive spirit, Serena became one of tennis' most exciting players. However, it was her off-court persona that launched Serena's branding bonanza. With a charismatic smile, warm personality, and fierce determination, Serena was an immediate fan favourite, attracting a huge following of loyal supporters as well as a significant cadre of hopeful sponsors.

As Serena's career went from strength to strength, her influence on sport marketing grew along with it. As a sponsored athlete, she became a spokesperson for an assortment of brands, such Nike, Gatorade, Wilson, and Beats by Dre, all of which reported significant boosts in sales and brand awareness as a result. But the impact on sport marketing and product sales was just the beginning of Serena's sway. As an African American woman in a predominantly white, male-dominated sport, Serena faced significant challenges. Instead of backing down, however, she stepped up and worked throughout her career as champion of social causes and a powerful voice for change. She has been an outspoken advocate for women's rights, racial equality, and social justice, using her platform to raise awareness and effect change.

From a sport marketing viewpoint, Serena Williams is not just an athlete but a brand. Her name, image, and reputation are valuable assets that have been carefully cultivated and managed over the course of her career and have incorporated everything from her fashion choices to her social media presence. In fact, every aspect of Serena's public persona has been designed to reinforce her brand and appeal to her target audience. As an individual with uncompromising social principles, Serena's brand features authenticity. This has helped to build trust and loyalty amongst her fans and followers, who see her as a genuine and relatable figure beyond the tennis player with an undeniable association with excellence and winning.

QUESTIONS

1. 'Serena William's brand has also been carefully crafted to appeal to a diverse range of audiences. She is a trailblazer for women, African Americans, and other underrepresented groups, and her message of empowerment and inclusivity has resonated with people around the world. Her brand is inclusive and welcoming, and it encourages people of all backgrounds to aspire to greatness and to believe in themselves'. Do you agree with this statement? Explain why or why not.
2. In what ways has Serena Williams permanently changed sport marketing and athlete branding, especially for women?
3. Consider to what extent an athlete is also a sport marketing brand. Describe the brand attributes for Serena Williams using key words.

What makes sport marketing special?

Sport marketing is a complex and nuanced sub-discipline within mainstream marketing requiring a specialised approach to sport-related products and services. As an earlier section of this chapter highlighted, the sport industry compromises numerous sectors, and each of them has peculiarities that need to be thoroughly understood. Yet it is possible to identify some common features of sport marketing that tend to distinguish it from mainstream or generic marketing approaches. These features will arise throughout the text as critical elements that affect the choices made within a sport marketing context.

To begin with, most sport products and services have some association with a heightened emotional appeal because sport consumers and fans usually feel a deep connection with their favourite teams or athletes. Sport marketers employ the emotional connection to create strategies and campaigns that best appeal to fans' passion and loyalty. For example, in football (soccer), teams like FC Barcelona and Liverpool have a global fan base that is emotionally invested in the success of their team irrespective of their location. Sport marketers leverage emotional connections to sell tickets, merchandise, and other related products. This is because sport fans rarely lose their sense of team or club identification.

Sport marketing is often deeply intertwined with the culture and identity of its fans and supporters, creating an emotional connection that can drive significant revenue and growth for sport organisations. As a result, sport marketing practitioners work hard to promote the emotional connection with fans, which can deliver a huge yield in terms of brand loyalty and engagement. As subsequent chapters demonstrate, this can be achieved through a range of tactics including storytelling, social media, community events, and athlete branding that create a sense of belonging and loyalty. In addition, sport marketers aim to create unique experiences for fans. For example, sport events are often marketed as entertainment experiences where the unique aspects of the event, such as the atmosphere, the location, and the personalities involved, are highlighted.

A second common feature of sport is its seasonality, which means that its popularity and demand can vary significantly throughout the year. As a result, sport marketers need to be agile and adapt their strategies to fit the season, as well as ensure that they can provide other products and services to maintain revenues during times where no games are being played. As an example, the NBA season runs from October to April, and sport marketers need to create campaigns that align with the different stages of the season. During the playoffs, for instance, sport marketers may focus on creating hype and excitement for upcoming games, but in the off-season, they might focus more heavily on recruiting new sponsors, re-packaging content for alternative forms of broadcasting, social media engagement, and promoting merchandise.

Another common feature in sport marketing is that its appeal often transgresses geographical boundaries. Sport has both local and international appeal because some sports enjoy popularity only in specific regions, while others have a global audience. As a result, sport marketers must appreciate the nuances of different markets and develop tailored campaigns that resonate with local fans. For example, American football is more popular in the United States, while European football (soccer) has a more global appeal. Moreover, the sport industry and its marketing have grown rapidly in most parts of the world. For example, Asia is currently the fastest-growing region, driven by rapid economic development, technological contact, and an increasing interest in traditionally western sports. Countries such as China, Japan, and South Korea are investing heavily in developing local sports leagues and hosting major international sporting events. The Asian market also presents a significant opportunity for global sport brands seeking to expand their reach, particularly in areas such as esports, soccer, and basketball.

Meanwhile, the Middle East is another region where the sport industry is growing swiftly, particularly in areas such as soccer and motorsports. Countries such as Qatar, Saudi Arabia, and the United Arab Emirates have invested heavily in hosting major international sporting events, such as the FIFA World Cup and Formula 1 Grands Prix, to promote their cities and attract tourism.

A more mature market, North America, continues to grow and evolve through new technologies and innovations, which has had the effect of fragmenting the industry. The rise of esports and virtual sports has presented new opportunities for marketers to engage with younger audiences and expand the reach of traditional sports.

Also mature, Europe remains a major player in the global sport industry, particularly in soccer, rugby union, and cycling. However, the industry is also evolving rapidly in response to changing consumer behaviours and digital technologies and the proliferation of mobile devices and social media, all allowing sport marketers to engage with fans and create immersive experiences both in-stadium and online.

One further implication from the ongoing global growth of sport and its marketing is that organisations need to carefully manage the complex relationships with different stakeholders such as athletes, fans, media, and sponsors and balance their expectations and demands. Sport marketing needs to ensure that all stakeholders are engaged with targeted messages and campaigns relevant to their interests and expectations. Currently, this imperative requires sport marketers to leverage the power of new digital technologies. As later chapters describe, approaches may include developing innovative marketing campaigns that utilise virtual reality, social media, wearables, smart devices, and other emerging technologies to enhance the fan experience and create a sense of community.

Finally, sponsorship and endorsements are a significant part of sport marketing, and they involve partnering with teams, athletes, and events to promote products or services. For example, Nike is an official sponsor of the NBA and has endorsement deals with some of the league's top players, including LeBron James and Kevin Durant. Sport marketers need to identify the right partnerships and endorsements that align with their brand and attract the target audience. Increasingly, sport organisations recognise their power as social agents and incorporate social responsibility into their sport marketing campaigns. Common examples include promoting healthy lifestyles, environmental sustainability, diversity and inclusion, women's sport, and disability sport.

CASE 1.5

Chinese Super League

The Chinese Super League (CSL) is the preeminent professional football (soccer) league in China. Its expansion has been impressive along with a corresponding escalation in the league's reputation for producing and recruiting high-quality players. Since its formation in 2004, the CSL's leaders and marketers have tried to enhance the brand through a succession of branding and product innovations. One prominent transformation occurred in 2016 when the CSL embarked on a rebranding exercise designed to position it as a football league of global standing, part of which meant appealing to football-loving audiences outside China, and especially Europe from where the league's clubs hoped to secure high-profile players. A new logo was designed to convey a more current, dynamic, and competitive image. The league also extended its name from the CSL to the China Football Association Super League to emphasise its close affiliation with the Chinese Football Association, a decision aimed at driving domestic football participation while signalling to the world the sport's national standing. To attract more international attention, the CSL signed a multi-year partnership agreement with global sport marketing company, Infront Sports & Media. Their expertise in media rights distribution and sponsorship management was employed to drive the CSL's exposure and commercial value.

With product innovation in mind, the CSL focused on recruiting high-profile and quality players from some of the world's standout leagues to play for clubs in the league. They made good use of the Asian Champions League competition format that had commenced in 2009, which allowed Chinese teams to compete against the top teams in other Asian leagues, thereby giving them a lift in exposure.

More recently, the CSL became a player in the transfer market, with clubs spending significant sums of money to sign international stars such as Oscar, Nicolae Stanciu, Carlos Tevez, and Hulk. In addition, the league also implemented a salary cap for foreign players, to ensure that clubs do not overspend on player wages and to encourage local talent development. Currently, the 18 clubs share 81 foreign players of 653 signed, where the total value on the transfer market is estimated at €152 m in 2023. The CSL's branding and product innovation strategies have been largely successful. Certainly, the standard of football has been increasing significantly while the league's rebranding exercise has helped to enhance its reputation and appeal to international audiences. Infront's partnership has also bolstered CSL's commercial value, with a significant rise in media rights fees and sponsorship revenues.

However, the CSL has also faced some challenges. In 2019, the Chinese government imposed tighter regulations on the spending of football clubs, leading to a decrease in transfer spending and a decline in the number of high-profile foreign players joining the league. In addition, the outbreak of the COVID-19 pandemic in 2020 also disrupted the CSL's operations, leading to a delay in the start of the season and the suspension of matches for several months. Ultimately several clubs suffered and folded when affected by lower revenues during the COVID pandemic or a change in the strategy of their owners. To make matters worse, a cadre of star players including Hulk, Jackson Martinez, Yannick Carrasco, Axel Witsel, Marek Hamsik, and Gervinho left the league, with scores of other Brazilian players heading back to South America.

QUESTIONS

1. Visit the Transfer Market UK, which provides an estimation of the transfer values of players in all the major leagues. Compare the most valuable players in the CSL against the most valuable in the biggest European leagues. What can you conclude about the positioning of the CSL and why? (www.transfermarkt.co.uk).
2. What would you focus on to further develop the CSL brand and its ability to attract great foreign talent and global audiences?
3. Explore the digital footprints of some of the biggest clubs in the CSL, including on social media. How are they seeking to appeal to an international audience?
4. Currently, international star players in the CSL are few compared to the abundant recruitment and spending around 2016. Also worryingly, there has been very little improvement for the China men's national team, having failed to qualify for the 2022 FIFA World Cup. How can CSL club marketers create new and alternative revenue streams to ensure that they can survive and prosper even if their owners falter?

Multidimensional nature of sport marketing

The earlier discussion suggests that sport marketing is multidimensional. First, it involves the application of marketing concepts to sport products and services, and second, it involves the marketing of non-sport products through an association to sport. Sport marketing therefore has two key features, which we will subsequently refer to as 'angles'.

The first angle is the application of general marketing practices to sport-related products and services. The second angle is the marketing of other consumer and industrial products or services through sport. Like any form of marketing, sport marketing seeks to fulfil the needs and wants of consumers. It achieves this by providing sport services and sport-related products to consumers. However, sport marketing is unlike conventional marketing in that it also can encourage the consumption of non-sport products and services by association. It is thus important to understand that sport marketing means both the marketing of sport itself, and the use of sport as a tool to market other products and services.

These two angles of sport marketing are central to understanding the full range of ways in which sport is managed from a marketing perspective. However, this is not the full story, since the previous dual-angle discussion tends to emphasise the selling part of sport marketing. This is a far too simplistic approach to the sport marketing issue. Before any transaction can occur, a lengthy strategic analysis must be performed to determine what sport consumers want, why they want it, and how these wants can be best delivered to them. As a result, sport marketing should also be seen as the collection of planning and implementation activities associated with the delivery of a sport product or service.

Prior to any sales, a sport product or service must hold a place in the mind of a consumer. In practice, this demands that a consumer is aware of the sport product or service and has responded to it in some – hopefully positive – way. The process of cultivating such a response is known as branding, and when a sport brand has grasped a firm place in consumers' minds, then it is said that it is positioned. The consequence of successful branding and the acquisition of strong market positioning is not merely a single transaction. Rather, sport marketing reflects the establishment of an ongoing relationship between a sport brand and its users.

With the introduction of these three further points, it is possible to devise a simple working definition of sport marketing.

> *Chapter principle 1.3*: Sport marketing is the process of planning how a sport brand is positioned and how the delivery of its products or services are to be implemented in order to establish a relationship between a sport brand and its consumers.

Different angles, different intentions

With a working definition of sport marketing specified, it is useful to return to the idea that there are two angles to sport marketing. To repeat, the first is that sport products and services can be marketed directly to the consumer. The second is that other, non-sport products and services can be marketed through sport. In other words, sport marketing involves the marketing *of* sport and marketing *through* sport. For example, the marketing *of* sport products and services directly to sport consumers could include sporting equipment, professional competitions, sport events, and local clubs. Other simple examples include team advertising, designing a publicity stunt to promote an athlete, selling season tickets, and developing licensed apparel for sale. In contrast, marketing *through* sport happens when a non-sport product is marketed through an association to sport. Some examples could include a professional athlete endorsing a breakfast cereal, a financial-services business sponsoring a tennis tournament, and a beer company securing exclusive rights to provide its products at a sport venue or event.

> *Chapter principle 1.4*: Sport marketing has two angles: one is the marketing *of* sport products and services, while the other is marketing *through* sport.

CASE 1.6

Super Bowl

The Super Bowl is the championship game and the jewel in the crown of one of the world's most valuable, popular, and professionalised competitions, the US NFL. It offers a remarkable example where the marketing of and through sport can be seen in a gigantic commercial collision featuring a spectacular sporting event product, the participating teams, sponsors, advertisers, broadcasters, media, and fans. The Super Bowl is also one of the most significant events in the United States, with an estimated 115 million viewers tuning in to watch in 2023, making it the most popular TV programme in US broadcast history at the time. Many other millions of fans also tune in from around the world. Globally, the social media views stretched towards 250 million, signalling the event's monumental digital signature.

Due to the astonishing audience reach the Super Bowl and its famous half-time entertainment commands, especially with domestic viewers, advertising during the event is the costliest television commercial time in the United States. With the Super Bowl as one of the biggest sporting events in the world, it has become a showcase for some of the most creative and innovative commercials in marketing history. Super Bowl commercials often feature celebrity endorsements, humour, and memorable catchphrases, and have become a cultural phenomenon. Also astonishing is the cost to purchase the airtime for a single 30-second Super Bowl commercial, which reached US$7 million in 2023. Of course, the cost of a Super Bowl commercial is determined by a variety of factors, including the expected audience size, the length of the commercial, and the placement of the ad within the broadcast. Advertisers typically purchase multiple spots during the game, with prices varying depending on the time slot and the size of the audience. Yet, despite the high cost of Super Bowl advertising, advertisers are willing to pay a premium for the opportunity to reach such a large and engaged audience. The Super Bowl provides advertisers with a unique opportunity to connect with consumers on a massive scale, with many viewers tuning in specifically to watch the commercials. In addition to buying the space, advertisers also tend to spend a significant amount to create something worthy of a Super Bowl, adding to the investment required.

In addition to the large audience, Super Bowl advertising also provides significant impact for brands, with many commercials generating significant buzz and media coverage in the days and weeks before and after the game. For example, memorable Super Bowl commercials like Apple's '1984' and Coca-Cola's 'Mean Joe Greene' spots have become iconic in the world of advertising and remain decisive marketing contributions decades later. More recently the advertisements themselves have often been geared to generate social media buzz and engagement, allowing the massive TV audience to spill over to digital platforms.

A handful of other sporting events can also secure similar amounts for advertising time during their most significant matches. For example, the cost of advertising during the FIFA World Cup can be similar to the Super Bowl. However, prices can also vary much more depending on the specific game or match, with lower-profile games or matches having much lower advertising costs. Similarly, the cost of advertising during the Olympics can also be sky high, with prices for a 30-second commercial during the 2020 (2021) Tokyo Olympics reportedly reaching as high as US$1 million. Other major sporting events, such as the NBA Finals and the MLB World Series, typically have lower advertising costs than the Super Bowl, with prices for a 30-second commercial during the NBA Finals hovering under US$1 million, and prices for a 30-second commercial during the baseball World Series reaching over $500,000. Super Bowl and other major sport event advertising demonstrates the power of marketing through sport, where the costs reflect the enormous value that the game provides to advertisers, who evidently believe that the yield justifies the investment.

QUESTIONS

1. At the Super Bowl, describe all the versions involving the 'marketing of sport' then do the same for 'marketing through sport'. Is the Super Bowl as important for commercial opportunities as it is for the game itself? Explain.
2. Visit YouTube and search for 'famous Super Bowl commercials'. Which of these advertisements have received the greatest number of views, and can you identify anything in common about these most popular ones?
3. What does the volume of social media views suggest about the composition of future viewing audiences attracted to watch the Super Bowl?

A philosophy of sport marketing

While thinking about what sport marketing encompasses, it is helpful to understand that it is a hierarchical concept. That is, there are levels at which sport marketing can be considered. At the broadest level, sport marketing embraces a *philosophy* – a set of beliefs, if you like – about how to *do* marketing. It is not just marketing managers or the marketing department of a sport organisation that can think in marketing terms. A marketing philosophy is about putting the needs and wants of the customer at the centre of all decisions. It is important to add that the needs of the customer must complement the goals of the enterprise. In business, the goal is to make a profit, but in sport organisations the most important goal is usually to win or attract attention to the sport or organisation. Marketing philosophy is concerned with creating a win–win situation for both the organisation and sport consumers, but it recognises that no one will win if consumers' needs are not met. This sport marketing philosophy threads its way through this text. Each chapter provides a sharp reminder of the importance of understanding and targeting customers' needs and working out the best alignment between an organisation's goals, the sport product's features, and the expressed needs of consumers.

> *Chapter principle 1.5*: The *philosophy* of sport marketing is to deliver products that best satisfy the needs of sport consumers.

At a second level, sport marketing may be considered a *process*. It is a process because it involves a series of activities and steps. For example, sport marketing involves research, analysis, planning, development, implementation, and evaluation. These processes are a common property of sport marketing and feature as the structural framework around which this text is written.

> *Chapter principle 1.6*: The *process* of sport marketing is the series of steps required to find opportunities, devise a strategy, plan the tactics, and implement and evaluate a sport marketing plan.

At the third level, sport marketing may be summarised as a set of principles because it adopts numerous ideas and concepts that provide specific guidance to those undertaking sport marketing activities. In each chapter, a set of sport marketing principles are highlighted to provide clear guidance as to how the processes of sport marketing can be used in practice.

Finally, at the most operational level, sport marketing principles can be implemented with the aid of tools, which are devices and activities used in day-to-day practice. Direct selling is a tool, and so are price discounting, targeted advertising, and press conferences.

> *Chapter principle 1.7:* Sport marketing can be described as a philosophy (a set of values that drive the marketing function), a process (a linked series of activities), a set of principles (rules and guidelines) and tools (techniques).

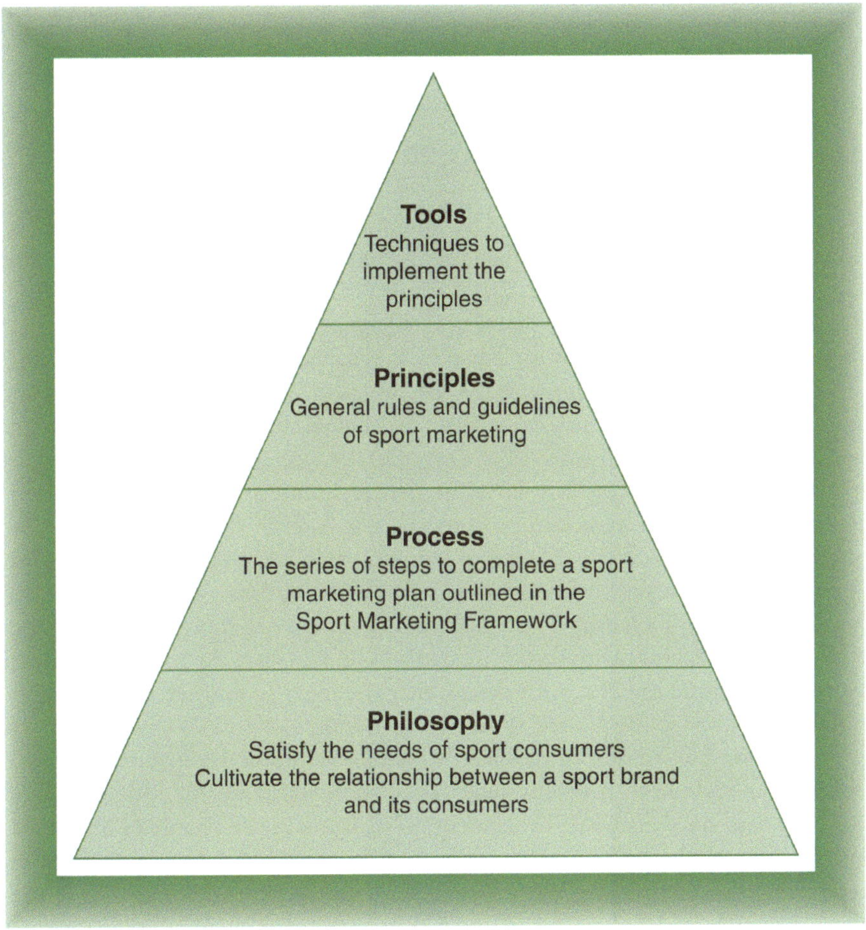

FIGURE 1.1 The structure of sport marketing

To summarise, this text adopts the sport marketing philosophy that consumers' needs are met when they match features of a product or service where the ultimate goal is to cultivate an ongoing relationship between a sport brand and consumers. The remainder of this text structures this philosophy around a sequence of sport marketing processes that reflect the organisation of the chapters. Within each chapter, sport marketing principles are presented to help steer the implementation of sport marketing processes. In addition, tools are offered as specific, recommended techniques. The four levels are represented in Figure 1.1.

> *Chapter principle 1.8:* The principles of sport marketing provide the rules and guidelines for the implementation of the Sport Marketing Framework process, while the tools of sport marketing are specific activities designed to help execute the principles.

CASE 1.7

Tokyo Summer Olympic Games 2020

The Tokyo 2020 (2021) Summer Olympic Games showcased the host city and nation to the world with the aim of enhancing its reputation through city and nation branding. Japan's hosting of the 2020 Olympic Games, held in Tokyo in 2021 due to a COVID-19 delay, brought this aim under heavy scrutiny. Was the investment in hosting the Olympics worth it for Japan from a nation branding perspective?

It could be argued that hosting the Olympics in Tokyo did provide an opportunity for Japan to broadcast its culture, technological-savvy, event prowess, and inviting hospitality to the world. For example, the opening ceremony emphasised Japan's history and culture, as well as the new and innovative technologies used at the event, such as the hydrogen-powered Olympic torch that signalled the country's commitment to sustainability and innovation. In addition, the event provided a 'home-ground' advantage for Japanese athletes to perform, with Japan winning a total of 58 medals, including 27 golds, and setting new Olympic records in several sports. From an economic perspective, it could be said that the Games provided a significant domestic impetus with the country spending an estimated US$15 billion on the event.

Conversely, the decision to go ahead with the Olympics during a pandemic was controversial and raised concerns about the health and safety of athletes and officials. This may have affected the perception of Japan as a responsible and reliable country, particularly as the Games had been postponed due to the dangers. Further, the event's organisation was not entirely textbook sport marketing, with a senior official resigning in the lead-up to the Games following negative publicity. Also, since the event was still mired in COVID concerns, the actual volume of visitors to Tokyo turned out to be negligible because tourists and fans were banned from attendance for safety reasons. But perhaps most worryingly, an enormous city and national financial investment had been expended that could have been directed elsewhere into critically needed infrastructure, the environment, or social welfare. Instead, Tokyo was left with an assemblage of magnificent venues in danger of being severely underused in the future.

In the long run, it will be important to assess the economic and reputational impact of the event, as well as how Japan was able to leverage its success in hosting the Olympics to enhance its nation branding efforts in the future.

QUESTIONS

1 Before COVID-19, the Tokyo city government estimated the economic legacy of the Games to be worth around US$109 billion. Part of their calculations included the impact from foreign spectators and post-Olympics visitors to Japan who had been inspired to travel because of the Games. This estimation was ultimately

overstated because foreign spectators were not allowed, but do you think that the long-term city and national branding outcomes could still have made the investment worthwhile?

2 Did you watch any of the Tokyo Games? If so, did watching the event shape your perceptions of the city and country? Do you find the idea of visiting Japan and Tokyo more attractive than prior to the Games?

3 The Tokyo Olympic stadium is now used for soccer and rugby matches as well as cultural events. Also, the athletes' village has been converted into apartments for commercial sale. Moreover, since fans were excluded from the Games, there was a huge surge in the sales of big screen televisions in Japan that has been estimated at around 30%. Consider what other beneficial outcomes have come from the event that might be less obvious than tourism.

What is to follow?

The marketing of sport may appear at first to be like general marketing. However, sport marketing does have differences to other forms of marketing. For example, the sport product is often highly inconsistent and unpredictable because it is not possible to predict the outcome of a sporting match or control the quality of play. In many other industries, the failure to guarantee the quality of a product would be disastrous. Another significant difference is that few products can evoke the emotional attachment and personal identification that sport commands. To be successful in sport marketing, it is necessary to understand general marketing as well as the unique circumstances of sport.

There are two aspects of sport that are pivotal to understanding its unique circumstances: the sport market and the sport consumer. Chapter 2 introduces the special features of sport with an emphasis on the three sectors associated with sport: the government, the not-for-profit, and the corporate sectors. Chapter 3 introduces the various types of sport consumers including those who utilise sport as a consumer product and those who actively engage in sport. The chapter also reveals the idiosyncratic motives and behaviours of sport consumers as well as the factors that influence their behaviour.

Once the sport market and the sport consumer are described, it is possible to move on to the process of sport marketing. Chapter 4 provides an overview of the four stages of the sport marketing process: (1) identify sport marketing opportunities; (2) develop a sport marketing strategy; (3) plan the marketing mix; and (4) implement and control the strategy. Figure 1.2 illustrates the Sport Marketing Framework. It is helpful because it offers a structure through which the logical sequence of sport marketing is implemented. A detailed guide to stage one is contained in Chapter 4. Stage two is provided in Chapter 5.

> *Chapter principle 1.9: The Sport Marketing Framework* provides a detailed explanation of the four stages of the sport marketing process: (1) identify sport marketing opportunities; (2) develop sport marketing strategy; (3) plan the marketing mix; and (4) implement and control the strategy.

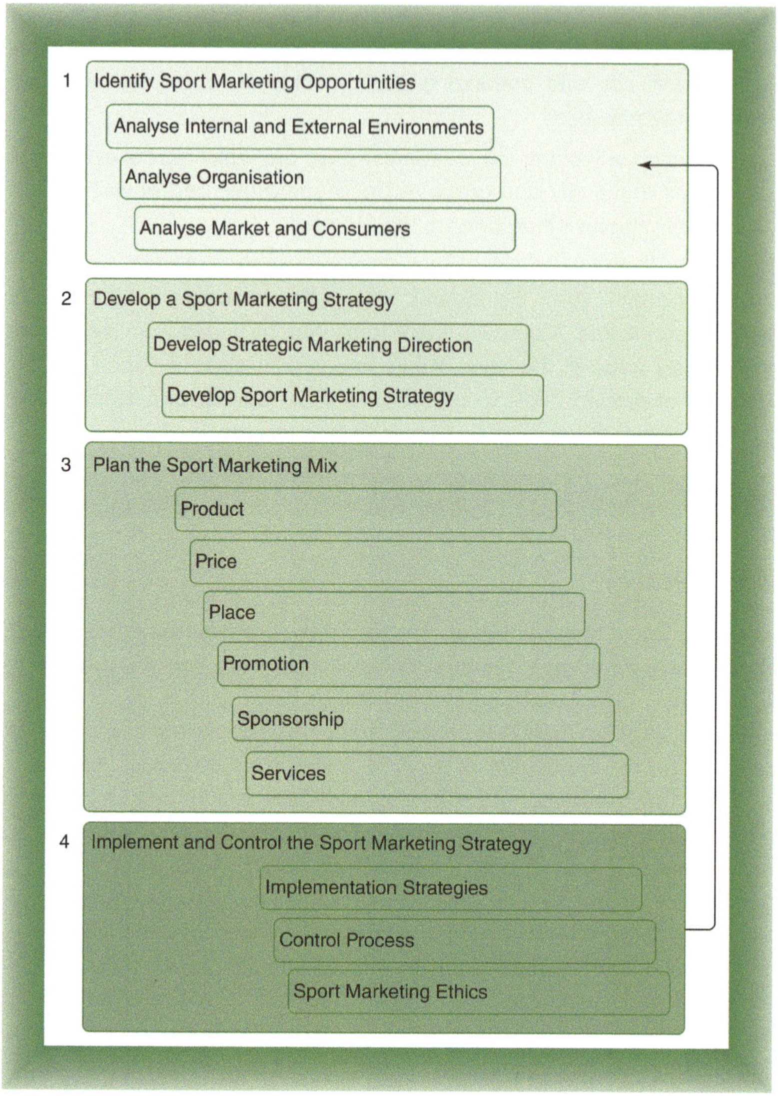

FIGURE 1.2 The sport marketing framework

Chapter 6 explores the first elements of the sport marketing mix. It introduces the key elements of the sport product, and outlines product-related marketing strategies. Chapter 7 specifies the second element in the sport marketing mix. The chapter is structured around a step-by-step pricing approach. Chapter 8 tackles the third dimension of the sport marketing mix. It highlights the basic concepts and issues of sport distribution and pays particular attention to the centrality of the sport venue, and media and broadcasting. Chapter 9 highlights the final component of the marketing mix. The chapter identifies the purpose of promotions, reviews its key elements, and describes promotions planning. Building on the promotion of sport, Chapter 10 presents the process of locating sponsors, the nature of sponsorship associations, the management and leveraging of relationships, and the evaluation process. Chapter 11 augments the sport marketing mix by examining sport services. This chapter introduces the specific aspects of services marketing and the idiosyncrasies of the sport service. It describes the techniques of quality service and customer satisfaction management as well as customer relationship marketing.

The world of sport marketing is changing rapidly, and the way in which the marketing mix and sponsorship are deployed is subject to constant new media platforms, technologies, and opportunities. Chapter 12 focuses on the current marketing context relevant to sport. This includes the key social and digital media technologies and their implications for the way in which sport consumers engage in the marketing process.

Chapter 13 explains the final stage of the Sport Marketing Framework. It introduces readers to the activities associated with setting up feedback mechanisms for determining whether the implementation process is successful. Chapter 13 also summarises the key processes and principles that are addressed in the text. It concludes with a discussion of the ethical responsibilities of sport marketers.

Finally, a reminder that a comprehensive case study summary appears in the Appendix at the end of this book.

PRINCIPLES SUMMARY

- Chapter principle 1.1: Marketing is more than promotion, advertising, personal selling, or sales gimmicks.
- Chapter principle 1.2: Marketing aims to create an exchange where the customer gives up something for a product or service.
- Chapter principle 1.3: Sport marketing is the process of planning how a sport brand is positioned and how the delivery of its products or services are to be implemented in order to establish a relationship between a sport brand and its consumers.
- Chapter principle 1.4: Sport marketing has two angles: one is the marketing of sport products and services, while the other is marketing *through* sport.
- Chapter principle 1.5: The *philosophy* of sport marketing is to satisfy the needs of sport consumers.
- Chapter principle 1.6: The *process* of sport marketing is the series of steps required to find opportunities, devise strategy, plan the tactics, and implement and evaluate a sport marketing plan.
- Chapter principle 1.7: *Sport marketing* can be described as a philosophy (a set of values that drive the marketing function), a process (a linked series of activities), a set of principles (rules and guidelines) and tools (techniques).
- Chapter principle 1.8: The *principles* of sport marketing provide the rules and guidelines for the implementation of the Sport Marketing Framework *process*, while the *tools* of sport marketing are specific activities designed to help execute the *principles*.
- Chapter principle 1.9: The *Sport Marketing Framework* provides a detailed explanation of the four stages of the sport marketing process: (1) identify sport marketing opportunities; (2) develop sport marketing strategy; (3) plan the marketing mix; and (4) implement and control the strategy.

REVIEW QUESTIONS

1 What is the basic philosophy of all marketing?
2 How does marketing differ from selling?
3 When and why did marketing emerge as a crucial management competency?
4 How is sport marketing different from general – that is, generic – marketing?
5 Explain the difference between marketing *in* sport and marketing *through* sport.
6 What are the steps in the Sport Marketing Framework?
7 Provide a definition of sport marketing in your own words.
8 What do you think is the ultimate goal of sport marketing?
9 Does this 'ultimate' goal generally deliver more benefits than costs to society?

RELEVANT WEBSITES

Chinese Football Association (www.thecfa.cn/CFAsuper/index.html)
Drone Racing League (www.thedroneracingleague.com)
Major League Eating (www.majorleagueeating.com)
Transfer Market UK (www.transfermarkt.co.uk)
World Wrestling Entertainment (www.wwe.com)

FURTHER READING

Dees, W., Walsh, P., McEvoy, C. D., McKelvey, S., Mullin, B. J., Hardy, S., & Sutton, W. A. (2021). *Sport Marketing*. Human Kinetics.

Lee, Y. H., & Watanabe, N. (2019). Sports economics and management of Asian sports business. *Journal of Global Sport Management*, *4*(2), 121–127.

Shilbury, D., & Rowe, K. (2020). *Sport management in Australia: An Organisational Overview*. Routledge.

Woods, R., & Butler, B. N. (2020). *Social Issues in Sport*. Human Kinetics Publishers.

Zhang, J. J., Breedlove, J., Kim, A., Bo, H. H., Anderson, D. J., Zhao, T. T., Johnson, L. M., & Pitts, B. G. (2021). Issues and new ideas in international sport management: An introduction. In J. J. Zhang, B. G. Pitts, & L. M. Johnson (Eds.), *International Sport Business Management* (pp. 1–15). Routledge.

CHAPTER 2

Sport markets

LEARNING OUTCOMES

At the end of this chapter, readers should be able to:

- describe the scale and scope of the sport industry.
- identify the differences between the three sport sectors and their roles in sport marketing.
- explain the unique features of sport products.
- describe how the special features of sport impact upon sport marketing theory and practice.

OVERVIEW

A market is, from a business perspective, a place where buyers and sellers interact to facilitate an exchange. In the sport context this can include consumers, or fans, who are ostensibly purchasing an experience, or consumers, buying an array of products and services from gym memberships to sporting memorabilia. This chapter provides an overview of the structure and operation of sport markets, which are far bigger than many people imagine. It does this by first discussing the general nature of the sport industry, and then its three core sectors more specifically. These sectors are the government, not-for-profit organisations, and the corporate sector. A review of the scale and scope of different sport markets is presented, while this chapter ends with an examination of the special features of sport, and how they often combine to present a unique and challenging marketing environment.

THE SPORT INDUSTRY

To understand sport markets, it is important to consider what constitutes the sport industry which they operate within, as well as the concept of industries more broadly. The term industry can be defined as an assembly of markets where similar, or closely related,

DOI: 10.4324/9781003391319-2

products and services are offered to consumers. These offerings bring about the potential for an exchange which can occur physically, or remotely depending upon the types of products or services being sought. As such, industries are often categorised according to the types of products and services they offer. The result is that there can be a wide range of organisations involved in an industry including commercial or corporate entities, non-profit organisations, associations, manufacturers, wholesalers, retailers, government agencies, and small businesses. From a sport marketing perspective, it is useful to remember that in a single industry the products and services produced satisfy similar consumer needs and wants. Consequently, the sport industry includes all the suppliers of products and services that satisfy the needs of sport consumers. The important point is that the sport industry constitutes a vast marketplace where consumers can acquire products and services that are associated with a multitude of sports with each sport offering a different and often quite unique experience to its participants and fans.

It is easy at first to get caught in the trap of thinking narrowly about what the sport industry comprises. For example, on first impressions the sport industry may appear to encompass little more than sport venues, gymnasiums, clubs and teams, leagues, athletes, sporting apparel, merchandise, sporting associations, and mega events like the Olympic Games. While this is a good start, there are many other organisations that form part of the sport industry. Some examples include:

- government departments of sport and recreation, at state or county, and federal or national level;
- the media, including print, television, streaming services, and an array of online applications;
- educational organisations such as universities and private providers that teach sport management programmes;
- researchers and consultants who study the sport market or consumers, as well as exercise physiology and sport medicine;
- the transport and construction sectors that contribute to the building of sporting venues;
- corporations and private enterprises that contribute to sport through sponsorship;
- sport governing bodies at a variety of levels from community to international who provide processes and structures to facilitate the playing of sport and the rules that apply;
- volunteers who assist in the operation of sport clubs and associations by taking on administrative, coaching, and officiating responsibilities.

One way of thinking about the composition of the sport industry is to visualise it as a series of steps that begin with the supply of raw materials that are used to create sport products and services through to their delivery and marketing at a specific place or destination. Figure 2.1 provides an example of a 'value chain' for the sport industry. It is called a value chain because at each step there is the addition of new value to the sport product. The diagram shows that government has a broad impact across all areas of the sport industry. Not only do they provide money to support sport organisations but they also help to create and maintain many of the physical facilities and venues, such as parks and stadiums,

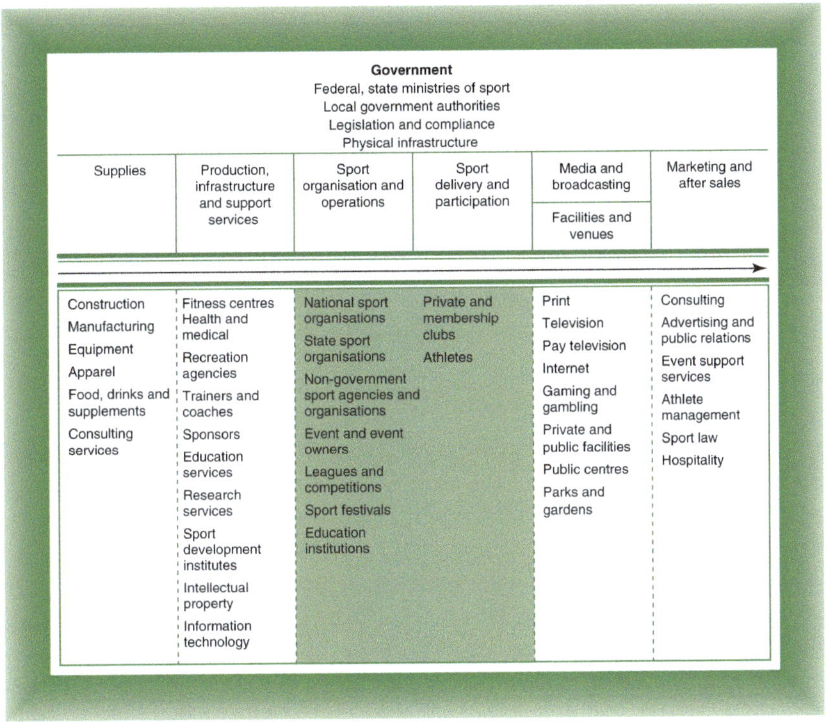

FIGURE 2.1 Value chain of the sport industry

in which sport activities take place. In addition, governments enact legislation and policies that affect sport in many ways. For example, they set laws that regulate how and when media can cover sport events. Many other types of government legislation can affect the individuals and groups involved in the sport industry, such as corporate law, contract law, taxation, and intellectual property rights.

The next level down in Figure 2.1 shows seven different categories of producers, suppliers, consumers, and others who are involved in the sport industry. Underneath each is a list of examples for that category. The shaded area shows the activities and groups that are commonly associated with the sport industry. These may be seen as the core sport products and services. Figure 2.1 shows that there is a lot more to the sport industry than just the core. For example, to the left of the shaded core are input activities contributing to the development of the core sport products and services. To the right of the shaded area are activities related to the distribution and marketing of sport products and services.

The size of the sport industry can be measured in a variety of ways. For example, one way is to count how much money is spent on sport directly, such as on sporting goods, the building of venues and organised sporting activities. Another approach involves determining how much money government and private businesses contribute to sport by way of grants and sponsorships. Other approaches still would be to examine how much consumers spend on sport-related products and services per year, how many people participate in sport, how many people are employed in the sport industry and even how many volunteers provide their services. However, it is extremely difficult (if not impossible) to calculate accurate statistics on these aspects of sport, let alone put them together to provide some measure of the sport industry. The sport industry is just too large and fragmented that it is not practical to locate and study them all.

CASE 2.1

Clearinghouse for Sport

Information on sport markets can be challenging to collate given the diverse number of stakeholders involved and the numerous ways a market can be defined. Each country tends to have its own system which reflects the way sport is governed and operated.

While almost all countries hold sport up as an important part of their social and cultural fabric, Australia takes sporting interest to an extreme considering it a critical part of identity. The state of Victoria has two public holidays dedicated to sporting pursuits (one a football match, the other a horse race), and the country is home to a vast array of major sporting events that belie its population and geographical location. This includes having a third city, in Brisbane, host the Summer Olympic Games in 2032, following on from Melbourne in 1956 and Sydney in 2000.

Not surprisingly the country also boasts a plethora of information around the various sport markets and industries that exist, however getting a sense of the size of sport marketing in Australia is challenging given the various ways that sport can be measured or divided. While certainly in the tens of billions of dollars (it is estimated to contribute about AUD$14 billion to the Australian economy), the economic impact is perhaps less important to how participation in sport, as fan or player, contributes to social wellbeing. Sport is well known for its physical benefits, but it also contributes to a sense of community spirit, camaraderie, and provides an escape that improves quality of life and enhanced wellbeing more generally.

A central point for sharing information and knowledge about sport in Australia is the 'Clearinghouse for Sport' (Clearinghouse) which uses the federal government's Australian Sports Commission as a central repository for storing a wide range of information and data that can be used by all sectors including interested individuals.

The Clearinghouse is home to a vast array of information making it helpful to understand the size and scope of a market such as sport, although various aspects such as media and gambling remain difficult to explore since they are connected to sport in tangential ways. It may be helpful for those readers who are not overly familiar with Australia to seek out similar information in their own home country to compare to Australia. Comparisons need to be made with caution given the measurement parameters are likely to be very different, however they can shed some light on how sport markets and industries differ around the world. The US market in sport, for example, is quite corporate in its orientation, often favouring private ownership of teams, which is quite different to the Australian and European models where membership and community involvement is often paramount in leagues.

QUESTIONS

Visit the Clearinghouse (www.clearinghouseforsport.gov.au) and explore the links provided there.

1 What does the available data highlight about the contribution of sport to the Australian economy and its community?
2 The Clearinghouse indicates that more than 10% (3 million) Australians volunteer in the sport and active recreation sector each year. What motivations are behind this commitment and how can marketers operating in the non-profit, government and corporate sectors use this information to advance their own goals?
3 The investment in sport by the government sector is often linked to providing a legacy, especially when it comes to major events. Australia and its cities are host to a plethora of major events including the 2023 FIFA Women's World Cup, the 2027 Rugby World Cup, and the 2032 Summer Olympic Games. How do these events, or others you may have noted, leave a legacy?

The multi-sector nature of the sport industry

In looking at the sport industry value chain, it becomes clear that different kinds of industrial activities are involved, all of which coalesce to make sport work. Without one of these sectors, it is very challenging, although not impossible, for a sport to succeed on a broader level. Even the most commercially rigorous and successful of sports require a vast infrastructure to succeed. From the complexities of the world game of football, which is overseen by a governing body in FIFA in grand tournaments but played with as much passion on public beaches, to jogging through a park track maintained by a local municipality and then entering a half-marathon sponsored by an international company, sport has many actors in its industry who create the networks which allow it to prosper. In general, they fall into three broad categories.

First, there are those associated with the government, which are collectively referred to as the public sector including national, state/county/provincial, regional, and local governments. Connected to these various levels are quasi-government institutions and agencies that are involved in the development of sport. These bodies typically receive government funding but have differentiated legal status to allow them to operate with some autonomy and more closely to that of a business, despite the ultimate government oversight. They can, for example, determine government sport policy, seek ways to bolster competitive performance of elite athletes, or encourage health compliance or exercise in the community. Undoubtedly around the world governments of all levels and their agencies are intrinsically intertwined with sport. Often because sport is seen as a desirable conduit for public health, or to generate tourism, or positive perceptions, governments will take their connection to sport extremely seriously. Some countries like Australia see a strong reflection of their national image in sporting endeavours, while regions in the world such as the Middle East are increasingly investing in sport as a mechanism to create new bases for tourism and influence.

The second kind of activity is undertaken by the non-profit or voluntary sector. This group is made up of local clubs, community-based associations, universities and colleges, governing organisations, and international federations. In the non-profit sector, the focus is on the development of sport through organised competition and participation, with a heavy emphasis on the regulation and management of sport. The non-profit sector is important for many sports as it provides a backbone to facilitate participation at junior levels that can often translate into adult fandom. While many teams around the world playing in elite leagues are now fully professional, some retain a special corporate status to minimise tax or operate under special antitrust provisions to facilitate activities such as revenue sharing, player movement, and media deals. An important part of this sector are the volunteers who are critical to allowing sport clubs to function. At the junior or community level the reliance on volunteers is especially critical.

The third and final set of activities is the purview of the professional or corporate sport sector. This has become an increasingly important group in recent decades as sport has become more commercialised, attracting the interest of a wide array of parties who see potential profits from the unique nature of sport, including the passion of its fans. Members of this corporate group are commercially focused, comprising professional clubs, leagues, and major events. Some of these can be many decades old, while others may be just emerging. In addition, this group includes an increasing number of corporations that have a financial interest in sport, such as equipment and apparel manufacturers, sport retailers, media companies, telecommunications providers, investors, management companies, rights holders, and sponsors. In fact, any organisation with the primary purpose of making a profit from an association with sport may be placed in this category.

As Figure 2.1 shows, the three sectors mix and mingle, their activities intersecting regularly. In fact, sport would struggle to be produced in a sustainable way without the cooperation of all three sectors. To begin with, the government or public sector provides the context in which sport is undertaken. Often this includes financial support and the provision and maintenance of sport venues and facilities for non-profit sector activities, or to attract the private sector for events that are seen as mutually beneficial. Equally, non-profit sport is expected to deliver social and community benefits and may also drive interest in more professional events. The regulatory environment created by government also affects corporate sport because professional leagues generally require the use of public venues and often seek government funding citing community impact as the rationale for this investment. Corporate sport is also dependent on community sport because they provide the playing, coaching and administrative talent to lower levels of leagues and associations. Reciprocally, parts of the corporate sector seek marketing benefits through an association with non-profit sport by providing much needed funding through sponsorships. In general, it is important to remember that the activities of the three sectors bleed into each other. For example, some high-profile non-profit sport organisations are professionally managed and behave as corporate entities. There is also some ambiguity about where large non-government, non-corporate entities such as the International Olympic Committee, or large universities in North America, fit in. The next sections focus on the marketing implications that relate to each of the three sectors and their primary activities.

Government Sport Sector

In general, governments choose to get involved in sport because of its potential to deliver social, economic, and political benefits. For example, sport can provide health benefits for participants as well as social cohesion. It can also stimulate economic activity and bolster civic pride. For some governments, sport is advantageous because it can cultivate national identity and solidarity, which tends to be helpful for the re-election of politicians and in developing national goodwill. Although the policy approach taken by a government towards sport can change radically depending on its ideological orientation, all governments influence sport in at least four ways.

First, governments at various levels provide funding and facilities for sport. This includes funding for national sport organisations and Olympic campaigns, and the construction and maintenance of major and local sport, recreation, and leisure facilities. Second, governments can be directly involved in the development of sport via training institutes and elite testing facilities. Third, governments can deliver sport-, health- or physical activity-related programmes, or just promote lifestyle campaigns. Finally, governments can take responsibility for aspects of sport compliance, such as anti-doping, as well as the composition of the general regulatory environment. A few further comments on this last element are warranted.

The term 'regulatory environment' refers to the nature of competition within an industry. Unlike more traditional industries, the sport industry is often allowed by government to pursue anti-competitive practices, including significant restrictions on the rights of players including such mechanisms as salary caps on what they can be paid and drafts that regulate who they will play for. This occurs because many governments accept that sport performs poorly under normal market conditions. As a result, although league regulation may be anti-competitive when compared to other business types, it is generally not considered unreasonable, or against the public interest. While member teams are highly competitive and concerned with on-field dominance, they also understand that their long-term viability depends on a high-quality and well-balanced competition where teams are of comparable strength and ability. Government regulations allow sport teams in some leagues to band together and operate for the greater good. This can provide substantial barriers to entry for competitor products, although these are not insurmountable if the marketing of a new league is done well.

Governments regularly employ marketing principles to support their sport objectives. Typically, governments do not get directly involved in marketing sport, but often spend considerable money on promoting the benefits of sport or its locations. For example, governments use marketing to attract large sport events to specific locations, with many cities now featuring quasi-government organisations tasked with luring and promoting major events. They also employ marketing to promote the social and health benefits of sport participation or an active lifestyle.

Non-profit Sport Sector

In the Western world, where economies are centred on the interaction of capitalist enterprises and their customers, it is generally accepted that government will never be responsible for the bulk of the production, distribution, and sale of sport products and related services. The result has been the emergence of non-profit sport organisations that make up the gaps in between profit-oriented business and government. Non-profit sport organisations are therefore concerned with the public good rather than making money. However, since they are not administered by the government, non-profit sport organisations must find resources and expertise for themselves and must comply with government regulations about their legal status and conduct. As a rule, non-profit sport organisations are highly specialised in that they tend to evolve to fit a particular community sporting need. They are also administered mainly by volunteers. Non-profit sport organisations are the backbone of sport.

Non-profit sport organisations develop communities, social networks, and local groups through the provision of specialised sport products and services. Typically, these services revolve around the organisation of sport competitions and the subsequent development and management of players, coaches, and administrators, along with the code itself. However, there are also professional service organisations, lobby groups, event organisers, and governing bodies. Sport and recreation organisations can be classified into three different kinds of non-profit groups. The first includes amateur sport, training, fitness and sport facilities, and sport competitions and events. The second includes recreation and social clubs such as country clubs and leisure clubs. The third includes service clubs that use sport as a vehicle for social development. Of these three groups, the first is the largest as it incorporates a vast number of sport clubs and their associations. In some countries, and particularly in the United States, school and college sport is the most prevalent form of non-profit sport.

Non-profit sport organisations face numerous marketing challenges. To begin with, they are often cash-poor, which means that they cannot pursue expensive advertising or other major promotional activities. Another challenge is that they do not necessarily have access to sport marketing expertise and rely on the goodwill and service of volunteer staff. A final problem is that many non-profit sport organisations have rich but cumbersome amateur traditions that do not lend themselves to attractive marketing. Non-profit sport organisations consequently focus their marketing initiatives on low-cost activities that emphasise the benefits of participating in sport. Some have recognised the importance of differentiating their products and services from others, and work hard to create a relationship between their brand and sport consumers. In addition, some non-profit sport organisations are taking advantage of new technology and digital media platforms to inexpensively position themselves distinctively in a cluttered sport marketplace. Social media and associated apps have allowed sport organisations to organise the community around them and the events that they run. These platforms have also formed a basis for attracting the attention of governments and the corporate sport sector who value the grassroots approach of many non-profit bodies.

Corporate Sport Sector

The corporate or professional sport sector is characterised by the commercial imperative; the desire to make a profit from sport. As Figure 2.1 demonstrates, there are numerous places in which commercial enterprises can provide value-adding products or services associated with sport that can generate a financial return. At the hub of corporate sport are professional clubs and teams that compete in large national or international leagues, or athletes and teams that participate in large events. Although these organisations and athletes may not all be profit-maximisers, they nevertheless provide the core content that other profit-based businesses wish to associate with.

Professional sport teams are central to the concept of sport that is produced for profitable consumption and create a product that is sold, or marketed, to four groups: first, fans who support leagues by attending games, following games via various media platforms and purchasing league- and team-related merchandise; second, television and other media or broadcasting companies that purchase the right to show games as a programming option; third, communities that build facilities and support local clubs; and fourth, corporations that support leagues and clubs by increasing gate monies, purchasing teams outright, or providing revenues through sponsorships or other associations that seek to leverage a commercial relationship.

Professional sports leagues are just one part of the corporate sport sector, however. There is also an enormous amount of money to be made in the manufacture of sport-related products and services. The tangible product sector is growing at every turn and includes areas such as stadium construction, equipment manufacturers, sport apparel, and fashion labels. The equipment needed to play hockey, go sailing, participate in golf, and even compete in cycling events can cost participants many thousands of dollars. There are also professional sport services to be considered, which include advertisers, athlete and player managers, sport nutrition and supplement consultants, sport physicians, physiotherapists, event and sport tourism promoters, hospitality services, sponsors, and team franchise owners.

An increasingly important part of corporate sport is the concept of building a relationship with fans and other stakeholders through branding, since in such a competitive sports world it is crucially important to establish lasting emotional connections with consumers. For example, sport equipment and apparel manufacturers need to convince consumers that using their brand has benefits over using a competitor's brand, and even fans who stay loyal to one team over their lifetime are urged to connect through digital platforms if they cannot attend a match in person. Much of the branding emphasis of corporate sport revolves around the spectacle and entertainment value of the sport experience, and all the symbolism and imagery that go with it. It is rare to attend any sport event and not see corporate brands associated with it. These brands have their own marketing goals, seeking to achieve their objectives through sport given its power to amplify elements of life, like success and determination that are so well understood by consumers.

CASE 2.2

Forbes World's Most Valuable Sport Teams

Building valuable sport brands is challenging for marketers given the fiercely competitive nature of the entertainment industry. To gain an understanding of which brands are leading the pack, *Forbes*, one of America's leading business magazines, does a regular update of the world's major sport brands, providing a list of the 'World's Most Valuable Sport Teams'. Commencing in 2010 the list has had (to date) only three number one brands. First with English Premier League (EPL) stalwart Manchester United between 2010 and 2012, then Spanish La Liga giants Real Madrid between 2013 and 2015, and since 2016 the clear top team has been the Dallas Cowboys of the National Football League (NFL). The list is heavy with US sporting franchises across the NFL, the National Basketball Association (NBA), and Major League Baseball (MLB). The mix for 2022 included 30 NFL teams, 7 NBA teams, 5 MLB teams, 4 EPL teams, 2 La Liga teams, and 1 each from French Ligue 1 and the German Bundesliga.

Forbes assigns values to each of the teams using a formula that seeks to value the brand attached to each team. While this can capture the global nature of the markets many of these teams operate in, it also accounts for revenue streams coming into the franchises and thus reflects the enormous media deals associated with the NFL and the plethora of star players it generates. Building a valuable sport team requires more than just assembling talented players, however. It also requires operating in a league that has widespread appeal that attracts the investment of various stakeholders such as the media, corporate sponsors, and fans alike. The NFL are clearly masters of understanding their markets, locating their 32 franchises across America, including having three teams in the lucrative California entertainment market, the Los Angeles Rams, the Los Angeles Chargers, and the San Francisco 49ers. All up California has 15 elite sporting teams across various sports with 8 of these teams featuring in the Top 50 of Forbes' 2022 list.

In 2021, the NFL inked the most lucrative deals in sport marketing history, announcing a 10-year deal worth well over US$100 billion to run between 2023 and 2033 that would further existing partnerships with Amazon, CBS, ESPN/ABC, Fox, and NBC to provide widespread coverage of the league. While all networks will look to build digital content, the Amazon deal worth $1 billion per season alone gives it the rights to the 'Thursday Night Football' series of broadcasts which will help take the NFL to new markets given the reach of the online platform and its ambitions to further develop its streaming presence. The deal also gives the NFL an enormous footprint across the United States, with a wide variety of major networks all focused on maximising and promoting the league given their investment in it.

The strength of a sport brand is dependent on the ability of marketing campaigns to draw more public awareness, more media coverage, more members, more supporters, and more corporate partners. In addition, as this chapter highlights, is how well the league a team competes in is marketed. It is of limited value being the most successful team in a league given the marketing aspirations will soon exceed the opportunity. This may be the arguable case in French football where an infusion of money and a bevy of star players has seen Paris Saint-Germain (PSG) dominate a relatively strong league but not necessarily reach the dizzying heights of international club rivals such as Barcelona, Real Madrid, Bayern Munich, and Liverpool.

Part of this may be attributed to win-loss records in defining success, including the UEFA Champions League which has become a de facto measure for achievement in Europe for football teams. For a professional sport club its trophy cabinet is critical. In football, Real Madrid, Barcelona, Liverpool, and Bayern Munich have massively valued brands, and they don't come from just having a nicely designed stadium, a lovely combination of club colours, a highly distinctive club logo and motto, or even a well-respected chairman of the governing board. Ultimately high brand values, especially in professional football, are built on a foundation of winning and high-profile success. This is why Crystal Palace and Bournemouth are unlikely to ever have the same brand value as Manchester United and Arsenal in the EPL. Good marketing will make a difference, but a marketing campaign will only be effective in the long run if the product is also perceived as being of high quality. In sport, this is measured by trophies and often far more so than profit and loss statements.

QUESTIONS

Locate the most recent Forbes Most Valuable Sports Team ranking and based on your reading and review of this list, how would you respond to the following questions?

1. What makes for a strong sport team brand?
2. Despite their unquestioned power, not all NFL teams make the Top 50 list. Identify some teams which did not and suggest an explanation for this.
3. The Forbes article says nothing about sporting goods suppliers. If sporting goods suppliers were included, then (at least) two businesses would most likely need to be included. Who would these be and why?
4. What brands were you surprised by on the list – either being on it or not being on it – outline why this was the case.

Sport markets

Within each of the three sectors described above there are a multitude of markets that exist and the possibility of many more that could be added if entrepreneurs see an opportunity to connect the various players. Markets are all about a place, tangible or intangible, that facilitates exchange, and the broad nature of the concept of sport and the similarly vast size of the industries that surround it make new markets inevitable. The best way to view a market is through the eyes of its constituents, rather than seeking to apply artificial categories.

Take, for example, the non-profit sport sector. Around the world there are hundreds of sports being played, and in most instances these sports are governed by international associations, national associations, and in some cases state and provincial associations. Each of the sports on their own can be viewed as a market where the suppliers of the services are seeking customers – that is, participants at the most basic level – to use their services. This means that there are markets for services associated with athletics, badminton, basketball, cricket, exercise programmes, football, field hockey, horse racing, ice hockey, rock-climbing, rugby, tennis, and volleyball. The list goes on. And, within each market, there are clubs and venues offering an array of different experiences. Tennis clubs, for instance, may offer weekend competitions, weekday competitions, competitions with modified rules, gender-specific competitions, or mixed-gender competitions. Similarly, there are a multitude of markets within one sport type. For example, athletics is an international discipline that features in its own World Championships and is part of the Summer Olympic Games but it is made up of a series of basic events including jumping, throwing, and running. This latter event has a multitude of styles, and thus potential markets, from professional leagues through to organised community events such as the weekly five-kilometre 'parkruns' that occur on Saturday mornings in over 20 countries.

The point to make here is that while sport markets are unified by their emphasis on physical activity of one sort or another, they can also be very different. Participation can involve playing the game, but it can also involve watching others play, or how a game is played, including where, when, and how. It can involve the use of complex technologies such as motorcycles and sailboats on one hand, and simpler technologies such as sport socks and jump ropes on the other hand.

THE SPECIAL FEATURES OF SPORT PRODUCTS

Sport, whatever its features and idiosyncrasies, has an extraordinary ability to command attention, interest, and loyalty. In some extreme instances, where injury is common or violence is excessive, it can lead to disapproval. Most people, however, value sport, entrenching it into their social and cultural fabric as a mainstay of life. Some people go even further by claiming that sport is a sacred space because it takes people out of their ordinary existence and transports them to a world where anything is possible – a marketing message often latched onto by brands seeking to exploit sport's unique properties. Others have views that are more circumspect and merely suggest that sport is character-building, provides participants with a solid moral compass, and thus its purpose is far loftier than doing business and making profits. For these people, sport is special and unlike other activities that our daily lives offer up to us.

Some sport commentators believe that when sport becomes a business, and thus focuses on marketing at the exclusion of other aspects, it loses its most important qualities, which includes a sense of history, tradition and continuity, a passionate connection to clubs and players, and even just the belief that sport gives life a little more variety and a lot more meaning. Sport marketers who accept the view that sport has an emotional resonance missing in many other products, tend to believe that managing sport is a difficult task, and thus that standard business and marketing practices do not translate easily to sport. This is because the emotions inherent in sport force managers to avoid decisions that could compromise long-standing traditions, cause fan dissatisfaction, or reduce volunteer participation. Sport is additionally framed by a plethora of rules and ethical standards that can be hard to navigate from a purely business perspective, and the element of control over the sport marketing product often rests with coaches or athletes rather than marketing managers given these practices and traditions. Additionally, sport often has a moral aspect to it and thus notions of fair play and cheating are always front and centre. People who believe sport is a unique enterprise also argue that the commercialisation and professionalisation of sport have damaged its community foundations and ethical base.

On the other hand, to some commentators, sport, whether played at the elite and professional level or at the local-community level, remains just another form of business that delivers entertainment to the masses and/or enjoyment to the participants. They argue that sport expresses a form of leisure that, like any other product, is valued because it not only delivers a fit and healthy body if played on a regular basis but also provides an unpredictable performance experience. In each case, the product will have a benefit and to secure this benefit the users of a sport product will be prepared to pay a specific price. And more sales mean that the supplying organisations will make more money by keeping more customers happy and satisfied. This is the market at work.

From such a viewpoint, good business practices are needed to help keep sport organisations alive; any benefits that sport might confer (e.g., health benefits, character-building opportunities, and a sense of belonging) will be lost forever if an organisation cannot remain profitable by operating in a business-like manner. As a result, those who believe sport operates as just another business take the view that standard marketing practices are the most appropriate way of dealing with the operation of sport. Instead of seeing sport as a unique enterprise, they believe that sport is a client-based service business, operating within a specific, but not necessarily unique business marketplace. This means they also take a corporate view of volunteers and traditions. For example, volunteers are a 'human resource' of an organisation, who must be inducted, rewarded, trained, and counselled like any other member of staff in any other commercial enterprise.

Both perspectives can be true. Sport is undoubtedly a special kind of product but it still operates in a business context that demands professionalism and accountability. Most sport marketers hold the view that sport organisations, whatever their size or scope, can no longer be managed as fun and games, or separated from the wider commercial world. Even non-profit clubs, for example, must perform financially if they want to survive as an on-going concern in the highly competitive world of sport and alternative entertainment products. Sport is not so unique that it cannot be put in a commercial framework. But it is not just another form of commercial entertainment either. Sport is business, but it is a special form of business. The key is to understand the special features of sport and their relevance to meeting the needs of sport consumers.

In the next section, the special features of sport products and sport experiences are outlined. It emphasises the point that those factors that make sport appealing to consumers, can in other situations make the products extremely unattractive. For example, going to a boxing match as a spectator is more exhilarating when the result is uncertain – anything can happen and, in many instances, the more unusual the experience the better it is. However, buying a washing machine on the basis that the outcome of the wash will be uncertain does not make any sense, since the expectation for reliability and certainty drive what really matters. Even in a service experience, consumers would expect a hotel to be clean and comfortable, an airline to be safe and punctual, and a hairdresser to be proficient and pleasant. As a result, sport's features are important for sport marketers to understand and to manage where possible. Like many service businesses, as we explore in Chapter 11, managing expectations will be highly important. From a marketing perspective there is a continual demand to balance sport's need for uncertainty on one hand, against the need for rules that will provide a regular quality outcome on the other. While fans love the unexpected, sport marketers can fear the unknown it generates.

> *Chapter principle 2.1*: Sport is a special form of business. A standard marketing approach does not always work, so sport marketers must also understand the special features of the sport market and build these into their strategic planning and operations.

Emotion and passion

Sport can stimulate an emotional response in its consumers of the kind rarely elicited by other products. Imagine bank customers buying memorabilia to show allegiance with their financial institution, or consumers identifying so strongly with their insurance company that they get a tattoo with its logo. We know that some sport followers are so passionate about players, teams, and the sport itself that their interest borders upon, or even becomes, obsession. This addiction provides the emotional glue that binds fans to teams and maintains loyalty even in the face of on-field failure.

While most marketers can only dream of having customers that are as passionate about their products as sport fans, the emotion stimulated by sport can also have a negative impact. The emotion and passion that fans have often empowers them to express their negative opinions strongly and clearly to clubs. While we would not critique the performance of the marketing manager of the toothpaste we use, we almost certainly have an opinion about our favourite team's administration, given the investment we have made emotionally, as well as perceptions that fans often have that they could run a club just as well given their inherent passion. Sport's emotional intensity can, from the organisational perspective, mean that teams and leagues have strong attachments to the past through nostalgia and tradition. As a result, they may ignore efficiency, productivity, and the need to respond quickly to changing market conditions. For example, a proposal to change club colours to project a more attractive and marketable image may be defeated because it breaks a link with tradition. Similarly, a coach or manager can be appointed based on their previous loyalty to the club rather than because of a capacity to manage players better than the other applicants.

> *Chapter principle 2.2*: Sport can elicit an emotional response in its consumers that is rarely found in other businesses. It can stimulate immense loyalty, but also strong attachments to nostalgia and club tradition as well as provide strong feelings to contribute a voice on matters affecting the bonds that have been built.

On-field versus off-field success

One of the most significant differences between not-for-profit sport organisations – especially those that participate in competitive sport settings – and commercial businesses, are the ways in which they measure performance. Commercial businesses may have many goals but their main purpose is to maximise profits. For example, Coca-Cola and PepsiCo are fierce retail competitors but in the same year they could both produce a large profit and claim it a success. That is, they can all win with no apparent losers. However, sport is different. Sport club members and fans judge performance based on trophies, championships, premierships, pennants, cups, and rankings. For every winner there are many more losers. Moreover, a large annual profit might not seem like a success to sport clubs if they finished the season at the foot of the rankings. For the most part sport clubs, and importantly their fans, value winning over expanding profits. In fact, many fans despise profits in sport as they believe it comes at the direct expense of winning – such as not investing enough in new talent, facilities, or coaching. It is also important to note that on-field and off-field successes do not always go together. A sport club may bankrupt itself by paying high salaries for players and coaches to secure a championship. On the other hand, they may succeed financially by placing a ceiling on player payments but not perform on the field of play because of their scarcity of playing talent. Finding the balance between success on and off the field remains an important consideration in many sporting teams, and clubs are always looking for an elusive advantage that allows them to maximise success while minimising cost. One of the most famous examples was outlined in the 2003 book 'Moneyball' by Michael Lewis, which later became a Hollywood movie. It tells the tale of the Oakland Athletics Major League Baseball team, which used advanced sport data and statistical analysis to recruit high performing but lower cost players using key metrics.

Competitive sport clubs and organisations must manage competing demands. On the one hand, they need to maximise profit in order to invest in their competitive activities. On the other hand, they need to perform on the field of play no matter what the cost. However, as the sport and leisure industry become increasingly competitive, and more alternative entertainment options are available to consumers, sport organisations become more pressured to focus on profits and cash flow. Marketing is one avenue to help support revenue without compromising an emphasis on sport performance.

> *Chapter principle 2.3*: Sport organisations measure their success both on and off the field of play and the two are not always happy partners. On-field success refers to achievement within sport competition. Off-field success refers to financial stability and profitability.

A level playing field

In most business settings it is desirable to put competitors out of business. Both British Airways and Qantas would be better placed if Ryanair and Virgin respectively were either available for takeover or were pushed into insolvency. Fewer competitors mean more available customers, which in turn leads to higher profits. Paradoxically, and despite our observations in the previous section, this is not always the case in sport. In fact, sport organisations that compete in leagues regularly demand the opposite. That is, they rely on the health of their competitors for their own success. This is because most fans are more attracted to a close contest where the winner is unknown in advance. Dominating a league or competition can be self-defeating because the interest of fans can fade, and corporate backers may look for more appealing products into which to invest. It is therefore often in the interests of the big teams to prop up the operations of the less powerful teams. In motorsport, the wealthier teams are often restricted in how they use their greater resources enabling the less wealthy teams to stay in touch within a sport that is heavily dependent on technological innovation and advancement.

Overall, sport leagues attract higher attendances and viewers when it is difficult to predict who will win a sporting contest. Ironically, to remain successful, leagues and competitions need as many of their clubs to be competitive as possible. When the outcome of a match is highly predictable, it will not attract large crowd numbers and eventually it will reduce ticket, media, and sponsorship revenue. A healthy, competitive balance between teams remains essential. Sometimes this will require a radical transfer of resources from wealthy clubs to poorer clubs, which of course rarely happens in the private business sector. Some sport codes and leagues have implemented policies to encourage competitive balance. For example, salary caps for players, rules about sharing revenues, and regulations regarding how players are to be drafted to teams, are all designed to maintain a competitive balance between teams.

Many of these factors work against a marketer in a successful team as it becomes almost inevitable that a downslide will occur in pursuit of a level playing field. It does however offer sport marketers the potent element of 'hope' as a marketing weapon which can be harnessed to excite and enthuse stakeholders. The pursuit of a level playing field will typically mean a unique mix of collaboration and competition is needed, and we explore this more fully next.

> *Chapter principle 2.4*: Sport organisations that compete in leagues and competitions rely on the health of their competitors for their own success. Sport consumers are more attracted to attend games where there is a balanced competition, providing the basis for unexpected outcomes that captures the essence of sport as a game.

Collaboration and competition

As noted earlier, teams and clubs depend on the continued on-field and off-field success of their opponents. If a league becomes divided into two groups, one of wealthy and high performing teams and another of poor and low performing teams, this will ultimately damage all the clubs involved and the competition. In practice, clubs must cooperate with their rivals to deliver what their consumers want, while at the same time competing with them for sporting success; this cooperation and competition in an industry is sometimes called 'coopetition', a portmanteau of the terms.

Sport clubs need their opposition to remain successful and may cooperate to share revenues and trade player talent to maintain competitive balance. In most industries, businesses would not be allowed to cooperate in this way; it is considered anti-competitive, or *cartel-like* behaviour, and there are often laws that prohibit it. But in sport, cartel arrangements are common. For example, clubs may share revenue, prevent other clubs from entering the market, collectively fix prices and generally limit the amount of competition.

The idea of regulating sport leagues to keep a fair and balanced competition has become common in sport. To achieve this, regulators often adopt three key structural principles. First, they establish an independent decision-making body to regulate the member teams or organisations, such as the Fédération International de l'Automobile (FIA) for motorsport, and the English Football Association for football. This decision-making body makes rules that address how players or teams are recruited and allocated, the number of teams allowed in the competition, where the teams are located, the length of the playing season, the design of the fixtures, and admission charges. Such rules can help to ensure that no team monopolises the best players, and that each team has a reasonable chance of winning. Other regulations set by the central body may even involve changing the rules of the game itself to make the sport more attractive to new markets or different forms of distribution (such as streaming services). For example, the Olympic Games in 2008 decided to schedule the swimming finals in the morning, rather than the normal evening slot, to maximise prime-time television viewing in the large viewing market of the United States, and its associated broadcasters and sponsors. The regulating body is usually able to enforce disciplinary action upon those who breach the regulations.

Second, sport regulators impose rules designed to minimise costs and maximise profits. For example, they enforce policies to restrict the ability of teams to bid for players, set limits on player salaries, and determine the distribution of shared revenues such as broadcasting rights. In principle, policies are designed to ensure that teams can not only acquire their fair share of quality staff, coaches, and players, but can also retain them.

Third, sport regulators aim to increase revenue through marketing efforts. They may try to expand the consumer base for their sporting product, improve the overall attractiveness of the product, or generally try to improve the image of the league in the community. The market, for example, could be expanded by admitting new teams to the league, extending the playing season, or playing games at different times of the week. Regulators may also spend money on improving the quality of the game through programmes to develop player skills, or by upgrading venues to make them more fan-friendly, or safer for athletes. Governing sport bodies also use their market power as sole owners of the sport competition (or monopolists) to maximise broadcast and sponsorship rights fees by negotiating as a single entity rather than through individual teams.

> *Chapter principle 2.5*: Sport leagues and competitions implement policies to encourage competitive balance. In essence this is a form of 'coopetition' a portmanteau capturing the situation where teams cooperate and compete at the same time in the belief that this is for the greater good. Policies often include salary caps for players, rules about sharing revenues and regulations regarding how the athlete labour market is to be shared between teams.

Variable quality

Commercial businesses aim for predictability and certainty, especially when it comes to product quality. But predictability and certainty are not always valued in the sporting world, especially when it comes to the delivery of professional sport competitions. From a spectator's perspective, the sport experience is usually better when unpredictable. Neutral fans want to see the underdog succeed and unlike a movie or play where the ending is fixed, the perceived 'magic' of sport is often linked to the notion that anything can happen. Sport events depend on this unpredictability in order to attract people to the game. When the results of games cannot be predicted, attendances at sporting contests are likely to be higher, as are the profits of leagues. However, the lack of predictability also leads to significant variability in the quality of sporting performances. Many factors can contribute to the variability of the sport product, including the weather, player injuries, the venue, the quality of the opponents, the closeness of the scores and even the size of the crowd. A cricket match can be exhilarating, boring or even frustrating, but fans still must pay the same price. A boxing contest may be over in 10 seconds and fans will have differing view as to whether that was value for money or not. Sport marketers may attempt to overcome this by 'improving' the product in systematic ways, such as including a star player, offering premium seating, or providing other forms of entertainment and attractive facilities to surround the actual sport itself and extend the notion of the product that is being consumed. The uncertain nature of sport contests is just one element of a total experience, although it is an important element for financial success.

> *Chapter principle 2.6*: Unpredictability can be advantageous in the competitive sport product because it makes sport more attractive. It can also make the sport marketer's job infinitely harder as they have to deal with a variety of factors that can impact the product quality and that are outside their control.

Product and brand loyalty

Strong loyalty to sport products and brands accompanies the emotional attachments that sport consumers develop for their favourite teams, events, players, and equipment. A good test of loyalty for conventional products can be seen in whether consumers are prepared to keep purchasing the product even when its price rises, or the price of competing products falls. For the most part this continuance of demand, which marketers refer to as loyalty, occurs in sport as fans invest an enormous amount of time and energy in their favourite sport products, creating a lifetime bond. In fact, sport fans often see their team as an extension of themselves; a part of their self-identity. It is almost unheard of for a person to swap to supporting a different team in a league, such is the cradle to grave mentality of fandom.

When sport consumers passionately support a particular kind of sport, a specific competition, or a specific team (or brand), a low cross elasticity of demand exists. This is an economic term that means it is difficult to substitute (or replace) one sport product for another. Most sport competitions have an inelastic demand and thus a high degree of product loyalty. Even if fans are unhappy about the result of a game, the winning margin, or the standard of refereeing, it is unlikely that they would change their sporting preferences. If, for instance, a supporter's football team is playing away from home and the match is not televised, they would probably not go to a hockey or bocce game instead, regardless of whether the venue was attractive, and the ticket was free. The situation is quite different for most other products. If a consumer bought a computer but felt unsatisfied with its quality, they would be likely to change brands or retail outlets next time. In team sports, the substitution of products occurs infrequently, although it can be more common for sport products such as equipment or apparel where typical variety seeking behaviours common in the marketing of many products can be observed.

It might seem that the low degree of product substitution in sport could only be an advantage to sport organisations. However, there are drawbacks. For example, it can be difficult for a new sport, team, or brand to enter the marketplace and wrestle fans away from their existing loyalties. Where does a new team get its fans from if they already have allegiances to other teams in the league? Another obstacle is that sport consumers maintain a reluctance to increase their sport watching because of reduced ticket prices or increased personal income levels. This means that marketing efforts need to be innovative about how to attract and convert fans as some conventional marketing tactics are ineffective.

> *Chapter principle 2.7*: In competitive sport there is a low cross elasticity of demand where it is difficult to substitute (or replace) one sport league, team, brand or competition for another. This can have advantages for sport marketers by locking fans in for extended periods, but also make those fans impervious to marketing tactics or create challenges in obtaining new fans.

Identification

Some sport consumers identify so strongly with their sporting heroes that they seek to emulate them. Supporters may wear the same club uniforms, colours, and sport clothing brands as their heroes. Many businesses such as sport equipment and clothing manufacturers have recognised the power of sporting identification, which can come in various levels, and regularly market their products through successful athletes. Of course, sport identification is the driving power behind sport sponsorship. By seeking an association with sport, sponsors try to claim some of the loyalty that fans possess for sports, teams, and players. The issue of fan identification is a very important concept in sport marketing as it goes to the heart of how fans relate emotionally to the athletes and teams that they follow. As such it is discussed in much further detail in Chapter 3.

> *Chapter principle 2.8*: Product loyalty is strong due to the emotional attachments that sport consumers develop to sport products and brands. This identification is based upon psychological attachments to being part of a group, or having a connection to the ambitions of a sporting team where hope is vested. There are various levels of identification that can exist, allowing sport marketers to segment the market on a key variable. It also provides a critical point of attachment for stakeholders such as sponsors who seek to leverage identification.

Blind optimism

Despite their allegiance to tradition and history there are some situations where sport consumers and marketers have a high tolerance for change, particularly when they involve personnel (such as players and coaches) and competitive success. For example, even when a star player moves from one club to another, their supporters are likely to remain loyal to the original club, possibly even booing that player if they return wearing the uniform of another team. Usually, the emotional bond that joins fans to their clubs means that they will put up with countless changes to its personnel and predictions for improvement in the future. This is an important variable for sport marketers to understand since sport organisations rarely pass up the opportunity to trade players and remove coaching and support staff where it might lead to more competitive performance. Similarly, sport marketers are perennially selling the future in their communications, knowing that fans often perceive significant changes to coaches and players with a rebirth of hope and ambition.

> *Chapter principle 2.9*: Sport consumers identify with teams, clubs, brands and athletes, and see them as extensions of themselves. They have faith that with enough input and change anything is possible, and that improvement is always just around the corner.

Fixed supply schedules

A supply schedule refers to the ability of a business to change their production rates to meet the demand of consumers. Some businesses can increase their production level quickly to meet increased demand. Running a factory for an extra shift might not be an issue for a company making breakfast cereal, however service-orientated businesses like sport have little extra capacity to engage when the opportunity arises. Sporting clubs have an inflexible (inelastic) production capacity. They have what is known as a *fixed supply schedule*. It is worth noting that this is not the case for sales of clothing, equipment, memberships, and memorabilia. But clubs and teams can only play a certain number of times during their season and even then, this schedule is often at the mercy of a separate process out of their hands. If fans and members are unable to get into a venue, that revenue is lost forever. Although sport clubs and leagues may have a fixed supply schedule, it is possible to increase the number of consumers who watch in other ways. For example, the supply of a sport product can be increased by providing more temporary seats, changing the venue to a larger one, extending the playing season or even through media distribution. Many teams have become truly global be ensuring that fans not only have the chance to view the team in person by moving matches to new geographical locations, but also extending reach via new media platforms that open new revenue and engagement opportunities.

> *Chapter principle 2.10*: The competitive sport product is restricted by a fixed supply schedule making it difficult to change production rates in order to meet the demand of customers but can be overcome through alternative distribution channels and adjustments to capacity where possible.

This chapter observed that sport requires professional marketing but with an appreciation of the special features of the sport market. The financial and business sides of the sport product need to be balanced with an understanding of its emotional power. Sport is a business, but a special kind of business. It is important for sport marketers to understand the unique features of the sport market because they have an influence on the development of a marketing programme.

CASE 2.3

Parkrun

Running for fun and fitness is popular right across the planet. Of all the natural sports that exist, running is arguably the purest. There is something deceptively simple and elegant in moving a body, under natural motion, quickly from one point to the other. To make it a competition, or sport, you only need to see who can do it the fastest, with set distances and a range of conditions providing different challenges.

The concept of running is steeped in tradition, with countless stories in a range of outlets attesting to its universal appeal. Perhaps the most famous is that of Pheidippides, the Athenian messenger who in 490 BCE ran 40 kilometres from the battlefield of Marathon to announce the incredible victory over the vastly larger Persian army (shouting 'Nike' the Greek word for victory as he did). He is said to have dropped dead from exhaustion at that point – and the legend was borne. Pheidippides was part of a group of specialist athletes in the Greek army, capable of running long distances day to day to swiftly deliver messages. The story suggests he ran hundreds of kilometres before the fateful journey from Marathon, which is now immortalised in the naming of one of athletics premier distance events. The marathon at the Olympic Games is perhaps the most famous, with it starting in 1896 and tracing the route between Marathon and Athens. Fittingly it was won by a Greek, Spyridon Louis, who completed the race in under three hours. The event has been a feature of the Games since and has also spawned an annual conglomeration of events that punctuate the sporting calendar of major cities around the world, including in London, Boston, New York, Berlin, and Tokyo. For many people running a marathon, particularly one of the big city ones, becomes a lifelong ambition, and the sport of ultramarathon has expanded in recent years as organisers turn races into larger distances, including the 245-kilometre Spartathlon in Greece that was inspired by the legend of Pheidippides and his run prior to the Battle of Marathon from Athens to Sparta to seek military help.

Beyond the marathons, cities around the world have also sought to capture the interest in running by promoting a vast array of fun runs covering a range of mixed distances. These events often feature elite athletes who lead the pack in pursuit of victory, however the vast number of participants are everyday runners and joggers, often attired in fancy dress and running simply for pleasure, charity, or to be a part of something. Latching onto this phenomenon is the 'Parkrun' concept which features a free 5 kilometre run on Saturday mornings held in thousands of local communities in over 20 countries around the world. Run entirely by volunteers, Parkrun is now considered the largest mass-participation sporting event on the planet, capturing the interest of over a quarter of a million runners each Saturday morning, and introducing many of these people to the simple pursuit of running.

The factors that motivate people to participate in a sport are often very different to those that turn them into fans. People will participate in a sport such as running because they want to get fit and keep their bodies in shape. They want to consume a 'physical activity experience' and might not even consider it a sport. Fans are more interested in consuming a 'sport watching experience', or maybe a 'sport entertainment experience' and generally want to do it in the company of others as a group activity. But, when you think further on this matter, there are in fact some motivational overlaps between participation in sport and fandom. The main overlap is the social connectedness that comes from both participating in sport and watching others play it. Even in a relatively solo sport such as running, the group and social component is prominent as the success of Parkrun and other running events have indicated. There is also the escape factor, which means both participation and watching provides a way of getting away from the stresses of life and throwing oneself into a world quite different from work or the family home. Some sport markets do this better than others, as we see in the following chapters.

QUESTIONS

1. Has Parkrun created a new market or simply changed an existing one?
2. From a marketing perspective what are the factors that have made Parkrun such a significant success?
3. How does a city hosting a major marathon involve the three sectors (non-profit, government, and corporate) discussed in this chapter?

PRINCIPLES SUMMARY

- Chapter principle 2.1: Sport is a special form of business. A standard marketing approach does not always work, so sport marketers must also understand the special features of the sport market and build these into their strategic planning and operations.
- Chapter principle 2.2: Sport can elicit an emotional response in its consumers that is rarely found in other businesses. It can stimulate immense loyalty but also strong attachments to nostalgia and club tradition as well as provide strong feelings to contribute a voice on matters affecting the bonds that have been built.

- Chapter principle 2.3: Sport organisations measure their success both on and off the field of play and the two are not always happy partners. On-field success refers to achievement within sport competition. Off-field success refers to financial stability and profitability.
- Chapter principle 2.4: Sport organisations that compete in leagues and competitions rely on the health of their competitors for their own success. Sport consumers are more attracted to attend games where there is a balanced competition, providing the basis for unexpected outcomes that captures the essence of sport as a game.
- Chapter principle 2.5: Sport leagues and competitions implement policies to encourage competitive balance. In essence this is a form of 'coopetition' a portmanteau capturing the situation where teams cooperate and compete at the same time in the belief that this is for the greater good. Policies often include salary caps for players, rules about sharing revenues and regulations regarding how the athlete labour market is to be shared between teams.
- Chapter principle 2.6: Unpredictability can be advantageous in the competitive sport product because it makes sport more attractive. It can also make the sport marketer's job infinitely harder as they have to deal with a variety of factors that can impact the product quality and that are outside their control.
- Chapter principle 2.7: In competitive sport there is a low cross elasticity of demand where it is difficult to substitute (or replace) one sport league, team, brand or competition for another. This can have advantages for sport marketers by locking fans in for extended periods, but also make those fans impervious to marketing tactics or create challenges in obtaining new fans.
- Chapter principle 2.8: Product loyalty is strong due to the emotional attachments that sport consumers develop to sport products and brands. This identification is based upon psychological attachments to being part of a group, or having a connection to the ambitions of a sporting team where hope is vested. There are various levels of identification that can exist, allowing sport marketers to segment the market on a key variable. It also provides a critical point of attachment for stakeholders such as sponsors who seek to leverage identification.
- Chapter principle 2.9: Sport consumers identify with teams, clubs, brands and athletes, and see them as extensions of themselves. They have faith that with enough input and change anything is possible, and that improvement is always just around the corner.
- Chapter principle 2.10: The competitive sport product is restricted by a fixed supply schedule making it difficult to change production rates in order to meet the demand of customers but can be overcome through alternative distribution channels and adjustments to capacity where possible.

REVIEW QUESTIONS

1. What does it mean from a marketing perspective to say that sport is a special form of business?
2. In what ways can sport products be differentiated from other products?

3 Why is it important for sport competitions to have competitive balance?
4 What are the various markets, large and small, available to an international body responsible for the governance and promotion of swimming?
5 Is the role of a sport marketer harder or easier than the marketer of a fast-moving consumer good sold in a supermarket?
6 Explain various reasons why corporate sponsors would want to be associated with sport.
7 What does it mean from a marketing perspective to say that sport has a low cross elasticity of demand where it is difficult to substitute (or replace) one sport league, team, brand, or competition for another?
8 What are some of the ways in which sport organisations can get around the fixed supply schedules associated with sport competitions?

RELEVANT WEBSITES

Australian Sports Data (www.clearinghouseforsport.gov.au)
Forbes magazine (www.forbes.com) (search 'sport teams')
Parkrun (www.parkrun.com)
Plunkett Research (www.plunkettresearch.com) (search 'sport')
Sports Business Daily (www.sportsbusinessdaily.com)
Statista (www.statista.com) (search 'sport')

FURTHER READING

Hums, M. A., Kluch, Y., Schmidt, S. H., & MacLean, J. C. (2023). *Governance and Policy in Sport Organizations*. Taylor & Francis.

Smith, A. C. T., & Stewart, B. (2010). The special features of sport: A critical revisit. *Sport Management Review*, *13*, 1–13.

CHAPTER 3

Sport consumers

LEARNING OUTCOMES

At the end of this chapter, readers should be able to:

- identify the different motives consumers have for buying sport products and services.
- explain the effects of each motive on sport consumption.
- highlight the external factors that can influence the behaviour of sport consumers.
- specify how the external factors can be influenced by sport marketers to change consumer attitudes and behaviours and enhance product usage.

OVERVIEW

Sport consumers are driven by a range of aspirations, incentives, and benefits to join clubs, compete in tournaments, attend games, buy merchandise, and watch sport on television. This chapter explains the factors that motivate sport participants and fans and provides advice on how to best communicate with consumers through marketing processes. It also distinguishes between two different categories of motivation, one of which is internal to the consumer and one of which is external to the consumer. Both factors are important to understand since they can radically change the ways in which sport consumers might perceive the utility of a sport product and can thus lead to quite different patterns of sport goods consumption.

BECOMING A CONSUMER

We are all consumers. We all have needs, wants, and desires, and will go to great lengths to satisfy them. We also like to think that we are rational when making decisions to purchase goods and services and acting out our consumption preferences. Economists make this assumption when they construct their models of consumer behaviour. They propose that consumers are continually seeking product information, and regularly weigh up the

DOI: 10.4324/9781003391319-3

costs and benefits of buying one brand over another. And this is also the way we like to see ourselves. That is, we are ruggedly autonomous individuals, shrewd and street-smart, but also intellectually hard-headed with an innate ability to identify false claims, expose exaggerated proclamations, and pick out fictitious testimonials. Although the modern consumer is constantly inundated with advertisements delivered through multiple channels, ranging from traditional television advertisements to highly targeted sponsored posts in an Instagram story, they are not immune to the persuasive efforts of an effective marketing campaign. Today's consumers are value driven and identify with products that convey authenticity in marketing. For example, environmental sustainability is an important issue for consumers in Generation Z, thus they seek out and purchase from brands that limit their environmental impact. For example, Patagonia is a company that produces outdoor leisure wear and could resonate with this generation as it has had a sustainable mission since its inception in the 1970s. The company makes clothing with percentages of recycled polyester that is designed to last for decades, thus reducing waste. Consumption has gone beyond the purchase of goods and services to meet our daily needs. People now use consumption to create a lifestyle and build an identity. In short, we are what we consume. Sport consumption is no exception.

SCOPE AND SCALE OF SPORT CONSUMPTION

Consumption takes place in markets and sport consumption is no different. Sport markets, like all other markets, will function only if there are some people who are willing to sell goods and services, and other people who are prepared to buy them. There are multitudes of sellers in sport markets, some of whom are intent on maximising profits, and others who are more interested in delivering something of value to members of their community. Lululemon Athletica Inc. desires to create products that allow individuals to live longer, healthier lives by producing high-quality yoga, running, and other athletic apparel. The company is also the fourth largest in athletic apparel, accessories, and footwear organisations globally in terms of revenue, making it a highly profitable business. The International Paralympic Committee (IPC) is also a large global business, but its mission is non-profit driven. The IPC instead seeks to promote inclusivity in the world through parasport and offer para-athletes the opportunity to achieve sporting success. Both Lululemon and the IPC operate in the supply side of different sports. One market is focused on sporting gear, while the other is more concerned with the promotion of social inclusivity through mega sport events.

Of course, markets have another side, which is all about demand. Demand is crucial to the operation of markets since without demand there will be no supply. Lululemon has become successful because it has convinced consumers that its premium sports gear delivers high-quality value and longevity. Its functional value is built on a foundation of innovation, with a transitional gym-to-leisurewear design that can be both attractive and practical, while its symbolic value arises from the belief that Lululemon's products imply social status through their premium price points. The IPC has become successful because people believe its biennial sport event delivers inclusive, highest-quality athletic performance in an array of sports, while bringing awareness to global issues surrounding disability.

CASE 3.1

Nielsen's Sports Consumption Evolution Report

Market demand drives decisions by sport properties and organisations that are connected to the sport industry. One such related industry is the media industry, which regularly bids for the rights to broadcast various sport content to consumers. Consumers, in turn, drive demand in terms of the variety of ways they choose to consume sports content. Shifts within the past several years, in part due to the COVID-19 pandemic, have resulted in new habits for sport consumption emerging, with the biggest factor including flexible delivery across a variety of devices.

To assist sport media organisations within the changing sport consumption landscape and offer insights into how sports fans choose to consume content, Nielsen Media Company provides a variety of measurement tools to track audience behaviour. These tools include meters that can detect audio and visual content and identify what individuals are watching, streaming meters that operate like wireless routers to track streaming content, content recognition software from 'smart' TVs, and return tracking data provided from satellite TV boxes. Consumer insights can also be gathered via survey methods that are performed on a rolling basis. These audience insights are then compiled into reports that are available for media organisations to purchase and use to inform content delivery.

One such example of this research is Nielsen's 'Year in Review: Sports Consumption Evolution' report. This report gathered global sports consumption data from various media markets on events and leagues such as The French Open tennis tournament, La Liga in Spain, The NBA, The 2020 Tokyo Olympic Games, and the 2020 UEFA European Championships. Key findings from the report highlight the diversification of content provided to fans, perhaps as a result of sporting competitions being halted during the COVID-19 pandemic. Of note was the utilisation of historical, or classic games, virtual sporting events, and community-driven events such as 'watch alongs' to facilitate connections with, and between, sport fans. The pandemic also accelerated the use of online streaming platforms as well as the generation of sport content that could be delivered through this format. Video has also played a significant role in sport consumption with almost all sport properties showing increases in video views across the social media platforms of Facebook, Instagram, and YouTube. When adding in the wildly popular video-based platform, TikTok, growth in video views increases further. Certain sport properties saw their video views double while simultaneously engaging the hard-to-reach Generation Z audience.

Post pandemic, there was a return to a more recognisable sports schedule, however, the flexible approach to content delivery continued. Sport organisations continued to offer content that could be streamed or consumed via cable or satellite TV, while also expanding streaming-based options such as over-the-top (OTT) content that could be consumed via mobile phones, tablets, or computers. While global sporting events are still popular in terms of sports consumption, digital and social media-based sport consumption is driving growth, thus a varied strategy to sport consumption is necessary for future success.

QUESTIONS

1. How would you develop a content delivery strategy to meet the growing demands of sport consumers?
2. Would you put more emphasis on OTT and streaming-based video content or focus on traditional forms of broadcasting? Explain your rationale?
3. Taking into consideration the demand for video content, what platforms (e.g., Facebook, YouTube, TikTok) would you utilise to market a sport property to consumers?

CATEGORIES OF SPORT CONSUMERS

There are numerous ways of defining sport consumers, most of which revolve around identifying different kinds of sport products or services. However, the first point to make is that there is a difference between sport consumers and sport stakeholders. A consumer is an individual or group who uses a sport or sport-related product or service in exchange for a direct (such as cash to buy a ticket to a game) or indirect (such as purchasing a television in which sport is one form of entertainment) payment. A stakeholder is an individual or group who has an interest or agenda in a sport product or service. For example, sport media organisations – both traditional and digital or streaming – are stakeholders in that they broadcast content related to sport products and services, but they are not consumers. Sport consumers are the end-users, in this example fans viewing the sport broadcast. Sport consumers can be differentiated into four categories.

First are *sporting goods consumers*. These retail consumers buy sport products including, for example, equipment, apparel, books, magazines, nutritional and health supplements, games, merchandise, memorabilia, and licensed products. A sporting goods consumer is anyone who purchases a physical product that has a sport-related aspect or purpose. This may range from the direct, such as the latest carbon-fibre based running shoes, to the indirect, such as a health- and fitness-related sport wearable devices like WHOOP, which can monitor an individual's physiological outputs.

Second are *sport services consumers*. These consumers utilise a sport-related service or experience excluding viewing or participating in sport directly. Sport-related services include education, gambling, specialised coaching, medical services, and recreational and health activities such as those offered by pools, gymnasiums, and leisure centres.

Third are *sport participants and volunteers*. These consumers are actively engaged in sport as participants or in unpaid organisational and support roles. This includes all participants in school, recreational and organised club sport, even if the sport participation is virtual such as is the case with esports.

Fourth are *sport supporters, spectators, and fans*. These consumers take an active interest in the performance of sport mainly, but not confined to, the elite or professional level. The activities of sport supporters, spectators, and fans include attendance at live sport or viewing sport on television, via the internet, or on a proprietary sports app. These sport consumers are highly complex because they may use sport products and services in ways that other, less intense consumers do not. For example, fans may actively engage in 'second screening' when viewing sports, which involves not only watching the match in person or on a single device but also viewing the same match on a second – or sometimes even a third – device such as a mobile phone or tablet. This is done to obtain additional information about the match. In some instances, particularly committed fans may become 'fanatical' or abusive when their behaviour and level of engagement steps outside of normal social expectations. Of course, most sport participants and volunteers are sport fans as well and utilise different kinds of sporting goods and services. For this reason, it is best to assume that sport consumer motivations are multi-variable and complex. It is easier to categorise kinds of sport consumption than kinds of sport consumers. Furthermore, based on these categories of consumption, the motives of sport supporters, spectators, and fans are the most complex and need to be explored further.

> *Chapter principle 3.1*: A sport consumer is an individual who purchases sporting goods, uses sport services, participates, or volunteers in sport and/or follows sport as a spectator or fan.

SPORT CONSUMER MOTIVES

Even though the topic of sport consumer motives can be complex, it is pivotal to understanding sport marketing in the current, competitive environment. Sport marketers need to appreciate the many reasons why consumers are motivated to buy sport-related products and services. Without this knowledge, tailoring products to consumers' needs becomes difficult. The more a marketer understands about sport consumers, the easier it is for them to design enticing marketing.

Sport consumers attend games, follow clubs and teams, and buy products for a multitude of reasons. As a result, we may look at sport consumer behaviour from a range of perspectives. One common approach in business, but typically outside of a marketing orientation, is to consider sport consumption behaviour from an *economic* viewpoint. This view suggests that people behave rationally and use sport products and services that meet their quality and value needs. The problem with this view, of course, is that sport consumers do not necessarily behave in rational ways because they have an emotional connection to the sport products they consume. Employing the example of Lululemon utilised earlier, an economic perspective toward consumption would align with purchasing a functional, reasonably priced pair of leggings that meet the individuals' needs, and not the higher-priced pair of Lululemon leggings. Considering consumer behaviour from a *psychological* and *social* point of view can prove rewarding. A psychological perspective suggests that people's attitudes and motivations (or desires) will predict what they buy. A social perspective suggests that people may be influenced by their social circumstances such as purchasing luxury leisurewear items from Lululemon if they see other individuals in their boutique fitness facility wearing them. The forthcoming section examines sport consumer behaviour mainly from a psychological and social perspective. It also focuses on the fourth group of consumers identified in the previous section because their consumption decisions are the most complex and furthest removed from rational expectations based on economic factors. This group of sport supporters, spectators, and fans will simply be referred to as sport fans.

BECOMING A SPORT FAN

There are many possible benefits that sport fans may experience through watching, talking, reading, and thinking about sport. This section considers what it is about sport that has captured the attention and passion of so many people for so long. There has been a considerable amount of research examining the psychological and social reasons (often called *psycho-social* motivations) why sport fans consume sport products. Here, the reasons are summarised into three different groups of motives: (1) psychological motives, (2) socio-cultural (social and cultural) motives, and (3) self-concept motives.

> *Chapter principle 3.2*: Sport fan motives for consuming sport products and services can be summarised into three categories: (1) psychological motives, (2) socio-cultural motives, and (3) self-concept motives.

Psychological motives

The psychological reasons (or motives) that drive sport fans to consume sport products and services are connected to the interest and enjoyment that they derive from sport. Sport can fulfil numerous emotional and intellectual needs for the sport consumer. For example, sport can be stimulating, can help to release stress, can be an escape, and can provide entertainment and visual pleasure. In other words, sport can stimulate positive feelings and thoughts for the sport consumer. Each one of these motives is explained further next.

Stimulation

Sport can be a stimulating, psychologically energising activity. It generates excitement and even anxiety, both of which can encourage the body to produce adrenaline. It also allows fans to shout and vent aggression in a socially acceptable way and to experience intense sensory stimulation. Imagine the stimulating effect of watching the 2022 FIFA World Cup final between Argentina and France live. After 90 minutes of back-and-forth action, the game went into extra-time and was ultimately decided by kicks from the penalty spot. Images from fans celebrating Argentina's eventual win captured the stimulation – from both excitement and anxiety – those fans experienced.

Escape

The stimulation provided by sport can provide consumers with a distraction from the ordinary routine of everyday life. The collisions, body contact and action offered by many sports can attract fans who want to escape from their highly organised and regulated work environments into a world of passion, spontaneity, and uncertainty. After all, sport gives spectators an acceptable place to shout, scream, and sing or dance, where their normal work or family roles might not. Sport can also provide a release and a diversion from a stressful lifestyle. For many fans, sport watching is the ultimate 'escape experience'.

Aesthetic (Visual) Pleasure

Sport watching offers aesthetic (or visual) pleasure to fans. Sport fans are often prepared to pay to witness excellence, such as skilful play or memorable moments. Some fans may also be motivated by the physical conditioning associated with elite-level sports. For fans who participate in recreational versions of popular sports, the sacrifice and dedication associated with keeping oneself in peak-level condition can provide motivation and admiration. For example, a recreational boxer may appreciate the time and effort required to maintain the fitness levels and physique of a professional boxer when they watch them on TV.

Drama and Entertainment

Sport can provide entertainment and drama. Through watching an engaging contest, fans can be part of a theatrical experience. The scale of many sporting venues, the sight of thousands of fans in club colours, and the use of lively half-time entertainment all enhance sport's dramatic qualities. Some events, such as horse racing, for example, have blended sport performance with fashion, theatre, and a carnival feel to maximise the dramatic atmosphere.

> *Chapter principle 3.3*: Psychological motives for sport fans include the opportunity for stimulation, escape, aesthetic pleasure and a sense of dramatic entertainment.

Socio-cultural motives

In addition to the psychological interest and pleasure that sport fans receive from consuming sport, they may also experience social and cultural benefits. Sport encourages fans to gather into groups such as families, fellow team supporters, and state and national 'cheer' squads. It provides fans with a social gathering place, as well as activities to share and common topics to talk about. In some cases, local fans will gather at pubs or restaurants to watch their favourite teams play, with the establishment then becoming associated with that sports team.

Family and Social Interaction

Sporting events and activities provide an opportunity for families and friends to spend time together in an organised and pleasurable way. A sport experience can help sport fans fulfil family needs or spend time with friends. It is important for sport marketers to realise that if a spectator is motivated to attend a match because of these reasons, then the type of game they attend or the teams that are playing may be irrelevant. Alternative activities may easily substitute for the sport experience, and still allow the consumer to meet their family and social needs. Alternatively, when members of the family are fans of the same team, perhaps having the fandom passed down from generation to generation, the type of game or teams that are playing could be increasingly relevant, resulting in a higher likelihood of commemorative purchases.

Cultural Connections

Fans use sport as a form of cultural connection and celebration. Sport can help fans connect to their national, racial, or ethnic culture, or even a subculture that they belong to (a social group that shares beliefs and behaviours). Spectators may like to attend games that are relevant to their heritage, or where some athletes are from ethnic or racial groups they identify with. Sport can also provide meaningful symbols, rituals, and 'mythical images'. The Super Bowl, for example, uses important rituals, such as the playing of the national anthem of the United States and the drama and spectacle of the half-time show, to convey special meaning to participants and spectators. For sporting clubs, the theme song, club colours, insignia, and mottos fulfil the same function by providing powerful images representing belonging to the group. Watching, reading, talking, and posting on social media about sport can create a feeling of familiarity that comes from participating in a seasonal ritual. There are also weekly rituals that include the match, the post-game commentary, the mid-week preview, and the pre-match media analysis, which are repeated reliably from season-to-season and delivered to the consumer through a variety of ways.

Economic benefit

Another kind of socio-cultural benefit for sport fans is the possibility of gaining money through gambling on sport. This is a potential advantage that is not part of the game itself, but one of the 'extras', or an external benefit that needs a social and cultural system to operate. Sport gambling has been the beneficiary of innovation and deregulation recently. Digital forms of gambling on the internet and sports betting applications available on mobile phones have dramatically increased the ease with which individuals can place sports bets. Additionally, the removal of gambling restrictions in the United States, specifically the repeal of the Professional and Amateur Sports Protection Act of 1992, commonly referred to as PASPA, allowed for state sanctioned gambling in all states. This has resulted huge growth in the global sport betting industry. Underpinning the economic viability of sport gambling is the rapidly increasing market for the collection and analysis of sport data. Sport analytics companies can now market to and partner with major sport gambling companies to provide the data that establishes the odds in sport betting.

> *Chapter principle 3.4*: Socio-cultural motives for sport fans include the opportunity for family and social interaction, cultural connections, and even economic benefit.

Self-concept motives

While psychological and socio-cultural motives help describe why a fan is attracted to sport, not all fans experience the same degree or strength of identification. The degree to which a fan identifies with a team is an important issue, since it may predict their loyalty. It is therefore useful to differentiate between psychological and self-concept motives, as the former describes attraction, and the latter strength of sport identification. Psychological motives are internal to individuals whereas belonging motives are a function of a sport consumer's interaction with sport. Fans with a stronger identification have sport more deeply embedded in their self-concept. A fan's identification with a team could be motivated by a need to belong to a group or a tribe, or by a desire for vicarious achievement.

Belonging and Group Affiliation

Sport consumers may feel a need to belong to a group. They may also be motivated to develop a sense of identity that is connected to the group, or to identify with something bigger than themselves. These fans want to feel part of a tightly bound community that shares a common interest. They may also develop a sense of personal identity partly through a connection to teams and athletes. If a sport fan develops a strong feeling of connection to a successful team or player, they may use that success to pretend that they too are successful; they share the warm after-glow of victory. This can be illustrated by sport fans using the terminology 'we' when describing performance, such as 'we played well in the match'. It is important to note, however, that the depth of identification fans possess can vary significantly. On the one hand, there may be 'fair-weather' fans whose attendance at events will correspond to team success. On the other hand, there are the passionate supporters who will remain loyal to their favourite teams and clubs even when the teams are performing poorly.

Tribal Connections

Sport fandom can also be used to recreate ancient ceremonies and primitive social rituals. For example, team sports such as football provide strong tribal connections, with athletes acting as the tribal heroes, and rituals such as pre- and post-game ceremonies. The fans themselves are the tribal followers who have conflicts with other tribes (other team's fans) and show their tribal colours and loyalty by wearing club colours. Of course, there are also tribal chants and team songs that help to bind the fans together and to intimidate rival tribes. For example, it is common for fans to develop specific chants for players on their team within the English Football Leagues. Additionally, certain songs are associated with specific teams and are played either before or after a match. Examples include Liverpool FC fans starting every match at their home stadium of Anfield by singing Gerry and the Pacemaker's song, 'You'll Never Walk Alone.'

Vicarious Achievement

Sport fans can develop a psychological attachment to sports, teams, and players. This connection can assist fans to develop a feeling of being strong, important, and successful. The term vicarious achievement refers to a sense of accomplishment that is felt second hand, through the success of someone else. Some fans may experience an increase in self-esteem when their team is winning. Others may feel a sense of confidence and skilfulness by learning team statistics and club history. Given that sport fans feel successful when their team is successful, the reverse occurs when they must deal with the disappointment of scandals and poor team performances. In these situations, fans may be a little less eager to publicly announce their support of the team, and they might even downplay the failure of the team. This can be exemplified by hearing some fans disassociate from the team when they play poorly by referring to the players as 'they' and stating 'they played poorly last night' to other fans. Fans can compensate for a team's poor performance by developing strong feelings of closeness with fellow fans, being critical of other successful teams, voicing criticism of umpiring or refereeing decisions, or by being blindly optimistic that things will get better. On occasion, when feelings from a poor performance become overwhelming, attempts to be critical of other successful teams can go too far, resulting in abuse directed at players. Recently, with digital forms of communication enabling unprecedented levels of access to athletes, growth in the amounts of online abuse directed at players has resulted and this remains a significant issue within sport. High-profile cases include abuse directed at American gymnast Simone Biles after she withdrew from an Olympic competition, as well as racist abuse directed at Marcus Rashford, Bukayo Saka, and Jadon Sancho after they missed penalty kicks for England during the finals of the 2020 UEFA European Championships.

Chapter principle 3.5: Self-concept motives for sport fans include the opportunity for belonging and group affiliation, tribal connections and vicarious achievement.

CASE 3.2

Hope United

Social media can offer fans the opportunity to express adoration for their favourite teams or athletes, but conversely it can provide an outlet for abusive comments directed at these individuals. If athletes perform poorly, do not display enough effort, or advocate for a social issue that conflicts with fans' personal views or expectations, the result can include a variety of abuse through social media platforms. This results from fans misdirecting their frustrations toward the athlete. Highlighting the amount of abuse, in a BBC Sport survey of 537 elite-level British athletes, 30% reported having received abuse on social media.

Attempts to reduce online abuse directed toward athletes have included efforts between football clubs, players, athletes, and media organisations in the United Kingdom. For example, a four-day 'black out' boycott of social media in 2021 was coordinated to call attention to the issue. Another example of an initiative to call attention to online abuse is the Hope United campaign by telecommunications company EE. This endeavour involved the formation of a squad of high-profile professional women's and men's football players to raise awareness of online abuse as part of a media campaign, while also providing educational services for individuals to recognize online abuse as a hate crime.

Specific to the Hope United campaign are initiatives to demonstrate how to report, block, and filter abusive content on various social media platforms. Supporters can also purchase a Hope United jersey, which features a unique design specific to each of their featured players with all proceeds going to partner organisation The Cybersmile Foundation, which focuses on tackling online abuse and bullying, as well as promoting digital wellbeing. Other partner organisations include internet Matters, Football v. Homophobia, and Glitch. Internet Matters was founded by broadband providers to offer parental resources to assist with online safety for children. Football v. Homophobia challenges sexual-orientation and gender-based discrimination in football, while Glitch focuses on online safeguarding initiatives through education.

QUESTIONS

1. Search for an example of online abuse in sport that has occurred in the last year. Outline how this event occurred and how the relevant sporting authorities dealt with it.
2. How can sport marketers utilise belonging and group affiliations to counter online abuse? Could codes of conduct be written into fan groups to counter this behaviour?
3. Could you, as a sport marketer, investigate forming an anti-abuse fan group to counter this behaviour? How could this be marketed to fans to capitalise on self-concept and socio-cultural motives for sport?

INFLUENCES ON SPORT CONSUMER MOTIVES

The motives just described help to explain why a fan may be driven to consume sport. But not all sport fans will be motivated by the same reasons. Some may be motivated by a desire for entertainment while others may be motivated by deep feelings of connection to a group.

Research on sport consumer behaviour has revealed some of the variables that influence the motives that fans hold. This research indicates that a sport fan's reasons for buying a sport product may be affected by demographic variables, or their age, education, income, gender, race, sexuality, or marital status. For example, younger fans are more likely to be motivated toward sport through the desire to belong to a group than older fans. Fans with higher levels of education are less likely to be motivated for economic gain, bolstering self-esteem, stimulation, or group affiliation.

In the past, research suggested that males and females may be motivated to consume sport for different reasons. Males, for example, were more likely to be motivated by economic factors than females, as well as for reasons of escapism, psychological stimulation, aesthetic pleasure, and self-esteem. Females, however, were more strongly motivated to consume sport for family and social reasons. In recent years, however, some research has shown that motivations do not differ significantly between male and female sport fans, with both groups being most motivated by physical skill and achievement.

While research into these kinds of factors can be informative, as a sport marketer it is important to remember that not all research provides the same result, as demonstrated by the different results of male and female sport consumer motivations. In addition, some researchers have found that gender differences may be more pronounced in some cultures or racial groups than others. There may also be other reasons to think carefully about the results of research. After all, it is likely that the sport fans targeted in one research study are different to those studied in others.

The key issue to remember is that different sport fans will be motivated to consume sport for different reasons. Some reasons for consuming sport will lead to greater loyalty than others. Self-concept motives may stimulate stronger feelings of allegiance. Also, fans' reasons for buying a sport product may be affected by their age, education, income, gender and race, although there is enough evidence to suggest that these demographic variables do not influence motivation in a uniform way. One approach to assist in understanding sport fans better is to examine and classify their behaviour rather than their motivations. This is easier because behaviour is tangible and measurable irrespective of the motivation that stimulated it.

> *Chapter principle 3.6*: Fan motives for consuming sport are affected by their age, education, income, gender, race, sexuality, and marital status, but these demographic variables do not always influence motivation in a uniform or predictable way.

UNDERSTANDING SPECTATOR BEHAVIOUR

Some fans watch sport for no other reason than to see their favourite team contest the game. These *passionate partisans* are loyal to their team and get despondent when their team loses and elated when it wins and are prepared to incur inconvenience (a wet day, or a long, slow trip to the stadium) to savour the fruits of success. They form the hardcore support base of sport, and their moods and identities are bound up with the successes and failures of their favourite teams. Such fans are heavy purchasers of memorabilia and club merchandise and will be great defenders of club history and traditions. They also possess a significant personal investment in their preferred club and its season-to-season performance.

There are also many sport fans who are more interested in supporting a winning team than blindly following their team through 'thick and thin'. These *champ followers* share some of the emotional highs and lows of the passionate partisan but are less reliable and fanatical. The champ follower's allegiance will change according to whatever team happens to be the top performer. Alternatively, champ followers often remain hidden from public view (are non-attendees) until their favourite team starts winning and they become vocal and active supporters but drop off when their team begins to lose again. Sometimes these fans are also referred to as bandwagon fans or glory hunters, depending on the cultural context in which the term is used.

A third category is the *reclusive partisan*, whose interest in the game and commitment to the team is strong, but who attends infrequently. The reclusive partisan is opinionated, and apparently loyal to their team, and could become a passionate partisan again if others can influence them or through media-saturation coverage of the event.

The common motive shared by each of the above categories is fans' desires to see their team win. Their dominant concern is not whether it is likely to be a close contest or whether it will be skilful, dramatic, or entertaining, but the likelihood of success. They are attracted to team performance or team quality. Such sport fans are parochial.

There are at the same time many sport fans who, while notionally committed to a particular team, are more interested in the game or sport itself and attend more frequently than the reclusive partisan, but less frequently than the passionate partisan. These fans may be considered *theatregoers*. The theatregoer is motivated to seek entertainment through a pleasurable experience. However, entertainment from this viewpoint involves more than drama and half-time shows. It also includes comfortable and proximate viewing conditions, easy access, the availability of complimentary services, a close contest, and the participation of star performers. The theatregoer is attracted to comfort, enjoyment, excitement, sensory stimulation, and uncertainty of outcome. Since their team and game loyalty initially begins at a low level, most theatregoers will attend less frequently than passionate partisans unless the likelihood of exciting and pleasurable contests continues throughout the season. At the same time, a few theatregoers will put such high value on their sporting experiences that they will become regular patrons. In this respect, theatregoers may be described as either *casual* or *committed*.

Like the theatregoer, the *aficionado* will be attracted to games that are expected to be exciting and contain star performers. However, unlike most theatregoers, aficionados attend frequently because of their strong attachment to the structure of the game and its athletic practices. They will attend games that provide high skill levels, tactical complexity, and aesthetic pleasure, even if they are likely to be one sided or unexciting. Some aficionados would call themselves purists because they would attend their match of the day, which may or may not include the top performing teams. The aficionado will also be attracted to a quality venue since it will accentuate a quality performance. Both the aficionado and the theatregoer will show only moderate concern about who wins or loses. Their dominant concern is game performance or game quality, and not the likely success or failure of a particular team.

While each of the fan categories has an interest in the game or sport, there are significant differences in the ways in which their interest is expressed. Different incentives will activate different segments. A change to the structure or conduct of the competition that attracts more of one type of fan may be resisted by another type. For example, while theatregoers are likely to attend more games where the stadiums are comfortable, games are expected to be close and competitive, and where complementary entertainment is provided, passionate partisans and champ followers may think that such changes undermine the essential nature and traditions of the game and lessen the expectation of success. Similarly, while theatregoers may be excited about the sensory delights that they see

TABLE 3.1 Sport fan categories

Type of spectator	*Motivation*	*Behaviour*
Aficionado	Seeks quality performance	• Loyal to game rather than team, although will usually have a preferred team • Attends on regular basis • Puts emphasis on aesthetic or skill dimension
Theatregoer (casual and committed)	Seeks entertainment, close contest	• Only moderate loyalty to team • Frequent losses create lack of interest only in team • May attend other games
Passionate partisan	Wants team to win	• Loyal to team • Short-term loyalty undiminished by frequent losses • Strongly identifies with, and responds to, team's success and failure
Champ follower	Wants team to win	• Short-term loyalty • Loyalty a function of team success. • Expects individual or team to dominate otherwise supports another team or spends time elsewhere
Reclusive partisan	Wants team to win	• Loyalty not always translated into attendance • Strong identification but provides latent support only

arising from new rules designed to speed up the game, an expanded league, or the relocation of one team to another city, passionate and reclusive partisans are likely to view such adjustments as treachery, and in extreme cases sever their relationship with their club. It should be noted that all fans could vary according to their personal profile and depending on the sport in question. Thus, one individual may be a casual theatregoer when it comes to rugby, but a passionate partisan when observing football. Table 3.1 summarises the five categories of spectators, their motivations, and behaviour.

MARKETING IMPLICATIONS

For the sport marketer, the previous categories highlight the different segments that comprise the sport fan market. They reinforce the importance of supporting the passionate partisan and the aficionado. However, it is clear from the categories that the motivations of partisans and aficionados are quite different. The categories also demonstrate the potential for increased attendances provided by the theatregoer, champ follower, and reclusive partisan. In each case, the provision of appropriate incentives may be used to generate greater frequency of attendance. The theatregoer would be attracted to comfortable seating arrangements, colour and drama, the availability of appropriate food and drink, and the expectation of an exciting contest, whereas the reclusive partisan and champ followers would be most attracted to games in which their teams had a good probability of winning and were in the championship race. For champ followers to maintain interest, in contrast to passionate partisans, it would be necessary to have a competition where playing talent was distributed equally among the teams, and where the championship race was close for most of the season. Reclusive partisans would also be influenced by the social context in which the sport operates, and a strong media campaign emphasising the cultural significance and fashionability of the event may be effective in this case.

Sport marketers are faced with the difficult task of ensuring that the sport product provides for good watching conditions, a balanced competition, uncertainty of game, and seasonal outcome (exciting high-quality games played in attractive surroundings), and that the loyalty of partisan fans is maintained (by ensuring the ongoing viability of teams within strategically positioned regions and districts that fans can use to establish a sense of identity and community). While changes to the structure of a sport competition (such as new recruiting laws, the relocation of teams or the merger of clubs) are likely to weaken the loyalty of partisan supporters, it must be weighed against the attraction that such changes have for the other spectator categories, particularly the theatregoers.

> *Chapter principle 3.7*: Sport fans can be classified according to the sources and dimensions of their attraction to the sport, and their frequency of attendance.

EXTERNAL FACTORS THAT INFLUENCE SPORT CONSUMPTION

Even when fans are strongly connected to their team or club, they will not always regularly attend games or watch them on television. The reasons for attending matches and events may also be influenced by other factors, such as the type of sport involved, the balance of the competition, the uncertainty of outcome and the likelihood of a certain team winning. Other important factors include the venue and facilities, weather conditions, prices, income levels, special experiences, promotional factors, and the availability of alternative activities. Each of these factors will be briefly examined along with its potential influence on sport fan behaviour.

Type of sport

Different sports attract different types of fans, and different fans are motivated by different factors. The type of sport that a fan follows reveals something about their motivations. Fans of individual sports such as tennis and swimming are more likely to be motivated by an interest in particular athletes, compared with fans of team sports such as football, basketball, and volleyball who are more likely to be motivated by a sense of personal belonging to a team. In addition, fans who prefer non-aggressive sports such as baseball are more likely to be motivated by aesthetic concerns than fans of aggressive sports such as American football and boxing, who are more interested in vicarious escapism.

Balance and uncertainty

Some fans will be influenced by the anticipated closeness of the competition. More fans will attend games when they expect a close contest, which will be affected by the quality of the opposing team or athletes. Closer contests tend to be expected later in the season or during events when semi-finals and finals are played. In general, the closer the expected result of the match, the more attractive a game will be to fans. When fans are uncertain about who might win, they are likely to be more enthusiastic about attending, and tend to have more intense experiences when they do.

The likelihood of winning

Although some fans appreciate a close contest, others are preoccupied with winning. Since fans can receive a sense of personal satisfaction in identifying with a winning team, they will attend or watch games more frequently if they believe their team has a strong chance of winning. In contrast, a team that consistently loses will have difficulty attracting a large following. In general, winning teams and athletes will attract more spectators than losing teams and athletes. There are some instances, however, where fans enjoy watching teams that they dislike lose.

The venue

Sport venue features and facilities can have a strong impact on a fan's decision to attend a sport event. A facility will attract fans if it is able to provide an attractive setting, a convenient layout, good signage, a visually appealing scoreboard, comfort, a better view of the contest, and easy accessibility. Parking, the quality of food and beverages, childcare facilities, and other entertainment options can also influence a fan's decision to attend. The expectation of a large crowd can also be a motivating factor.

CASE 3.3

Chase Center San Francisco

The Golden State Warriors, a team in the North American National Basketball Association (NBA), played its home games at the Oracle Arena in Oakland, California from 1971 until 2019. Located outside of the city centre of Oakland near the Oakland International Airport and just off a busy freeway, the stadium was difficult to access from most parts of the Bay Area of California without a car. The surrounding area offered very little in the way of restaurants, shopping, or other forms of entertainment, meaning attendees of events at the arena would arrive specifically for the game or event, and then leave directly afterwards.

In 2012, the team announced it would build a new venue across the bay in San Francisco, and seven years later the state-of-the-art Chase Center finally opened in the Mission Bay neighbourhood of the city. The move to San Francisco meant that fans attending Warriors games would be able to use public transportation to access the stadium, and the neighbourhood surrounding it was filled with restaurants, nightclubs, and shops. The new location also made it easier for tourists to attend Warriors games, as the new venue is in a popular area of the city where people from all over the world visit each year. Along with the location of the new facility, the features of the stadium also made it an attractive proposition for fans considering attending a Warriors game.

The Chase Center is built on 11 acres of land, much of which was converted into restaurants, offices, hotels, and shops along the San Francisco Bay waterfront. Fans have access to food and beverage options within the arena ranging from microbreweries, wine bars, steak restaurants, and a bakery. The Chase Center is also home to an art collection featuring over 300 pieces from local artists. Finally, fans who attend Warriors games have access to Wi-Fi 6E throughout the entire arena, the fastest Wi-Fi currently available. The Warriors have their own smartphone app that fans can use in the stadium to pre-order meals at the venue, access statistics and game replays, and purchase items such as tickets and food. The Warriors also use augmented reality to stream images onto fans' smartphones. This allows fans to 'wear' the Warriors' championship rings, for example, and take screen shots to share on social media. The Warriors' move from Oracle Arena in Oakland to the Chase Center in San Francisco provided fans with easier access to the stadium, greater options for entertainment before and after a game, as well as world-class technology within the stadium. This case provides a prime example of how venues can be used to successfully market sport events and draw fans into games.

QUESTIONS

1. Visit the Chase Center website (www.chasecenter.com) and browse all the leisure and entertainment options available on-site at the venue. Imagine that you are planning to attend an evening Golden State Warriors game. What other things would you do at the venue before the game?
2. Aside from the Golden State Warriors games, what other events take place at the Chase Center?
3. What design features in the stadium are likely to enhance the sport fan experience?

Weather

The weather can affect match attendances by influencing both the conditions under which fans watch the game, and the quality of the game. A waterlogged ground will not only inconvenience many fans but may also produce slow-moving and boring games. This has encouraged many venues in rain-prone cities to construct retractable roofs or provide undercover seating. However, good weather may also be a problem if it means that people may be attracted to alternative leisure activities. For example, a temperate climate and proximity to water-based activities may lure fans away from sport.

Price

To some extent admission prices to sport events can have a predictable effect. While admission prices are typically fixed during the regular season, between seasons and during finals they can change significantly, impacting on a fan's decision to attend. Broadly speaking an increase in admission prices will lead to a reduction in crowd numbers. However, some evidence suggests that price increases have only a minor influence because sport fans are unusually loyal consumers. This relates to the point made earlier that sport has a low cross elasticity of demand. Sport fans may be unlikely to substitute one sport league, team, or competition for another, even if the price of their preferred competition rises.

Income levels

The income levels of fans can have a direct effect on what kind of leisure they prefer. As the income of fans rises, there is often a decrease in match or event attendances. More income usually means people have more choices to participate in alternative leisure activities, such as travel, restaurants, and the theatre.

Special experiences

Special experiences will generally gain the attention of fans. The experience may involve the participation of a star player or personality, or the likelihood of a record-breaking performance. It may also involve the expectation of a dramatic or even violent encounter, or the anticipation of highly skilled and aesthetically pleasing play. These experiences can give sport fans a feeling that they are getting value for money. Special experiences can also include the availability of reserved seating, access to a private box, and the opportunity to meet a celebrity. The contest itself is just part of the total package.

Promotional factors

Promotional strategies, particularly when accompanied by admission concessions, sales vouchers, and merchandising discounts, are important influences on fans' decisions to attend sport. Advertising, direct mail outs, give-away prizes, the promotion of upcoming games, entertainment and the provision of premium seating can all increase crowd sizes.

Alternative activities

The availability of alternative activities will also influence sport fan decisions. While this factor is unlikely to explain week-to-week variations in attendances, it can explain a decline in attendance over a longer period. Fans have become increasingly mobile and are able to choose between a huge number of leisure and entertainment alternatives. In addition, home entertainment options such as computers, game consoles, and pay television are the biggest threats to live sport. The choice between competing leisure activities has never been more expansive.

> *Chapter principle 3.8*: Fans' decisions to attend or view sport may be influenced by external factors, such as the type of sport involved, the balance of the competition, how uncertain the outcome is, the likelihood of their team winning, the venue and facilities, weather conditions, prices, personal income levels, special experiences that are being offered, promotional factors and the availability of alternative activities.

CASE 3.4

Barmy Army

English sport fans have a reputation for being actively engaged in the games they watch. In many instances they become an integral part of the event. English cricket has had its fair share of supporter and fan collectives, one of which has become a permanent feature of its international cricket matches. It all started during the 1994–1995 Ashes series, which is a biennial Test cricket series played between England and its arch-rival Australia. The English cricket team was not having great success, but they had a group of loyal and highly visible fans who attracted a significant amount of media attention. The Australian media labelled this lively group England's 'Barmy Army'. The group and name became so popular that it became a registered trademark in late 1995.

Nowadays, the Barmy Army entourage comprises a colourful ensemble of fanatical cricket supporters who liven up the game with their songs, merchandise, and banter, and who are prepared to travel to all of England's overseas matches in support of their team. While some supporter groups in sport can be considered intimidating and prone to disruptive behaviour that resembles a kind of mob mentality, the Barmy Army strive to project a different and far more inclusive identity. Regardless of race, age or gender, any English cricket fan can become a part of the Barmy Army. An adult membership costs £35 per year, or a lifetime membership costs £325. Membership benefits include priority ticket access to all England games, attendance at special events, and discounts from sponsoring brands. The group boasts a membership of over 40,000 fans and the leaders are vocal about their desire to have a diverse and inclusive group. Barmy Army marketing focuses on recruiting people by emphasising the fun of being involved, the social connectivity, their vibrancy and colour, and most vividly of all, the cleverness and catchiness of their songs and chants. The group has its own social media accounts to help share their activities and messages with nearly 400,000 X (formerly Twitter) followers and over 150,000 on Instagram.

Barmy Army emblazoned cricket merchandise has become a successful business venture and the group has enhanced their exposure with guest appearances on television. These entrepreneurial activities provide a unifying influence on most fans. On balance, the Barmy Army has added an attractive dimension to the game. Cricket is a commercialised commodity and its coverage on television focuses not only on the game, but also on the overall atmosphere. Broadcasters can easily identify the animated Barmy Army, and the guaranteed attention provides an attractive location for perimeter advertisers. Realising the potential to attract attention, the Barmy Army has progressed beyond rigid commercial interests, and has assumed a benevolent persona, demonstrating social sensitivity through charity work. Over the past 25 years, the group has raised over £500,000 for various charities. In 2022, it became official partners with a charity called the ACE Programme, launched by the Surrey County Cricket Club to respond to the rapid decline of Black cricket players in England. The programme provides talent pathways, an elite academy, and workforce development for young people of African and Caribbean heritage in the United Kingdom.

The Barmy Army has thus become an integral part of England cricket matches, essentially ingraining itself as part of the product offering. It is now so successful and well known that it can attract its own sponsorship. The Barmy Army has also become a social entrepreneur by getting involved in philanthropic causes. The Barmy Army has created its own style of fandom that is highly appealing and has subsequently become a permanent fixture of the international cricket scene and experience.

QUESTIONS

1. Visit the Barmy Army's website at www.barmyarmy.com. What is the Barmy Army and what is its overall purpose?
2. What factors and needs led to the formation of the Barmy Army?
3. While the Barmy Army can enhance the sport consumer's experience, is it also possible that it may detract for some? Explain why, or why not.
4. Look at some of the Barmy Army's social media accounts (i.e., Facebook, X, and Instagram). What types of posts does the group make to try to recruit new members?

PRINCIPLES SUMMARY

- Chapter principle 3.1: A sport consumer is an individual who purchases sporting goods, uses sport services, participates, or volunteers in sport and/or follows sport as a spectator or fan.
- Chapter principle 3.2: Sport fan motives for consuming sport products and services can be summarised into three categories: (1) psychological motives, (2) socio-cultural motives, and (3) self-concept motives.
- Chapter principle 3.3: Psychological motives for sport fans include the opportunity for stimulation, escape, aesthetic pleasure, and a sense of dramatic entertainment.

- Chapter principle 3.4: Socio-cultural motives for sport fans include the opportunity for family and social interaction, cultural connections, and even economic benefit.
- Chapter principle 3.5: Self-concept motives for sport fans include the opportunity for belonging and group affiliation, tribal connections, and vicarious achievement.
- Chapter principle 3.6: Fan motives for consuming sport are affected by their age, education, income, gender, race, sexuality, and marital status, but these demographic variables do not always influence motivation in a uniform or predictable way.
- Chapter principle 3.7: Sport fans can be classified according to the sources and dimensions of their attraction to the sport, and their frequency of attendance.
- Chapter principle 3.8: Fans' decisions to attend or view sport may be influenced by external factors, such as the type of sport involved, the balance of the competition, how uncertain the outcome is, the likelihood of their team winning, the venue and facilities, weather conditions, prices, personal income levels, special experiences that are being offered, promotional factors and the availability of alternative activities.

REVIEW QUESTIONS

1. Identify and describe the different kinds of sport consumers.
2. Define and distinguish between (1) psychological motives, (2) socio-cultural motives, and (3) self-concept motives.
3. Choose one variable from age, education, income, gender or race, and speculate on how it might influence sport consumption.
4. Why are sport fans often distinguished on the basis of their consumption behaviour?
5. List the five different types of sport fans and provide a brief comment on the best way to market sport to each.
6. What is the difference between an internal factor and an external factor when it comes to their influence on sport consumption?

RELEVANT WEBSITES

Barmy Army (www.barmyarmy.com)
Chase Center (www.chasecenter.com)
EE Hope United Campaign (www.eehopeunited.co.uk)
Nielsen Sports (www.nielsensports.com)

FURTHER READING

Sarver Coombs, D., & Osborne, A. C. (2022). *Routledge Handbook of Sports Fans and Fandom*. Routledge.

Smith, A. C. T. (2023). *Football on the Brain: Why Minds Love Sport*. Margin Press.

Wann, D. L., & James, J. D. (2019). *Sport Fans: The Psychology and Social Impact of Fandom*. Routledge.

CHAPTER 4

Sport marketing opportunities

LEARNING OUTCOMES

At the end of this chapter, readers should be able to:

- describe the key marketing activities required to identify sport marketing opportunities.
- explain the elements and purpose of a SWOT analysis.
- conduct a macro and micro environmental analysis.
- describe the process and importance of a competitor analysis.
- identify some of the introductory issues associated with market research, including its application and importance to identifying marketing opportunities.

OVERVIEW

This chapter examines the ways in which sport marketing opportunities can be identified and exploited. This will be done by constructing a Sport Marketing Framework. The Sport Marketing Framework begins by identifying marketing opportunities and then proceeds to developing a strategic marketing strategy that involves planning the sport marketing mix, and implementing and controlling the sport marketing strategy. This chapter provides detailed guidance for undertaking the first stage of the Framework: identifying sport marketing opportunities. Included are details on the three parts of stage 1: (a) analyse internal and external environments; (b) analyse organisation; and (c) analyse market and consumers.

THE SPORT MARKETING FRAMEWORK

The Sport Marketing Framework describes the stages and activities of sport marketing. It is the backbone of all sport marketing efforts. The Sport Marketing Framework is made up of four stages and is illustrated in Figure 4.1, with stage 1 of the process,

DOI: 10.4324/9781003391319-4

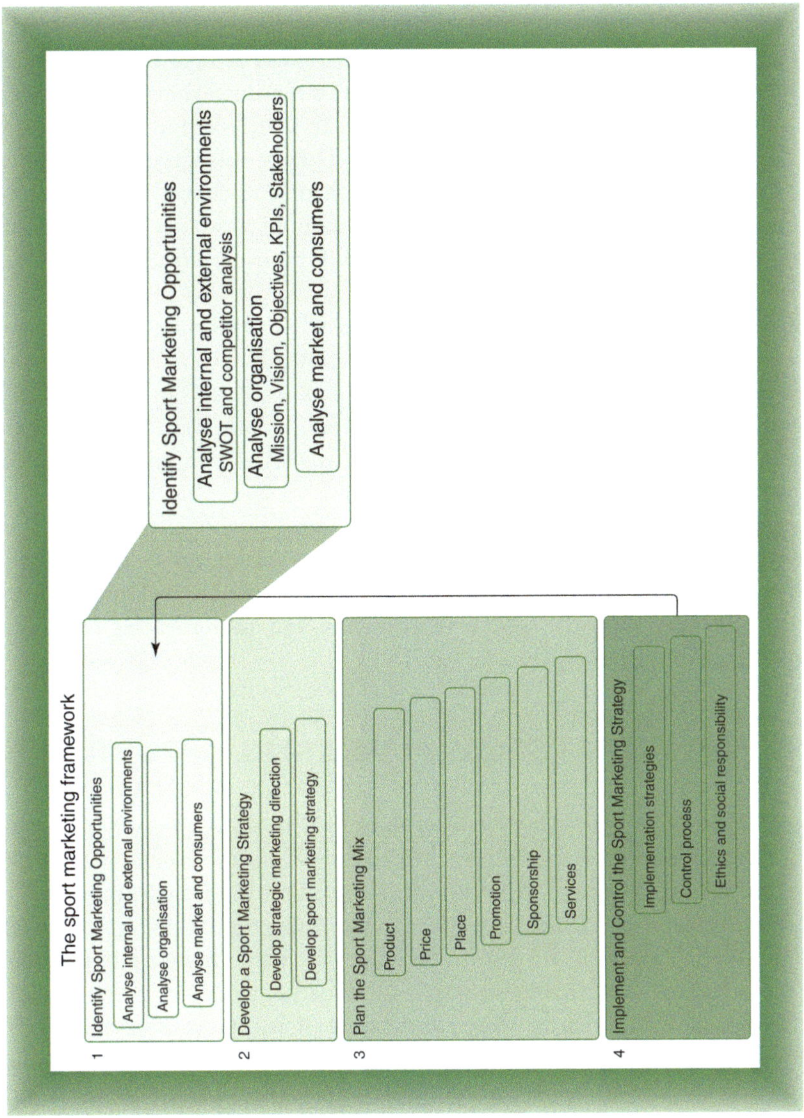

FIGURE 4.1 Identify sport marketing opportunities

'Identify Sport Marketing Opportunities', highlighted. Stage 1 involves three parts. First is the analysis of conditions in the external marketplace (such as competitors' activities, technology, legal restrictions, and the economic climate) as well as the internal environment of a sport organisation (such as its strengths and weaknesses). Second is the analysis of the sport organisation's unique position, such as its mission, vision, objectives, performance measures, and stakeholders. Third is the analysis of the market and its consumers via market research.

Once stage 1 is completed, the assembled information is used to undertake stage 2 of the Sport Marketing Framework – 'Develop a Sport Marketing Strategy'. Stage 2 involves making key decisions about the strategic direction a sport marketing programme should take considering the analysis performed in stage 1. During this stage, it is important to establish the strategy within the boundaries of both objectives and performance measures to later evaluate whether the marketing programme has been successful. Stage 2 also involves determining the specific tactics that will be used during the strategy, such as how it will position (differentiate) the sport product or service in the market, exactly who it will be targeted towards (segmentation), and what marketing mix decisions (this is a term covering the elements of product, pricing strategies, promotional strategies, and distribution systems) will be employed to implement the strategy. In stage 3 of the process, the sport marketing mix is documented in detail. Finally, stage 4 involves putting the plan into action and making sure it remains on track through systematic evaluation and modification.

> *Chapter principle 4.1*: The Sport Marketing Framework describes the four stages of sport marketing: identifying sport marketing opportunities, developing a sport marketing strategy, planning the sport marketing mix, and implementing and controlling the sport marketing strategy.

STAGE 1: IDENTIFYING SPORT MARKETING OPPORTUNITIES

The first step of the Sport Marketing Framework recognises the importance of conducting preliminary research and analysis before it is possible to make sensible marketing decisions. For example, it is essential to know what opportunities exist in the marketplace, what competitors are doing, what a sport organisation is good at doing, and what consumers want. The first stage of the sport marketing process is therefore to identify sport marketing opportunities. This involves analysing the market and consumers, as well as the organisation for which the plan is being constructed. It is important to realise that the three parts of stage 1 should be conducted at approximately the same time, as the three analyses are interconnected.

Analyse internal and external environments

The first activity in stage 1 prescribes an analysis of the internal and external environments in which a sport organisation is placed. The internal environment refers to the unique circumstances of the sport organisation for which the plan is developed. A sport marketer must therefore determine the strengths and weaknesses of their sport organisation. For example, a local rugby club may be strong in terms of its positive community profile and the support it receives from a regional association providing access to a well-organised competition structure. However, the club may be weak in financial terms and may have difficulty in attracting young players.

The external environment refers to the marketplace in which a sport organisation operates. This includes the immediate sport industry as well as the national and international context. In fact, it is important to understand the industry-related external environment, the nature of competitors, and the broad national and global environment. In the example of a local swimming club, an analysis of the external environment may reveal that swimming is not a popular sport in the region, or that there is limited government support for its development. These external factors may also have a strong influence on the specific strengths and weaknesses of a sport organisation.

In the following section, the tools for conducting internal and external analyses will be explained in detail. These tools include a SWOT analysis (with external environment analysis) and competitor analysis (with the Five Forces Analysis).

> *Chapter principle 4.2*: The first step in identifying sport marketing opportunities is to analyse the internal and external environment using the tools of SWOT analysis (with external environment analysis) and competitor analysis (with the Five Forces Analysis).

CASE 4.1

Youth Olympic Games

Many professional sport organisations undertake a marketing audit to identify current organisational strengths and weaknesses relative to their rivals. They also look towards the future in relation to exploring environmental opportunities and reducing threats. One of the most common planning tools used by organisations is a SWOT analysis. Below, you will read about the International Olympic Committee's (IOC) Youth Olympic Games (YOG). Following the case, you will be asked to conduct a SWOT analysis of the YOG.

The IOC is best-known for operating and governing the Summer and Winter Olympic Games, which are mega- and multi-sport events involving athletes from over 200 nations. Perhaps less well-known, however, is that the IOC also hosts an event called the YOG as well. First held in 2010 in Singapore, the YOG is designed to provide a high-level global sporting event for people between the ages of 15 and 18. The YOG also includes three educational components for participating athletes, focusing on protecting athletes, working on performance, and helping athletes in aspects outside of sport. The YOG was first envisioned by former IOC President Jacques Rogge, who wanted to design an event that would help tackle childhood obesity and encourage young people to participate in sport. To achieve these goals, each YOG includes initiatives involving children who are local to the area where the YOG is hosted. For example, during the 2018 Summer YOG in Buenos Aires, Argentina, over 250,000 local children participated in sport programmes offered through the YOG, such as introductory classes to various sports.

Like the Olympic Games, the YOG takes place every two years, alternating between a Summer and a Winter edition. The YOG has been used to test new sports that the IOC is considering introducing in the Olympic Games. For example, breakdancing was introduced in the 2018 YOG in Buenos Aires, and then subsequently became an Olympic sport at the 2024 Paris Olympic Games. In 2026, the YOG will introduce another new sport, wushu, which is also sometimes known as Kung fu. It is a complete martial art as well as a full-contact combat sport. Several athletes who competed in the YOG have later gone on to compete in and win medals at the Olympic Games, such as Chinese freestyle skier Eileen Gu and Russian gymnast Nikita Nagornyy. For those athletes who do not continue their elite sporting careers post-YOG, the IOC hopes that participation in the YOG will help them to become better humans by learning about the Olympic values and other cultures.

QUESTIONS

1. Visit the website for the YOG (www.olympics.com/ioc/youth-olympic-games) to see where the next edition will be held. Then, using the information presented in the case, conduct a basic SWOT analysis of the upcoming YOG.
2. Identify the most important strength, weakness, opportunity, and threat.
3. Explain why the items in your SWOT were selected.

SWOT analysis: an analysis of the internal and external environments

One of the basic tools in this stage of the sport marketing process is known as the SWOT analysis. The term SWOT is an acronym for the words: *strengths, weaknesses, opportunities, threats*. A SWOT analysis examines the strategic position of an organisation from the inside (strengths and weaknesses) and the outside (opportunities and threats).

The SWOT analysis can be divided into two parts. The first part represents an internal analysis of an organisation, which can be summarised by its *strengths* and *weaknesses*. An organisation has control over its strengths and weaknesses. The strengths of an organisation include those areas in which an organisation does well and can be considered capabilities. The weaknesses of an organisation can include those areas in which it does poorly and can be seen as deficiencies. The second part of the SWOT technique concerns external factors. These constitute elements that the organisation has no direct control over and can be summarised as *opportunities* and *threats*. Opportunities include environmental circumstances that can be used to an organisation's advantage, while threats include unfavourable situations in the external environment that need to be avoided or otherwise taken into consideration.

The strengths and weaknesses of a sport organisation, along with the opportunities and threats it faces, will influence the options available for a marketing plan. As a result, the SWOT analysis is used to identify the major issues that mitigate strategic options. A good rule of thumb is to look for no more than five factors under each of the four headings so that the most important issues are given the highest priority. One of the most common mistakes made when conducting a SWOT analysis is getting caught in needless detail and losing sight of the 'big picture'. Another common mistake is including external factors in the strengths and weaknesses sections, which should only focus on internal factors, and conversely, focusing on internal factors in the opportunities and threats sections, which should only focus on external factors. It is also important not to focus only on sport-related matters, but to consider general organisational and business factors.

Strengths and Weaknesses

The analysis of strengths and weaknesses should be focused on present-day circumstances. To recap, strengths can be defined as resources or capabilities that a sport organisation can use to achieve its strategic ambitions. Common strengths may include committed coaching staff, a sound membership base, a good junior development program, or management staff with sound business skills and knowledge. Weaknesses should be seen as limitations or inadequacies that will prevent or hinder the strategic direction from being achieved. Common weaknesses may include poor training facilities, inadequate sponsorship, a diminishing volunteer workforce, or a weak financial position.

Opportunities and Threats

While strengths and weaknesses should be focused on the present-day situation, opportunities and threats should be future-oriented. Opportunities are favourable situations or events that an organisation can use to its advantage to enhance its performance. For example, common opportunities include new government grants, the identification of a new market or potential product, or the chance to appoint a new staff member with unique skills. Threats, in contrast, are the unfavourable situations making performance more difficult in the future. Common threats include inflating player salaries, potential new competitors, or unfavourable trends in the marketplace such as the increased popularity of other entertainment options. Table 4.1 summarises the SWOT technique.

The next section will introduce the many factors that need to be considered when evaluating the external environment to determine the opportunities and threats an organisation faces. This is followed with an explanation of how to perform a competitor analysis and Five Forces competitor analysis.

TABLE 4.1 SWOT guidelines

Strengths	• Resources (e.g., finance, staff, volunteers) • Skills (e.g., talents of management, staff, and volunteers) • Advantages (compared with competitors)
Weaknesses	• Lack of resources (e.g., finance, staff, volunteers) • Lack of skills (e.g., among management, staff, and volunteers) • Disadvantages (compared with competitors)
Opportunities	• Favourable situations in the external environment • Weaknesses of competitors
Threats	• Unfavourable situation in the external environment • Unfavourable trends in leisure and entertainment

CASE 4.2

Lawn Bowls

Lawn bowls is played around the world but enjoys its highest popularity in nations that were once part of the British Commonwealth. The oldest green (playing surface) that is still used is in Southampton, England, and was established in 1299. Throughout history British kings and knights have played the game. Older age groups traditionally played the sport, although it is now beginning to attract younger participants.

Lawn bowls has a lot going for it. It is played outdoors on beautifully manicured grass. It is easy to play, but also requires skill to perform at a high level. According to the British Heart Foundation, it is possible to walk up to three miles during a game, which provides players with important exercise. Lawn bowls also offers a workout to one's arms during the act of bowling. The game provides a strong after-game experience, where friendships are formed, and social networks are established. Its customs and protocols deliver an appropriate level of discipline, while also allowing creativity to thrive. It is inclusive and is one of the few sports that has impeccable gender balance. Neither does it discriminate between social classes. So, why has it faced so many problems in attracting new members over recent years?

The core problem revolves around the average age of club members. Lawn bowls has a history of attracting older adults, and as a result, anyone in their fifties who plays it is considered young. This is the public image of the game, and even though more young adults are becoming involved, and doing well at the elite level, this stereotype persists. The average age of lawn bowls players varies from one country to the next, ranging from approximately 55 in England to 45 in Canada, and around 30 in Australia. One of the reasons that the demographic may be trending younger in Australia is the proliferation of 'barefoot bowls' in recent years. This new form of lawn bowls involves playing bowls in a relaxed manner with no shoes, no dress code, and no strict regulations. Instead of becoming members of bowls clubs, barefoot bowlers largely pay an hourly fee to play, and tend to spend more at the bar than traditional players. The barefoot trend has not caught on with such intensity in other countries yet. From a marketing perspective, the challenge for lawn bowls revolves around rebranding the game and recasting it as a whole-of-life sport for all demographics where equity, inclusivity, and social connectedness are its key values.

QUESTIONS

1. What are the most attractive aspects of lawn bowls?
2. What sports and games are its main competitors?
3. What new markets and players could lawn bowls target?
4. How might lawn bowls go about seeking out these new markets and new players?

External environment analysis

The external environment is made up of several factors, including an organisation's competitors, the sport industry, and the wider environment. These are illustrated in Figure 4.2.

The largest circle in Figure 4.2, the macro (or broad) external environment, comprises the political, economic, legal, technological, social, and physical environments. Imagine, for example, that there has been a change over time in the demographic make-up of a region. Such changes may impact the kinds of sports that are considered most popular and likely to attract participants. In a population with a greater proportion of older people, sports such as lawn bowls and golf may have an improved opportunity to expand their participation bases.

Figure 4.3 summarises the six factors that form the macro external environment of a sport organisation. It is important to understand the demands, constraints, and possibilities that each of these elements might bring to the sport organisation. Each of these will be described next.

Political Environment

Government policy influences the ways in which sport organisations can operate. For example, as you will read about in the next case, sport policy in some countries such as

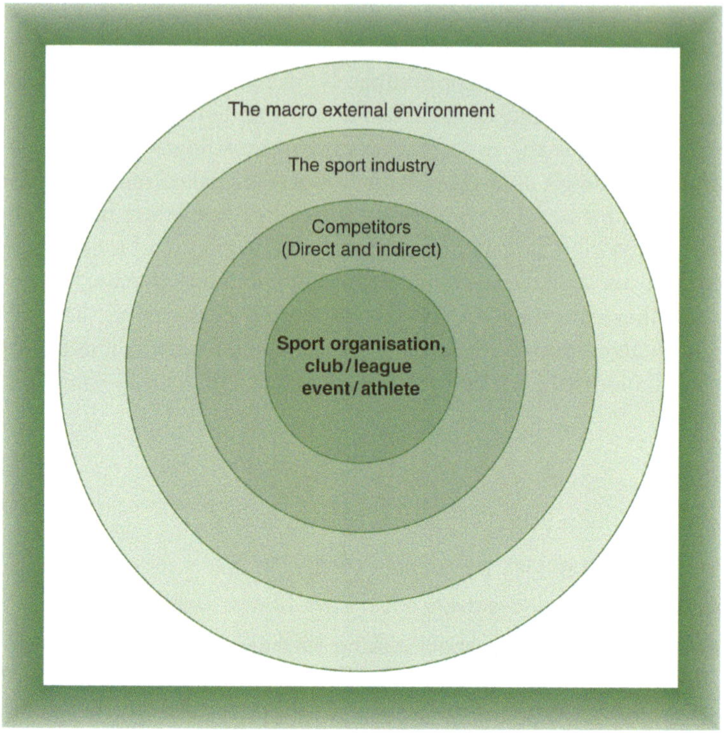

FIGURE 4.2 External environments of a sport organisation

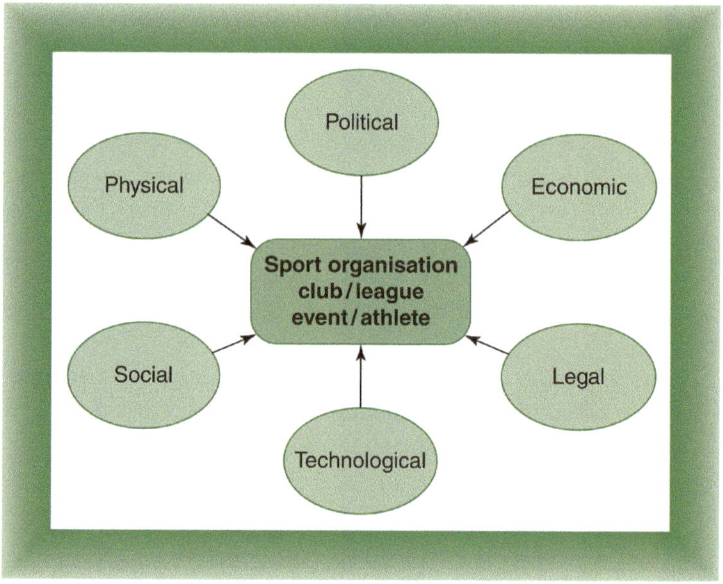

FIGURE 4.3 The macro external environment

New Zealand put a high priority on the development of elite sport, which may be supported by millions of dollars of funding. Government influence can also be relevant in attracting major events to cities.

CASE 4.3

Sport New Zealand

Most Western nations now have government agencies that administer the national government's sport development policies. Sport New Zealand (Sport NZ) is a central government agency in the small country of 5 million people. Sport NZ's mission is to see 'Every Body Active', or to ensure that everyone in the nation takes part in some form of physical activity. In addition to encouraging participation in sport and recreation, Sport NZ also operates High Performance Sport New Zealand (HPSNZ), which is responsible for leading the country's elite sporting system. HPSNZ hopes to inspire the nation by seeing more New Zealand athletes winning medals on the world stage (e.g., at World Championships, Commonwealth Games, Olympic and Paralympic Games). Clearly, Sport NZ has two very different major organisational goals; one related to the participation and wellbeing of everyday citizens and one related to high performance elite sport.

To help fulfil its commitment to ensuring all New Zealanders are active, Sport NZ conducted research on sport participation of its citizens. The organisation found that those between the ages of 12 and 14 are most active (98% of both males and females), with participation experiencing a steady decline as the population ages (62% of males and 61% of females are active by age 75+). Sport NZ identified three areas to help encourage more life-long participation: advocacy, collaboration, and investments. Advocacy takes the form of promoting the importance of health and wellbeing to one's life, collaboration involves developing strategic partnerships with organisations offering sport participation opportunities, and investments focus on capitalising on opportunities to boost communities and test pilot programmes for involvement.

In terms of investment, HPSNZ has its own strategy designed to develop elite talent within New Zealand sport. In the past, New Zealand invested heavily only in sports that it believed had the best chances of winning world or Olympic medals, whereas its latest strategy invests $273 million NZD into a greater number of sports, athletes, and coaches throughout the country in the years leading up to the 2032 Summer Olympic Games to be held in nearby Brisbane, Australia. The new strategy also includes funding for approximately 920 athletes per year, an increase from the 559 athletes previously funded. While Sport NZ and HPSNZ are still focused on winning on the world stage, the new strategy moves the organisation's focus away from being purely performance-based and instead provides more financial security to more athletes and giving attention to athletes' wellbeing.

QUESTIONS

1. What is the overall responsibility of Sport NZ?
2. Based on what you know about Sport NZ, what priorities does the New Zealand government have for sport?
3. What does HPSNZ seem to value in its latest investment strategy?
4. Why would national governments want to fund sport?

Economic environment

The economic environment is made up of two elements: the macroeconomic and the microeconomic. Macroeconomic elements represent the big picture as they describe the economy on a national level. Microeconomic elements represent the detailed picture at the organisational or consumer level.

Macroeconomic factors provide a broad picture of economic issues that might affect a sport organisation. When employment levels and consumer spending are higher (in times of prosperity), consumers tend to spend more money on sport. During times of recession or depression, consumers may not be as likely to spend money on sport. However, it is possible that during these low economic times consumers will still choose to spend money on sport for entertainment and distraction. Sport can be a powerful way for people to temporarily escape from their everyday worries and stresses. The way that sport organisations will be affected may vary greatly from one organisation to another.

One of the most important microeconomic elements relevant to sport organisations is consumer income levels. Naturally, a consumer's income level will have an influence on whether they can afford to purchase a sport service or product. When economists talk about income, they often use the terms gross income, disposable income, and discretionary income. Gross income is how much money people earn before any tax or expenses are taken out. Disposable income is how much money is left over after tax has been paid. Finally, discretionary income is what remains after tax had been paid and all the necessities of living have been bought (e.g., housing, food, transportation). As sport is not a necessity of life, consumers pay for sport products out of their discretionary income. Therefore, the greater the amount of discretionary income that a consumer has, the more money they may potentially spend on sport if they wish. It is true, however, that some sport fans are so dedicated that they consider spending on sport as important as spending on the essentials of living.

Legal environment

The legal aspect of the macro external environment can include legislation passed by government, as well as the regulations set down by sport associations, and national and international sporting bodies. Governments create legislation (laws) designed to implement and enforce the policies they set (see Political Environment section). For example, the government sets laws that regulate how and when broadcasters can cover sport events. Many other types of government legislation can also affect the individuals and groups involved in the sport industry, such as company law, taxation, patents and copyright, and contract law. The smaller regulatory bodies relevant to sport organisations can include associations, leagues, and international federations. The International Gymnastics Federation (FIG), for example, sets rules about how international gymnastics competitions should be run. WADA (the World Anti-Doping Agency) is another international example. WADA sets regulations regarding the types of substances athletes are permitted to use in sanctioned sport competitions and establishes the standards of punishment for non-compliance.

Technological environment

Technology has had a substantial impact on the way sport organisations operate. For example, social media has revolutionised sport marketing and communication, medical technology has improved sport medicine techniques and virtual reality has made it possible for a fan to feel as if they are watching a sporting event live and in-person from the comfort of their own home. Technological developments are so important to the marketing of sport that Chapter 12 further explores its implications.

CASE 4.4

Netflix: Drive to Survive

Formula One (F1) had its first world championship race in 1950 in the United Kingdom and has since become the most popular form of motorsport in the world. This elite level of racing has at times had challenges engaging with some audiences, however, and hasn't been able to rest on its laurels. In 2017, Liberty Media acquired the series for approximately $8 billion USD and began an aggressive branding strategy to bring some motorsport fans back to F1 and attract up new audiences.

As part of its new strategy Liberty Media aimed to target motorsport fans in the United States and increase fan engagement with the drivers and the people running the teams. One of the primary mechanisms to do this was the introduction of a documentary series (docuseries) on the popular streaming platform Netflix called 'Drive to Survive'. The series first aired in 2019 and the high-quality content brought audiences an immersive experience in which they felt as though they were inside the teams' cockpits, learning about the lives of many of the drivers, and other key personnel within F1. Using a narrative approach highlighting the season that has just finished, the Drive to Survive formula is one of high production values, extraordinary access, exhilarating visuals and sounds, and a documentary-drama approach that seeks to wring emotion out of the sport and its participants.

Following the first season there was a 40% increase in F1 viewership within the United States, and the US Grand Prix in Austin, Texas was the most-attended three-day F1 event ever with 400,000 attendees. Following the popularity of the first Netflix series, F1 continued to pursue this strategy, releasing the second season of Drive to Survive in 2020, and has continued to release new seasons each year since. According to Front Office Sports, a sport business media outlet, content has been key to F1's success and growth to become the most popular motorsport in the world. Utilising a global streaming platform such as Netflix has allowed the sport to reach audiences all over the world, and the rich content has brought fans closer to their favourite drivers and teams.

QUESTIONS

1 What audiences do docuseries like Drive to Survive appeal to? Which, if any, of these are likely to be converted to following F1?
2 What sports lend themselves best to a streaming series, such as F1's Drive to Survive? What other examples of similar series can you note?
3 What elements do docuseries like Drive to Survive contain that can help the marketing of the sport they are aligned to? If you were starting a similar series for another sport, what are these key elements that you would wish to include?

Social Environment

The social environment can include the culture of a region as well as its prevalent social trends and demographics. Different cultures and changing cultural trends can have an influence on whether sport is a valued activity, what kind of sport is appreciated, and even how sport and competition should be organised. Cricket, for example, enjoys great strength in England, Australia, New Zealand, India, South Africa, and the West Indies (all previous colonies of the British who introduced the game). It is common for sport consumers from other countries, however, to report that the game is too slow and boring. Social issues may also include demographic trends, which refer to the changing composition of a population in an area.

Physical Environment

The physical environment can include the unique geographical features of a region, the weather, and the built facilities available. On the coastlines of Australia, for example, the warm climate and accessible beaches offer the opportunity to participate in sports such as surfing, stand-up paddleboarding and kite surfing. In many European countries, in contrast, the Alpine formations and cold environment during winter provide ample options for a variety of snow sports to be enjoyed. Weather factors, such as the availability of water, can directly impact on the kinds of sporting surfaces that can be easily managed. For example, golf courses and other turf surfaces require significant water resources to be maintained.

Changing weather patterns may represent a significant threat to sport grounds and events, with drought being an obvious example. Finally, the availability of sporting facilities can also present unique opportunities and threats to a sport organisation. In a country such as England, for example, there are numerous facilities and grounds available for polo to be played, whereas few such facilities exist in China and Indonesia.

CASE 4.5

Ski Dubai

Ski Dubai is an indoor ski resort in the desert nation of the United Arab Emirates (UAE) comprising 22,500 square metres of ski space. Ski Dubai offers visitors the opportunity to take part in downhill skiing, bounce down a snowy hill in an inflatable zorb (ball) or on an inflatable tube, zipline over the ski slope, or have a personal experience interacting with penguins. It allows people in the Middle East to experience the joys of winter snow sports without traveling to Europe or other traditional ski and snow areas such as Colorado in the United States. Since Ski Dubai opened in 2005, two additional facilities have opened in the Middle East as well; Snow Abu Dhabi and Snow Oman, illustrating the desire of Middle Eastern residents to have more traditional winter sport experiences.

This example starkly shows how a sport facility can provide a service that operates in direct contrast to the geographical features and weather of the local environment. The average daily temperature in Dubai during January is 24°C/75.2°F and the average daily temperature rises to 41°C/105.8°F in July. This hardly seems like the kind of environment for snow sports, but despite this massive climatic constraint, a 400-metre indoor ski slope has been built. There are 23 mega-scale air conditioners to help keep the temperature at around 2°C/30°F. The Dubai desert ski resort is the ultimate novelty sport experience. However, it has a major drawback. It is costly to run, and these costs will only escalate as the local authorities aim to win their 'fight' against the environment. This fantasy sporting escape may enhance the city's image as a 'can do' place, but at what cost?

QUESTIONS

1. What motivated the city of Dubai to build a ski park?
2. Who is their target market, and what aspects of the ski park would attract this market?
3. Why would a sport consumer with an interest in snow sports visit Dubai, and not a natural snow resort such as the ones in the Swiss or Austrian Alps?
4. What additional value would a sport consumer get from a few days at the Dubai ski park that could not be secured at a traditional ski resort?

The Sport Industry Environment

Sport organisations should look at how the general external environment influences their specific industrial environment. Figure 4.4 provides a summary of the specific sport industry environmental factors that may influence a sport organisation's marketing decisions. The combination of an analysis of broad, external environmental factors and the sport industry external environment should complement the opportunities and threats component of the SWOT analysis.

> *Chapter tool 4.1 SWOT and external environment analysis*: A SWOT analysis is used to examine the strategic position of an organisation from inside (strengths and weaknesses) and outside (opportunities and threats). The OT part of the analysis is supported by examining the macro (or broad) external environment, which is made up of the political, economic, legal, technological, social and physical environments, as well as the sport industry environment, which is made up of media, finance, staff and members, commercial, government and leagues, and public groups.

Direct and Indirect Competitors

Although direct and indirect competitors are external factors, their assessment is so important that it typically constitutes a separate activity. Competition occurs when numerous sport organisations attempt to meet the needs of the same group of consumers.

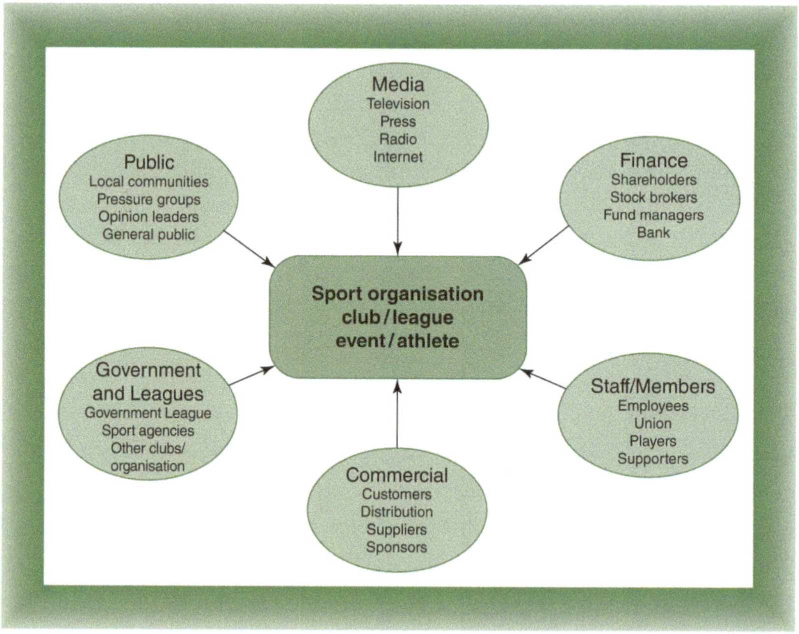

FIGURE 4.4 The sport industry (micro) external environment

The sport apparel segment offers an example of an extremely competitive sport market where large numbers of manufacturers and sellers try to attract the same consumers to buy their products.

A sport organisation must understand its competition for several reasons. First, competitors may have weaknesses to be exploited. Second, competitors may have strengths that could represent a threat, or alternatively provide helpful lessons. Third, competitors change over time. By analysing the competition, a sport organisation considers some of the opportunities and threats that it needs to manage.

There is a difference between direct and indirect competition. Direct (or immediate) competition can be defined as the competition that occurs between sellers who produce similar products and services. The example of sporting shoe manufacturers provides a good illustration. Direct competition can also exist between two products that consumers consider substitutable. Instead of purchasing Under Armour apparel, a sport consumer might choose to buy New Balance instead. These products have differences to one another, but they are similar enough that the consumer could substitute (replace) one for the other. Secondary competition occurs when sellers produce substitute products that meet consumer needs in a different way, such as going to a netball game instead of a football match. Here, the consumer need reflects the desire for entertainment rather than the experience of watching a particular sport.

Indirect competition occurs between sellers who produce *different* products and services that either satisfy similar consumer needs or encourage consumers to seek the satisfaction of different needs. In the case of sport, other forms of entertainment are a strong source of indirect competition. For example, movie theatres, music concerts, cafés, shopping centres, restaurants, and even television offer alternative ways that consumers could choose to spend their leisure time. Figure 4.5 illustrates the levels of direct and indirect competition.

The level of intensity in competition, where entry into the market is dependent on timing and speed, and understanding the response from competitors are very important, and have made the gathering of intelligence an advantageous commodity for sport organisations. No sport can operate in a vacuum. The diversity of competition, whether it is direct or indirect, is much more complex than it first appears. Direct competition in most professional sport leagues is similar in terms of a specific product offering, technology, or target markets. Direct competition can also be more general in that the product or technology may be the same but different segments of the consumer market are targeted. For example, when the Women's Super League (WSL), an English professional women's football league, was first established in 2011, it was marketed as a niche product separate from the men's game targeting families. Indeed, even in 2023, the percentage of WSL fans who watched only WSL (and not the men's Premier League) was 55%. The strategy of targeting different consumers from the men's game seems to be successful for the WSL. On the other hand, indirect competition is often different and overlooked in a competitor analysis. When women's netball in Australia developed a semi-professional league in 2008 there was a notable increase in interest and attendance from male sport fans, satisfying a sport consumer's need differently. Alternatively, it can shift the sport consumer's discretionary spending elsewhere, such as the purchase of digital devices and services to support an individual training strategy rather than employing the

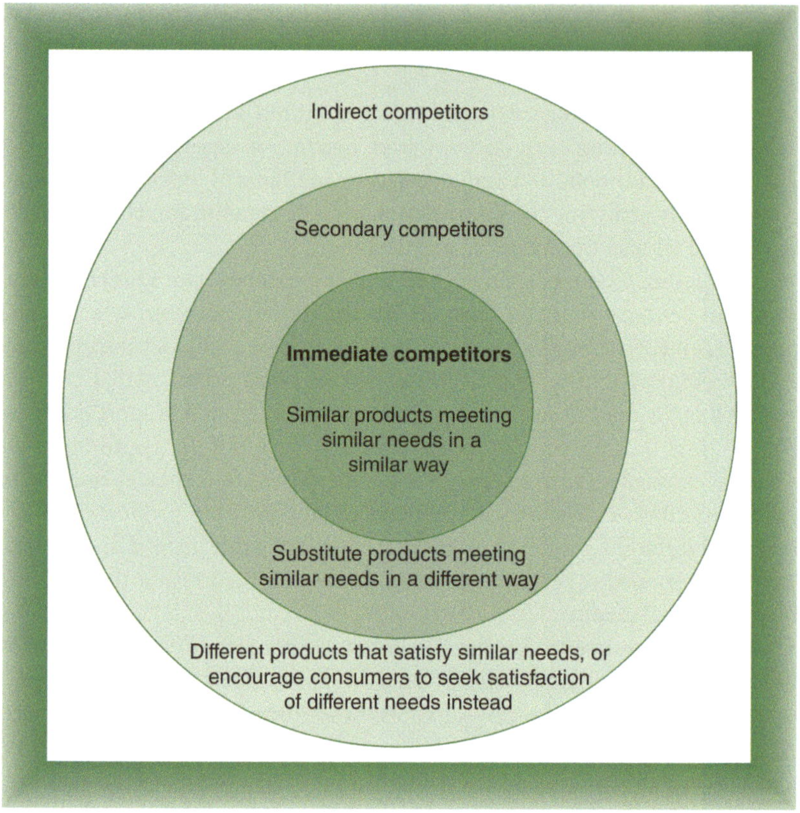

FIGURE 4.5 Types of competitors

services of a personal trainer. Latent competition can take the sport marketer by surprise and change the competitive playing field appreciably. Understanding where the competition is, where your customers are going and where they access information are all part of building strategic intelligence.

Competitor Analysis

Because competitors can have a large impact on the strategy a sport organisation develops, sport marketers must analyse competitors in a careful and systematic manner. In conducting a competitor analysis, it is critical to assess competitors' strategies, strengths, vulnerabilities, and resources, as well as their forthcoming actions. The recommended aspects of a competitor analysis are reproduced in Table 4.2.

Five Forces Analysis

In addition to conducting a competitor analysis, it is advisable to conduct a Five Forces Analysis. Originally developed by Michael Porter, the Five Forces Analysis is the most

TABLE 4.2 Dimensions of a competitor analysis

Dimension	*Description*
Geographic scope	What region or location do they operate in with emphasis on overlap?
Mission and vision	Do they intend to maintain their current market position, or do they have a vision to change their situation? What are their ambitions for the future?
Objectives	What are their short- to medium-term goals?
Market share and position	Are they a small player, a medium player or a virtual monopolist?
Strategy	What methods are they using to gain an advantage over their competition?
Resources	What are the amount and availability of resources?
Target market	To whom do they market their products and services?
Marketing mix approach	What products and services do they offer? What promotions, pricing, and distribution strategies do they use?

common tool for describing the competitive environment and can be adapted to the sport industry. As can be seen from Figure 4.6, this analysis examines five forces driving competition in the sport industry. Understanding the competitive situation in a sport sector is a particularly helpful way of determining whether it is an attractive one in which to conduct business, and whether there is scope for existing or new products to be developed. In other words, it may help to identify future opportunities and threats. Although businesses would consider a lower level of competition better than a higher one, the situation is often not as straightforward for sport organisations. Sport organisations rely on close on-field competition to keep consumers interested. Competitive threats, however, may come in many forms, such as new leagues or sports entering the market, substitute products available to consumers, and the potential for buyers and suppliers to exert their bargaining power.

Intensity of Rivalry among Industry Competitors

In general, greater rivalry will be present where there are more sport organisations offering similar products and services. The rivalry between Nike and Adidas is an excellent example of extreme rivalry. College basketball teams in the United States are another example, as would be different soccer clubs in any one country's professional soccer league. While one club is unlikely to be able to 'steal' supporters from the other, there would be significant competition between them for media exposure, corporate sponsorship, players, and

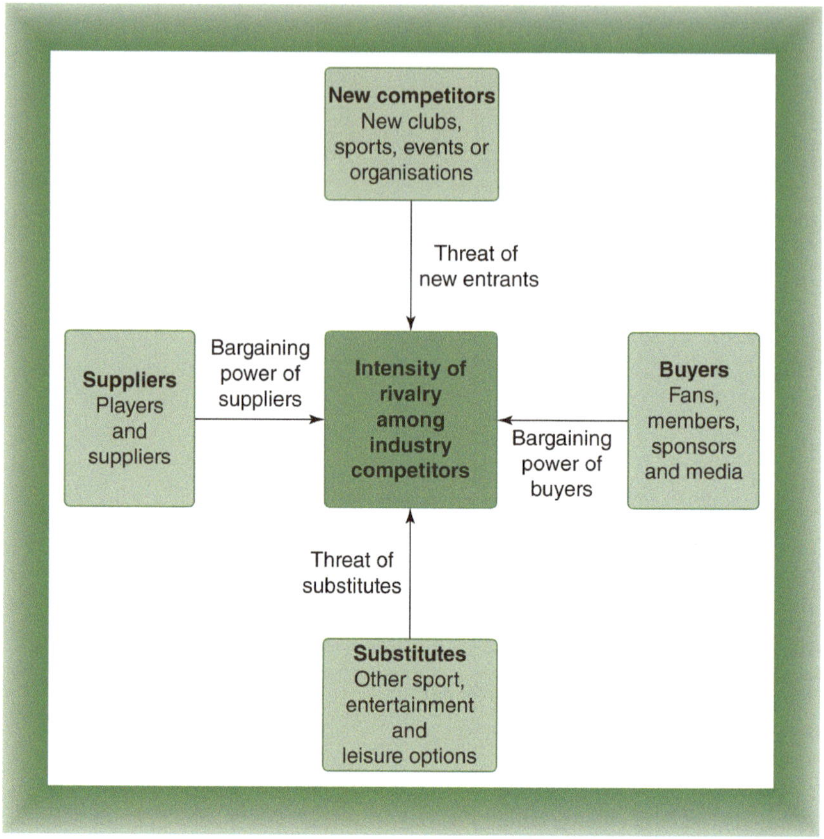

FIGURE 4.6 Five forces driving sport industry competition

coaches/managers. Intensity of rivalry appears at the centre of the diagram not only due to its significance, but because the other four forces can all contribute to its magnitude. Typically, the outcome of a Five Forces Analysis is represented in terms of the intensity of rivalry among industry competitors.

The Threat of New Entrants

Every sport organisation is faced with the possibility that at any time new competitors can enter their industry sector and offer substitute products. Of course, in some forms of professional sport, it seems unlikely that new clubs or teams could enter the competition. There are typically regulations dictating how many teams are allowed in the competition, and it may be difficult to generate a supporter base if fans hold strongly to the history and traditions of the competition. However, in other segments of the sport industry, there are often new organisations entering the marketplace, such as new sport facilities, leisure and recreational centres, events, sport apparel companies, and new equipment manufacturers. In general, the greater the threat of new entrants, the higher the intensity of rivalry among industry competitors.

The Bargaining Power of Buyers

Buyers of sport products and services include individuals, groups, and organisations. Fans, sport club members, corporate sponsors, and the media are all examples of parties that purchase sporting goods and services. The nature of competition in the environment will be affected by the strength of the bargaining power of buyers. The term 'bargaining power' refers to the influence that buyers must exert pressure on suppliers to reduce prices. For example, judging by the high ticket prices of some professional leagues, fans have little bargaining power. Also, when the bargaining power is low for media broadcasters, they may have to pay extravagant sums of money to secure the rights to broadcast an event. In contrast, when bargaining power is higher, the costs of rights will be lower. For most sport organisations, however, the main buyers are fans, and since fans do not usually work together to increase their bargaining power, it remains limited. In general, the greater the bargaining power of buyers, the higher the intensity of rivalry among industry competitors.

The Bargaining Power of Suppliers

Like buyers, suppliers may also be able to use bargaining power to force sport organisations to pay more for the inputs they require. When suppliers of raw materials threaten to raise prices or withdraw their products or services, they are attempting to improve their bargaining power. For example, suppliers of inputs to sport organisations include equipment and materials manufacturers. The most significant example of suppliers using bargaining power in sport has come about in relation to players, who can be thought of as suppliers of sport talent. As some professional player groups have become unionised, they have tried to put pressure on leagues and clubs to raise their salaries and salary caps. This has been successful in some instances where the player groups have been well organised. In 2002 in the United States, for example, players in Major League Baseball threatened to strike if their salary demands were not met, which forced the league into negotiations. In contrast, a similar dispute led the North American National Hockey League to cancel the entire 2004–2005 season. In general, the greater the bargaining power of suppliers, the higher the intensity of rivalry among industry competitors.

The Threat of Substitute Products and Services

Some competitors may not provide the same product but may offer alternatives or substitutes. As the sport industry expands, it is more common for different sports to compete with one another to meet similar needs of sport consumers. Other forms of leisure and entertainment also threaten to attract sport consumers' time. In general, the greater the threat of substitute products and services, the higher the intensity of rivalry among industry competitors.

> *Chapter tool 4.2 Competitor and Five Forces Analyses*: In order to conduct a competitor analysis, it is important to be mindful of the three different categories of competitors: immediate/direct competitors, secondary competitors and indirect competitors. When considering the *what* and *how* of competitors, it is important

to consider their geographic scope; vision, mission and objectives; market share and position; strategy; resources; target market; and marketing approach. It is also advisable to conduct a second type of competitor analysis: the Five Forces Analysis which comprises: (1) the intensity of rivalry among industry competitors, (2) the threat of new entrants into the marketplace (for example new clubs or leagues), (3) the threat of substitute products in the marketplace (such as other forms of entertainment), (4) the bargaining power of buyers (such as the media, sponsors and spectators) and (5) the bargaining power of suppliers (including players/athletes).

ANALYSE THE ORGANISATION

The second stage in identifying sport marketing opportunities is to analyse the organisation. To do this, it is necessary to understand the purpose, aims, and goals of an organisation in addition to the needs of its stakeholders. There are four tools that help to analyse the organisation. They are mission statement, vision statement, organisational objectives, and stakeholder analysis.

An analysis of the organisation will provide important information about the strategic direction it intends to pursue. It is important, for example, to understand the mission, vision, and objectives of an organisation, which indicate why an organisation exists, and what it is aiming to achieve. After all, the marketing efforts of an organisation are designed to fulfil its mission and achieve its objectives. It is possible that the information acquired during the organisational analysis may be considered useful to the internal (SW) analysis that contributes to the SWOT evaluation. This is one of the reasons why the three parts of stage 1 should be conducted at around the same time.

> *Chapter principle 4.3*: The second step in identifying sport marketing opportunities is to conduct an analysis of the organisation. This requires four tools: mission statement; vision statement; organisational objectives; and stakeholder analysis.

Mission statements

A mission statement identifies the purpose of an organisation. It should describe why an organisation was set up, what services and products it provides, and to whom they are provided. If a mission statement is not documented in writing, it can be easy for organisational members to be confused about the purpose of the organisation, or to have different ideas about what it should be. It is not uncommon for players, members, spectators, staff, coaches, media, sponsors, and government representatives to have different ideas about what constitutes the 'right' purpose. When it is recorded as a single, short statement (preferably a single sentence), this mission delivers a powerful declaration of the organisation's intentions. When developing a marketing plan, the mission statement offers fundamental guidance in the development of a strategy, as it should be consistent with the stated purpose of the organisation. For example, imagine that a community sport organisation states that its mission is to provide access to physical activities for people with an intellectual disability in each area. This basic guidance would be a useful starting point in developing a marketing plan. Many sport organisations possess mission statements, so their consideration is a simple task within an organisational analysis.

> *Chapter tool 4.3 Mission statement*: The sport organisation's mission statement should be reviewed in order to guide the identification of sport marketing opportunities. The mission statement reveals the purpose of an organisation: why it was created, what services and products it provides, and to whom they are provided.

Vision statements

Having a vision for the future is an important part of an effective sport organisation. A vision for the future is like a clear mental image of how a sport organisation would like to see itself in approximately three to five years' time. A vision statement is a written record of this future image, usually no longer than a sentence. It states the medium- to long-term goals of a sport organisation, or in simple terms, what it wants to achieve in a given time. It tends to be ambitious and bold, serving as a roadmap for the organisation to use while making decisions relating to its long-term goals. The vision is, of course, essential information before a marketing strategy can be devised. For example, if a sporting apparel manufacturer has the vision 'to be the number one brand of quality sporting clothes to the luxury market', it would be inappropriate to develop a marketing plan that involved providing budget goods and discount prices.

> *Chapter tool 4.4 Vision statement*: The sport organisation's vision statement should be reviewed in order to guide the identification of sport marketing opportunities. A vision statement is a written record of the desired achievements of an organisation in the future.

CASE 4.6

Under Armour

Mission and vision statements are important for organisations at all levels to define their reason for being and what the organisation's intentions are. Upon review of several sport organisations' websites, it is evident that most have a mission statement, but fewer have a publicly stated vision statement. Under Armour, however, is an exception. The American-based apparel, shoe, and equipment manufacturer lists its mission as, *'Under Armour makes athletes better'* and its vision statement is, *'Under Armour's vision is to inspire you with performance solutions you never knew you needed and can't imagine living without'*. In addition to listing its mission and vision, Under Armour also lists five core values for the company, which include: (1) love athletes, (2) celebrate the wins, (3) stand for equality, (4) act sustainably, and (5) fight on together.

Under Armour was founded in 1996 by Kevin Plank, a former American football player for the University of Maryland. Plank became tired of having to change the T-shirt he wore under his football uniform due to the sweat it accumulated. He noticed, however, that his compression shorts wicked away the sweat and managed to stay dry when he was playing. Plank therefore developed a prototype of a microfiber moisture-wicking shirt that football players could wear under their uniforms instead of cotton T-shirts. The products quickly took off, especially with American university football teams, and by 2005 the company became publicly traded and offered a wide variety of apparel options for athletes, with shoe options quickly following in 2006. Over time the organisation partnered with high-profile athletes such as NBA basketball star Steph Curry, NFL star Tom Brady, and multiple Olympic medallist skier Lindsey Vonn. True to its mission, Under Armour has been committed to making athletes better ever since its first prototype was created in Plank's grandmother's basement.

QUESTIONS

1 Based on what you learned about mission and vision statements in this chapter, how might you revise Under Armour's two statements to best reflect what a mission and vision statement should be?
2 How do Under Armour's stated values match with its mission and vision?
3 The connection between Under Armour's mission, vision and high-performance athletes is evident. How do you think these two statements serve general sport consumers, though?

Organisational objectives

If a vision statement shows the medium- to long-term ambitions of an organisation, organisational objectives are the stepping stones along the way to this destination. They are the targets that must be reached to make the vision a reality. For example, imagine that a hockey club sits at the bottom of the championship ladder but has a vision to finish in the top three. As might be expected, achieving this vision within one season is unrealistic. Therefore, an objective might be set to improve by three places in the following season, as a stepping stone to the ultimate goal. It is essential that these objectives are measurable, which means that they must be specific enough to be able to determine with certainty that they have been achieved. For example, the objective 'to be the best team' is not measurable, as this goal does not clearly state what being the best means. For example, does it mean the team that wins the most games, the team with the greatest number of new players joining, or the team with the most amount of money in the bank? In sporting clubs, objectives are normally set in each of the major operational areas, such as on-field performance, youth development, finances, facilities, marketing, and human resources. Just as with mission and vision statements, the objectives of an organisation help sport marketers to know where exactly to target their efforts so that they align with the broader goals of the organisation. In fact, they should provide marketers with more specific information about how to apply the mission and vision to the marketing plan.

> *Chapter tool 4.5 Organisational objectives*: A sport organisation's objectives should be reviewed in order to guide the identification of sport marketing opportunities. Organisational objectives are targets that must be reached in order to make the vision a reality.

Stakeholder analysis

Before an analysis of the organisation is complete, its stakeholders need to be considered. Stakeholders are all the individuals, groups, and other organisations that have an interest in a sport organisation. These stakeholders might include employees, players, members, the league, association or governing body, government, community, facility owners, sponsors, broadcasters, and fans. The obvious question this list raises is: who is the sport marketer going to try to make happy? The needs of different stakeholders will vary, and each will lead to corresponding implications for a marketing strategy. An interesting example is the case of some professional sport clubs, such as football clubs, that tend to focus on winning to the exclusion of all other priorities, including sensible financial management. While this may make members and fans happy in the short-term, other stakeholders may not be happy, such as governing bodies, leagues, and employees, who are more likely to be interested in the financial sustainability of the organisation. In a stakeholder analysis, the bargaining power of the different stakeholders should be weighed up. For example, some stakeholders, such as sponsors and government departments, may withdraw their funding if their needs are not met.

A careful analysis of the goals and objectives of each stakeholder in their affiliation with the sport organisation must therefore be completed before a strategic direction can be set. A marketing strategy can be strongly influenced by the beliefs, values, and expectations of powerful stakeholders. It should be noted that sport consumers might also be considered stakeholders of sport organisations. However, an analysis of customer needs is part of market research, which is outlined in the forthcoming section.

> *Chapter tool 4.6 Stakeholder analysis*: A stakeholder analysis involves assessing the diverse agendas of all individuals, groups and organisations that have an interest in a sport organisation.

ANALYSE MARKET AND CONSUMERS

The third step in identifying sport marketing opportunities refers to gathering information about the market and the consumers it contains. Market research is the process of learning about the marketplace and what consumers want, assessing their desires and expectations, and determining how to entice consumers to use a sport product. Market research is also used to ascertain whether sport consumers have reacted to a marketing plan as expected. In other words, market research is a way of evaluating the success of a marketing program.

Market research is concerned with answering several general questions about the market, such as:

- Who are the sport organisation's customers?
- What do these customers need and want?
- In what manner and how often should customers be contacted?
- Which marketing strategies elicit the most favourable responses from customers?
- What responses will each type of marketing strategy elicit?
- What mistakes have been made?

These questions are only a starting point because market research can have quite specific uses. Figure 4.7 highlights the potential applications of market research. As Figure 4.7 indicates, there are five applications of market research. The first is to determine specific information about the market: who are the customers, and what do they want? The other four areas represent what is known as the *marketing mix* (product, price, promotion, place). Market research can help not only to identify the best strategies in these areas but also to evaluate how successful they have been once implemented.

The more detailed the information obtained from market research, the easier it is to design an effective marketing program. However, the greater the detail, the higher the cost of the market research. Thus, the difficulty facing small and resource-challenged sport organisations is that market research can often prove expensive, time-consuming, and expertise intensive. For these organisations, the answer lies with finding a rapid and inexpensive approach, while avoiding the pitfalls of poor research, which include:

- using an unrepresentative sample;
- asking irrelevant questions;
- ignoring selected answers;
- 'stacking' questions so that they force certain types of responses that are 'leading' and include biases;
- failing to accept criticism.

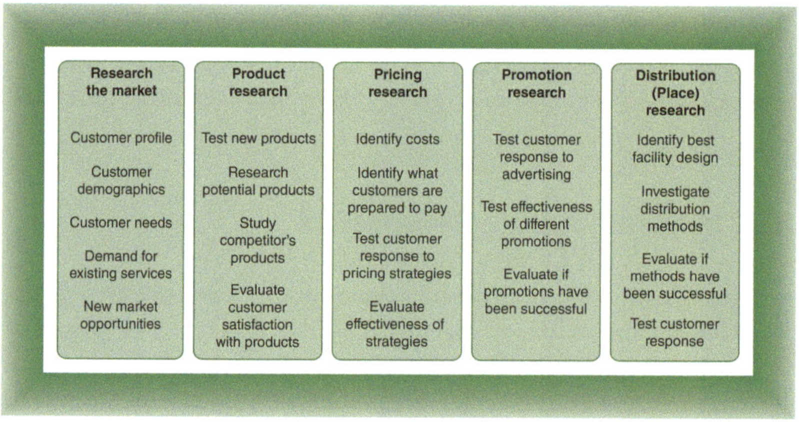

FIGURE 4.7 Applications of market research

Different types of market research

There are two types of market research: *quantitative* and *qualitative*. Quantitative research involves numerical information. This information tends to be superficial and is usually gathered from a diverse and large sample of people. Qualitative research involves non-numerical information (such as words from an interview with a consumer). Qualitative information tends to be more in-depth and is usually gathered from a narrow and relatively small sample of consumers. To better understand the differences between quantitative and qualitative research, it is helpful to consider some examples of each.

> *Chapter principle 4.4*: The third step in identifying sport marketing opportunities involves acquiring information about the sport market and consumers. Market research is the process of collecting information in order to learn about the marketplace and what consumers in general, and a sport organisation's customers specifically, want. It involves two kinds of information: quantitative or numerical and qualitative or non-numerical.

Quantitative Research

The most common method for gathering quantitative information is to use a survey or questionnaire. A survey/questionnaire may use multiple choices or scaled responses (see below) questions. This means that the consumers can give brief responses to set questions regarding specific topics. It is possible to survey a large group of consumers this way and to analyse the results with the help of a computer spreadsheet or statistics software programmes. Questionnaires are most often web-based and are distributed via email, text messaging, or through a sport organisation's bespoke mobile application.

An example of a scaled response survey question:

Question: How would you rate the seating quality at this venue?

(please circle the number that best represents your response)

1	2	3	4	5	6	7
Poor		Average		Outstanding		

Quantitative research should be used when a sport organisation already knows something about its customers and would like to refine this knowledge with greater precision. For example, if a sport organisation already knows that there are four main reasons why their customers employ their services, then they can use questionnaires to establish the relative importance of each. In addition, questionnaires can help to estimate how many customers share each of these reasons for using the service. Quantitative research can also be used to evaluate how satisfied customers are with the product, pricing, promotion, and place (distribution) strategies of a sport organisation. Furthermore, quantitative research techniques are valuable for constructing demographic profiles of customers (gender, age, marital status, education, etc.) or of a general segment of consumers.

There are obviously situations in which quantitative research is not a useful method. If a sport organisation does not know anything about its customers, it is not advisable to give them a survey with inflexible questions to try to get to know them. This is because the set questions and topics on a survey may miss the mark altogether and may not give customers the opportunity to share their unique perspectives. Also, it is often desirable to find out about complex issues, such as the motivations behind customers' consumption behaviours, which cannot be revealed using the relatively superficial information that a survey elicits. Circling a number or ticking a box on a questionnaire will not help a sport marketer get to the heart of consumer opinion and behaviour. For example, a survey may show that a netball club has a married, middle-aged female player with three children who plays because she enjoys the game, wants the exercise, and is relatively happy with the quality of service. However, it is unlikely to tell us that she is thinking about taking up basketball because her kids play, it is less stressful on her knees, that she will not play next season because a business commitment will take her overseas for several months, that her sister is an expert in marketing and specialises in non-profit organisations, that she would like to try coaching a junior netball team, that she finds it annoying that the showers in the changing rooms constantly leak, and that weekends are not a very convenient time to play games after all. While some of these questions can be answered by questionnaires and surveys, designing a survey that is so comprehensive would be impractical. For these reasons, a sport organisation may choose to undertake a qualitative approach as a first step in its market research process.

> *Chapter tool 4.7 Quantitative market research*: Quantitative research involves the collection of numerical information through a survey or questionnaire and should be used when a sport organisation already knows something about its customers and would like to refine this knowledge with greater precision.

Qualitative research

Qualitative research is a method of acquiring information that is non-statistical but in-depth. Because qualitative information is more detailed, complicated, and time-consuming to collect, it is usually gathered from a narrow and relatively small sample of sport consumers. The results obtained through qualitative research can also be used later to help construct a quantitative survey, if required. There are several effective and inexpensive approaches to qualitative market research that can provide rich and detailed information about the market and its consumers. They include:

1 interviews and focus groups;
2 suggestion boxes; and
3 complaint analysis.

Interviews and focus groups

One of the fundamental tools of qualitative market research is the interview, which can be conducted in a one-to-one situation or with numerous respondents at the same time. One efficient method is known as the focus group where a group of customers from the group being studied are gathered in an informal setting and encouraged to talk about specific issues. To be successful, the focus group should be conducted by an interviewer who has the skills to coordinate the group without inhibiting, intimidating, or leading the respondents so that ideas can flow freely and all opinions are expressed. Sessions should always be recorded (audio or video) so that they can be evaluated for important themes after the event.

Suggestion boxes

A suggestion box is a simple tool that can work if taken seriously. It is important to both the research process and good relationships with customers that the suggestions are read regularly and acted upon. It is usually best to document all suggestions (anonymously) and place responses in a prominent place within the organisation where readily accessible to all customers, members, and staff. It is also best not to make excuses if there is a genuine problem, and the actions taken to improve the situation should also be identified. Nothing is worse than a suggestion box with a rusty lock, so there is no point in pursuing this form of customer feedback without the commitment to deal with the suggestions promptly and systematically. With the prevalence of online communication mechanisms in today's sport industry, it is also possible for organisations to offer consumers an online version of a suggestion box, welcoming their feedback via a form on the organisation's website or social media outlets, or through the online reviews written by consumers on the organisation's website or other third-party sites.

Complaint analysis

This method is cheap and relatively easy to implement. Customer complaints can provide an insight into the elements of the product or service that are not meeting customer needs. With this information, it is possible to consider how to change and improve the situation, hopefully leading to improved customer satisfaction. Complaint analysis involves encouraging customers to contact employees directly if they have a problem or a complaint, or to use the online methods mentioned earlier in the section on suggestion boxes. Organisations should encourage complaints to be made either directly via an employee or a private online feedback form, as it will reflect negatively on the organisation if consumers write negative reviews on the website or other third-party sites. It is advisable to respond to every complaint with a personal and formal letter, email or social media response thanking customers for highlighting the problem and providing them with information about how the problem will be resolved.

> *Chapter tool 4.8 Qualitative market research*: Qualitative research involves the collection of non-statistical, but in-depth information through interviews and focus groups, suggestion boxes or complaint analysis.

SPORT MARKET OPPORTUNITIES

The information that was obtained in stage 1 of the Sport Marketing Framework, and its subsequent analysis, should highlight potential market opportunities. A market opportunity is a situation where a new or modified product or service can be introduced that meets an unfulfilled sport consumer need. However, it is first necessary to establish whether the

TABLE 4.3 Product-market expansion grid

	Existing product	*New product*
Existing markets	Market penetration	Product development
New markets	Market development	Diversification

opportunity is worth capitalising upon. Once decided, the target consumer group can be identified, along with a solid idea of where the sport product or service can be placed within the context of a marketplace that already contains sport products and services.

> *Chapter principle* 4.5: A market opportunity is a situation where a new or modified product or service can be introduced that meets an unfulfilled sport consumer need.

A useful tool for examining the marketing opportunities available is the Product-Market Expansion Grid. The grid provides a summary of the opportunities available for 'selling' a particular product or service. The Product-Market Expansion Grid is shown in Table 4.3.

Market penetration is the first possible type of market opportunity. It is an opportunity to increase 'sales' by attracting more consumers without sacrificing the old. An example of a market penetration opportunity in the horse-racing industry would be to attract even more males over the age of 50 to attend race meetings. It is therefore a 'more of the same' approach.

Market development is like market penetration in that the product remains the same. However, with market development the aim is to expand the target market to reach a wider range of consumers. A market development approach therefore promotes the product or service to existing markets as well as to a wider range of consumers. In the horse-racing example, a market development opportunity could be to attract more of the existing customers (males over the age of 50) as well as a wider range of consumers (such as women over 50 as well).

The third category, *product development*, involves marketing to the same consumers with a new version of the product or service. This new or modified product is 'sold' to the same target market as the existing product, such as Twenty20 cricket and beach volleyball.

The final category, *diversification*, involves marketing a new product to a new target market. It is an attempt to 'start-over'. Examples of diversification include indoor cricket, mixed netball, and modified rules versions of sport for children.

The Product-Market Expansion Grid provides alternatives to consider when going through the process of setting a strategic market direction, which is examined in the next chapter.

> *Chapter tool 4.9 Product-Market Expansion Grid*: The Product-Market Expansion Grid provides a summary of the opportunities available for 'selling' a particular product or service. It highlights four possibilities: (1) *market penetration* is an

opportunity to increase 'sales' by attracting more consumers without sacrificing the old; (2) *market development* is an opportunity where the product remains the same but seeks to expand the target market to reach a wider range of consumers; (3) *product development* is an opportunity involving marketing to the same consumers with a new version of the product or service; and (4) *diversification* is an opportunity involving marketing a new product to a new target market.

CASE 4.7

Oiselle

In the sport of running, apparel and shoe brands such as Nike, Adidas, Asics, Saucony, New Balance, and Brooks are all well-known. Despite numerous choices for consumers, Seattle, Washington-based Sally Bergesen saw a need in the market for women's running clothes that were designed for women, by women. Bergesen first set out to develop a pair of running shorts different from those that existed, and in 2007 she took her first product to market under the brand name Oiselle. The name means 'female bird' in French, and according to the Oiselle website it was selected for the brand because 'it alludes to that feeling of weightlessness that most athletes know and love. That sense of flight - when the legs go fast and the heart goes free'.

Oiselle quickly developed a loyal customer following from women runners who were impressed by the brand's attention to detail when it came to designing performance clothing that fit a woman's body better than many other brands. Simple product attributes differentiated Oiselle's apparel from its competitors, such as the inclusion of multiple pockets in easy-to-access locations in its shorts to hold runners' nutrition gels, keys, or phone; thumb holes in its long-sleeve shirts and sleeves that folded over a runner's hands to provide warmth in cold weather conditions; and smooth-waisted, non-puffy shorts designs. Other brands have since attempted to incorporate similar features, but due to Oiselle's success in building a brand community many female runners have remained loyal to Oiselle much to the dismay of the brand's competitors.

By 2016, Oiselle was sponsoring elite female track and field athletes and Bergesen appeared in an issue of *Outside* magazine with the headline, 'The woman who took on Nike with running shorts'. The article discussed Oiselle's keys to success in developing a fiercely loyal customer base, one of which was the community it developed among its consumers. For a small annual membership fee, Oiselle customers could join an exclusive club, The Volee, which gave them access to product discounts, exclusive merchandise such as a Volee racing tank top and backpack, and the opportunity to join other women in their cities for weekly group runs and social gatherings. And when a woman travelled from one city to another for work or a vacation, she could use Oiselle's exclusive members-only online platform to connect with the Volee group in another city in order to join their group runs. Additionally, Oiselle harnessed the power of user-generated branding to promote its ever-growing product line. When a runner tagged a photo of herself on social media wearing Oiselle clothing and used the hashtag #FlyStyle, Oiselle would put the picture on its website on the same page as that item of clothing so that other runners could see how it looked on someone who may have a similar height or weight to themselves. This further enhanced the sense of community and connection runners felt with the brand, a feeling that other running brands did not always foster with their customers.

QUESTIONS

1 Based on the case above, and any background research you can conduct on Oiselle, analyse Porter's five forces in relation to Oiselle's competitive marketplace.
2 What differentiates Oiselle in the crowded running apparel marketplace?
3 What can other sport brands learn from Oiselle to develop more loyal fan/customer bases?

PRINCIPLES SUMMARY

- Chapter principle 4.1: The Sport Marketing Framework describes the four stages of sport marketing: identifying sport marketing opportunities, developing a sport marketing strategy, planning the sport marketing mix, and implementing and controlling the sport marketing strategy.
- Chapter principle 4.2: The first step in identifying sport marketing opportunities is to analyse the internal and external environment using the tools of SWOT analysis (with external environment analysis) and competitor analysis (with the Five Forces Analysis).
- Chapter principle 4.3: The second step in identifying sport marketing opportunities is to conduct an analysis of the organisation. This requires four tools: the mission statement; vision statement; organisational objectives; and stakeholder analysis.
- Chapter principle 4.4: The third step in identifying sport marketing opportunities involves acquiring information about the sport market and consumers. Market research is the process of collecting information in order to learn about the marketplace and what consumers in general, and a sport organisation's customers specifically, want. It involves two kinds of information: quantitative or numerical, and qualitative or non-numerical.
- Chapter principle 4.5: A market opportunity is a situation where a new or modified product or service can be introduced that meets an unfulfilled sport consumer need.

TOOLS SUMMARY

- Chapter tool 4.1 SWOT and external environment analysis
- Chapter tool 4.2 Competitor and Five Forces Analyses
- Chapter tool 4.3 Mission statement
- Chapter tool 4.4 Vision statement
- Chapter tool 4.5 Organisational objectives
- Chapter tool 4.6 Stakeholder analysis
- Chapter tool 4.7 Quantitative market research
- Chapter tool 4.8 Qualitative market research
- Chapter tool 4.9 Product-Market Expansion Grid

REVIEW QUESTIONS

1 Differentiate between the four stages of the Sport Marketing Framework.
2 Identify the three parts of identifying sport marketing opportunities. Provide a general explanation of their respective functions.
3 For a sport organisation you know well, write a brief mission statement and vision statement.
4 What are the different kinds of sport marketing objectives?
5 Under what circumstances would it be advisable to use a qualitative approach to collecting market research information?
6 Devise an original example for each category in the Product-Market Expansion Grid.

RELEVANT WEBSITES

Bowls Australia (www.bowlsaustralia.com.au)
Bowls England (https://www.bowlsengland.com)
Bowls New Zealand (https://www.bowlsnz.co.nz)
Formula One (https://www.formula1.com/)
Oiselle (https://www.oiselle.com/)
Ski Dubai (https://www.skidxb.com/en-ae/ski-dubai)
Sport New Zealand (https://sportnz.org.nz/)
Under Armour (https://www.underarmour.com)
Youth Olympic Games (https://olympics.com/ioc/youth-olympic-games)

FURTHER READING

Karg, A., Shilbury, D., Westerbeek, H., Funk, D. C., & Naraine, M. L. (2022). *Strategic Sport Marketing* (5th ed.). Routledge.

CHAPTER 5

Sport marketing strategy

LEARNING OUTCOMES

At the end of this chapter, readers should be able to:

- explain the process of determining a strategic marketing direction.
- identify the main considerations when developing strategic marketing objectives.
- outline the factors critical to setting performance measures.
- describe the importance of determining a core marketing strategy.
- define the terms market positioning and market segmentation.
- discuss the importance of market segmentation.
- identify the main approaches to market segmentation.
- describe the process and importance of market positioning.
- outline the major elements of the marketing mix.

OVERVIEW

This chapter explains stage 2 of the Sport Marketing Framework, which comprises two parts: (a) develop strategic marketing direction and (b) develop sport marketing positioning. This chapter includes guidance on the process of setting marketing objectives and performance measures, developing a sport marketing strategy, determining market positioning and market segmentation strategies, and preparing to devise the marketing mix.

STAGE 2: DEVELOP A STRATEGIC MARKETING STRATEGY

The second stage of the Sport Marketing Framework is to 'develop a sport marketing strategy' and is highlighted in Figure 5.1. The first step of stage 2 requires the development of a strategic marketing direction by identifying marketing objectives and performance measures.

> *Chapter principle 5.1*: The second stage of the Sport Marketing Framework is to develop a sport marketing strategy. This requires two steps: (a) to develop a strategic marketing direction, and (b) to develop a sport marketing position.

DOI: 10.4324/9781003391319-5

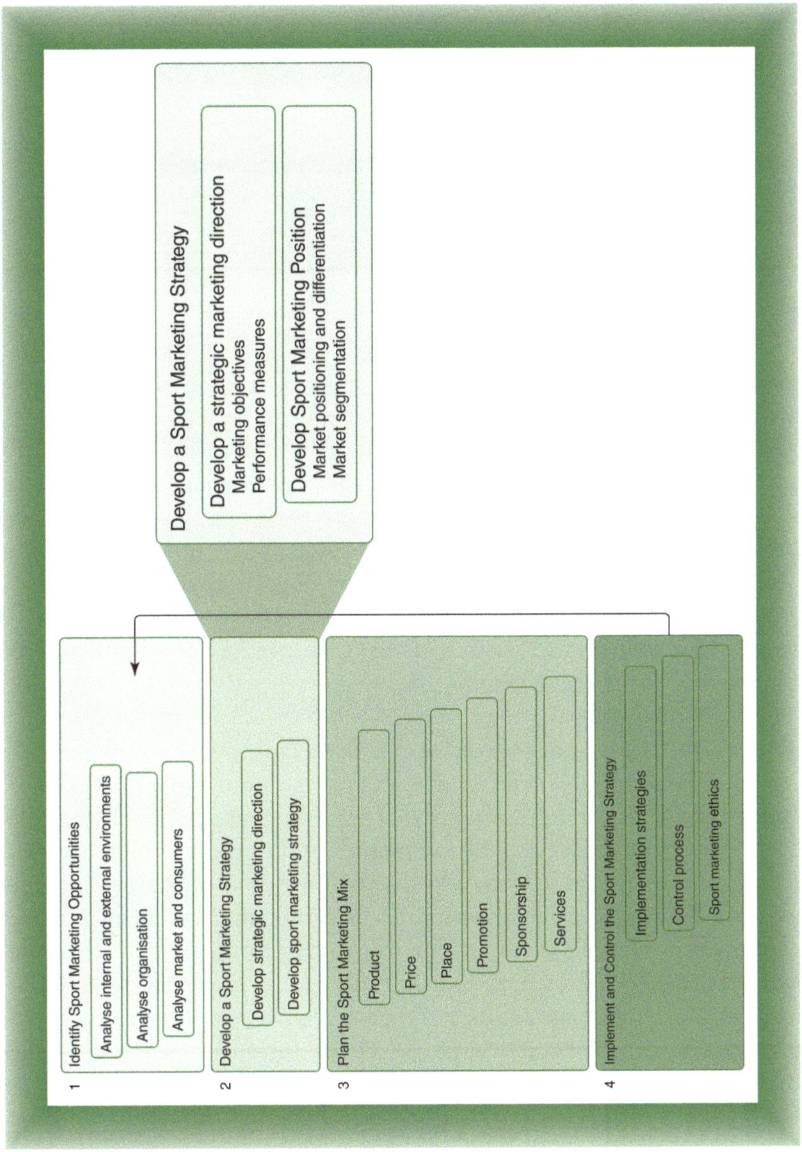

FIGURE 5.1 Develop a sport marketing strategy

DEVELOP A STRATEGIC MARKETING DIRECTION

There are two steps involved in developing a strategic marketing direction. First, marketing objectives need to be developed. Second, performance measures need to be assigned to these objectives. Both are outlined in the following section.

> *Chapter principle 5.2*: Developing a strategic marketing direction involves constructing marketing objectives and setting performance measures.

CASE 5.1

Esports

In general terms, when one thinks of the word 'sport,' active forms of play, whether organised or unorganised, may come to mind. Efforts of physical exertion and perhaps skill are involved, either individually or within a team-based format. There may also be perceived benefits that one associates with sport, such as physical or mental wellbeing. At a competitive level there are teams, leagues, and formal governing bodies to supervise competition. Additionally, there could be business aspects for professional sport that generate revenue such as ticketing, marketing and sponsorship investments, and broadcasting rights. How would you position and develop a strategic direction for a sport that shares many aspects with traditional sports, but has one key defining feature – the electronic nature of the competition? This is the case with esports.

Esports involves video games played competitively for spectators who are viewing the competition in-person at an event or watching through live-streamed video. As mentioned above, there are several shared elements between traditional sports and esports – professional players, teams, leagues, and even governing bodies. For example, the Korean Esport Association (KeSPA) was one of the first governing bodies dedicated to video game and esports regulation and was formed after the Korean government realised the popularity of gaming competitions. There is also an International Esports Federation that includes global members. In addition to similarities between traditional sports and esports from a performance perspective, they also share similar business activities that provide various streams of revenue for esports competitions and events.

Within esports, competitions can include team-based multiplayer online battle arenas (MOBAs), first person shooter style games, and virtual recreations of traditional sports. The popularity of esports could be attributed to a larger demographic of fans who grew up playing video games, as well as shifts in their relationship with viewing traditional sports through OTT and streaming offerings.

The most popular esports games that emerged early in the 2010s were League of Legends, Starcraft II, and Defense of the Ancients 2, commonly referred to as DOTA 2. Smaller tournaments built around DOTA 2 eventually grew into large, formally organised tournaments that occur on an international level. The international prize pool for DOTA 2 in 2021 was more than $40 million USD, which shrank to just under $19 million USD in 2022, but remains the largest international prize pool.

Beginning the move towards positioning esports alongside traditional sports in the mind of the consumer is esports inclusion within the Olympic Games. While not on the official list of competitions for the Paris 2024 Games, the International Olympic Committee (IOC) hosted an Olympic Esports Series (OES) in 2023. The series consisted of one week of events, including global virtual and simulated sport competitions that were streamed live for fans. The competition brought together the IOC, international federations, and game publishers, placing esports alongside traditional sports within the pinnacle of sporting competition.

QUESTIONS

1. Do you think inclusion of esports as part of the Olympic framework positions esports as a 'legitimate' sporting competition?
2. How should esports capitalise on increased awareness post OES competitions to further establish their standing in the competitive sport market and mindset of the consumer?
3. What elements of esports would you highlight to market it to casual fans and help with positioning?
4. How would you begin to establish a strategic marketing direction for esports? Where should the sport 'be' in terms of awareness, recognition, and positioning for consumers?

MARKETING OBJECTIVES

The word objective means an aim or goal. A marketing objective is a goal that a sport organisation may realistically achieve as the result of its marketing strategy. It is typically summarised in the form of a short sentence that describes what will be achieved because of marketing activities. Marketing objectives represent a guide through all the coming stages of the marketing framework. They should offer a clear direction to follow when it comes to conceiving the rest of the marketing plan. This means that the importance of marketing objectives is paramount. It is critical to think about marketing objectives carefully, and to document them clearly. They should provide everyone in a sport organisation with a clear direction so that all marketing activities are carried out in line with predetermined goals. As indicated in Table 5.1, there are four broad categories of marketing objectives that sport organisations may pursue: participation, performance, promotion, and profit.

TABLE 5.1 The four main categories of sport marketing objectives

Category	*Examples of marketing objectives*
Participation	• To increase the number of members in a club • To increase the number of clubs in a sport or competition • To increase the number of consumers using a service • To improve spectator levels at a competition or event • To expand the number of club administrators or officials • To expand the number of volunteers involved • To increase the volume or frequency of consumer use of the product or service
Performance	• To increase market share • To increase the range of products or services on offer to consumers • To improve customer satisfaction and service quality
Promotion	• To promote a health and wellbeing message • To improve the public 'image' of the organisation • To increase customer awareness of the product/service
Profit	• To increase product or service sales • To increase profit margins • To acquire new sponsorships or grants • To increase annual profit or surplus (or decrease expenses or deficit) • To increase the amount that sales revenue exceeds costs • To improve the ratio of cost to revenue

Privately owned sport facilities such as gymnasiums, recreation centres, and boutique fitness studios will have *profit* as their main objective. This would also be the main aim for sport equipment and apparel manufacturers such as Under Armour, and professional sport clubs that operate as franchises such as in North America, and as public companies. In fact, the corporate or professional sector of sport is interested primarily in profits. Any other objectives that these organisations might develop would remain subservient, or a means to achieving a greater profit. In theory, a privately owned professional club may want to sign up more club members, but only so that they can make more money. However, most business managers understand that the fastest route to profit in professional sport is to win.

On the other hand, many sport organisations will not have profit as their main objective. For example, sport clubs and community-based clubs will have *performance* and *participation* objectives. National sport associations, such as the International Gymnastics Federation (FIG), and government sport agencies such as the Australian Sports Commission may also be interested in *promoting* messages about healthy lifestyles. Sport organisations that are member-based are set up as non-profit organisations and therefore will not pursue profit as their main objective. It is still important for them to make sure they are earning enough money to cover their costs, which can then be reinvested into the organisations, or perhaps earn a little more to spend on developing new services or buying new equipment. However, for them, profit should be a means to an end, not their primary objective. Some recommendations when it comes to writing good sport marketing objectives follow.

WRITING MARKETING OBJECTIVES

1 *Marketing objectives should match organisational objectives.* Marketing objectives should help the sport organisation to achieve its overarching organisation objectives. In fact, marketing objectives should be stepping stones along the way that will help the organisation to realise its overall vision.
2 *Objectives should be realistic.* Marketing objectives should be plausible and within reach, especially considering the resources available to a sport organisation.
3 *Marketing objectives should focus on action.* Marketing objectives should say what is going to be done. This is why the examples in Table 5.1 begin with the word 'To'.
4 *Marketing objectives should be narrowed down to the most important.* By narrowing objectives down to as few as possible, the sport organisation will be better at focusing its energy on what really matters and not scattering resources too broadly. Five or less is a good ambition.
5 *Marketing objectives should be prioritised and ranked from the most important to the least important.* An organisation should know which objectives are the most important. To do this it will need to discuss and consult within the marketing department, and with the other managers of the sport organisation.
6 *Marketing objectives should be documented.* There should be a record to review at any time in order to ensure that focus remains on the objectives and so that they can be evaluated at a later stage of the Sport Marketing Framework and possibly revised, if needed.
7 *Marketing objectives should be clear, specific, and measurable.* If objectives are not clear, it becomes difficult to know exactly what is wanted. For example, the objectives in Table 5.1 are clear, such as the aim 'to increase membership levels'. But, if it was 'to improve participation', then this would not be clear, as the kind of participation desired is left unsaid (membership numbers, spectator levels, number of volunteers, etc.). An unclear objective also makes it difficult to determine whether an organisation has achieved what it wanted. As a result, all marketing objectives need to be measurable.
8 *Marketing objectives should be time-focused.* Without a time focus it is impossible to determine when further marketing activities should be undertaken.

Chapter tool 5.1 Marketing objectives: A marketing objective is a goal that a sport organisation wants to achieve as the result of its marketing strategy. There are four different categories of marketing objectives that sport organisations may pursue: participation, performance, promotion, and profit. All marketing objectives should be consistent with organisational objectives, realistic, action-oriented, narrowed down and ranked in order of importance, documented, clear, specific, and measurable, and time-focused.

PERFORMANCE MEASURES

Once objectives have been set, it is important to add performance measures. The word measure refers to a way of estimating, calculating, or assessing whether an objective has been achieved. It usually involves finding a way to quantify or put a number to an objective. For example, imagine that one organisational objective is 'to increase sales.' A possible

TABLE 5.2 Examples of performance measures

Common examples of marketing objectives	*Possible performance measures*
To increase club membership	To increase membership from 100 to 150 members by January 2025
To increase the number of people who use our service	To increase the number of people who use our service to 100 customers per month by July 2025
To improve spectator levels at a competition	To increase spectator levels to an average of 30,000 spectators per game, by December 2025, as measured by ticket sales
To increase customer satisfaction levels	To increase customer satisfaction levels to 7/10 as rated by them on an bi-annual customer satisfaction survey
To increase profit	To increase profit to $250,000, calculated at the end of the 2025 financial year
To increase awareness of our sport product	To increase the number of people who have heard of our product in China to 50,000, as measured by market research

performance measure would nominate the amount of the increase and the time period in which it is to be accomplished, say by 5,000 product units in six months. This performance measure has added a quantity to the objective and has also made it easy to determine whether it has been reached or not. Some further examples appear in Table 5.2.

> *Chapter tool 5.2 Performance measures*: Performance measures quantify or put numbers to objectives in terms of magnitude and time so that their specific achievement is transparent.

CASE 5.2

Name, Image, and Likeness

Within the United States sport market is the unique positioning of collegiate (or university) sports as a second-tier athletic competition. Within this framework, collegiate sports operate as a talent development system for professional sport leagues, while generating significant amounts of revenue for their respective universities in terms of ticket and merchandise sales, as well as branding. Collegiate sports would have performance and participation as the main objectives within their mission, although the profit objective is also extremely relevant. The two most popular sports for collegiate athletic programmes are basketball and American football. These competitions feature long-standing rivalries between teams, capitalising on the history and drama within these fandoms. In exchange for participation, male and female athletes are placed on scholarships, which include free college tuition (i.e., the cost of attending university in the United States), room and board, meal stipends, and other associated costs.

The governing body of collegiate athletics in the United States is the National Collegiate Athletic Association (NCAA),which has always required an amateur status for all athletes. Thus, while athletes received tuition funding, as well as financial assistance with living expenses, they were prohibited from individually profiting in any other way from their athletic performances. This arrangement was viewed as somewhat inequitable, as the popularity and revenue generated from collegiate sports – particularly NCAA basketball and football – began to grow with the broadcasting of national competitions. For example, the television broadcast rights for the College Football Playoffs are valued at $450 million USD a year. The premiere tournament for collegiate basketball, the NCAA's annual competition called 'March Madness' is valued at $8.8 billion for the TV broadcast rights, which is paid to the NCAA directly.

The monies resulting from these competitions highlighted the inequities prohibiting student athletes from earning additional revenue, while their institutions benefit financially. For example, a well-known, successful student-athlete wearing a particular jersey number would earn their institution monies from merchandise sales but did receive a portion of this revenue personally. This situation, changed, however, through the help of a court ruling, and subsequent policy change within the NCAA called Name, Image, and Likeness (NIL).

As a result of the significant revenues the NCAA and universities were receiving from collegiate athletic competitions, a group of former collegiate athletes filed a lawsuit against the NCAA to be able to market and profit from their own images. This lawsuit challenged the NCAA's prohibition on how universities compensate athletes, specifically, the restriction of trade and commerce. The case was decided by the Supreme Court, the highest court in the United States, which ruled in the athletes' favour, thus granting collegiate athletes the right to market their NIL, much like professional athletes are permitted. This included engaging in sponsorships and other deals with various sport brands, making collegiate athletics in the United States more reflective of their actual profit objectives. In turn, collegiate athletes could now develop sport marketing strategies to capitalise on their personal brands.

QUESTIONS

1. Do you think compensating collegiate athletes in the form of free university tuition, room and board, and a supplemental living stipend is fair or equitable compared to the monies they earn for universities and the NCAA?
2. How has social media and digital marketing contributed to the increased opportunities for athletes at all levels?
3. Search for a popular university athlete on Instagram. Based on your search, can you find any instances of NIL marketing on their feed?
4. Would you consider this type of marketing 'authentic' or that it aligns with this athlete's personal brand based on their Instagram profile?

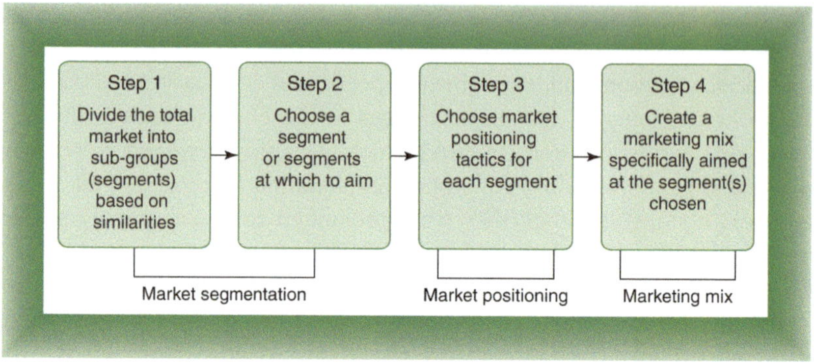

FIGURE 5.2 Develop sport marketing positioning

DEVELOPING SPORT MARKETING POSITIONING

The process of constructing a sport marketing position involves four steps. Steps 1 and 2 involve market segmentation, step 3 introduces a market positioning strategy, and step 4 leads to a marketing mix. This section overviews these steps, including a detailed explanation of market segmentation and market positioning. The development of the marketing mix is examined in detail over the six forthcoming chapters. Figure 5.2 illustrates the four steps of developing sport marketing positioning.

> *Chapter principle* 5.3: Developing a sport marketing position involves four steps: market segmentation (1, 2), market positioning tactics (3) and devising the marketing mix (4).

CASE 5.3

Smart Sport Stadiums

A popular trend within the sport industry is to build or update current stadiums to increase game day fan experiences. Various technologies are being incorporated into new and existing stadium designs to enhance mobile phone connectivity, offer seamless ticketing and security features, streamline food and beverage services, as well as reduce overall carbon footprints for green initiatives and sustainability. Not only does this increase the experience of local fans but can also act as a form of marketing for the sport organisation as part of a travel experience. Examples of such stadiums can be found across the globe and have been designed for various sport offerings.

The Mercedes-Benz Stadium in Atlanta, Georgia, is a multi-purpose arena in the United States that is home to the National Football League's Atlanta Falcons and Major League Soccer's Atlanta United FC. It features a seamless cashless transaction system that decreases wait times for food and beverage transactions, a technology that became widely utilised in the post-COVID-19 sports era. This cashless system enables customer relationship management data tracking through a scanned loyalty barcode, allowing the sport organisations to build a profile of who that fan is and their preferences for products or services in a particular location in the stadium.

Another example is the Johan Cruyff Arena in the Netherlands, home to AFC Ajax in Amsterdam, which features a bespoke blockchain ticketing app for ticket sales and distribution. The system allocates tickets to the near 55,000-capacity stadium via mobile phones. To access the tickets, fans then use a barcode that is only activated if the ticket holder is within a specified range of the stadium. This utilisation of blockchain ticketing technology prevents the secondary market resale of tickets while also prohibiting counterfeit tickets. If a ticketholder cannot attend the match, then they can return tickets via the platform, which will then be redistributed to another fan who is near the stadium at no cost. Within a season, approximately 20% of ticket holders do not attend, which amounts to roughly 10,000 fans. Thus, ticket redistribution does not directly generate profit, but instead decreases no-shows. Where it does increase revenue is through associated food and beverage sales as the increase in the availability of tickets results in more fans attending matches.

The Melbourne Cricket Ground, which is home to Australian Football League (AFL), cricket, and international football matches, features a data analytics and artificial intelligence (AI) customer service system that builds personalised fan profiles. These profiles are then employed to offer individualised information on public transport, parking, and direct fans to the best gates to facilitate seating. In addition, a cashless transaction system includes in-seat ordering with a system called 'WaitTime' that uses cameras and AI to recommend the quickest and nearest lines for food and beverages.

Finally, Tottenham Hotspur Stadium was built in London with enhanced mobile connectivity to allow 65% of individuals in attendance to stream live video. The stadium is also built with sustainability in mind to reduce electrical usage. LED signage and real-time monitoring for preventative maintenance, temperature control, and lighting conditions all reduce its carbon footprint.

QUESTIONS

1. Are smart stadiums a consideration to fans traveling to view sporting events? What types of strategic market research could you conduct to help answer this question?
2. As a sport marketer, what features within a stadium would you strategically choose to promote to increase attendance?
3. Using your target market analysis, would you segment ideal stadium features to different groups within the overall fan base?

MARKET SEGMENTATION

Not all sport consumers are the same. Different people are motivated to consume sport for different reasons. It is also true to say that different sports or events will attract different kinds of consumers. For example, esports appeals to a different crowd than badminton. This means that sport marketers must understand the kind of consumers that are currently attracted to their products and services, as well as the kind of consumers they might like to attract in the future.

Market segmentation is the process of categorising groups of consumers together, based on their similar needs or wants. A market is the total group of potential consumers for a product, and can include retailers, businesses, government, media, and individuals. Market segmentation therefore involves breaking down this total group into smaller groups based on something that the consumers have in common, such as their age, gender, interests, behaviours, or needs. Market segmentation recognises that it is not possible for a sport organisation to be all things to all consumers. Once a sport organisation has selected a particular segment or segments of the market, it can customise its product and marketing strategies to meet their specific needs. By breaking down sport consumers into different segments (or sections), it is possible for a sport organisation to use its limited marketing resources more effectively.

Imagine the marketing situation of a women's focused boxing club. A forthcoming Olympic Games might provide an opportunity for them to market their facility at a time when many people are watching and thinking about sport and fitness, as women's boxing was introduced as an Olympic sport during the 2012 London Olympic Games. One non-segmented (mass marketing) approach would involve advertising the boxing club on traditional broadcast television, thereby reaching a large but diverse group of people. However, this type of traditional television advertising is extremely expensive and may not be the best use of money. Another disadvantage of this idea is that a portion of the people who will see the promotion will not be interested in the boxing club because it serves a specific target market – women. The advertisement is wasted on consumers who do not fit the target market. The alternative approach would be to target the specific segment (or a couple of segments). For example, some research undertaken by the boxing club might reveal that stay-at-home mothers, as well as single women who live within 20 kilometres of the facility have a strong interest in getting fit, gaining strength, and learning how to defend themselves. A marketing programme could be tailored to these consumers by offering a range of classes during the day and advertising the facility through targeted digital media marketing on streaming platforms and social media. Depending on the boxing club's resources, it may also be possible to consider developing food and beverage facilities or negotiating an agreement with local business to offer customers of the club a discount when they visit to encourage socialising following the classes.

THE PROCESS OF SEGMENTATION

Market segmentation comprises two parts. First, the market must be divided into subgroups based on a common feature. This can be done with the help of market research, as discussed earlier in this chapter. Second, the target segment must be determined in order for the segment(s) chosen need(s) to be substantial enough to justify all the efforts associated with developing and implementing the marketing strategy. It is equally important that the segment identified is different from the general market. If the needs of all the consumers in the total market are very similar, it might not be necessary or profitable to try to break them down any further.

WAYS OF SEGMENTING SPORT CONSUMERS

There are six ways of grouping consumers together for segmentation, illustrated in Figure 5.3. Consumers are often grouped together into the following categories: demographic, socio-economic, lifestyle (psychographic), geographic, product behaviour, and benefits. Each is described in the following paragraphs.

Demographic segmentation

Demographic segmentation is the most conventional and common in sport marketing. Demographic variables include age, gender, ethnic background, and what stage of their working 'life cycle' a consumer occupies. Sporting apparel, for example, is often targeted towards consumers based on their gender and age. Think of traditional gym inspired clothing for men and women. For example, crop tops are designed and marketed towards a female demographic and create a body-positive image. They could also be targeted towards specific sports, such as boxing, which has historically featured this type of athletic wear. Alternatively, men's athletic apparel could feature more tank tops or T-shirt designs, as well as shorts instead of tights or leggings.

The life cycle category is less obvious than age and gender. Traditionally, life cycle refers to the conventional stages of life from being single, married with children, 'empty-nesters' (couples with adult children who have left the family home), retired, and the elderly. In addition to these traditional stages, sport marketers recognise relatively new categories such as married without children, same-sex couples, single parents, blended families, and the separated or divorced. The life cycle stage of a consumer will naturally make a

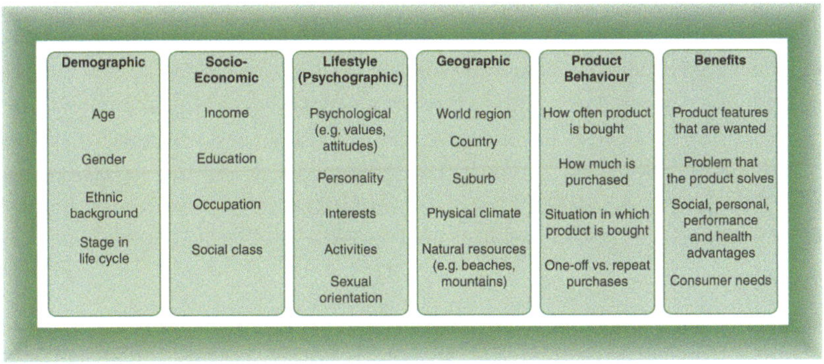

FIGURE 5.3 Categories for segmenting sport consumers

difference to how, when, and why they spend money on sport products. A single, working adult may have more income to spend on season tickets to sport events, whereas parents of young children may prefer to buy a membership to the local club so that their child can participate in youth sport every week.

A consumer's ethnic background refers to their race, nationality, or religion. It is important for sport marketers not to think of the ethnic background of different groups in stereotypical ways, but to try to understand their unique behaviours. The major national soccer leagues in Australia and the United States possess a strong ethnic fan base. Both countries have large numbers of immigrant populations – California's Hispanic and Latino communities are an example. For a person who emigrates to a new country, the sport that they enjoyed in their country of origin can become an important link for them. It connects them not only to their personal history, but also to a new community, which may share similar experiences of settling in a new country.

Socio-economic segmentation

Socio-economic segmentation refers to aspects of a consumer's social or economic circumstances, such as their income, the highest level of education they have achieved, and their occupation. These kinds of factors are often grouped together under demographic segmentation. However, they have been separated out here for clarity.

Income is a popular way to segment markets. How much money a consumer earns (and their disposable income) is likely to have an influence on their purchasing behaviour. A family living on a tight budget is unlikely to buy a season membership to their local cricket club. The sport apparel industry tends to be highly segmented with brands such as Gymshark providing functional, yet reasonably priced products. On the opposite end of the spectrum are higher-priced speciality stores that offer middle-to-high income customers brand names with the latest imported fashion colours and designs. Brands within this category could be Lululemon or Sweaty Betty, which are marketed as premium items.

A person's education, income, and occupation are often strongly related. The higher the level of education a person achieves, the more likely they are to earn more and work in jobs with higher status. It can also be true that the higher a consumer's or their family's wealth, the more likely they are to be able to afford an education that can lead to more prestigious employment. Some sports have been associated with certain social class segments. For example, football has traditionally been seen as a working-class game in the United Kingdom, while basketball is considered working class in the United States. Golf and rugby union are typically classified as middle-class activities, and downhill skiing and horse racing are perceived as sports of the rich. Of course, the popularity and accessibility of these sports can shift and change over time. In wealthier developed nations, the average income is significantly higher than in developing countries, and many consumers spend significant sums of money on the technologies necessary to access sport and entertainment.

Lifestyle (psychographic) segmentation

Lifestyle factors refer to consumers' day-to-day routines and their general way of life. These can be influenced by a consumer's personality, their interests, activities, and their opinions.

TABLE 5.3 Segmentation examples

Opinions (about)	*Interests*	*Activities*	*Personality*
Politics	Family and children	Work	Values
Education	Home	Leisure and entertainment	Attitudes
Environment	Career	Self-care	Beliefs
The future	Art and culture	Holidays	Hopes
Religion	Sport and leisure	Hobbies	Habits
Social issues	Achievements	Home tasks	Expectations
Money	Travel and languages	Volunteering	Temperament
Morality	Community support	Social events	Reactions to situations
War	Charity	Community activities	Ways of thinking

For example, a consumer's activities include what they do for leisure, socialising, sport, hobbies, and holidaying. Their interests may include family, home, recreation, fashion, and/or a desire to achieve. It is possible to segment consumers based on lifestyle factors as Table 5.3 demonstrates.

Geographic segmentation

Sport consumers can be segmented according to their geographical residence. Geographical segments might include local (such as a suburb or state/county/province), national and international regions. A local swimming club, for example, might target their services to individuals who live within a 10-kilometre radius. The environment, climate, and natural resources in a region can also provide the basis for segmentation. For example, the mountains in Whistler, Canada mean that there are a large variety of snow sports available to residents (and tourists), while the beaches in Costa Rica provide plenty of opportunity for warm water sports, such as surfing.

Product behaviour segmentation

It is possible to segment sport consumers based on their buying behaviour. For example, consumers may display similarities in how much and how often they purchase certain sport products, the situations in which they buy sport products, and how loyal they are to certain sport brands (such as whether they repeat purchase, or just buy once-off). For example, people may buy products exclusively from Nike, Adidas, or Puma. Sport consumers who have a strong emotional connection to a brand or team, and who see it as an extension of themselves, are more likely to be loyal. This means that they are more likely to repeatedly buy tickets to games and purchase memberships and memorabilia, even if the team is performing poorly. Other consumers may be more interested in sport as a form of entertainment or socialising. These consumers will probably engage with sport in situations where their friends are involved, where special events and promotions are offered, and where additional entertainment options are available. Another example of behaviour segmentation in sport may be found in customer usage, such as heavy users, medium users, and light users of a product. In this instance, heavy users are the consumers who buy life memberships or season tickets, compared with light users who attend games casually. Chapter 3 provides a detailed set of sport fan categories based on sport consumption behaviour.

BENEFITS SEGMENTATION

A final way that sport consumers can be segmented is based on the similar benefits that they seek from using a sport product or service. For example, a particular sport shoe brand might have carbon plates as a technological innovation in the shoe, resulting in more return force generated per stride, less energy expenditure, and faster racing times. These qualities are appealing to one group of consumers, while another group of consumers may be more interested in the colours and fashion appeal of another brand. Different sport products offer different advantages, such as social, personal, performance, or health benefits. Some of the consumers who are interested in one aspect of a brand's features or benefits can be grouped together, usually based on the underlying needs that are being met, such as performance, fitness, entertainment, or belonging.

APPROACHES TO USING SEGMENTATION

In addition to the six kinds of segmentation, there are three main ways of using segmentation. In step 2 of the segmentation process, it is possible to choose one or more than one segment. It is also possible not to choose any at all. The three ways of using segmentation are focused segmentation, multiple segmentation, and undifferentiated segmentation. Focused segmentation occurs when only one segment is chosen with one corresponding marketing mix. Multiple segmentation involves the selection of more than one segment, with a unique marketing mix for each. Finally, undifferentiated segmentation occurs when a sport organisation decides not to choose a segment at all, but rather considers the total market as a single and unvarying consumer group. Figure 5.4 highlights where these three approaches fit within the four-step process of developing marketing positioning. Each is explained in further detail next.

Focused segmentation

Focused segmentation involves selecting only one of the market segments that has been identified and developing just one marketing mix with which to communicate to

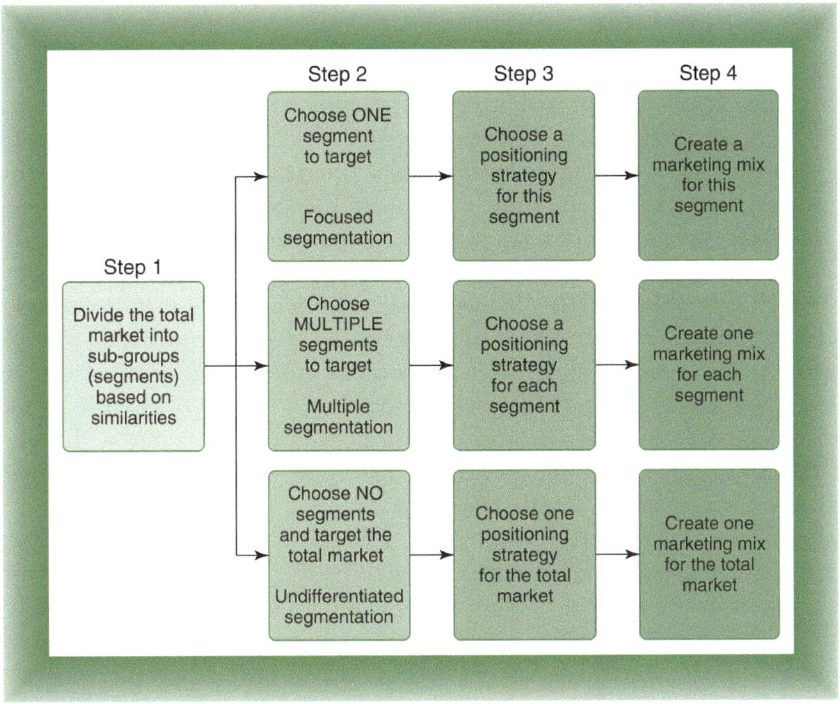

FIGURE 5.4 Sport marketing segmentation approaches

that segment. The result is that the organisation's marketing targets one segment, an approach sometimes called niche marketing, or concentrated segmentation. For example, a wearable sport technology company might focus their efforts on a single segment of the market, such as elite distance runners, and develop an innovative product specifically targeted to meet their needs. One instance of this would be Polar's H-10 chest strap heart rate monitor. This product is intended to be marketed towards elite runners with specialised training requirements, such as keeping their heart rate within a specific zone, and delivers high levels of accuracy. While intended for a specific market, if the product meets their needs, then consumers tend to be very loyal to this product and overall brand.

There are some advantages to focused segmentation. By choosing one segment to emphasise it is possible to develop a highly specialised marketing mix perfectly tailored to meet the segment's needs. It also means that a sport organisation can direct all its resources towards the single market segment, making it more cost effective. However, there are also disadvantages to focused segmentation. There are dangers if the market segment turns out to be too small, or if it shrinks over time. Using the example above, elite distance runners are a small section of the overall running market. Also, another sport organisation might start to market to the same focused segment, but with more resources. Focused segmentation is powerful but risky.

Multiple segmentation

Multiple segmentation means choosing more than one segment and developing a separate and unique marketing mix for each one. However, not all the elements of the marketing mix need to be changed for each market segment. For example, different promotions may be employed for each segment, but the same product, price, and distribution options may remain. Multiple segmentation can help to spread the risk if one of the segments is too small, shrinks in size over time, or was a poor choice in the first place. However, there are also disadvantages to using multiple segmentation. The main disadvantage is that it can be expensive. This is because it takes money, time, and resources to create a new marketing mix for each segment. For example, it might mean that a sport organisation must develop new products, invest in several different promotional programmes, distribute its products in different ways, and research different pricing strategies. It is often wise to limit the number of segments chosen, particularly for smaller sport organisations with constrained resources. Except for large national or multinational organisations, it is probably imprudent to choose more than two or three segments.

Again, utilising Polar as an example, the research and design innovation, time, and market research necessary for multiple segmentation can be a costly endeavour, but was ultimately worthwhile when they developed the optical heart rate monitor. Designed to be worn on the arm, Polar had to develop an entirely new product to widen segmentation from elite distance runners to all levels of runners, swimmers, and even recreational athletes participating in high-intensity interval training (HIIT) classes. Whereas the H-10 chest strap delivers high levels of accuracy it can be uncomfortable and not all athletes need this level of monitoring. The optical heart rate monitor worn on the arm provided slightly less accurate heart-rate monitoring capabilities, but with a more convenient placement and design, which opens the market to increased utilisation.

Undifferentiated segmentation

Undifferentiated segmentation reflects the decision not to choose a segment at all, but rather to consider the entire market as a group of potential consumers. A sport organisation employing this strategy would develop one marketing mix for all consumers. Sometimes this approach is called mass marketing. It may seem uneconomical to follow the three steps of the segmentation process if only to decide not to proceed with any segmentation. However, one of the benefits of the segmentation process is that it reveals important information about consumers. Regardless of which segment is selected, or even none, it is always helpful to know as much about the market as possible. Another reason to follow the segmentation process is that it will help to reveal whether choosing one, more than one, or no segment at all will be most advantageous. For example, if a sport marketer discovered that there is little difference between segments in the market, it might be best to use undifferentiated segmentation. This was the main challenge within the wearables market. Health and fitness consumers tend to be widely varied in their needs; thus, mass marketing and undifferentiated segmentation were difficult to achieve. Perhaps the closest to undifferentiated segmentation within the wearables could be Fitbit and their activity tracker. A base model wearable, it was able to capture a large section of the health and wellness market that was interested in general fitness, while missing the individuals with more tailored or advanced fitness tracking needs, as they were a smaller subsection.

As with the previous two approaches to segmentation, undifferentiated segmentation has advantages and disadvantages. Like focused marketing, it can be more resource effective because it requires an investment in the development of only one marketing mix. One of the disadvantages of undifferentiated segmentation is that it is harder to stand out from competitors.

TARGET MARKET

Target marketing is a term used in sport marketing in reference to the way an organisation chooses one or more segments in which to target or aim its marketing mix. The segment(s) selected are like the numbers on a dartboard, where marketers take aim with a marketing mix. When the segmentation process is complete, a target market (or segment) should be the outcome.

> *Chapter tool 5.3 Market segmentation*: Market segmentation describes the process of categorising groups or segments of consumers together, based on similar needs or wants. There are several important elements to the effective use of segmentation as a marketing sport tool. First, the segment(s) chosen need(s) to be big enough to justify the effort of developing and implementing a marketing mix. Second, the segment chosen should be different enough from the other segments in the market to justify the effort and resources. If they are not different enough (and all the consumers in the total market are very similar already), then it may be more advisable to use an undifferentiated approach. In addition to these suggestions, there are four relevant issues to consider when choosing a segmentation approach:

It is important to estimate how easy it will be to reach the chosen segment. Is there a way to communicate with them? Can it be done via the media, internet, social media, or another means? Is there a way of getting the sport product to them? If they cannot be reached, or there is no way to distribute the sport product to them, then they are not the right segment to choose.

A sport organisation must consider the resources it can apply to the marketing process. Multiple segmentation can be expensive and time consuming, and it therefore may not be the best approach for a small and/or new organisation to employ.

The segmentation approach should also reflect how much a sport organisation knows about consumers. If it is a new enterprise, and/or offering a new product, it may not know much about its consumers yet, and its potential consumers may not yet be aware of the sport organisation and its products. Such circumstances would make it difficult to follow a multiple segmentation approach, which would demand considerable information about consumers.

The level of competition a sport organisation has in the market is likely to influence the choice of segmentation approach. If there is little competition, an undifferentiated approach might be satisfactory and, of course, cost less. However, in a market with fierce competition, multiple segmentation or concentrated segmentation would be helpful. This is not the only way to deal with competition. The way a product is positioned in the market helps to separate it from competitors.

MARKET POSITIONING AND DIFFERENTIATION

After the target market has been identified, a positioning strategy must be devised for use with each segment. Market positioning refers to how a sport brand is perceived by consumers relative to its competitors. For example, do consumers consider a sport brand as a luxury and high-quality product, or as a basic and value-for-money product? Do they see it as conservative and reliable, or exciting and dynamic? Positioning considers the fact that consumers will compare a product with others in the market. It assumes that they will put each product into a position in their minds; they will find a place where it fits compared to others.

The outcome of successful market positioning is a *differentiated* sport brand or product. If a sport brand or product has been differentiated it means that each target market segment attributes a specific value or set of features to it that are unique and special compared to competitors. In short, a differentiated sport brand or product stands out from the rest.

As reproduced in Table 5.4, there are numerous different positioning tactics that a sport organisation can choose from to best appeal to the target segment. Each positioning strategy will create a different perception in the minds of consumers. A positioning strategy is strongly connected with the concept of branding, where it is reinforced, amplified, and extended. Sport branding is considered in Chapter 6.

> *Chapter tool 5.4 Market positioning*: Market positioning is the process of attributing a sport brand or product a distinctive value or set of features for each target market segment compared to its competitors. The outcome of market positioning should be a differentiated sport brand or product. There are eight tactics of market positioning that a sport marketer might consider:
>
> 1 product features
> 2 product benefits
> 3 specific product use
> 4 product user
> 5 price and quality
> 6 against competitor
> 7 product class
> 8 hybrid positioning.

TABLE 5.4 Positioning tactics

Positioning tactics	*Method*	*Examples*
Product features	Focus on the unique features of the product	Unique features of sport shoes could include a comfortable fit, carbon plate inserts for performance, or a cutting-edge fashion design. Most sport codes have unique features in the way a game is played, such as soccer, cricket, tennis, and football
Product benefits	Tell customers what they will get out of the product or service	Health, fitness, social contact, fun, entertainment
Specific product	How can consumers use or apply the product?	Consumers could go to a game to socialise with friends. What does the product do in specific situations?
Product user	Focus on the personality of the user	Show women enjoying working out at a boutique Pilates studio to encourage more women to sign up for the classes. Show how the product can be used by people whom the user relates to
Price and quality	High price may reinforce quality and low price may reinforce value	Making sport accessible for families through discounted ticket packages or appealing to those with high disposable income because it is exclusive, such as box seating
Against competitor	Show consumers how the product or service is better than its competitors	Position the product or service as a market leader, an innovator; emphasise a superior product or better price. For example, the WHOOP wearable
Product class (associate or disassociate)	Position the product as belonging to a particular class or category of products. Tell consumers it is associated or connected to this category. Or, highlight the product as being revolutionary or innovative, and in a class of its own. It is incomparable with other products	Promoting a sport event as a once- off experience. Watching the Olympic finals events live in stadium could fall into this category
Hybrid positioning	Using several elements of different types of positioning	High-quality and innovative product; a unique experience

CASE 5.4

User-Generated Content

High levels of social media utilisation have resulted in brands incorporating consumer-generated content into their social media feeds as a form of promotion. This is a result of the oversaturated, competitive nature of social media marketing where brands struggle to be seen. Another challenge is that today's consumers are more sceptical, particularly Generation Z, with consumers almost two and a half times more likely to view content created by other individuals compared with traditional branded content.

Incorporating user-generated content (UGC) into an organisation's overarching brand image is known as user-generated branding (UGB). The benefit of UGB is that traditional forms of branding and marketing can be viewed as more forced and less authentic on social media, while brands promoted by individuals who utilise the products through UGC can be viewed as more trustworthy and authentic. UGC can include all form of social media content, including photos, videos, reels, and stories, often acting as testimonials for products.

UGC can be produced by a variety of sources, including general customers, brand loyal consumers, employees, and dedicated UGC creators, also known as influencers. The most organic form of UGC can be provided by customers, as they are the individuals who have decided to post content related to a particular brand. Photos of new purchases or videos unboxing new items can be powerful UGC. One step further than general consumers are brand loyalists, and while they may organically share branded content with more frequency, their continued posting demonstrates a genuine enthusiasm for a product. Although employees may not seem like a source of social media content, employee-generated content (EGC) can provide behind-the-scenes footage or testimonials illustrating why individuals work for a particular company. This can provide further justification for consumer support. Finally, UCG creators or influencers are individuals who have been recruited to provide content. This content appears authentic as they are not employees of the organisation, however, they are being paid to generate content due to their brand reach and significant followings. It's a form of traditional marketing that is designed to appear organic and authentic.

One major sports brand that has incorporated UGC into their digital marketing strategy is Adidas. In one instance, Adidas needed to update their approach to a road race due to the COVID-19 pandemic. The Adidas City Runs race was initially planned as a 1-hour loop around London, but pandemic restrictions prevented the racers from gathering at the start. Thus, Adidas shifted gears to a virtual format where runners could compete and start from their various locations. To engage runners during the event, and create a sense of community, a social media dashboard was employed by Adidas to gather and publish UGC from the race participants.

This was accomplished by using hashtags and gathering mentions of the event on social media, with Adidas publishing these highlights to the Adidas City Runs website. By promoting the hashtag and mentions to race participants, Adidas was able to create a community and drive content for promotion.

QUESTIONS

Search your favourite sports brand on Instagram (or utilise Adidas' Instagram account) and see if you can find instances of UGC and answer the following questions:

1. What forms of UGC do you see utilised by this brand?
2. Can you classify the types of UGC into the four types of general consumers, brand loyal consumers, employees, and dedicated UGC creators?
3. Imagine you worked for your favourite sport brand as a digital marketer, how would you go about searching for organic content to post on their Instagram feed?

INTRODUCTION TO THE MARKETING MIX

The final part of this chapter is a brief introduction to the marketing mix, which is explained in detail in the six subsequent chapters. After a sport organisation has divided the total market into subgroups (step 1), chosen a segment(s) (step 2), and identified a positioning strategy for that segment (step 3), it must then develop a marketing mix for each segment. The marketing mix is a set of strategies and activities that cover product, price, promotion, and place (distribution). These are commonly referred to as 'The Four Ps'. The fact that these four elements are grouped into a set, or a 'mix', is important, because they should be coordinated together in an integrated fashion. In this text, further to the four Ps, services, and sponsorship each receive a chapter of their own. This is because sport services and sponsorship demand quite unique marketing strategies. Table 5.5 illustrates the marketing mix and their composition.

Product

It is easy to think of the word *product* as referring to a physical, manufactured item. For example, Head produces tennis racquets. However, the term product can also refer to services, ideas, and the benefits that a sport organisation offers consumers. Many sport organisations offer a service, such as a form of physical activity like boxing, entertainment via sport matches, or an experience. There is often no physical product to take away, but a sport organisation might offer some intangible benefits such as a lifestyle, a social group or even a belief system. The product can also include design, packaging, and merchandise.

TABLE 5.5 Marketing mix composition

Product	*Price*	*Promotion*	*Place*
Service/product/ facility	Level	Advertising	Location
Quality	Concessions	Sponsorship	Distribution
Features and options	Special offers	Event signage	Availability
Design and packaging	Season tickets	Exhibitions	Sport facilities
Benefits	Payment methods	Sales promotions	Accessibility
Ideas and intangibles	Social costs	Personal selling	Public transport
Licensing/merchandise	Customer time	Publicity	Parking
Brand name	Market sensitivity	Direct marketing	Media distribution
Product image	Legal constraints	Promotional licensing	Internet distribution
Resource management	Pricing objectives	Branding	Manufacturers/ wholesalers/retailers
Staff	Break-even analysis	Public relations	Ticket distribution

Marketing the sport product is explained in detail in Chapter 6 and is heavily associated with branding. Sport services are considered in Chapter 11.

Price

The price refers to the cost that a consumer must pay to receive a product or service. This is usually thought of as the literal cost in monetary terms. To develop a pricing strategy, it is important to consider pricing goals and match them to pricing techniques. Devising a pricing approach is considered in Chapter 7.

Place

Place is concerned with where consumers access the sport product or service. It is another word for distribution. Place is therefore about the way a product is made available to consumers; how it gets from the place where it is produced to the place where the consumer buys and consumes it. For physical, concrete products, place is concerned with the practical issues of getting a product from producers to consumers through a supply chain, along with any other stops along the way such as wholesalers and retailers. In recent years the internet has provided new, more efficient ways of distributing and delivering products. With the internet, there does not necessarily need to be a retail outlet or shop, as consumers can buy directly from wholesalers, manufacturers, and through individual people (such as on Shopify or Squarespace), or even through social media, as most retailers link to online stores through their organisational bios.

When it comes to services, sport may be delivered to people via pay, cable or satellite television, free-to-air television or through OTT and streaming platforms. It may also be delivered in person by a sport organisation, such as local competitions and sports health practitioners. Place also includes different ways of getting tickets for a game or event, such as through a secondary market service provider such as StubHub, and decisions about where to locate sport facilities. Perhaps the most important aspect of place marketing is the way the sporting venue is used to augment the sport consumption experience. Place is considered in Chapter 8.

Promotion

Promotion is about communicating with consumers, getting a message across to the marketplace. Promotion therefore includes advertising, sponsorship, signage, exhibitions, sales promotions, personal selling, and publicity. These are examined in Chapter 9. Chapter 10 examines sport sponsorship as part of a promotional strategy.

CASE 5.5

Angel City FC and Corporate Social Responsibility

Angel City FC, a team based in Los Angeles, California announced in 2020 its intent to join the National Women's Soccer League (NWSL) as the newest team in 2022. The ownership group includes many female investors, including actor Natalie Portman, technology investor Kara Nortman, and media and gaming entrepreneur Julie Uhrman. Its first season saw the team draw a significant amount of fan interest, with four sold out home games, and a league-leading average attendance of more than 19,000 per game.

Angel City FC's mission extends beyond its on-field performance and success, focusing heavily on a community-driven business model with a corporate social responsibility (CSR) marketing strategy as a key component. This type of marketing strategy is based on connecting with like-minded customers who support businesses that align with their core values and feel they make a positive impact with purchases. By taking a community-driven business approach and engaging in CSR initiatives, Angel City FC seeks to align with fans who identify with community engagement as a core feature of sport. For example, the club employs a sponsorship model where 10% of contributions from each corporate partner is donated to an LA community organisation. These community organisations operate in areas such as education, food security, sports equity, LGBTQ+ support, and gender equality. The community engagement efforts are focused in three main areas: essentials, which include basic items for families to function; equity, providing information and resources to marginalised groups; and education, encouraging individuals to choose areas for growth.

Demonstrating the impact of the various community outreach initiatives performed by Angel City FC, the following results were highlighted as part of their ongoing CSR efforts. By mid-2023 Angel City FC delivered 485,195 meals via Doordash, trained 70 coaches in partnership with Gatorade, completed 3 SOAR Fellowships with Birdies shoes, funded 4 female entrepreneurs courtesy of Jane Walker of Therabody, distributed more than 1,000,000 pounds of fresh food and updated 8 school garden programs in partnership with Sprouts Farmers Market, donated 22,000 sports bras by Nike, coached more than 2,350 youth players with support from Yaamava and Gatorade, established a 3-year partnership with PlayEquity Fund, and sponsored a week of trans pride celebrations with Heineken.

QUESTIONS

1. What are the strategic benefits from establishing a community-based mission for an organisation and combining it with a CSR marketing focus?
2. Are there any downsides that you could foresee emerging from this strategic marketing approach by Angel City FC?
3. Can you think of any other sport organisations or properties that take a similar approach to marketing initiatives?

PRINCIPLES SUMMARY

- Chapter principle 5.1: The second stage of the Sport Marketing Framework is to develop a sport marketing strategy. This requires two steps: (a) to develop a strategic marketing direction, and (b) to develop a sport marketing position.
- Chapter principle 5.2: Developing a strategic marketing direction involves constructing marketing objectives and setting performance measures.
- Chapter principle 5.3: Developing a sport marketing position involves four steps: market segmentation (1, 2), market positioning tactics, (3) and devising the marketing mix (4).

TOOLS SUMMARY

- Chapter tool 5.1 Marketing objectives
- Chapter tool 5.2 Performance measures
- Chapter tool 5.3 Market segmentation
- Chapter tool 5.4 Market positioning

REVIEW QUESTIONS

1 How is the information acquired from stage 1, identifying sport marketing opportunities, used for stage 2, developing a sport marketing strategy?
2 Identify the key criteria in devising a good sport marketing objective.
3 What is the relationship between sport marketing objectives and performance measures?
4 What are the different kinds of market segmentation options?
5 When should each kind of market segmentation be used?
6 What is the purpose of market positioning?
7 How does market positioning influence the marketing mix?

RELEVANT WEBSITES

Adidas Running London (www.adidas.co.uk/adidasrunners/community/london)
Angel City FC (www.angelcity.com)
International Esports Federation (iesf.org)
Johan Cruyff Arena (www.johancruijffarena.nl/en/home/)
Korean eSports Association (www.e-sports.or.kr)
Melbourne Cricket Ground (www.mcg.org.au)
Mercedes-Benz Stadium (www.mercedesbenzstadium.com/)
NCAA Name, Image, and Likeness Policy (www.ncaa.org/sports/2021/2/8/about-taking-action)
Olympic Esports (olympics.com/en/esports)
Tottenham Hotspur Stadium (www.tottenhamhotspur.com/the-stadium/)

FURTHER READING

Chadwick, S., Chanavat, N., & Desbordes, M. (2016). Routledge Handbook of Sports Marketing. Routledge.
Hoye, R., Smith, A., Stewart, B., & Nicholson, M. (2015). *Sport Management: Principles and Applications* (4th ed.). Elsevier.
Karg, A., Shilbury, D., Westerbeek, H., Funk, D. C., & Naraine, M. L. (2022). *Strategic Sport Marketing*. Routledge.

CHAPTER 6

Sport products and branding

LEARNING OUTCOMES

At the end of this chapter, readers should be able to:

- define the term sport product.
- outline the key characteristics of sport products.
- explain the sport product continuum.
- define the term product augmentation, and describe augmentation strategies.
- identify the process of new product innovation and development.
- explain the concept of the product life cycle.
- describe the process of building a sport brand.

OVERVIEW

The purpose of this chapter is to explore the first of the six elements of the marketing mix: the sport product. It will introduce the key components of the sport product and will outline product strategies that can be used within the marketing mix, including product augmentation, new product innovation, and sport branding. The combination of product, innovation, and branding has become one of the most critical aspects of sport marketing as it provides the foundations for differentiation; that is, how sport organisations seek to stand out as being uniquely favourable compared to competitors, and as a result, cultivate a loyal fan following and strong brand value. Several trends are instructive to consider, many of which have already appeared prominently in earlier chapters. Perhaps the most evident is the continuing global reach of sport. As sport competitions and teams become more globally accessible, they adapt their products and branding efforts to appeal to fans in different regions, and through non-traditional channels. One pioneer, for example, is the NBA which opened basketball academies in several countries, and partners with local media companies to broadcast games in multiple languages, while football (soccer)

DOI: 10.4324/9781003391319-6

clubs such as Manchester United and Real Madrid have established large fan bases in Asia and North America mainly through new technologies and delivery platforms. With the rise of digital media, sport organisations have been leveraging technology to enhance their branding and fan engagement, typically incorporating social media and streaming platforms to promote its players and events.

Other technological developments have featured in sport product strategy too. For example, in tennis, the Hawk-Eye system uses high speed cameras to track the ball and provide more accurate line calls, while in many football codes teams use player tracking data to optimise tactics and reduce injury risk. In cycling, the use of power meters and real-time performance data has transformed training and race strategy. Further, equipment and gear innovations have been driven by materials science and engineering advances. For example, in golf, the development of lighter, more forgiving clubs has made the game more accessible to amateur players while pushing the elite level to higher levels.

Product innovations have also come in the form of rule changes and new formats designed to make the sport's performance attractive to new generations of fans, better aligned with apps and other streaming platform channels, or more accessible to fans or participants previously excluded. For example, basketball has created a new 3-on-3 format, while cricket's Twenty20 product, emphasising quick scoring and fast-paced action, has become the most popular form of cricket since its introduction in 2003, and the exemplar for many other sports seeking to attenuate declining viewers of traditional product forms. In motorsport, the Formula E racing series has experimented with new event formats, such as indoor street circuits and 'fan boosts' giving fans the opportunity to vote for their favourite drivers, in the process giving them added on-track advantages. As an odd contradiction, some sport organisations have sought to re-engage older generations by experimenting with nostalgic product innovations by reviving old logos, colours, traditions, rituals, and values with the hope of evoking a sense of past loyalty.

As observed in previous chapters, sport organisations have placed greater importance on environmental sustainability, incorporating eco-friendly practices into their product offerings as well as their branding profiles. For example, the Seattle Mariners became the first Major League Baseball team to eliminate plastic straws in their stadium, while the Formula E racing series promotes itself as a carbon-neutral alternative to traditional motorsport. Responsible product innovations and branding have further addressed social awareness too. For example, the Dakar Rally, an annual off-road race, has partnered with the United Nations to raise awareness of the importance of sustainable energy and reduce the event's carbon footprint. In football (soccer), the Common Goal initiative encourages players and teams to donate a percentage of their salaries to social and environmental causes. Finally, and allied to the social and sustainability movement in sport branding, athletes and players have moved aggressively to reclaim their personal brands, promote social causes, and engage authentically with fans. For example, soccer star Megan Rapinoe is an outspoken advocate for LGBTQ+ rights and racial justice, while basketball player LeBron James launched the More Than a Vote initiative to combat voter suppression in the United States.

CASE 6.1

TikTok

TikTok is a controversial but immensely popular video-sharing social media platform and a go-to destination for sports fans, athletes, and teams to engage with each other. TikTok has also employed various product innovations to enhance its positioning, the most evident associated with its almost exclusive focus on short form video content. Like other social media platforms, TikTok relies on AI-driven learning software algorithms in its backend that recommends content to users based on their interests and behaviour on the platform, thereby personalising content to suit users' preferences.

The company has also created some functionality innovations that have proven to be popular aspects of the platform. An example is the 'Duet' feature, which gives a user the chance to create videos and post them alongside another user. It's an especially relevant product feature for sport marketing as it encourages athletes and teams to engage directly with their fans, create new challenges, and promote their brand. For example, the Dallas Cowboys NFL team used the Duets feature to create a challenge where fans could participate in a dance-off with the team's cheerleaders. Such initiatives have become commonplace public relations activities for sport brands.

A further product innovation TikTok introduced involves augmented reality (AR) effects. AR effects include filters that allow users to create videos that look like they are playing in a game or that show a team's logo or jersey. These effects have also been used by athletes and teams to create engaging content that promotes their brand. Yet another innovation comprises a live-streaming option that enables users to engage with their followers in real-time. It has been used by athletes and sport teams to broadcast live events, such as training sessions, Q&A sessions, and behind-the-scenes footage. With the aid of this series of product innovations, the platform offers a hub for users to post videos of themselves attempting various sport-related challenges, some of which entice prominent athletes and teams to participate as well, sharing the videos on their own social media accounts.

QUESTIONS

Visit the TikTok site (www.tiktok.com/) or app to help answer the following questions:

1 What sport-related challenges have become popular among TikTok users and how have they helped to promote the platform as a brand for sports marketing?
2 What AR effects TikTok introduced for sport-related content and how have they been used by athletes and sports teams to create engaging content?

3 How has TikTok's live-streaming feature been used by sport organisations to connect with their fans in new and innovative ways?
4 How has TikTok's marketing approach differed from other social media platforms when it comes to sport-related content?

STAGE 3: PLAN THE MARKETING MIX

Sport product: goods and services

Chapters 4 and 5 explained the first two stages of the Sport Marketing Framework. This chapter concentrates on the first of six elements in stage 3, Plan the sport marketing mix: the concept of the sport product, and product strategies that can be used in sport marketing. The additional elements of stage 3 are presented in the forthcoming five chapters. Figure 6.1 highlights stage 3 and its major components within the Sport Marketing Framework.

What is a sport product?

A product is usually conceived as a physical good that has been manufactured; something that can be held and touched, such as a sporting shoe, football, or baseball cap. However, the term product can also refer to services and ideas. In fact, the word product is used in sport marketing in several ways including as (1) a good (physical item), (2) a service, (3) an idea, and/or (4) a combination of these. Each is explained next.

Sporting Goods

In the sport industry, examples of physical products include sport shoes, tennis racquet memorabilia, golf balls, and skateboards. There are also goods that are not only used exclusively for sport but can be used along with sport or as part of the sport experience. These include sunglasses, caps, T-shirts, watches, gym bags, sporting apparel, and sunscreen. These items are all tangible, which means that they can be experienced physically by the senses of sight, touch, taste, smell, and hearing.

Sporting Services

Sport services, on the other hand, are not tangible. Patrons of sport services receive benefits in the form of an intangible experience. For example, services are offered in the form of fitness and recreation opportunities, entertainment through live or televised matches, physiotherapy or coaching. These services are not physical objects that can be purchased and removed. Sport organisations cannot make extra services and store them away for consumers who may wish to buy them later. There are four important differences between sport goods and services that are highly relevant to sport marketing. These are tangibility, consistency, perishability, and separability.

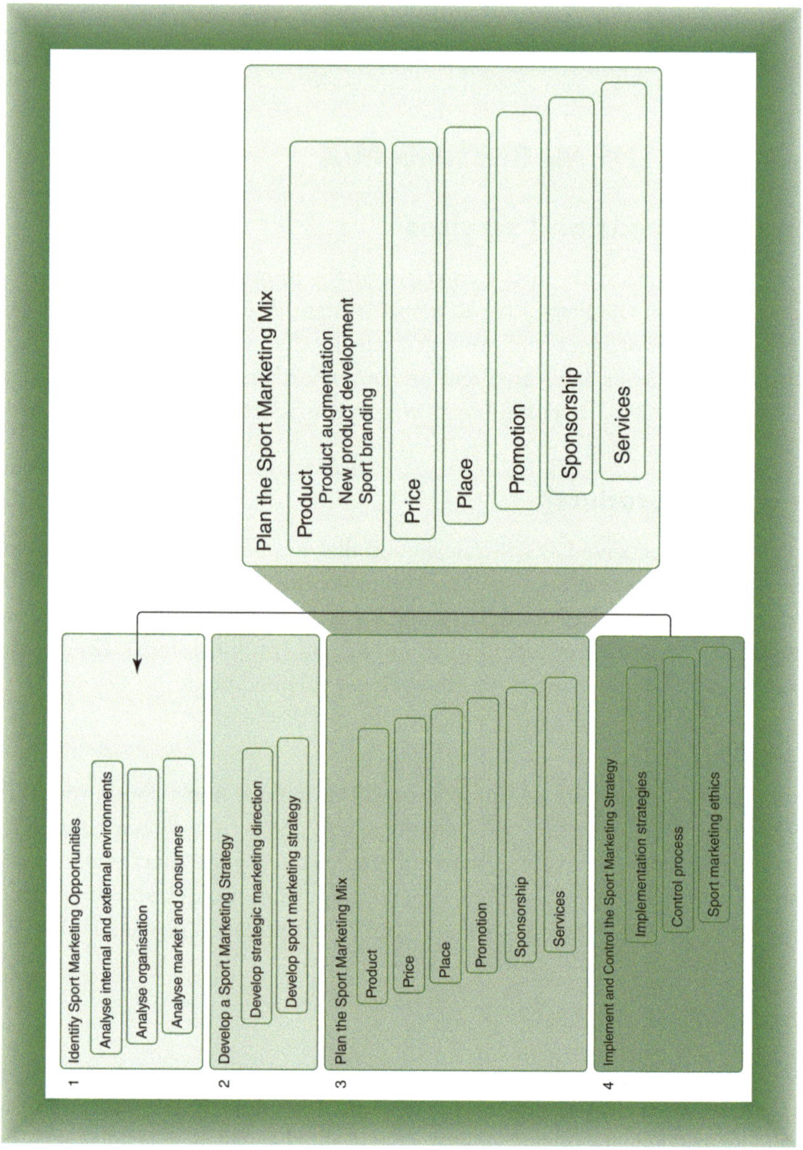

FIGURE 6.1 Plan the marketing mix

Tangibility

Sporting goods are tangible when they are physical and are experienced by the senses. From a practical viewpoint, sport product tangibility means that a consumer can take the product away with them for use later, and most often, for repeated use. Services are intangible because they are not physical and cannot be taken home to keep. Services are experienced for a period rather than owned.

Consistency

Consistency is another way by which sport goods and services can be separated. Consistency refers to how reliable the quality of the product is from one time that it is purchased and used to the next. Sporting goods usually have a high degree of reliability. There is not much change in the quality of a sporting shoe or a football of the same brand and model from one version to the next. On the other hand, sport services are likely to have more variable quality. The service quality of a sport experience may change depending on who is providing the service as well as the special conditions of its offering (e.g., weather). The fact that the quality of a sporting match will change from one time to the next has already been addressed in Chapter 2. Of course, an athlete may perform brilliantly in one competition or game, then fail miserably at the next. When this issue of variability in the sport product was discussed, it was emphasised that sport marketers should focus their attention on the quality of those parts of the service or product that they have some control over, such as service quality, prices, food and beverages, and the venue.

Perishability

Perishability refers to whether a sport product can be stored and used at another time. Sporting goods (such as clothing and equipment) are not perishable. Basketballs, cricket bats, and bicycles can be stored if they are not bought by a consumer without any damage to the product. Services cannot be stored. For example, it is not possible to hold on to unsold tickets to a sport contest to sell them at another time. Once the game has been played, any seats that were not filled are lost forever.

Separability

Separability is a term that is used to describe whether the creation or manufacture of a sport product happens at the same time as when it is consumed. Naturally, sporting goods are made prior to their use. For example, a hockey stick is made, delivered to a wholesaler and/or retailer, placed on the shelf or online, and ultimately bought by a consumer. The quality of the good (the hockey stick) is separated from the quality of service at the sport store where it is bought. It is also possible to separate the item from the person selling it, although sometimes one can affect the other. Sport services, in contrast, are made and consumed at the same time. At a live sport event, entertainment benefits are created while it is consumed by fans. It is also more difficult to separate the service from the person providing the service.

> *Chapter principle 6.1*: Sport goods may be differentiated from services on the basis of four factors: tangibility, consistency, perishability and separability.

Ideas

Although it might sound strange, ideas can form the core of some sport products. One example is when a consumer buys a gymnasium membership with the idea of becoming slimmer or more muscular. Another example is the power of sport in providing a sense of identity and vicarious achievement for fans. From this viewpoint, sport stimulates consumers to feel (emotional response) and to believe certain things (thinking response). At sport events, it is not just goods and services that are offered to consumers. There may also be ideas that are sold to consumers, such as those relating to belonging and success.

A combination of goods, services, and ideas

In practice, most sport products and services are a mixture of tangible and intangible elements. Many physical products have a service or idea element. In fact, sport consumers frequently buy products because of the intangible benefits they deliver. Equally, many services are sold together with something tangible to take away. For example, a membership to a football club may come with a package including club stickers, badges, and regular newsletters. In many instances, a sport consumer buys a mixture of goods, services, benefits, and ideas. There are also examples of sport services being transformed into sport products, such as live games that have been recorded for later sale, online streaming, or YouTube content. In sport marketing, it is common to combine products and services, and the tangible and intangible, to provide a more flexible, textured, and appealing set of materials to sell to sport consumers.

> *Chapter principle 6.2*: A sport product is the complete package of benefits presented to a sport consumer in the form of physical goods, services and ideas, or a combination of these to produce a sport experience.

THE SPORT PRODUCT CONTINUUM

Although sport products may feature a mixture of tangible and intangible elements, some sport products are mainly tangible, and some are mainly intangible. The sport product continuum is a useful tool to help show that products can be defined along a continuum (or a scale) with *mainly tangible* products on one end, *mainly intangible* products on the other end, and a mixture of the two in the middle.

As Figure 6.2 demonstrates, some products are mainly tangible, such as tennis balls and fitness equipment. Although they might provide intangible benefits that consumers want, these products depend on their tangible or physical elements. Take away the physical object and the product is essentially gone as well. In contrast, suburban tennis competitions or surfing lessons are examples of products that are mainly intangible. Even if there is a physical good supplied as part of the service (such as a racquet or surfboard), the product depends on its intangible service element. Take away the service, such as all the volunteers and administrators, and the product is untenable. Finally, a sport event provides a good example of a product that is a mixture of tangible and intangible elements. The intangible elements of a baseball game include what happens on the diamond, while the tangible elements include

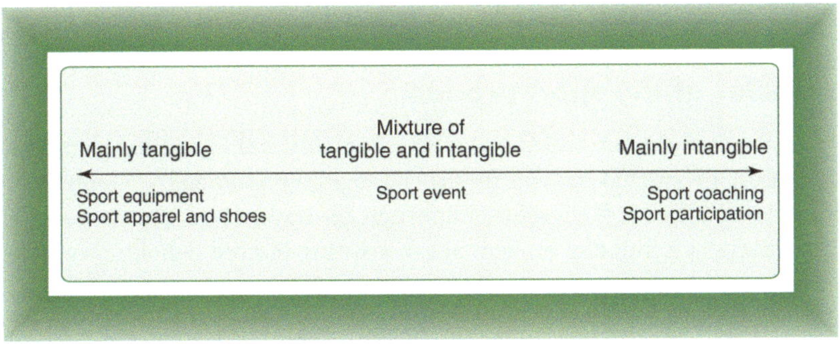

FIGURE 6.2 The sport product continuum

the food, beverages, and merchandise that are offered as part of the experience. Fans are usually looking for all these elements in a sport event, not just one or the other. For sport marketers, it is a useful exercise to locate all their products on the sport product continuum.

Mainly tangible and mainly intangible products

Products that sit exclusively at either end of the continuum can present sport marketers with unique challenges. Imagine, for example, the difficulties associated with marketing a tennis ball. There is little to make one brand of tennis ball stand out from others. One common approach is to use pricing to form a point of differentiation that can make the product more appealing for economic reasons, but it is also easy for competitors to copy this tactic. As a result, sport marketers try hard to add intangible value to their tangible products, such as the use of a famous tennis player to endorse a brand of tennis balls, or by emphasising that the product has a unique feature or quality.

Similarly, mainly intangible products are challenging to market. Consider, for example, golf lessons. When the consumer has nothing tangible to take away with them, there is no definitive reminder of what they have bought. It may be difficult for them to judge or remember what the quality of the lesson was because the advice given was essentially intangible and easily forgotten. One way to overcome these difficulties is to include some tangible elements such as brochures on certain golf skills or rules, or even bonus golf balls with the service name or logo. One pivotal tactic in sport marketing is to try to move products away from either of the extremes of the continuum, and to create a mixture of tangible and intangible elements. Sport events, for example, may emphasise the physical qualities of the venue, as well as opportunities to purchase memorabilia and merchandise. Many sport events make more profit from these tangible value add-ons than they do from the core entertainment product of the game itself. For example, it is common at sport events for consumers to spend more money on merchandise and food and beverages than they do on the entry ticket.

> *Chapter tool 6.1 Sport product continuum*: The sport product continuum is a useful tool to help show that products can be defined along a continuum (or a scale) with mainly tangible products on one end, mainly intangible products on the other end and a mixture of the two in the middle.

PRODUCT AUGMENTATION

Key variables of the sport product

Sport products possess many benefits as well as tangible and intangible elements. In addition, if the sport product is lacking in either tangible or intangible elements, it can be more difficult to market. It is therefore important to think of the sport product as being a complete package or a 'bundle' of elements, consisting of core benefits, product features, and the augmented product, as illustrated in Figure 6.3.

Core Benefit

The core benefit represents the principal advantage that the consumer receives from buying and using a product. For example, if a consumer buys a sports car, the main benefit is transportation. If a consumer buys a T-shirt, the main benefit is a covering for the body. If a consumer buys a ticket to a sport event, the main benefit is the entertainment value or experience the consumer receives because of attendance. Finally, if the consumer buys a service, such as a sport physiotherapy session or a sport skills lesson, the core benefits are physical treatment of an injury, or instruction on how to play a sport, respectively.

It is easy to underestimate the importance of the core benefit of a product and focus on the other variables such as features (actual product) or add-ons (augmented product).

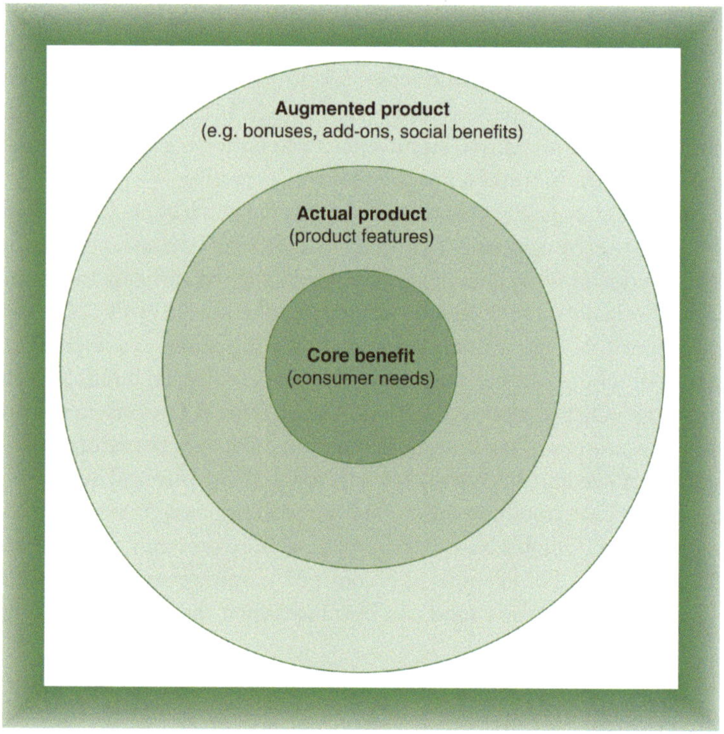

FIGURE 6.3 Key variables of the sport product

The core benefit is the most *fundamental* benefit of the product; if it does not meet the needs of sport customers, then it is unlikely to be successful. It is always important to understand the main need that the consumer has, or the primary benefit that they get from using the product. It is no use adding frills to a product if it does not meet the basic needs of consumers in the first place.

Actual Product

The actual product refers to the features of the product. The features of a merchandised sport T-shirt, for example, could include the colour, sizing, fabric, and pattern. The product features of a sport event could include the venue, facilities, the participating athletes or players, and the scoreboard. The features of a sport physiotherapy service could include the length of time of the appointment, and where the treatment is performed (e.g., at home or at a clinic). Paying attention to the features of the product can be one way of making it stand out against competition. If the core benefit of the product is something that people want, then developing the right features can help amplify a product's effects or allow it to be better matched to the specific needs of consumers.

Augmented Product

The word augmented means improved or increased. When a product is augmented, it is made better in some way. The augmented product refers to any extras or extensions that are added to the actual features of the product. These may be additional benefits, bonus extras, or even the image of a product. A sport T-shirt may be augmented by adding a bonus cap (an extra or add-on); it may also be improved in the eye of the consumer by being a particular brand that they think is fashionable. A sport event could offer extras such as merchandise, programmes, fanzines, posters, multimedia downloads, and autograph signing opportunities. A sport lesson could include a bonus-free lesson after every 10. Finally, in the case of the sport physiotherapy session, the therapist could offer information brochures, or provide a reminder call the day before the appointment. It is important to remember that aspects such as the status, image, or social appeal of a product are all examples of augmentation.

Understanding how sport products can be augmented is particularly useful in markets where there is substantial competition, or where different products have similar core benefits and product features. The market for sport shoes provides a prominent example. The core benefit of shoes (a covering protection for feet) is the same no matter who makes them. Different manufacturers try to create different product features, such as colour schemes, air pockets for shock absorption, or Velcro straps. However, these features are often quickly copied by competitors. One of the most effective ways of making sport shoes stand out is through the image of the product. Many manufacturers such as Nike and Adidas use athlete sponsorship to give the product an association with success, exclusivity, or style.

It is not as easy as it might appear to differentiate between the three variables of the sport product. Sport consumers might have different motivations for their consumption decisions. For example, although the core benefit of a sports car is transportation, it is probably reasonable to conclude that it is not actually the benefit of transport that is compelling in such a purchase. Rather, the features of a sports car make its transportation benefit much more appealing. In addition, augmented product add-ons such as belonging to a sports car club might provide a further set of advantages that add to the satisfaction of a consumer.

> *Chapter principle 6.3*: Sport products should be seen as a bundle of benefits comprising the core benefits, actual product features and the augmented product.

These three variables of the product are interrelated and should be manipulated as a group.

CASE 6.2

Goalball

Goalball is a Paralympic sport for players with visual impairments. It is a physically demanding and highly competitive sport that requires both athleticism and strategic thinking. The sport involves two teams of three players who face each other across a court that is 9 metres wide and 18 metres long. The aim is to roll a basketball-sized ball with bells inside across the opponent's goal line. Players listen for the ball and attempt to block it with their bodies. Goalball was devised in the aftermath of the Second World War for visually impaired veterans to play. To make the sport accessible to athletes with visual impairments, a unique set of product features were incorporated. First, the ball itself has bells inside it, allowing players to track its movement by sound. It's larger and heavier than a traditional volleyball, around the size of a basketball, making it easier to block and defend. Second, players are all required to wear eye coverings during matches to ensure that all participants have the same level of visual disengagement. The eyeshades create a level playing field, reduce any advantage held by partially sighted athletes, and provide an opportunity for sighted players to get involved as well. Third, the court is demarcated with tactile lines and boundary ropes rather than visual markings, allowing players to orient themselves and navigate the playing area through touch alone.

From a product strategy and sport marketing perspective, goalball has several key attributes that make it appealing, the most important being its inclusivity given that anyone can play irrespective of visual status. Another attribute has to do with the sport's highly competitive and intuitive nature where anyone can immediately engage without having to learn a lot of rules, but at the same time demands skills, strategy, and teamwork to excel. Goalball therefore appeals to athletes who enjoy the challenge of a mentally and physically demanding sport without having to invest years in learning complex rules or a lot of money on sophisticated equipment. Finally, goalball enjoys immense loyalty among its players with visual impairments as it offers an opportunity to showcase tremendous skills and strategy, at the same time promoting a sense of empowerment and self-confidence, especially for young participants who may have been excluded from other sports.

QUESTIONS

1 Imagine you are tasked with marketing goalball. Visit YouTube to watch some games being played if you are unfamiliar with the sport. Devise a campaign that emphasises the sport's product attributes. Use the following suggestions as a starting point to build upon:

a) **Inclusive sport:** You could create a campaign that showcases the inclusivity of goalball, highlighting the unique adaptations that make it accessible to athletes with visual impairments. This could include images of athletes with varying degrees of visual impairment competing on an equal playing field, along with messaging around the importance of inclusive sports.

b) **Competitive athletes:** You could create a campaign that emphasises the competitive nature of goalball, highlighting the speed, agility, and strategic thinking required to succeed in the sport. This could include images of intense game action, along with messaging around the mental and physical challenge of the sport.

c) **Empowering athletes:** You could create a campaign that focuses on the empowerment of athletes with visual impairments, highlighting the sense of pride and accomplishment that comes from competing in a challenging sport. This could include images of athletes celebrating after a win or completing a difficult play, along with messaging around the importance of self-confidence and empowerment, especially for young players.

d) **Endorsements:** Consider how you might employ athlete endorsements or partnerships with other sport or disability organisations to promote the sport and create a sense of excitement and interest around it.

SPORT PRODUCT INNOVATION

Sport marketers may consider the possibility of new product development through a process of innovation. Developing a new product can be expensive and risky. Every year there is a proliferation of new sport products introduced to the market, but only a small fraction of these is successful. If a new product is a failure, the sport organisation has lost time and money, and perhaps even some of its reputation. But what does it mean to develop a new product? A new product does not have to mean a brand-new product. In sport marketing, a new product can take many forms, such as the improved performance of an existing product, new functions added to an existing product, a new way to use an existing product, combining existing products, or a new look or design for a product. Whatever form the new or revised product takes, it arises through a successful process of innovation.

Innovation has come to mean many things from simple creativity to complex manufacturing. For us, from a sport product perspective, innovation refers to the translation of a new idea into a tangible deliverable via a technology, physical product, or process-based service. Unlike an invention or a discovery, an innovation takes place on the real-world stage, either as a novel solution to an existing consumer problem, an improvement to a consumer experience, or even a completely new offering for a consumer to try that they had never contemplated before. Because innovation tends to be synonymous with inspiration, considerable mystery surrounds its cultivation. Here we explore the basics of the sport product innovation process and offer numerous examples of cutting-edge developments.

In sport, product innovations can be found in several forms. First, mobile technology is changing the way consumers and participants connect with sport. For example, smart devices allow consumers to watch and experience sport from anywhere and at any time. Participants, and especially elite athletes, can collect, store, and analyse a vast amount of training and performance data that offer vital clues for subsequent improvement. Second, sport product innovations have made a serious impact on the support systems for sport performance, such as sports medicine, rehabilitation, pharmaceuticals, nutrition, and supplements. Also, of course, sport managers and marketers can benefit from new innovations that augment audience size, consumer viewing experiences, broadcasting coverage and quality, media channels, regulation, rule enforcement and officiating, and general spectator safety and comfort. Finally, sport product innovations can wield new materials in combination with technological developments. For example, carbon fibre has been used to create inexpensive, lighter and stronger sporting equipment, such as tennis racquets, bicycles, and golf clubs. The material's high strength-to-weight ratio has revolutionised sport equipment, enabling players to achieve better performance and results at any level. In addition, wearable technologies have become increasingly popular in sports, with devices such as fitness trackers, heart rate monitors, and GPS watches now commonplace even for recreational athletes. These gadgets provide users with real-time data on their performance, allowing them to adjust their training and technique, not to mention the fun and novelty of playing with the devices. Likewise, smart equipment such as basketballs, footballs, and tennis racquets have sensors embedded inside them, which provide coaches and players with data on ball speed, spin, trajectory, and other metrics. Finally, with growing concerns over the environmental impact of manufacturing, there has been a shift towards using sustainable materials such as recycled plastics and organic fibres. Sporting companies have been exploring innovative ways to produce eco-friendly sport products.

As a result of these major opportunities arising from the application of innovations, sport marketers would be well advised to become conversant with the processes surrounding innovation. But this does not mean that sport marketers must await the development of new technologies. Instead, they can aggressively pursue new product innovations through the application of available ideas and tools in new ways. Many sports, for example, have developed modified versions of their games to attract new audiences, including formats specifically designed for children, and those exclusively conceived for maximum entertainment. For our purposes, innovation relates to product outcomes that are more attractive to a targeted audience. An innovation can be incremental in that it shifts the existing product in modest but important ways, or radical, where a product can be completely redesigned or even replaced by something consumers never expected.

> *Chapter principle 6.4*: In sport marketing, a new product can take many forms such as the improved performance of an existing product, new functions added to an existing product, a new way to use an existing product, combining existing products, or a new look or design for a product.

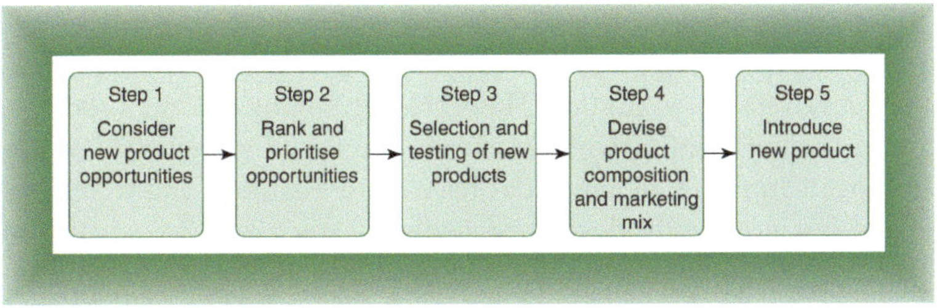

FIGURE 6.4 Steps of new product development

The process of new product development is usually coordinated by high-level managers in large sport organisations. However, irrespective of the level, it is important for sport marketers to understand the process to which they are expected to contribute. The process of new product innovation has five stages, which are shown in Figure 6.4.

CASE 6.3

Women's Professional Bodybuilding

Women's professional bodybuilding is a niche sport that has struggled to gain recognition and acceptance in the sport and fitness industry but has made numerous product innovations to address the challenges associated with its negative public perceptions. Women's bodybuilding emerged in the 1970s and up until relatively recently, the focus of the sport was on building extreme levels of muscle size and muscularity, characterised by radically low body fat, the combination of which often led to negative perceptions of the sport. However, the sport has transitioned to place more emphasis on aesthetics and athleticism and has started to gain more recognition and popularity.

One of the biggest challenges for women's bodybuilding was the lack of support from mainstream sport governing bodies and sponsors, who did not recognise it as a legitimate sport and therefore did not provide financial support or resources to athletes. Another challenge was the disapproving perception of the sport in the media. Women's professional bodybuilding was typically portrayed in a negative light, with the media often associating it with steroid use and other unhealthy practices like extreme dieting. Stereotyped and traditional gender expectations were also sometimes transgressed by the sport's participants, making their acceptance as role models more difficult.

An effective response implemented by governing bodybuilding authorities was to introduce new categories of competition in addition to the traditional and default bodybuilding division. For example, the 'figure' category was introduced in the late 1990s as a response to the public's desire for a more feminine and toned physique rather than the extreme muscularity seen in bodybuilding. Figure competitions are like bodybuilding competitions, with participants judged on their muscularity, symmetry, and overall presentation. However, the emphasis is on a more balanced and proportionate physique, with less stress placed on extreme muscularity and size. Participants in figure competitions have a more athletic and toned look, with well-defined but not overly developed bodies characterised by smaller waistline and more curves. Figure competitions exploded in popularity providing an opportunity for women who were interested in competing but were not interested in the extreme muscularity of traditional bodybuilding. The category has since become a staple in most bodybuilding competitions, including the prestigious Ms Olympia competition. So successful was the new fitness category that women's bodybuilding now encompasses as many as six different divisions, each with its own focus. These include wellness, bikini, figure, fitness, physique, and bodybuilding.

At the same time, the sport's athletes have made use of new technologies, platforms, and channels to communicate their experiences in bodybuilding. Primarily through social media platforms, many bodybuilders have become fitness 'influencers', showcasing their training, diet, and daily routines, giving fans a behind-the-scenes look at the sport. The personalised insight has humanised the athletes and broken down some of the negative stereotypes associated with the sport. A growing emphasis on promoting the health and wellness aspect of women's professional bodybuilding has also helped to transform public opinion. Many athletes are now focusing on maintaining a healthy and balanced lifestyle, and there is more focus on sustainable training and nutrition practices.

QUESTIONS

1 What specific marketing and public relations challenges has women's bodybuilding faced?
2 How has women's bodybuilding adapted its product-marketing strategies to overcome negative perceptions and stereotypes associated with the sport?
3 How has the emergence of new categories impacted the marketing and branding of women's bodybuilding?
4 What role have social media platforms played in the marketing and promotion of women's bodybuilding, and how have athletes and organisations wielded these platforms?

Consider new product opportunities

This first step of product innovation involves creating and collecting new product possibilities and ideas. While the product innovation process can occur either spontaneously or evolve almost unnoticed over a long period of incremental improvements, sport marketers can benefit from noting a series of steps typically present in any innovation outcome. Although beginning with a problem to be solved is a conventional and quite obviously sensible approach, innovation does not necessarily need something wrong to get it going.

If we consider, for example, some of the most significant sport product innovations of the last few decades, we will have to concede that many were not responses to problems. Rather, many came about through ingenuity, market testing, examining what competitors are doing, studying what is being done overseas, consulting with other staff and current customers, and starting with a strong pool of potential ideas. Or, to put it another way, product developers and marketers imagined new products and services impelled by thoughts on new opportunities. For example, some new product options are likely to have emerged in stage 1 of the Sport Marketing Framework. Consider the banned, full body 'sleeksuits' used in swimming to set a gamut of new world records, or the Ultimate Fighting Championship League, which redefined the sport combat entertainment experience. Both emerged in a cluttered product market, were anticipated, or were created as solutions to problem products or services. Opportunities are the engine of innovation. For this reason, product innovation begins with the desire for new value. Step 1 in the sport product innovation process therefore seeks to cultivate an abundant, diverse, and rich platform of potential concepts from which to conceive new value. It is important that the ideas remain unconstrained from the usual practicalities associated with convention, resources, and preconceived assumptions about what sport consumers want.

Rank and prioritise opportunities

The second step in new product innovation involves sifting through all the ideas that have been collected and only keeping the ones that fit with the marketing objectives of the sport organisation. It is also helpful to consider how well the new product ideas fit with existing products, and how they relate to current trends. This is not the stage to be concerned about financial realism. However, by the end of this step, new product opportunities should be ranked according to priorities determined by marketing objectives. In short, the lengthy set of ideas from step 1 need to be reduced to a workable handful. A range of methods can be employed, including voting and weighting systems, predetermined priority areas, expert advice, panels and workshops, and the product champions must quickly develop their ideas into testable prototypes. Subsequently, new product and service innovations should be tested as quickly and inexpensively as possible, in step 3, rapid prototyping and testing of new products.

Rapid prototyping and testing of new products

Step 3 of the process involves a more careful assessment of the ideas that were retained following step 2. In fact, the highest-ranking options should be identified and piloted to determine their potential in the market. This is the time to check feasibility by undertaking cost and financial estimates, and to conduct additional market research, or concept testing. Concept testing involves giving potential customers a description of the new product and asking them if they would be likely to buy it. It may also mean providing a prototype of the new product for customers to try. One powerful option at this stage involves creating a 'rapid prototype'.

Recently popularised and infused into marketing and business circles, rapid prototyping is a method of quickly testing an idea to see whether it could work before significant resources are expended in creating it for the market. Because rapid prototyping has been appropriated from designers, the process reflects the fluid and iterative methods they use in testing their nascent ideas. A prototype can range from a basic sketch or flowchart to a mock-up product or an unrefined but fully functional technology. The key is not in the finish but rather in the start. Most innovations never make it to the market because they take too long to develop or require too much investment without really knowing whether it will pay off or not. Rapid prototyping attempts to sidestep the development lag that most product innovations face. By quickly converting an idea into something tangible that can be tested – preferably by the same kinds of sport users and consumers who might buy it in the end – and subsequently refined and retested, the innovation process can be radically shortened. Often, the result is the choice to abandon the innovation. This is sometimes referred to as 'fast failure' or 'cheap failure' but reflects a positive outcome where resources have been protected from wastage in the light of early trials. In rapid prototyping, experimentation remains central, which leads to better design, faster.

It is important to understand that the rapid prototyping method does not seek to create fully functional products or services. But they do need to evoke an experience in users that will provide them with a first-hand insight into what it is like to try the new product. For example, a marketer might conceive a new process for sport consumers to purchase tickets to events through a mobile application. Instead of spending months and thousands of dollars on development, the marketer might simply construct some cards or offline screens reflecting the steps through which a consumer would use the application. By working with users to test the idea, the marketer can quickly ascertain whether their consumers have an appetite for the actual product. A prototype could range from the low fidelity, such as a series of sketches on paper, to high fidelity, such as a working application with limited functionality. The important issue is that users can be exposed to the kind of experience that the ultimate product seeks to elicit. Better prototypes duplicate the final product experience with greater precision than lesser prototypes. But even a poor prototype can be enough to provide sufficient feedback for a successive, refined version.

Most consumers find it difficult to imagine their responses to new product innovations in the absence of any tangible experience upon which to base their expectations. Prototypes vastly amplify the productivity of market testing and have therefore become a pivotal tool in the sport product development arsenal.

CASE 6.4

The Hundred

Launched in 2021, The Hundred is a professional franchise cricket tournament played in the United Kingdom. It comprises eight teams, each with both men's and women's squads, representing different cities across England and Wales. The Hundred was conceived with inclusivity as a priority where the men's and women's squads play at the same venues, on the same days. In terms of the product innovation, The Hundred was created as a new format of the game, with 100 balls per innings. The marketing strategy behind The Hundred revolves around creating a faster-paced and action-packed version of limited overs cricket. Its big ambition was that it would appeal to a wider audience, especially a new generation of young sport fans. The tournament founders believed that shortening a game to only 100 balls would make it much more engaging and exciting for those fans who find traditional cricket formats too long, slow, and dull.

One interesting feature of The Hundred's product strategy is its approach to team composition and player selection. A series of rules imposed by the competition ensures that all the teams must have a blend of established international stars, local talent, and up-and-coming players, the latter group being afforded a unique opportunity to display their skills against high profile players. Another feature involves a rule that allows the fielding team to take a strategic timeout of up to two and a half minutes, creating an opportunity for teams to regroup and plan their next moves. The strategy was calculated to give the game a novel tactical dimension that would escalate fan anticipation and tension. There were also some innovative applications of technology, like the use of a smart ball to provide data on its speed and spin while in flight.

To augment the excitement around the competition, organisers deployed an extensive marketing and promotion campaign, with a focus on digital and social media channels. They targeted a younger demographic by collaborating with popular music artists and influencers, as well as running a digital content series to showcase the players and the teams. Although the competition was delayed by the COVID-19 pandemic, it looks to be a promising new version of the sport, and full of product innovations.

QUESTIONS

1. How has The Hundred differentiated itself from existing cricket tournaments and other sport leagues in the United Kingdom and globally?
2. What specific marketing tactics has The Hundred employed to attract a wider audience, particularly younger fans and those new to cricket?
3. How do you think The Hundred will measure the success of its marketing efforts, and what metrics could it use to evaluate the impact of its campaigns on audience engagement?

Devise product composition and marketing mix

With the results of the new product's feasibility and market testing available, it is time to make a final decision about how to proceed. It is possible that the best decision is not to proceed and to choose the next highest ranked new product opportunity to investigate.

If the feasibility and testing results are promising, the final product composition should be determined. This involves specifying the core product benefits, actual product features, and augmented product composition. The other elements of the marketing mix will also need to be determined to provide the appropriate positioning strategy.

Introduce new product

Finally, if a sport product has successfully made it through all these stages, it is ready to be released onto the market. With this decision, an implementation plan will need to be created to support the deployment of all the variables in the marketing mix. The details of implementation are provided in Chapter 13.

> *Chapter tool 6.2 New product development*: The process of new product development involves five stages: (1) consider new product opportunities, (2) rank and prioritise opportunities, (3) rapid prototyping and testing of new products, (4) devise product composition and marketing mix and (5) introduce new product.

PRODUCT LIFE CYCLE

Sport products come and go. At first, they seem like the latest fashion, then consumers lose interest, and a new product takes its place. After a product has been on the market for a while, sometimes sport organisations change it in some way, creating a 'new and improved' version. These changes reflect the fact that every product has a life cycle. A product is 'born', introduced to the market, people learn about it and buy it, then they lose interest, and the product may 'die' or be changed or upgraded. The term *product life cycle* refers to the stages that a product goes through from first being introduced onto the market to its decline. There are four stages of the product life cycle as depicted in Figure 6.5: introduction, growth, maturity, and decline.

> *Chapter principle 6.5*: The term *product life cycle* refers to the stages that a product goes through from first being introduced onto the market to its decline. There are four stages of the product life cycle: introduction, growth, maturity, and decline.

Introduction

The introduction phase refers to the period when a product first enters the market. Many sport products fail at this stage, and/or they are changed as problems become apparent. Sales and usage usually increase slowly, and there may not actually be a profit for the organisation once the costs of product development and marketing are considered. Marketing costs are usually high because of advertising needs (the need to inform consumers about the new product and its benefits), the need to give consumers incentives to try the product and the need to encourage distributors to sell the product by giving them

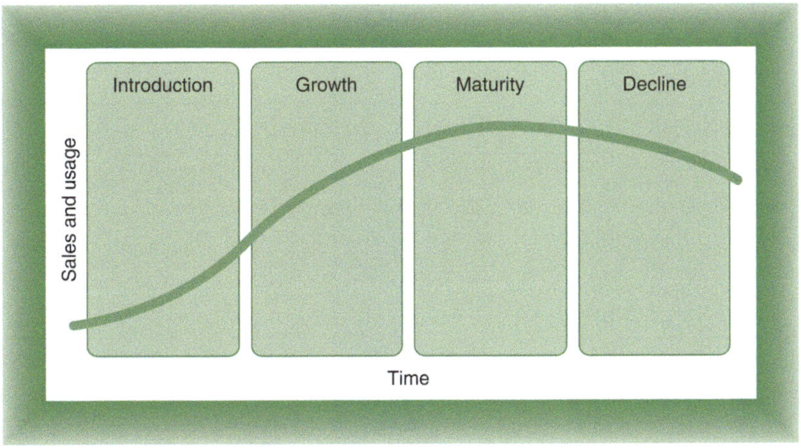

FIGURE 6.5 Product life cycle stages

attractive profit margins. The length of time that a sport product stays in this stage will vary greatly. For example, there may be a long introduction time if there are already plenty of other substitute products on the market.

Growth

Growth is the stage when the product has already attracted the awareness of the target consumers, and there is a rush or increase in sales. Profits usually rise quickly at this stage, however, so does the amount of competition.

Maturity

Once the product has been on the market for a long period, it is in the maturity phase. There are likely to be more competitors in the marketplace for the product and the producer may be forced to make some changes. This is normally the longest stage of the product life cycle. Gradually, profits or usage will decrease during this stage.

Decline

A product is in the decline stage when it experiences a drop in sales or usage as an enduring trend; how quickly sales drop will be different for every product and every situation. Eventually the product may be substantially changed or taken off the market.

Understanding the product life cycle is pivotal in sport marketing because different marketing strategies should be used during different stages of the cycle. Some examples are reproduced in Table 6.1.

> *Chapter tool 6.3 Product life cycle stages*: Different marketing strategies should be employed at each stage of a product's life cycle using variations to the mix including price, promotions, sponsorship, distribution, and services.

TABLE 6.1 Marketing strategies at each stage of the product life cycle

	Stage of the product life cycle			
Marketing mix	*Introduction*	*Growth*	*Maturity*	*Decline*
Product strategies	Narrow or single product option with ongoing changes to adapt to initial market feedback	More changes to product and more options to the range and variety	Introduce new variations of product to appeal to new segments	Products that are no longer popular are removed
Pricing strategies	High prices to cover high costs *or* low prices and discounts to encourage people to 'try and buy'	Reduce prices, especially if there are lots of competitors	Continue to reduce prices if number of competitors has increased	Continue to reduce price, unless there is not much competition
		If a low-price strategy was used in introduction, the price may be increased once some customer loyalty has been developed	Stabilise price if there is strong customer loyalty	
Promotional strategies	Advertising to develop awareness of product and its benefits	Emphasise the difference between the product and competitor's product	Increased promotion to distributors to continue to encourage them to sell product	Reduce or eliminate promotion and the costs associated with it
	Personal selling to distributors		Promote to new market segments	
	Incentives to encourage people to 'try and buy', such as offering samples			
Sponsorship strategies	High-profile athlete or team sponsorship for new product	Increase the range of sponsorship categories covered by introducing a greater range of endorsements	Reduce endorsements	No sponsorships

(Continued)

TABLE 6.1 (Continued)

Stage of the product life cycle				
Marketing mix	*Introduction*	*Growth*	*Maturity*	*Decline*
Distribution strategies	Offer good profit margins to distributors to encourage them to try selling the product, or use a short supply chain strategy such as the Internet	Build long-term relationships with distributors	May reduce the profit margins that are given to distributors	Stop using unprofitable distribution outlets and/or methods
		Increase number of distributors and/or different methods of distribution	May give incentives to distributors to encourage them to keep stocking product	
Services strategies	Introductory offers to build regular users	Heavy focus on service processes, quality, and customer satisfaction	Develop new aspects of services to renew point of differentiation	Retrain service deliverers to prepare for end of service delivery

SPORT BRANDING

The idea of branding is closely linked with positioning. A brand is like an identifying badge, often reinforced by a name or a logo that helps consumers recognise a product or an organisation. A brand becomes linked with consumers' opinions and perceptions of a sport product and organisation. A brand serves to remind consumers of its positioning compared to other products. Because branding and positioning are associated, it is important to keep branding, segmentation, and positioning strategies closely related. It is no use having a branding concept that emphasises luxury and quality, choosing a segment that is interested in value for money, and positioning the product as belonging to the 'x-treme' class of sports. In this example, the branding, segmentation, and positioning strategies do not match or complement one another. The result would be confusing and off-putting to consumers.

In a competitive industry such as sport, product sales can be affected by how easily a consumer can tell different products apart. Branding is one of the key strategies that sport marketers use to help their product stand out from the crowd. The way a consumer thinks about a product becomes a powerful form of reinforcement. Branding is therefore a way of augmenting a product by helping to create associated ideas that make it different. The added value that a product possesses because of its brand name and identity is called brand equity.

Brands can help consumers to remember products and can set off images in their minds. A powerful brand is one that has both a high level of recognition in the market, and strong associated imagery. Manchester United, Ferrari, Dallas Cowboys, Los Angeles Lakers, IOC, FIFA, and Nike are all examples of very powerful sport brands.

> *Chapter principle 6.6*: A sport brand is the symbolic representation of everything that a sport organisation seeks to stand for, leading to expectations about its value and performance. A brand can be portrayed as an identifying badge that triggers consumers to remember a product or an organisation. It can be a name, a design, a symbol (or logo), an image or a combination of these things. Branding is one of the key strategies that marketers use to help their product to stand out from the crowd by positioning it through associated ideas and concepts.

CASE 6.5

ESPN

ESPN is a market-leading sports media company that has been in operation since 1979 and has cultivated a global reputation for its comprehensive sports coverage, analysis, and entertainment. One reason that ESPN has been able to maintain its status as a market leader is because it has consistently introduced innovative product-marketing strategies. Although ESPN was a pioneer in its early years as a sport content specialist media company, it has been forced to reinvent itself repeatedly to maintain its position in an increasingly cluttered marketplace saturated with sport media options including traditional live free-to-air television broadcasters and packaged pay-per-view streaming services. To combat consumer fatigue and renew their cutting-edge standing, ESPN has launched regular new product innovations, several of which have become standard industry practice.

An early but seismic product innovation came in the form of multi-platform content. ESPN recognised that sport fans consume content across multiple platforms, so it created a comprehensive multi-platform product strategy. This offering contained live streaming, mobile apps, social media content, podcasts, and traditional TV broadcasts, collectively giving fans access to ESPN content no matter where they were or what delivery channel they preferred. ESPN was also one of the first major sport media players to engage deeply with social media to push its content and promote its brand to establish a clear identity as an organisation that comprehensively understood sport. To help this connection to fans, and now part of sport marketing history, ESPN developed its 'This is SportsCenter' campaign commercials in the mid-1990s, which featured athletes and ESPN personalities in humorous situations, and which became legendary viral content. The commercials remain available and enjoy remarkable viewing levels on YouTube. In fact, so successful was the campaign that it was revived in 2023. Another product innovation was the ESPN+ subscription streaming service, launched in 2018. The service offers exclusive content, including live events, documentaries, and original series. It's been a powerful new revenue driver for the company mainly because the mobile-friendly channel attracted a new generation of sports fans to engage with the content it already had. Along the way, ESPN has invested in cutting-edge technology to enhance the sports watching experience for fans and deepen their connection to the coverage. For example, the company uses advanced analytics and virtual reality to provide fans with a more immersive and informative experience, such as through 'MegaCast', which gives fans multiple viewing options during big events. More recently, ESPN announced the ESPN Edge Innovation Center, a collaboration with technology leaders Accenture, Microsoft, and Verizon, to explore how new technologies like 5G, augmented and virtual reality (AR/VR), and mobile edge computing (MEC) can revolutionise the fan experience of the future.

QUESTIONS

1. What motivated ESPN to pursue innovative product strategies?
2. How has ESPN leveraged emerging technologies to enhance its sports coverage and engage with fans?
3. What role do you think multi-platform content has played in ESPN's success as a sports media company?
4. How has ESPN's social media strategy contributed to the company's brand identity and fan engagement?
5. How has ESPN differentiated itself from competitors in the sports media industry?
6. What lessons can other companies in the sports media industry learn from ESPN's innovative product marketing strategy?

BRAND NAMES AND LOGOS

To recap, a brand can be many things, including a name, a design, a symbol, an image, or even a combination of these. A brand name and a brand mark (or logo) are two of the most common representations of a brand. A brand name is a word, a written label, or even a group of letters and/or numbers; it is usually something that can be verbalised rather than merely an image. The choice of brand name will put across (or symbolise) a unique idea. For example, some brand names might suggest strength and confidence, such as the All Blacks New Zealand Rugby Union team, while others might suggest boldness, such as Nike. If you do not agree with these connotations, it means that you hold a different brand identity in your mind.

There are several issues to keep in mind when choosing a brand name. It is important that it communicates ideas that an organisation would like its consumers to possess. It should be related to the kinds of benefits that consumers will get from the product. It is also useful if it is memorable and unique enough to be registered and trademarked.

A brand name should be easy to say, and easily translatable into another language. The Olympic rings and the Ferrari prancing horse are two well-known logos associated with sport. Some suggestions for a good brand name are as follows.

WHAT MAKES A GOOD BRAND NAME?

- Short
- Positive
- Easy to remember
- Easy to say
- Easy to recognise
- Unique
- Describes the product/product use/benefits
- Able to be registered or trademarked
- Translates into other languages.

BUILDING A SPORT BRAND

Sport branding is more than choosing a memorable name, or having an appealing logo designed. A brand must be sold to consumers if it is going to elicit the desired reaction. Brands have to be built. There are four steps to brand building as outlined in Figure 6.6.

> *Chapter principle* 6.7: Building a brand is a process made up of four steps including (1) establish brand awareness, (2) develop and manage a brand image, (3) develop brand equity and (4) develop brand loyalty.

Step 1: establish brand awareness

Brand awareness refers to the extent to which consumers recognise and remember a brand name. It is the first step of building a sport brand because consumers must be aware of a brand to understand its identity or image. The process of improving consumer awareness of a brand is one of the key roles of promotion, which is addressed in Chapter 9.

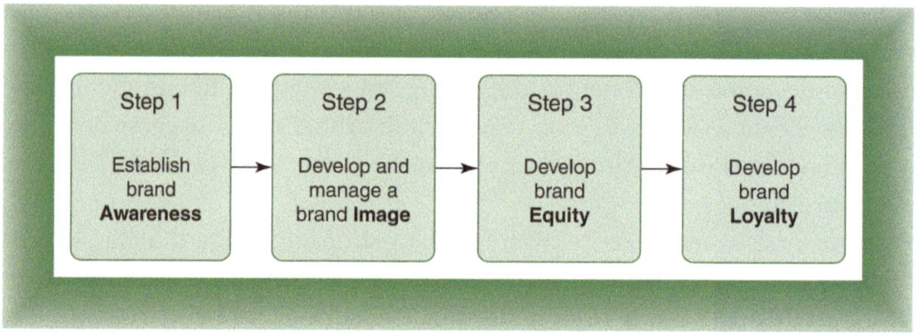

FIGURE 6.6 Building a sport brand

TABLE 6.2 Image variables and the marketing mix

Image variables	*Relationship to marketing mix*
Brand name	Product and promotion
Product features	Product
Product quality or performance	Product
Packaging	Product
Price point	Price
Advertising	Promotion
Promotion	Promotion
Sponsorship associations	Sponsorship (promotion)
Customer service	Place and services
Distribution channels	Place

Step 2: develop and manage a brand image

A brand's image is the way it is represented in the minds of consumers. For example, do consumers believe that it stands for reliability, luxury, adventure, or excitement? Once consumers are aware of a brand, it is essential to manage their perceptions of it. Managing a brand also means that continual effort needs to be made to remind consumers of the brand image. There are numerous variables that can be manipulated to affect consumers' perceptions of brand image. These are summarised in Table 6.2 along with the corresponding aspect of the marketing mix needed to introduce an effect.

CASE 6.6

Mumbai Indians

The Mumbai Indians are a professional cricket team that compete in the Indian Premier League (IPL), the world's most popular and lucrative Twenty20 cricket league. The team is owned by India's biggest conglomerate, Reliance Industries, and is captained by Indian cricket legend Rohit Sharma. The branding strategy of the Mumbai Indians is built around the team's core values – also known as its brand attributes – which declare a focus on innovation, consistency, inclusivity, and passion. These values are reflected in, and expressed through, the team's brand features.

A striking feature is the Mumbai Indians logo, which comprises a combination of blue and gold, with the team's name in bold letters. An important additional feature is the iconic Sudarshan Chakra, a symbol that is closely associated with Lord Vishnu, one of the most important deities in Hindu mythology. The Sudarshan Chakra represents the team's commitment to excellence and their desire to be a dominant force in the IPL. The team plays in blue and gold colours because they are associated with Reliance Industries, the franchise owners. The colours are especially relevant as they assist in building a strong brand identity and cultivate a sense of tribal community, continuity, and consistency across all team merchandise and marketing materials. The Mumbai Indians offer a wide range of merchandise, including jerseys, caps, T-shirts, and other accessories, all of which feature prominently the team logo, symbols, and colours. Another feature is the team's brand messaging, which for the Mumbai Indians scaffolds around the franchise's central brand attributes of innovation, consistency, inclusivity, and passion. The team's marketing campaigns focus on these values and refer to the same themes in all its public relations. Another manifestation of these values and attributes appears through the team's strong commitment to community engagement and its social programmes. For example, the 'Education for All' initiative provides educational opportunities to underprivileged children, while the 'MI Junior' programme aims to support young cricketing talent in the community. Social involvement bolsters the team's positioning and augments its community goodwill. Finally, the Mumbai Indians seek to offer home fans a memorable stadium experience at the Wankhede Stadium, where in addition to the buzzing atmosphere, they provide engagement activities where fans can meet players and participate in fun activities.

QUESTIONS

1. What steps has the Mumbai Indians taken to differentiate themselves from other IPL teams in terms of their branding strategy and features?
2. How does the Mumbai Indians merchandise offerings help to build their brand identity and create a sense of connection with fans?
3. How does the Mumbai Indians leverage their brand identity and core values in their marketing campaigns?

Step 3: develop brand equity

Brand equity is the added value that a sport product holds because of its brand name. Consumers are more likely to be loyal to a product if it develops high levels of brand equity. Brand equity can be influenced by several factors including consumer awareness, price, concepts, and ideas that consumers connect to the brand, the prominence of competitor's brands and their respective images, the nature of the products offered under the brand, and consumer loyalty. However, the most influential factor is perceived quality.

TABLE 6.3 Five elements of sport service quality

Service quality element	*Explanation*
Reliability	The ability to provide a service in a consistent and dependable way. How reliable a customer believes a service is depends on how strongly they believe their expectations of the service will be met every time
Responsiveness	The willingness to help customers and to provide them with the service on time
Assurance	The level of confidence and trust that a customer has in the service
Empathy	The ability to get to know customers and their needs, and to deliver a personalised service
Tangibles	Physical features of the service (e.g., information booklets, equipment, appearance of staff, facilities, sport venue)

This means that the most productive avenue to develop brand equity is by increasing awareness while controlling the quality of the products offered. Because of the differences between goods and services, there are additional issues to consider when it comes to service quality compared to goods quality. In fact, there are five areas that are commonly used to describe the specific aspects of service quality: reliability, assurance, empathy, responsiveness, and tangibles. Each is briefly described in Table 6.3 and explained in detail in Chapter 11.

There are also several important considerations when it comes to the quality of goods in comparison to services. There are eight elements of quality when it comes to physical goods. These are features, performance, reliability, conformity to specifications, durability, serviceability, aesthetic design, and product warranties. Each is summarised in Table 6.4.

> *Chapter principle 6.8*: Brand equity increases when consumers rate products as high quality. There are different elements of product quality for goods compared with services. There are five elements of *service* quality: (1) reliability, (2) assurance, (3) empathy, (4) responsiveness and (5) tangibles. There are eight elements of *goods* quality; these are (1) features, (2) performance, (3) reliability, (4) conformity to specifications, (5) durability, (6) serviceability, (7) aesthetic design and (8) product warranty.

Step 4: develop brand loyalty

When a customer is loyal to a brand, it means that they will choose it repeatedly in preference over alternatives offered by competitors. As explained in the previous section, the quality of a sport good or service will play a role in encouraging loyalty, and it therefore needs to be continually addressed. It is also useful to look at how easy it is for consumers

TABLE 6.4 Eight elements of sporting goods quality

Service quality element	*Explanation*
Conformity to specifications	Whether the goods meet the design standards of the manufacturer
Features	Whether the features of the product are high quality
Performance	How well the product carries out its main function (core product)
Reliability	How consistently the product performs
Durability	How long the product will last
Serviceability	How quickly and conveniently the product can be serviced if there are problems
Aesthetic design	Whether the design of the product looks to be of high quality
Product warranty	The guarantee of support if something goes wrong with the product

to buy the product on an ongoing basis. For example, is the product distributed in a way that is convenient for consumers to access? Sport organisations sometimes try to encourage loyalty by offering rewards to consumers for buying their product more than once.

BRANDING AND LICENSING

Licensing is an arrangement where a sport organisation allows another party to use their brand for a fee. The organisation that purchases the right to use the brand (called the licensee) will then produce a good, service, or promotion, and will give a percentage of the money they make or pay a fixed fee to the real owner of the brand (called the licensor).

Licensing is particularly common in sporting merchandise and apparel. Sport merchandise can include toys, collectible cards, board games, school supplies, clothing, magazines, and computer and console games. Sport clubs and leagues do not have the resources to make all these kinds of products by themselves. Instead, they may make an agreement with another company to make the merchandise for them, and, of course, they will want their sport brand or logo to be used. As a result, sport brands offer specific companies the right to use their brand. Also, both organisations will want to make money out of the agreement, so each of them will agree on a percentage of profits that they will receive.

Licensing is a very common product strategy in sport, and each year it generates billions of dollars in sales internationally. As with all strategies, there are opportunities and risks associated with licensing for both parties. These are outlined in Table 6.5.

TABLE 6.5 Licensing sport brands

	Opportunities	*Risks*
For the licensee	• An association with a prominent sport brand with an automatic level of brand awareness and equity • After heavy investment, the licensor can terminate the agreement	• Reliant on the continued (sporting) performance of the brand
For the licensor	• New markets become accessible through broader distribution network • More volume of the product can be made available • Increase brand awareness and equity through greater exposure of the brand to new consumers • No capital investment	• Out of control of the way their brand is portrayed and marketed • More difficult to manage quality of the product

NATION BRANDING

Sport has become an increasingly important tool for nation branding, with many countries using sports events and teams to promote their national identity and improve their international standing. For example, in the Middle East, countries such as Qatar, Saudi Arabia, and the UAE have been using sports ownership to enhance their global reputation and achieve their nation branding objectives.

One of the ways that Middle Eastern countries are using sports ownership for nation branding is through the acquisition of high-profile Western sports teams. Qatar's acquisition of French football club Paris Saint-Germain (PSG) in 2011 was seen as a strategic move to raise the country's global profile. PSG is a powerhouse in European football, and the Qatari ownership has given the country an opportunity to promote its image on a global stage. The team's sponsors have featured Qatari brands, such as Qatar Airways who became the shirt sponsor in 2022. In a similar way, the UAE's ownership of Manchester City Football Club has been employed to promote the country's image as a modern and progressive nation. The club's owners, Abu Dhabi United Group, have invested heavily in the club and helped transform it into one of the most successful football teams in the world.

Another way that Middle Eastern countries are using sport for nation branding is by hosting major sporting events. For example, Qatar hosted the 2022 FIFA World Cup, the first World Cup to be held in the Middle East. It invested heavily in infrastructure and in building state-of-the-art stadiums and facilities to host the tournament. The World Cup was seen as an opportunity for Qatar to showcase its culture, hospitality, and modernity to the world, although there were controversies surrounding the event from a safety and social viewpoint.

Saudi Arabia has also long used sport to promote its image, with the country regularly hosting major boxing matches and motor racing events. The Saudi Arabian Grand Prix, for example, was run for the first time in 2021, and promoted the country's tourism industry as well as displaying its modernity and progressiveness. The success of these initiatives has demonstrated the power of sport as a tool for nation branding and is likely to lead to more countries using sports ownership and major events to enhance their global reputation in the future. However, they have not been universally well-received, sometimes mired in controversy around social, cultural, and political differences.

CASE 6.7

City Football Group

The UAE's City Football Group (CFG) displays how a sport organisation, or a group, can be used for nation branding. CFG is a global football organisation that owns numerous football clubs in the United Kingdom, United States, Australia, India, Japan, Spain, Brazil, Uruguay, China, Belgium, France, and Italy including Manchester City FC, New York City FC, Melbourne City FC, Montevideo City Torque, Troyes AC, Lommel S.K., Mumbai City FC, Girona FC, Sichuan Jiuniu FC, Yokohama F. Marinos, Palermo FC, and Esporte Clube Bahia. The company was founded in 2013 and is majority-owned by the Abu Dhabi United Group, a private equity company owned by Sheikh Mansour bin Zayed Al Nahyan, a member of the royal family of Abu Dhabi.

CFG's ownership of football clubs has allowed the UAE to promote its image as a modern, progressive, successful, and Western-friendly nation. Manchester City Football Club has become a global brand, with the team winning multiple English Premier League titles and attracting some of the world's best players while under CFG ownership. CFG has invested heavily in the team, building a world-class training infrastructure and stadium. The group has also leveraged football to publicise the UAE's tourism industry. For example, in 2019, CFG partnered with the Abu Dhabi government to launch a new football tourism initiative called 'Football Abu Dhabi', which offered fans the chance to visit the emirate and experience the city's distinctive football culture, including stadium tours, training sessions, and visits to football clubs and facilities. The initiative has been successful in promoting Abu Dhabi as a global football destination and attracting more tourists. Part of the nation branding has been yielded from the CFG's commitment to philanthropy, in their case by using football to connect with communities. Examples include initiatives where CFGs football clubs have contributed to charity projects like building football pitches and supporting local development projects and events. CFG also specialises in youth development programmes, aimed at promoting and encouraging young football talent, where some of the participants can secure places in CFG club-aligned academies.

QUESTIONS

Familiarise yourself with the CFG's website (www.cityfootballgroup.com).

1. What role does sport play in the UAE's national branding strategy, and how does CFG utilise this to position itself in the market?
2. What specific sports events and initiatives has CFG sponsored or organised to enhance its positioning and nation branding strategy, and how have these efforts been received by audiences and stakeholders?
3. What is the messaging and tone of CFG's sport-related communications, and how does it reflect the company's broader brand values and image?
4. How does CFG integrate its sport-related positioning and nation branding strategy with its overall marketing and communications strategy?
5. What future plans does CFG have for its sport-related initiatives and partnerships, and how does it plan to continue utilising sport as a key positioning and nation branding strategy in the future?

CONCLUSION

In sport marketing, the product is an essential element of the marketing mix and refers to any tangible or intangible offering that satisfies the needs or wants of the target audience. The importance of the product in sports marketing lies with its centrality in shaping a unique and desirable offering that differentiates a sport organisation and its products from competitors. The product itself can be a physical item such as equipment, footwear, a jersey, merchandise, or a ticket to a game, or it can be an intangible offering such as a memorable game experience or a warm feeling of tribal belonging.

The application of the product in sport marketing involves developing a product strategy that aligns with the target audience's needs and wants. This includes conducting market research to understand the audience's preferences, desires, and expectations from the sport organisation's offerings. Such research can help inform product innovations, extensions, and augmentation, along with pricing, promotion, and place strategies as well. Furthermore, sport organisations utilise branding and packaging to enhance the product's appeal and create a unique identity that resonates with the target audience. Effective branding can help to increase brand loyalty and drive revenue through merchandise sales and ticket purchases.

Product innovation is an essential aspect of sport marketing, as it helps sport organisations to stay ahead of the competition by developing new and improved products or services that better satisfy the fans' needs and wants. In the sport industry, product innovations can take many forms, such as the introduction of new technologies, the creation of new game experiences, or the invention of new merchandise lines. For example, new high-tech wearables and tracking devices have revolutionised how athletes train and perform, while the creation of new game experiences such as esports, social media, and VR have delivered new revenue streams for sport organisations, and new forms of engagement for fans. In addition, sport organisations commonly develop mobile apps to provide fans with a more engaging and personalised experience. Such apps offer features such as live scores, news, highlights, and exclusive content. Some teams also provide mobile ticketing, allowing fans to purchase and manage their tickets directly from their devices.

Yet, product innovations can also come with risks, as introducing a new product or service can be costly and may not always lead to immediate success. For example, sport organisations are increasingly using apps, cryptocurrencies, blockchain, non-fungible tokens (NFTs), and other untested product extensions to generate new revenue streams. Sport organisations must carefully evaluate the potential costs and benefits of these product innovations and conduct thorough market research to ensure that the new offering speaks to fans.

PRINCIPLES SUMMARY

- Chapter principle 6.1: Sport goods may be differentiated from services on the basis of four factors: tangibility, consistency, perishability, and separability.
- Chapter principle 6.2: A sport product is the complete package of benefits presented to a sport consumer in the form of physical goods, services and ideas, or a combination of these to produce a sport experience.
- Chapter principle 6.3: Sport products should be seen as a bundle of benefits comprising the core benefits, actual product features, and the augmented product. These three variables of the product are interrelated and should be manipulated as a group.
- Chapter principle 6.4: In sport marketing, a new product can take many forms such as the improved performance of an existing product, new functions added to an existing product, a new way to use an existing product, combining existing products or a new look or design for a product.
- Chapter principle 6.5: The term *product life cycle* refers to the stages that a product goes through from first being introduced onto the market to its decline. There are four stages of the product life cycle: introduction, growth, maturity, and decline.
- Chapter principle 6.6: A sport brand is the symbolic representation of everything that a sport organisation seeks to stand for, leading to expectations about its value and performance. A brand can be portrayed as an identifying badge that triggers consumers to remember a product or an organisation. It can be a name, a design, a symbol (or logo), an image, or a combination of these things. Branding is one of the key strategies that marketers use to help their product to stand out from the crowd by positioning it through associated ideas and concepts.
- Chapter principle 6.7: Building a brand is a process made up of four steps including (1) establish brand awareness, (2) develop and manage a brand image, (3) develop brand equity, and (4) develop brand loyalty.

- Chapter principle 6.8: Brand equity increases when consumers rate products as high quality. There are different elements of product quality for goods compared with services. There are five elements of *service* quality: (1) reliability, (2) assurance, (3) empathy, (4) responsiveness, and (5) tangibles. There are eight elements of *goods* quality, these are (1) features, (2) performance, (3) reliability, (4) conformity to specifications, (5) durability, (6) serviceability, (7) aesthetic design, and (8) product warranty.

TOOLS SUMMARY

- Chapter tool 6.1 Sport product continuum
- Chapter tool 6.2 New product development
- Chapter tool 6.3 Product life cycle stages

REVIEW QUESTIONS

1. What is the difference between a sport product and a sport service?
2. Provide a simple definition of a sport product.
3. Sport products can provide both tangible and intangible benefits. Why do these present challenges for sport marketers?
4. What are the three variables of a sport product and provide an example of each for a sport product of your choice?
5. Identify the four stages of the product life cycle. Provide a brief description of the best marketing strategy to employ at each stage.
6. How does product innovation come about? Provide an example of a new innovation in a sporting product.
7. What is product prototyping and how does it apply to sporting products?
8. What is the relationship between branding and positioning?

RELEVANT WEBSITES

City Football Group (www.cityfootballgroup.com)
ESPN – www.espn.com
Goalball/International Blind Sports Federation (www.ibsasport.org)
The Hundred (www.thehundred.com)
International Federation of Bodybuilding (www.ifbbpro.com)
Mumbai Indians (www.mumbaiindians.com)
TikTok (www.tiktok.com)

FURTHER READING

Funk, D. C., Alexandris, K., & McDonald, H. (2022). *Sport Consumer Behaviour* (pp. 3–18). Routledge.

Pedersen, P. M., Laucella, P., Geurin, A., & Kian, E. (2020). *Strategic Sport Communication*. Human Kinetics Publishers.

Smith, A. C. T., Stavros, C., & Westberg, K. (2017). *Brand Fans: Lessons from the World's Greatest Sporting Brands*. Palgrave Macmillan.

Stavros, C., & Smith, A. C. T. (2021). *Sport Branding Insights*. Routledge.

Schmidt, S. L. (Ed.). (2020). *21st Century Sports: How Technologies Will Change Sports in the Digital Age*. Springer Nature.

Stoldt, G. C., Dittmore, S. W., Ross, M., & Branvold, S. E. (2020). *Sport Public Relations*. Human Kinetics Publishers.

CHAPTER 7

Sport pricing

LEARNING OUTCOMES

At the end of this chapter, readers should be able to:

- describe the strategic pricing process.
- outline the different pricing goals available to sport marketing managers.
- outline the factors that influence price sensitivity.
- explain what a break-even analysis is, and how to perform it.
- discuss other factors that influence pricing decisions.
- outline the different pricing strategies used in the sport industry.

OVERVIEW

The purpose of this chapter is to explore the second of the six elements in the marketing mix – price. This chapter is structured around a multi-step pricing process. Steps 1 and 2 provide guidance on setting pricing goals and analysing market sensitivity. The remaining steps include break-even analysis, the consideration of other variables that affect pricing, and the choice of pricing strategies for specific sporting goods or services.

PRICING: A MULTIFACETED ISSUE

Chapter 6 explained the first element of the marketing mix – the product – and this chapter expands the discussion to consider the second element of the marketing mix – price. The element of price and its components can be located in Figure 7.1 within the Sport Marketing Framework. In order to set the groundwork, there are four important terms to understand: price, value, revenue, and profit, which are reviewed in the following sections.

DOI: 10.4324/9781003391319-7

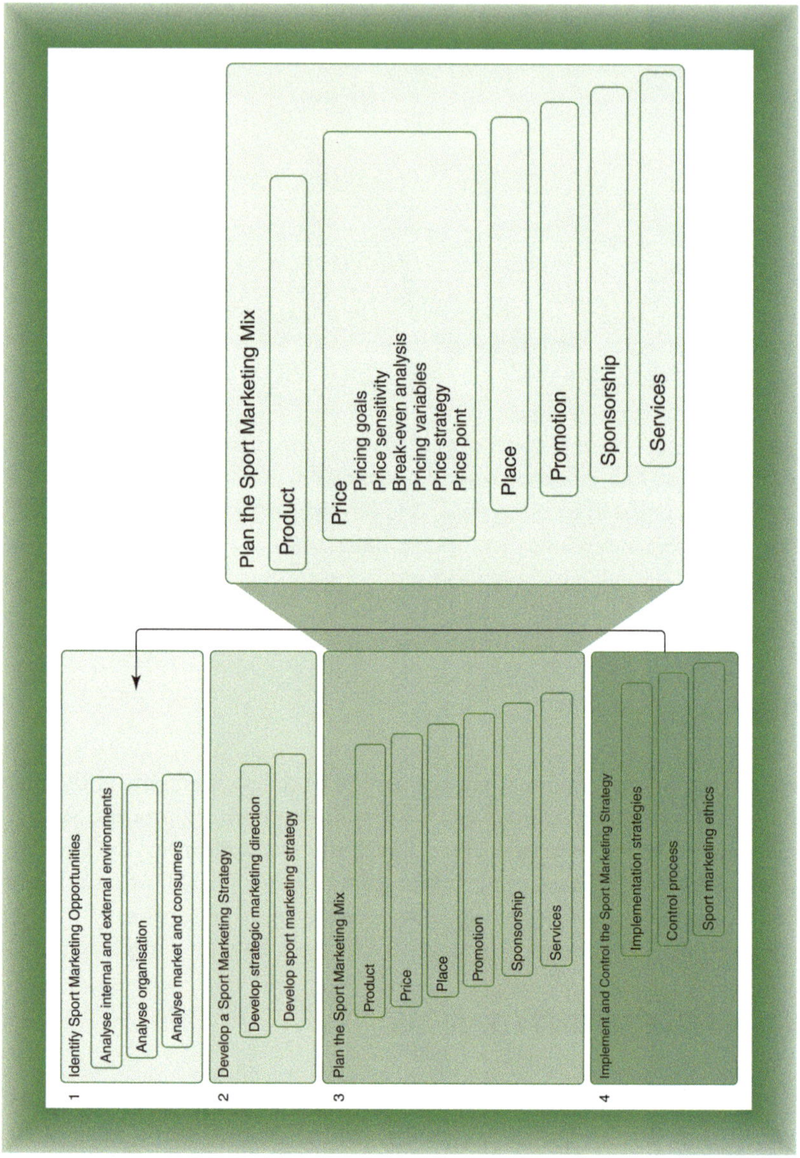

FIGURE 7.1 The sport marketing framework

It is easy to imagine that pricing a sport product (or service) simply involves working out what it costs to produce, then adding on a margin for profit. This is a useful beginning point, since price setting is crucially important when working out budgets and establishing the minimum price necessary to cover the costs of producing the product, getting it onto the market, advertising it, and finally selling it. Take, for example, a tennis coaching business, where the proprietor of the business and the senior instructor happen to be the same person. This multi-tasking requirement is a common feature of most small businesses. Setting the right price is crucial for this business since it may be the difference between making profits and incurring losses.

The example tennis coaching business has few options to consider. A coaching fee that will undercut competitors' fees is likely to secure few more tennis beginners, but if it does not cover the coach's costs of delivering the group instruction, it will make the business unviable. On the other hand, a premium fee that provides a handy surplus may look good on paper but may be so uncompetitive that no one takes up the service offer because it is too expensive. In this instance, the business has priced itself out of the market. The business is on the horns of a dilemma. However, there is a way out. The solution to this vexing issue is to design a product – in this case a tennis coaching programme – that offers value (with an accompanying fee, or price) that can be delivered within a cost structure that accommodates an operating surplus. This means there are at least two options to consider. The first is to run a low-cost business that delivers a basic no-frills discount programme to families on limited budgets, but who are committed to improving their tennis playing abilities. So, this programme is about learning the basics in a larger group in a low-rent, public court setting with little one-on-one instruction. Families with constrained budgets become the target market. Alternatively, the business could take on a more selective image, and thus charge a much higher fee, but offer a premium service at well-maintained clubs, and with smaller classes and the occasional personalised instruction. In this case, the target market is families with a bit more discretionary income, and who feel more comfortable in settings commensurate with their social aspirations.

As the above case shows, pricing sport products is a complicated process. In fact, the way that a sport product is priced will have a dramatic influence on the way that consumers perceive it. In addition, pricing tends to change continually, depending on a range of variables including a product's position in its life cycle. This tennis coaching case shows that pricing not only influences a sport product's profitability, but also communicates a powerful message to consumers about the brand and its image. A simple example can be found in the contrasting prices of general admission tickets (low price) versus corporate box tickets (very high price) to sport events. The variable ticket prices will immediately communicate different messages about the sort of experiences that a consumer might expect. The higher the price of the corporate box tickets, the more consumers would expect quality service, networking opportunities, lounge room style seating, weather protection, and quality food and alcohol. On the other hand, the cheaper general admission tickets will imply relatively poor seating arrangements, exposure to the weather, the likelihood of mixing with unruly fans, and long queues for food service. The difference in price is a key symbol that immediately signifies what consumers should expect. It also signals the social setting in which the experience will take place. This is very important to many people. However, when there is little difference in price, consumers expect little difference in the quality of the experience.

> *Chapter principle 7.1*: Pricing communicates an important symbolic positioning message to consumers about a sport product.

PRICING AND OWNERSHIP MODELS IN SPORT

Another aspect of sport pricing complicating decisions relates to the different ownership models in sport, and the different objectives that accompany each one. To begin with, sport-related enterprises can be privately owned, which, of course, is common in markets with competing businesses like sporting equipment, apparel, and energy drinks. In some cases, the most successful privately owned sport-related enterprises grow into global corporations backed by public share offerings. Whether owned by one person or by thousands of shareholders, private sport enterprises make pricing decisions based almost exclusively on profit-seeking aims. In some leagues like those in North America, the teams are privately owned franchises where one individual, group, or company owns the team and has complete control over its direction and operations. Not all team franchises pursue pricing based on the profit imperative, but all do treat their organisations as serious business ventures with serious financial obligations. A couple of the most famous privately owned sport teams include the New York Yankees, owned by the Steinbrenner family, and the Dallas Cowboys, owned by Jerry Jones.

Another type of ownership common in Europe and British Commonwealth nations like Australia is the membership model. Under this model, clubs and teams are not-for-profit enterprises owned by members who pay annual fees entitling them to vote in elections for a board of directors. Unlike private ownership, the membership model emphasises accountability to the members, who are generally fans of the club, as well as to its community and other stakeholders. While elite membership-based clubs participating in professional leagues often take a corporate approach to pricing, they still provide varying tiers of memberships and benefits at different price points to be more inclusive. Most membership-based clubs do not participate in professional or elite competitions and therefore rely heavily on membership fees to pay for the costs of running the club's operations. Pricing these memberships can be a tricky balance between making ends meet and encouraging as many memberships as possible.

Less common is the community ownership model found primarily in Europe. In this model, a team is owned by a group of fans or supporters who invest in the team and have a say in its operations. Community ownership provides a more democratic approach to sport ownership and can help to foster a stronger connection between the team and its fans. Examples of community-owned sport teams include FC Barcelona, which is owned by its members, and Borussia Dortmund, which is owned by its fans. Pricing works in a similar way as in the membership-based model.

A further model is characterised by government or nation state ownership. The model can be found in countries with communist, socialist, centralised, or constitutional monarchy governments. Pricing can be less a function of profit-maximisation and more focused on stability, performance, nation-state branding, or political identity. An example is the Saudi Arabian football club, Al Hilal FC, which is owned by the General Sports Authority (GSA) of Saudi Arabia, the government agency responsible for overseeing and promoting sports in the country. As a state-owned team, Al Hilal FC has access to significant financial resources and support from the government, which allows it to invest in top-quality players, coaches, and facilities. As a result, there is less emphasis on pricing for profit.

A final model is consortium ownership, wherein a group of investors or businesses collectively pool their resources to own a sport enterprise. Typically, consortium-owned sport teams are more sensitive to pricing pressures on fans as their desire to be a part owner of a sporting brand was unlikely to be motivated by profit or wealth. Yet, like all owners and custodians of sport teams, pricing decisions must accommodate commercial pressures. Examples of consortium-owned sport teams include Inter Milan and the Melbourne Storm rugby league team.

Ownership models are just one major influence on pricing decisions in sport marketing necessitating a unique approach. As noted in previous chapters, and especially in Chapter 1, sport's numerous idiosyncratic features mean that marketers must design pricing approaches that fit the specific challenges and unusual conditions of the sector. Pricing not only has to be right for 'customers' – the fans – but also with other stakeholders in mind too. It is instructive to consider the pricing tactics common in sport marketing before this chapter ventures more deeply into the process of setting a price.

A good first example is season ticket pricing, which is common to almost every sporting team's pricing toolkit. Using this approach, teams offer fans tickets to all or most of its home games, excluding finals, for a discounted price. Of course, the approach aims to encourage fans to attend multiple games and requires an upfront commitment, which is also advantageous for the team because it delivers a reliable revenue stream. In addition, season ticket fans are more likely to spend money on merchandise. Often a season ticket gives fans the chance to secure priority seating at playoffs or finals, as well as access to special events. Another example is pay-per-view pricing, which is commonly offered by major sporting events or team games where demand to watch the event is much greater than the available in-venue seating. Fans pay a fee to access a live broadcast or replay of the event through television or a streaming service for a set fee.

Sport marketers utilise variable pricing too. It features ticket or pay-per-view prices that vary according to the specific circumstances of the event or game, like who is playing, the seasonal importance, and even the day of the week. Higher prices are imposed where the anticipated demand to watch is higher resulting in an optimisation of the revenue for each event. Variable pricing explains why different games and events are not all the same price. A version of variable pricing known as demand pricing has become extremely sophisticated in recent years with the introduction of data analytic methods that are used to calculate and predict all the factors likely to affect demand for an event or game, as well as the maximum price that fans will be willing to pay. These are just a few of the common pricing approaches employed in sport marketing, where adjusting for the special features of sport must always be considered. Many further approaches to pricing are explained later in this chapter, including some more relevant to manufactured sport products, equipment, or other services associated with sport.

CASE 7.1

Peloton

Peloton is a US-based company within the fitness industry. Its chief product is what the company refers to as an 'integrated fitness platform', which comprises high quality equipment like stationary bikes, treadmills, and indoor rowers all equipped with internet-connected touch screens, which provide access to live streamed and on-demand fitness classes through a subscription service. Although fitness equipment remains a highly competitive product sector, Peloton's competitive advantage proved to be its pioneering approach to what has become known as 'connected fitness' where participants can stream a wide range of workouts on-demand in their own homes or join live group workouts with instructors and other participants from anywhere in the world. Connected fitness combines ubiquitous, high bandwidth connectivity with the attraction of being part of a common community, thereby combining the best of convenience, peer support, and professional instruction. The product also capitalised on the COVID-19 pandemic's enforced closure of fitness centres and facilities, thereby encouraging consumers to find alternative ways of exercising at home.

Underpinning Peloton's pricing model is a 'premium pricing strategy', which means that the company has positioned itself as a luxury item within the fitness arena. Fitting with this positioning, the company's equipment is high quality and high price compared with most comparable fitness equipment brands, or memberships to fitness centres and gyms. Aligned with the pricing strategy is the intention of targeting affluent fitness consumers who are willing to pay more for the unique combination of quality, convenience, and personalised instruction. To participate in Peloton streaming workouts, consumers not only have to purchase equipment, but also have to pay an ongoing subscription fee providing access to live and on-demand classes, music, and other features like performance and physical metrics. Peloton's 'value proposition' rests upon the unique experience it offers to consumers, which differentiates it from competitors, and validates the high-end pricing. Since Peloton requires the combination of equipment and services, its approach can be considered 'price bundling'. There are numerous options for consumers to select from in terms of streamed classes and fitness services with discounts offered when more are 'bundled' together. Other pricing tactics are critical to Peloton's marketing strategy. These include discounts for referrals for existing users who introduce new customers, financing options that allow new customers to acquire the equipment through loans, new products and features that nudge customers to upgrade their subscription plans, and discounts on partner/sponsor products like sporting apparel and music.

Despite soaring in value during the pandemic, Peloton overestimated the ongoing demand and faced significant challenges in 2022 that necessitated a dramatic response to their operations that raised questions over its medium-term viability and survival.

QUESTIONS

1. Peloton's pricing strategy is premium. Do you think the company is best to continue with this pricing strategy, or should it consider offering some lower priced options to reach a wider audience?
2. How do you think Peloton determines its pricing strategy for products and services, such as Peloton Bike+ and Peloton Tread?
3. Peloton has faced some backlash over the cost of its monthly subscription fee. Do you think it has been justified?
4. Peloton has expanded into numerous international markets. Do some investigations to find out if the company determines its pricing strategy for different markets or whether it adjusts its prices to reflect local market conditions?

Price

The price of a sport-related product represents what a consumer relinquishes in exchange for the product. A price should also reflect the value of a product. Generally, price is thought of in financial terms, but may include other things that a customer has to give up in order to obtain the product, such as time (e.g., waiting in a queue) or social costs (e.g., no longer having time to maintain membership of a club). This chapter on monetary pricing, but it is worth remembering that the other sacrifices a consumer makes to acquire a product may also have an influence on whether they buy it.

Value

A useful way to think about pricing decisions is to consider them in terms of value. In sport marketing, the value of a product is determined by how its price relates to the benefits that consumers believe they will receive in exchange. Value is expressed in terms of the following equation:

$$\text{Value} = \frac{\text{Benefits a consumer thinks they will receive from the sport product}}{\text{Price of the sport product}}$$

Chapter principle 7.2: The value of a sport product is the relationship between its price and the benefits a consumer believes they will receive from it.

The benefits of a product are what it offers the consumer, as described in Chapter 6. Consumers will feel that a product is of good value if the benefits received from it are equal to or greater than the price paid. With sport products, this can be a highly variable and individual assessment. Sport memorabilia provides an example. Consider a sport uniform that has been signed by the members of a prominent national cricket team. An unsigned uniform may sell for $200, so it would be reasonable to assume that a dedicated fan would pay considerably more for a uniform with players' signatures on it. Depending upon the popularity of this type of sport memorabilia, it is likely that some fans would pay up to $2,000. Many sport consumers are prepared to pay substantial amounts of money for unusual or special sport items. This is because the product has value to them. Value, and the benefits that go with it, is thus a very subjective concept, since people who are not sport fans would see little of value in a sport uniform soiled by graffiti. Both value and the perceived benefits of sport products vary considerably.

> *Chapter principle 7.3*: The price of a product is the amount of money a consumer must give up in exchange for a good or service. However, price is not the same as value, since value is the difference between price and the anticipated benefit. Although price is usually viewed in monetary terms, it may also include other consumer sacrifices in order to acquire a sport product, such as time or social cost. Additionally, in some instances the value secured from a sport product can be well in excess of its purchase price. This is a good position for a product to be in, since the expectation of getting more value for money will be an incentive to purchase the product.

Revenue and profit

Two further relevant pricing terms are revenue and profit. For product suppliers, revenue is the price that consumers pay for a product, multiplied by the number of product units sold. For example, if a sport venue sells tickets to an event for $38.00 each, and 45,000 tickets are sold, then revenue is $1,710,000. When the supplier's costs are removed from this revenue figure, the remainder is considered profit. In other words, profit equals revenue minus expenses.

On the surface, it is logical to assume that the higher the price, the more revenue earned, and the larger the resulting profit. However, in order to make a sale, the price of a product should not be higher than its perceived value to consumers. Problems emerge when the price of a product exceeds its perceived value. There is always a risk that an increase in price will force some customers to shift their spending somewhere else since the perceived value of the product may now be lower than the cost of securing it.

> *Chapter principle 7.4*: *Revenue* is the price that consumers pay for a product, multiplied by the number of units sold. *Profit* is revenue minus the costs of producing and selling the product.

STRATEGIC PRICING PROCESS

By calling the pricing process 'strategic', it is meant that setting a product's price should be planned with careful analysis and a consistent aim. The steps of the strategic pricing process are outlined in Figure 7.2. The remainder of this chapter will examine each of these steps in turn.

> *Chapter principle* 7.5: The strategic pricing process provides a structure for setting price. The process involves: (1) setting a pricing goal, (2) determining price sensitivity, (3) conducting a break-even analysis, (4) assessing pricing variables, (5) selecting price tactics and (6) setting a price point.

Pricing goals

Because different pricing strategies will achieve different outcomes, it is important to begin by determining what goals are being sought. It is essential to remember that pricing goals should support a broader product and brand positioning strategy, which in turn should underpin marketing objectives and the achievement of organisational objectives.

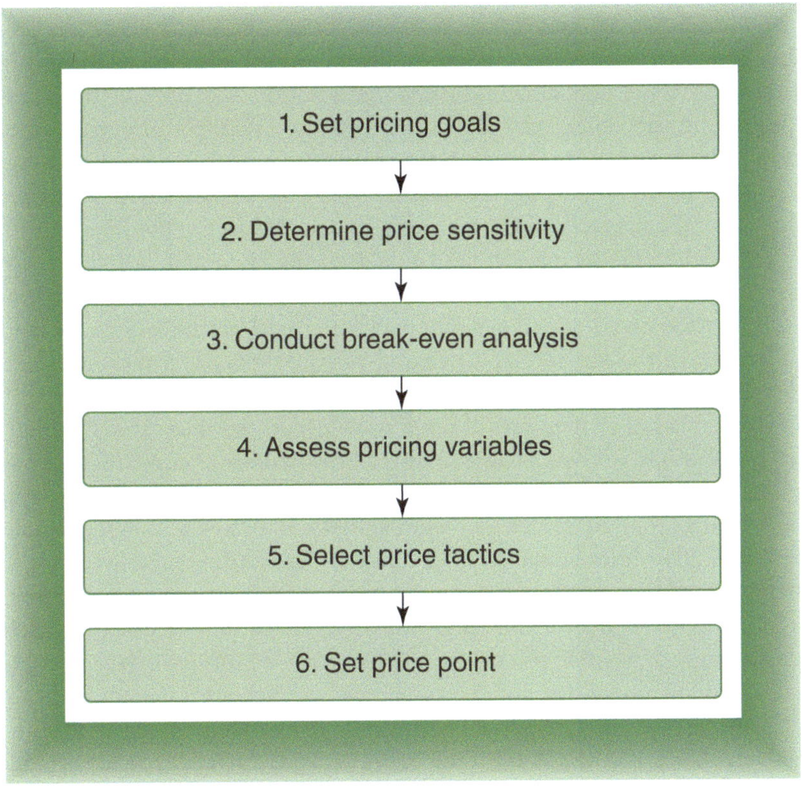

FIGURE 7.2 The strategic pricing process

There are two main types of pricing goals: (1) profit-based pricing goals and (2) sales-based pricing goals. Profit-based goals are focused on how much money a sport organisation earns after it has paid all of its costs. Sales-based pricing goals are focused on amount of sales an organisation makes. Both of these goals have a number of sub-goals, which are described next.

CASE 7.2

FIFA World Cup

The FIFA Men's World Cup is arguably the world's preeminent sporting event and is by most measures the most watched sporting contest as well, enjoyed by football fans from almost all parts of the globe with 5 billion fans tuning into the 2022 event, of whom 1.5 billion saw the final. The 2022 tournament hosted by Qatar was the 22nd time the event has been run, each time escalating in reach, popularity, and commercial value. For the Cup organisers and FIFA, ticket pricing represents a critical strategic decision to find the balance between full venues and maximised revenue.

Like all major sporting events, the World Cup ticketing strategy has a strong variable and demand pricing component, influenced by factors like the stage of the tournament, the participating teams, the location and time of the game, the seat position in the venue, and the venue capacity. As simple examples, tickets to the early rounds are lower cost than for the later rounds, while tickets to see the most popular teams are higher cost than those to see the teams with lower profiles. Because the circumstances of the tournament can change the combination of relevant variables like the teams that get through to the later rounds and the interests of the local audience, the event marketers utilise some dynamic pricing for unsold tickets where the prices are adjusted in real time based on contingent demand.

Underpinning the variable and demand pricing model is a more fundamental pricing philosophy established by the hosts. Often this broader philosophy reflects local factors relating to the costs of staging the event, the interest and affluence of local audiences, investments in upgrading facilities and other infrastructure, variable costs like security and accommodation, and the importance placed on maximising revenue versus other aims such as nation and city branding and filling venues. For example, the 2014 tournament in Brazil used a conservative variable pricing model depending mainly on location and popularity of the match, ranging from few hundred dollars (US) to over a thousand dollars. In 2018, the World Cup hosted in Russia introduced dynamic pricing for the first time, adjusting ticket prices according to the fluid nature of demand. The result was a much greater variability in ticket prices, even for the same match. As demand increased with proximity to the kick-off, with escalating interest, or with the importance of the match, tickets could double in value. Qatar's organising team decided to increase the cost of tickets to the final by 46% over the previous World Cup, but also reduced the price of the group stage matches at the same time. Notably, Qatari nationals were offered preferential access to tickets and discounts of around 50% compared to the prices charged to non-Qataris.

QUESTIONS

1. What factors do FIFA and the event organisers consider when setting ticket prices for World Cup matches?
2. What implications accompany a differential pricing strategy between local fans and visiting fans?
3. What issues would FIFA and the event hosts have to consider in trying to balance maximising revenue from ticket sales with the aims of ensuring that the World Cup is accessible and that the venues are full?
4. Can you think any new pricing strategies or ticketing innovations that might be used for future World Cup events, and why would they be a good idea?

Profit-based Pricing Goals

Profit maximisation means setting a price that will maximise the margin or difference between revenue and expenses. It does not automatically mean that prices should be set as high as possible. It is unwise for an organisation to set a price above the *perceived value* of the product. One of the potential problems with a profit maximisation goal is that it can encourage sport organisations to think in the short-term rather than the long-term. For example, it could lead a sport organisation to cut costs and wages as much as possible, and as a result lead to a lower quality product delivered by unhappy staff.

Satisfactory profit means a reasonable or realistic profit. What is reasonable and realistic will vary for different organisations and different product markets. It can be difficult to set a specific goal corresponding to how much profit is reasonable because it requires research into the market and competitors.

Target return on investment is the most common profit-based pricing goal. Target return on investment means that an earnings target is set for each specific market. Using this approach, a sport organisation would consider the amount of money it intends to make from selling a product, considering the amount they had to invest to develop and bring it to the market. Based on this calculation, a price can be determined. Naturally, a higher return on investment is better, but, of course, many sport organisations are not profit seeking and therefore choose a price that is sustainable rather than profitable.

Sales-based Pricing Goals

Market share is a measure of the percentage one product or brand has acquired of the total sales in a sector or part of the sport industry. Market share can be calculated in terms of revenue or in terms of how many units of the product are sold. It is not automatic that sport organisations with the largest market share make the biggest profits. While it is true that increasing market share can increase profit, some organisations with a low market share can survive and do very well. Market share tends to be a better measure for the sporting goods sector as sport teams and sport organising bodies are not oriented towards profit. Indeed, sport organisations participating in competitions will never hold the allegiance of all fans, and were they to, it would mean the end of the competition. However, it is reasonable that sport organisations oriented towards participation may find market share useful to gauge whether they are attracting more or fewer participants.

Sales maximisation refers to the goal of acquiring as many sales as possible. Sport organisations that pursue this goal are less concerned with profit, and are more focused on increasing the number of sales. For profit-oriented sport organisations, this goal is generally not a good long-term goal because it does not pay enough attention to whether the organisation is earning enough money to survive. It can be a short-term goal, however, if an organisation needs to generate some quick cash, or if it wants to sell off some old stock to make way for new products. For participant-based sport, sales can translate into participant numbers. For these organisations, as long as they can cover their costs, an increase in participation represents improved performance.

Chapter tool 7.1 Pricing goals:

- Profit maximisation: Setting a price that aims to maximise profit, but also making sure that it is not above the *perceived value* of the product.
- Satisfactory profits: A reasonable or realistic profit.
- Return on investment: A mathematical sum where net profit is considered in light of the investment in the product.
- Market share: How many sales or how much money an organisation makes as a percentage of the total sales/revenue in the market or a segment of the market.
- Sales maximisation: Trying to achieve as many sales as possible.

Price sensitivity

The second step of the strategic pricing process involves determining how sensitive consumers are to the price of the product. Price sensitivity is sometimes called *market sensitivity* because it refers to how sensitive consumers are (in other words how sensitive the market is) to changes in the price of a product. For example, if prices for a product rise, will customers be very sensitive and stop buying it, or will they ignore the price rise and keep spending their money? Price sensitivity is influenced by demand, supply, price elasticity, and the perceived value of the product.

Demand

Demand represents how many units of a sport product the market will want (the sum total of consumers) at a certain price. Usually, the higher the price for a product, the fewer

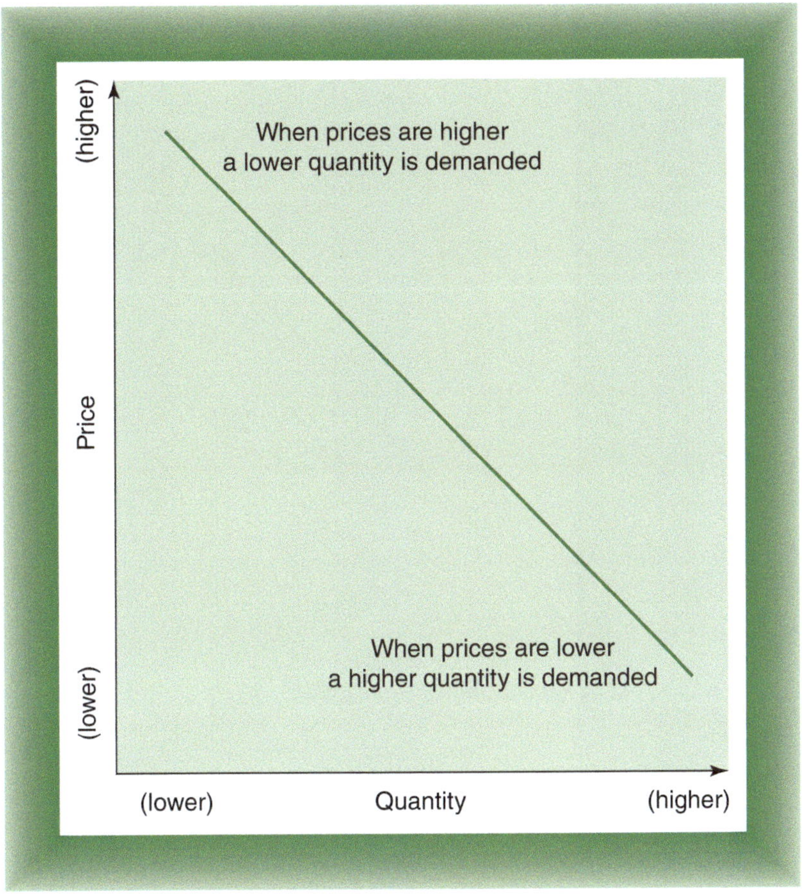

FIGURE 7.3 Demand for a product

goods or services consumers will want. Equally, the lower the price, the more goods and services customers will want. This relationship is shown in Figure 7.3.

Product demand is also influenced by product *substitutes* and *complements*. Product substitutes are products that can be used in place of another product. For example, if the price of a family ticket to the tennis increased dramatically, other products such as movie or theme-park tickets could be used as a substitute for a cheaper family outing. Product complements are those that are used together. For example, membership to a rock-climbing gymnasium and sales of climbing harnesses are complementary products. If the cost of a membership rises, the quantity of both products (memberships and harnesses) demanded by consumers would likely fall.

Supply

Supply represents the quantity of a product that is available in the market at certain prices. In principle, the higher the price of a product, the greater the returns to the supplier. Also, high prices signal for other organisations to enter the market and produce a similar product

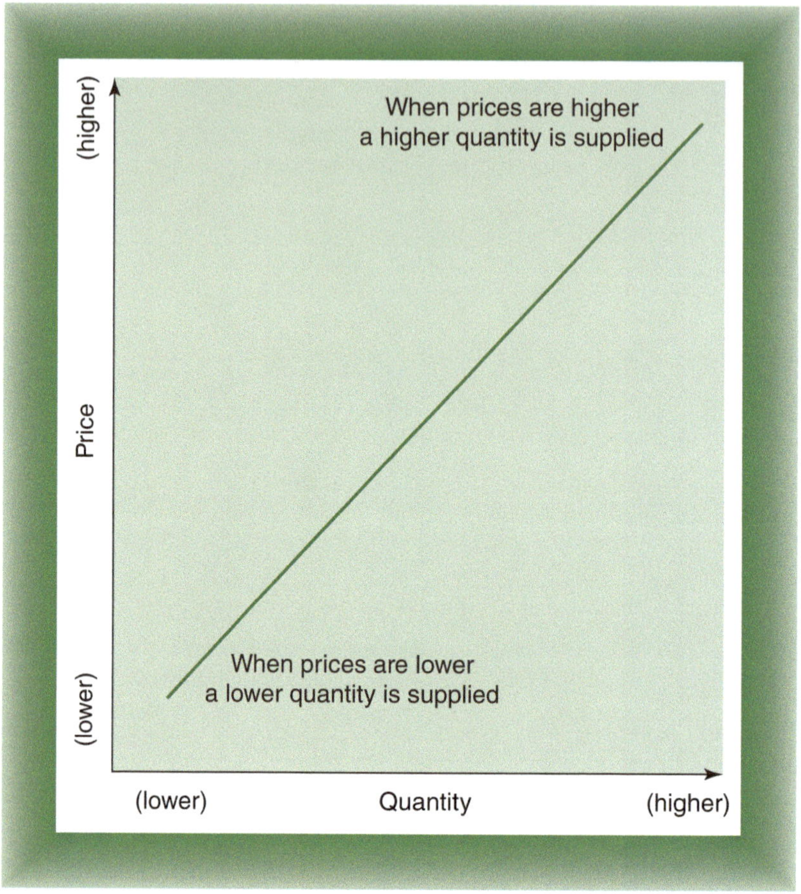

FIGURE 7.4 Supply for a product

themselves. In other words, a higher product price usually leads to a greater amount of the product being supplied to the market. This is illustrated in Figure 7.4.

The volume of a product supplied to the market will also be influenced by other factors, such as the prices of raw materials and resources, the number of competitors, and consumers' expectations about future prices and technology. For example, if the cost of cotton (a raw material) to make a sport branded T-shirt dramatically increased, then the number of T-shirts supplied in the sporting apparel industry would fall. Another example is that the volume of a product supplied to the market increases with growth in the number of competitors (suppliers) offering it.

The graph shown in Figure 7.5 illustrates the theoretical conditions when demand equals supply, also known as market equilibrium. At market equilibrium price, the quantity of the product that is produced by suppliers is the same as the quantity demanded by consumers. There is no excess product left unsold, and there are no consumers who want to buy the product but miss out. Of course, this is merely a theoretical possibility that is almost impossible to predict or achieve in practice. However, the concept of market

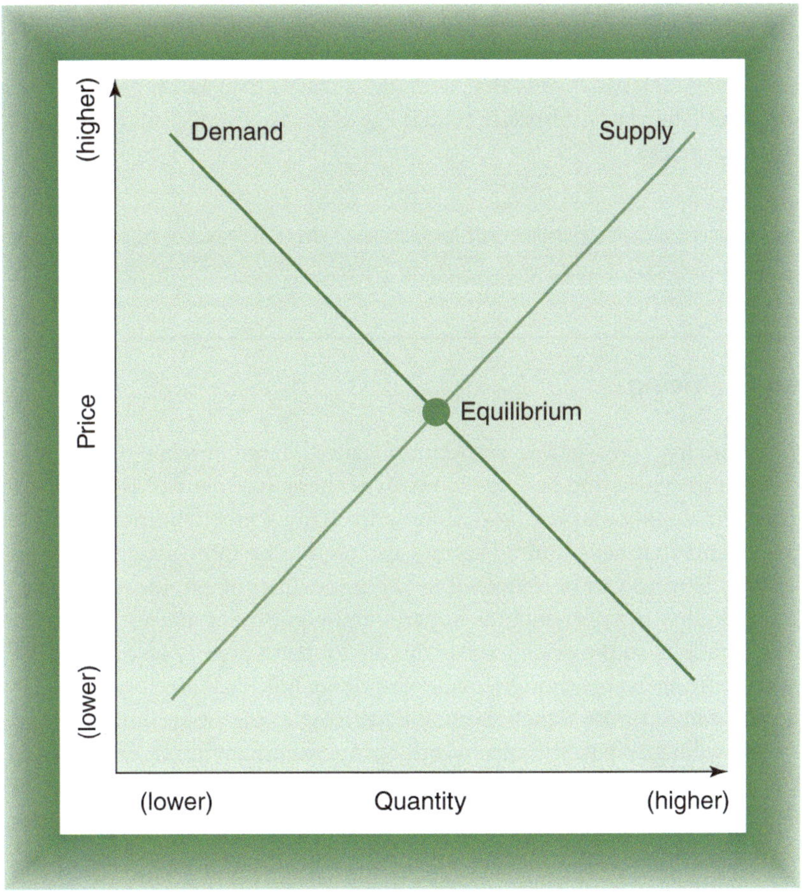

FIGURE 7.5 Market equilibrium

equilibrium helps to explain why sport organisations review the relationship between the volume of their product or service offerings and demand. Equally, sport organisations can deliberately influence demand by changing their pricing structure.

Price Elasticity

Price elasticity refers to how easily consumer demand for a product changes when there is a change in price. There are two different types of price elasticity: inelastic demand and elastic demand. In most competitive sport, inelastic demand is more prominent. This means that it is difficult to substitute (or replace) one sport league, team, or competition for another. Many sport fans are fiercely loyal to their team or their sport. Even if the price of tickets to games increases, loyal fans are unlikely to stop attending. They are thus insensitive to price changes. The other type of elasticity is elastic demand. This means that demand for the product will change dramatically, even when the price change is small. In this case, if the price of a product increases, consumers will buy less of it, but if the price falls, a higher quantity will be demanded. Demand for the product is like an elastic band. Being elastic means demand is sensitive and therefore responsive to price changes. On the other hand, being inelastic means that demand is insensitive, and therefore unresponsive to price changes. The classic response to manage elasticity in sport marketing involves the use of dynamic pricing.

CASE 7.3

Dynamic Pricing

Dynamic pricing, or what is sometimes called 'surge pricing' features prominently in sport marketing because it involves the adjustment of price in response to changes in supply and demand. Like with many scarce commodities, access to sporting events that have limited supply also tend to be more sought after, and this heightened demand can be reflected in the price. In contrast, most physical products associated with sport such as apparel and equipment are not constrained by supply limitations, so the pricing strategies do not focus heavily on demand. When it comes to sporting events though, dynamic pricing holds great relevance because its application can optimise ticket revenue by pricing at the upper limit of what consumers are willing to pay. It is also worth noting that many products affiliated with sport or tangentially connected to the delivery of sporting events and games can utilise dynamic pricing to exploit the demand for the sport product. For example, merchandise, food and beverages at games can increase, just as the price of taxis and accommodation can in locations hosting major events or games.

The use of dynamic pricing in major leagues and competitions is quite common. In the United States, for instance, Major League Baseball applies dynamic pricing for postseason games, ticket prices flexing according to the teams, venues, and the number of games each team has won in the 'best-of' series. A World Series game ticket could be as much as three times the price of a regular season ticket. During the season, many NFL teams employ dynamic pricing for single-game tickets, not only considering factors like the participating teams and season context, but also highly nuanced variables such as proximity to a public holiday, weather, and the availability of star players. All these elements are calculated, and optimal ticket prices predicted based on years of granular data analytics. In the National Basketball League, it has become more common for teams to utilise dynamic pricing for season tickets too, especially for when games fall on major holidays or where the results have postseason playoff implications. English Premier League ticket pricing makes heavy use of dynamic pricing for individual matches with a particular emphasis on the popularity and league table position of the competing clubs. When two of the heavyweight clubs meet, like Manchester City and Liverpool, ticket prices can escalate by 50%. Sometimes numerous factors intersect to elevate prices even more.

In the Indian Premier League, for example, dynamic pricing can lift prices sky high when the most popular teams meet in the finals.

Major sporting events also cater to dynamic pricing by planning for the opportunities it provides to calibrate demand and revenue. The Wimbledon tennis tournament, for example, schedules the highest seeded and most popular players on the centre court for their early rounds while the lesser-known players appear on the outer courts. Not only can the event charge more for the matches between the most popular players, but they can also sell many more tickets because the centre court has more capacity. For the Australian Open later rounds, the men's singles tickets are in the highest demand and therefore set at the highest price. Similarly, in major sporting competitions involving numerous sports like the Olympics, the most popular events command the highest prices, the most obvious examples being the finals of the men's 100 metres, and the opening and closing ceremonies. In another variation, this time in Formula 1, dynamic pricing is strongly influenced by the location of the race and the seating position on the track. For example, the Monaco Grand Prix may be able to charge higher ticket prices than many others given its famous connection to elite motorsport.

QUESTIONS

1. Explain the rationale behind using dynamic pricing in sport?
2. How does the dynamic pricing model work and what factors are taken into consideration when determining the pricing?
3. Do you think that sport marketers should strive to balance the need to generate revenue with ensuring accessibility for fans from different income brackets?
4. How can sport marketers ensure transparency and fairness in the pricing process for fans and customers?
5. What role do advanced analytics and data play in determining dynamic pricing for sporting events?

Perceived Value

The level of demand and supply, and the price elasticity of a sport product are not the only variables that influence how sensitive consumers are to changes in price. Consumer sensitivity to price change is also affected by the perceived value of the product. If consumers believe that a sport product has substantial benefits, or provides them with social status, then they may be willing to pay a price that is higher than the market average. Furthermore, if sport marketers can increase the perceived value of a sport product, then consumers may be willing to pay more for it, and the sport organisation may receive more revenue. Equally, some consumers will be willing to go without some product benefits in exchange for a cheaper price. For example, consumers may be willing to buy a T-shirt without a fashionable logo for the benefit of paying less. This means that the T-shirt producer can spend less money on marketing their logo, and sell the product for less.

Chapter tool 7.2 Price sensitivity analysis: Price sensitivity refers to how sensitive consumers are to changes in the price of a product. Consumers are considered price sensitive if they do not buy a product when the price is high, or if they buy more of a product when the price is low. The more sensitive consumers are, the more they will change their buying habits when the price changes. The process involves:

- examining how much of the same or a similar product is supplied and demanded at each price level. This may provide a guide in order to determine a realistic price that consumers are willing to pay. This is an assessment of supply and demand;
- considering how many product substitutes exist in the market. The more product substitutes, the more sensitive consumers will be to higher prices. This is an assessment of price elasticity;
- determining whether there are any product complements. It can be revealing to discover that sales of complementary products change corresponding to price changes of a sport product. This is an assessment of the price elasticity of the product;
- assessing the degree of perceived product value held by consumers. This is undertaken through market research.

CASE 7.4

HoverGlide

The HoverGlide backpack by Lightning Packs LLC presents an unusual pricing case in the marketing of a recreational product. The product itself is uniquely positioned as the first so-called zero gravity backpack featuring a novel suspension system that allows the pack to move on the wearer's back in a way that designers, Lightning Packs, claim feels like it is floating, thereby reducing impact and strain especially for runners and hikers. Perhaps even more interesting than the unique product attribute is the way that the backpack was priced, which came about through a crowdfunding campaign. Using the online crowdfunding platform Kickstarter, the HoverGlide backpack was offered at a discount when preordered to raise capital for the product's development and manufacture. The Kickstarter campaign successfully raised US$200,000, allowing the company to produce enough of the backpacks to sell through its website to the general public. While the Kickstarter backers secured their backpacks at a discount when making a pledge, the price of the HoverGlide has softened, although at more than US$300 it remains significantly higher than most competitors signalling a premium pricing strategy. Periodic sales promotions through the company's website and social media platforms offer the product at a modest discount too.

HoverGlide proved that crowdfunding need not only be for low-cost products within a sector but can also be effectively used to stimulate interest and capital towards premium priced, high quality, and novel market entrants. The approach seems to have created a sense that the backpack has distinguishing features unavailable in competitors' offerings.

QUESTIONS

What issues should a company consider when determining their pricing strategy when crowdfunding? Following are some examples to build upon, although you should also add several of your own:

1. **Funding goal:** Determine the minimum amount of funding needed to bring the product to market and set an appropriate funding goal that reflects this amount.
2. **Cost of production:** Calculate the cost of producing the product, including manufacturing, packaging, shipping, and any other associated costs.
3. **Markup:** Determine an appropriate markup that reflects the value of the product and the profit margin desired.
4. **Competitive pricing:** Research similar products on the market and set prices that are competitive, but also reflect the unique value proposition of your product.
5. **Backer rewards:** Create rewards for backers at different contribution levels and set prices that are reasonable and provide good value for the reward offered.
6. **Early-bird pricing:** Consider offering early-bird pricing for backers who contribute during the first few days of the campaign to incentivise early support.
7. **Shipping costs:** Consider shipping costs when setting prices for the product and rewards, and factor in any potential international shipping fees.
8. **Limited-time offers:** Consider offering limited-time discounts or promotions to incentivise backers to contribute at specific times during the campaign.
9. **Profit margin:** Consider the desired profit margin for the company and ensure that the pricing strategy supports this goal while still providing good value to backers.

Break-even analysis

The third step of the pricing process requires a break-even analysis to be conducted. Break-even analysis is used to determine how many product sales are needed in order to ensure that revenue is equal to the costs of producing the product. When a product reaches break-even point, its revenue is equal to its costs; there is no extra money left over (this would be a profit), and costs are not greater than revenue (this would be a loss).

The costs of delivering a product are usually divided into fixed costs and variable costs. Fixed costs are the expenses an organisation incurs in producing and delivering a product that will not change, no matter how much of the product is sold. For example, the cost of rent, equipment, and insurance are often constant for a sport organisation, no matter how many products are made or services delivered.

Variable costs are the expenses that change (either up or down) depending on how much of the product or service is made or delivered. For example, the cost of fabric for a sport apparel producer would increase if it had to buy more fabric to make additional T-shirts. Another example is the cost of staff in a service business; more staff are needed to deliver more services, which in turn costs the sport organisation more. Usually, an organisation will calculate how much it spends on variable costs per unit. For example, a sport shoe company might calculate that for every pair of shoes they make (one unit each), they spend $15 on variable costs (such as leather and shoelaces). Similar calculations can be performed as extra participants are added to sport events.

To calculate a break-even point, the following formula can be used:

$$\text{Break-even point} = \frac{\text{Total fixed costs}}{\text{Price per unit} - \text{variable costs per unit}}$$

For example, imagine the situation of a company that produces collectible sport cards. Its fixed costs (such as factory rental, printing equipment, and insurance) equal $450,000. The variable cost for each packet of cards (such as paper, ink, and packaging) is $1.50. It sells each packet for $10.00.

Step 1: Put the amounts for total fixed costs, price per unit and variable costs per unit into the formula.

$$\text{Break-even point} = \frac{450{,}000}{\$10 - \$1.50 \text{ per unit}}$$

Step 2: Take the variable costs per unit away from the price per unit ($10.00 minus $1.50 equals $8.50). This is called the contribution margin.

$$\text{Break-even point} = \frac{450{,}000}{\$8.50 \text{ per unit}}$$

Step 3: Divide the total costs by the figure on the bottom (remember, the figure on the bottom is the price per unit minus the variable costs per unit).

$$\text{Break-even point} = \frac{450{,}000}{\$8.50 \text{ per unit}}$$

Step 4: The outcome represents the number of units needed to break even.

Break-even point 52941 units

The company in the example needs to sell 52,941 packets of collector cards in order to break even. Determining the break-even point is advantageous in setting a price for a product because it means that the financial implications of various alternative pricing strategies can be explored. When these are considered in light of other factors that influence pricing, then a final price can be set.

> *Chapter tool 7.3 Break-even analysis*: A *break-even analysis* calculates the quantity of sales needed to ensure that revenue earned is equal to the costs of producing the product or service. At *break-even*, revenue is equal to costs. The costs of producing a product are divided into *fixed* costs and *variable* costs. Fixed costs are the expenses an organisation has that do not change no matter how much they sell of their product. Variable costs are the expenses that change (either up or down) depending on how much of the product is made. Break even: Total fixed costs/Price per unit less variable costs per unit.

Pricing variables

Armed with an appreciation of a price point required in order to break even, the next stage is to consider any other variables that could affect the price set. These other factors include the pricing strategies of competitors, any legal or technical boundaries that may be relevant to the pricing of the product, and the impact of choices associated with other marketing mix variables.

Competitor Pricing

The price that competitors charge for the same or similar products will offer an insight into consumer expectations. When considering the pricing approach of competitors, it is important to keep positioning and quality in mind. For example, some competitors will offer a product or service at the upper end of the quality scale, and will position the product with supportive marketing accordingly. It is helpful to determine which competitors' pricing strategies are most successful. In some cases, competitors' pricing levels will be unsustainable to match, and an alternative positioning approach will be essential in order to compete with a higher price.

Legal and Technical Boundaries

A pricing boundary is an encumbrance that restricts or limits the price that can be set. One prominent boundary placed upon pricing comes in the form of laws or regulations established by government or governing sport bodies that restrict or modulate the prices that can be set. For example, clubs in a sport league may be told by the league what prices they can charge for tickets. Alternatively, a local council may control the range of fees that a club passes on to its customers for using council facilities (such as a council-owned gymnasium or tennis court). In addition, in most countries there are laws that affect the way price can be structured. For example, price fixing (agreeing with competitors to each charge the same price) is illegal in many industries, although as noted in Chapter 2, many sport leagues are allowed to collude on prices. There are frequently laws preventing prices being set so low that they drive competitors out of business. This practice is known as predatory pricing. Further boundaries can be technical in nature, such as production methods, which limit supply, and environmental sustainability, which adds to costs.

Marketing Mix

All of the marketing mix variables should reflect the positioning strategy a sport brand selects. As a result, it is important to consider how the other marketing mix variables influence price setting. The approaches chosen with the other variables (product, promotion, place, sponsorship, and services) will influence the choice of the best pricing strategy. For example, the way that a product is distributed to consumers may affect the price that they are willing to pay. If a product is convenient to buy, consumers may be willing to pay a little more than normal for it. This is why food, beverages, and merchandise always cost more at a sporting venue than they do in other outlets. Also, sport services can be priced higher if a tangible product, such as a junior football programme, comes with a backpack, stickers, and a football. Finally, if a product is positioned at the top end of the market, it is advantageous to bolster the brand with a prominent sponsorship.

> *Chapter tool 7.4 Assess pricing variables*: Several environmental factors can influence the price set for a product, including the pricing strategies of competitors, any legal or technical boundaries, and the impact of the other marketing mix variables in the marketing plan.

CASE 7.5

Pay What You Can Pricing

FC United of Manchester is a football club established in 2005 by disaffected Manchester United supporters who were unhappy with the direction of their club and wanted to create a new club where fan involvement and community engagement were paramount. As part of their inaugural season launch, the club offered a 'pay what you want' ticket pricing strategy to its home matches to promote inclusivity, and place community values front and centre. The club's first home match attracted more than 3,000 fans, which was a record for attendance at a ninth-tier English football match. Although the pricing strategy was not financially viable, it remains in use for some home matches and has become a hallmark of the club's community-driven identity.

Similarly, Club Atlético Huracán, based in Buenos Aires, Argentina, is a South American football club that introduced a ticket pricing system allowing their fans to pay whatever they can afford to attend home matches. According to the club, the pricing approach is known as 'Fiel al Fortín', meaning 'Faithful to the Fort', the Fort being the nickname of the Huracán's stadium. It too was successful but temporary. Another example is the German club FC St. Pauli, which implemented a sliding scale pricing system for its tickets. Fans choose from a range of prices for their tickets, depending on their financial situation, and where the lowest price is set to make matches accessible to low-income fans, while those who can afford it are encouraged to pay more. This pricing system has been in place since the 2015–2016 season. English club Lewes FC did something similar with its 'pay what you can' ticket pricing system for both men's and women's matches. The club suggested a minimum price and encouraged those with greater means to pay above it.

Other variants can be found elsewhere like the US National Basketball League team, the Philadelphia 76ers, which uses a pricing system allowing fans to bid what they can afford for some single-game tickets. Fans can choose to pay the full price, or they can make an offer for a lower price. The team then reviews these offers and either accepts or declines them. Also in the United States, the Major League Soccer team, the Seattle Sounders, implemented what they called a community pricing system. Under this model, the team maintains a base price for its tickets, but its fans can choose to pay more if they want to support the community outreach programmes.

QUESTIONS

What questions should a club or team's sport marketers consider before introducing a 'pay what you can' ticket pricing strategy? Following are some examples. Based on these, come up with another two questions to consider.

1. Can the team afford to offer a pay-what-you-can pricing model? This pricing model may not be suitable for all teams, as it could result in lower revenues and potentially impact the team's financial viability.
2. Will this pricing model attract the desired audience? It is important to consider whether a pay-what-you-can pricing model will attract the target audience, or if it may attract individuals who are not interested in the team or the sport.
3. How will the team handle the logistics of a pay-what-you-can pricing model? This includes determining how to collect payments, how to monitor and regulate pricing, and how to ensure that the model is fair and transparent.
4. How will the team communicate the pay-what-you-can pricing model to fans and potential customers? It is important to effectively communicate the pricing model to ensure that it is understood and embraced by fans and customers.
5. What impact will the pay-what-you-can pricing model have on the team's brand and reputation? It is important to consider how this pricing model could impact the team's reputation and brand, and whether it aligns with the team's overall values and objectives.
6. How will the team measure the success of the pay-what-you-can pricing model? It is important to determine how the team will measure the success of the pricing model, whether it is through increased attendance, revenue, or other metrics.

Pricing tactics

The fifth step in setting a price is to select a pricing tactic. The pricing tactic should be directly related to the positioning strategy that is chosen for the product. As a reminder, market positioning refers to how consumers think and feel about a brand or product when they compare it with others. It is the image or perception of a sport brand or product. For example, consumers might perceive a brand or product as luxury and high quality, or as basic and value for money. Consumers might see a brand or product as conservative and reliable or exciting and changeable. Positioning takes into account the fact that consumers will place a brand or product into a position in their minds that is relative to others. The positioning strategy that is chosen will have an influence on the best choice of pricing strategy. For example, if a sport organisation has decided to position one of its products as high quality, it would be appropriate to set a premium price goal. A high price can help to give consumers the idea that the quality of the product is correspondingly high. There are a number of common pricing strategies that sport marketers should consider, which are outlined in the following subsections.

Prestige Pricing

In some situations, the quality or benefits of a product may be more important to consumers than price. The product may be so excellent, fashionable, or even essential that the price is less important. In the sport industry, examples of prestige pricing include exclusive memberships, special events, priority seating, celebrity seating, or special services. Because price is not the most important variable in the decision to purchase a product, prestige pricing involves setting a high price. It must be remembered that by setting a high price, a product appears to be exclusive and of high quality. Sometimes it can be effective to produce only a limited number of goods or provide a limited service in order to enhance the image of a product or service. For example, a gymnasium may decide to offer only premium-priced memberships, and give consumers higher quality service, state-of-the-art equipment and less crowding than competitors. One of the drawbacks of prestige pricing is that it will only appeal to a relatively small number of consumers. The power of prestige pricing is that it confers a psychological benefit by encouraging consumers to believe they are special because they have access to such an exclusive product. This is why a variation of prestige pricing is called psychological pricing, which emphasises the intangible quality of a special product.

Status Quo Pricing

Maintaining the status quo means keeping things the way they are. Status quo pricing aims to either keep prices at the same level or to meet competitors' prices. One advantage of this strategy is that it does not require much planning. It can be a useful approach against a competitor that is an established price leader. However, it is also worth noting that offering a lower price (and therefore better value) and a higher price (for a better product) are two ways of setting a product apart from competitors.

Price Skimming

Price skimming involves setting the highest price possible that consumers will pay for a new product. This can help an organisation to quickly cover the costs of product development and promotion. Price skimming will not work in all situations or for all products. It is best used when new equipment or technology is introduced, such as a brand-new golf club or a new exclusive service. Because price skimming is likely to reduce the total number of consumers who buy the product, it is not suitable for all products. Some sport products need a large volume of consumers in order to be successful (like ticket sales to a sport event). However, there are examples in sport where demand is so high for a prestige event that price skimming can be combined profitably with high volume. Good examples are the finals of major sport competitions and hallmark events, such as the Olympic Games opening and closing ceremonies.

Penetration Pricing

Penetration pricing is the opposite of price skimming because it involves setting a low introductory price for the product in the hopes of encouraging people to give it a first try. The word penetration is used to mean entry or access to the market. Penetration pricing can be effective in parts of the sport industry where there is a high level of competition, or where consumers already have strong loyalties to products. It is one way of developing some interest in a new product, or trying to increase its market share. After a certain amount of time, penetration pricing is usually replaced with a more standard price that can be realistically maintained. It is hoped that by this time, sufficient numbers of consumers will continue to use the product.

Cost-plus Pricing

The cost-plus pricing method is common in the sport industry. Using this method, the price is set by calculating the costs of the product, then adding a flat fee or a percentage (e.g., cost plus 10 per cent). If this method is selected, it is essential to have accurate information about fixed and variable costs.

Break-even Pricing

A break-even price is one that generates just enough money to cover the costs of the product. This may be a pricing tactic that is useful to non-profit or community sport organisations. It has the advantage of being a simple, consumer-friendly strategy. However, the danger is that consumers will become used to the 'cheap' price, leaving the organisation with little opportunity to change prices in the future, even if costs rise unexpectedly.

Competition Pricing

This means setting prices that copy those of competitors. In a highly competitive market, this may prove a useful strategy. It has the advantage of reducing the possibility of being undercut, but it does require a reactive rather than proactive approach. As such, it is best employed selectively.

Market Demand Pricing

Market demand pricing involves setting a price according to the level consumers are willing to pay at a given time. It has the potential of generating high profits for a sport organisation, but it may need to be changed over time because the price consumers are willing to pay changes. It is possible that consumers could feel exploited if they believe they are being charged high prices just because they will pay them. It may also leave an organisation vulnerable to the penetration pricing of competitors.

Discount Pricing

Discounting involves reducing or cutting a price in special situations. In the sport industry, discounts may be offered for long-term memberships, group or family concessions, frequent use or bulk purchases. It is used as a way of encouraging consumers to buy more than they otherwise would. Discount pricing can increase overall sales, and by selling more, an organisation can still earn a good profit even though the price per product is reduced. Of course, discounts can only be used occasionally if they are to be successful. Variations of discount pricing include sales and two-for-one offers.

Seasonal Pricing

Sometimes it is possible to price a product based on changes in demand that occur over a time period. In competitive sport, leagues often charge different prices at different times in the playing season; they may have different prices for off-season, preseason, regular season, and finals. This is one way that sport leagues can stimulate sales when they are not in the main playing season. Seasonal pricing can cause difficulty if the price needs to be set below cost to stimulate demand.

Off-peak Pricing

Like seasonal pricing, off-peak pricing involves setting different prices for different periods. Where seasonal pricing takes advantage of changes over the course of a year, off-peak pricing focuses on changes over the course of one day. Off-peak pricing is commonly employed in sport services where demand is centred on a particular period. For example, gymnasiums and leisure centres often provide discounted memberships for consumers prepared to use the facilities at low-demand times. One of the problems with this kind of pricing is that it can be difficult to control and manage.

Price Bundling

A more sophisticated but common pricing tactic is known as bundling, where numerous product benefits are included in one price. Bundling has been popularised through television advertising promising 'steak knives' and other extras when a product is ordered. In a sport context, bundling may include free merchandise with a product purchase, such as a sports watch with a sporting magazine subscription. Bundling is most common in memberships where consumers are offered a range of services and products in one package, such as access to a pool, social club, gymnasium, spa, and sauna for one price in a health club. Bundling is effective because it gives consumers the experience of receiving something extra for nothing. For sport marketers, bundling is popular because the extras offered are rarely expensive to include.

Discriminatory Pricing

Sometimes known as differential pricing, discriminatory pricing involves making changes to prices according to the category or segment of consumer to whom it is offered. As a result, this tactic is particularly useful for sport organisations that deal with a range of target segments. For example, a sport organisation might offer a less expensive membership to students, pensioners, or the unemployed even though the service and benefits are the same.

Exchange Pricing

Exchange pricing is a form of reciprocal trade where exchanges are made, such as corporate boxes, signage, tickets to events, and access to players and athletes, for 'everyday' items, including furniture and paper, as well as other necessities such as travel, accommodation, and advertising. This is a useful tactic for sport organisations because exchange pricing is effectively bartering, allowing asset-rich, cash-poor sporting organisations to 'save' their liquid finances. It is worth noting that in most countries, while legal, exchange pricing does incur tax.

Rocket and Feather Pricing

Rocket and feather pricing is the term given to pricing when the cost of the product increases quickly leading to a sudden and sharp increase in the price, but falls back down very slowly even when the initial cost impetus has gone. In some cases, the cost increase might be due to rises in production costs, such as from acute rises in labour, raw material, or energy costs in the manufacturing of sporting equipment or apparel. Similarly, costs can go up for sport-related services like pay-per-view or a gym membership. In sport, rocket and feather pricing can accompany sudden and significant surges in demand for a team or event, like when a previously underperforming team gets on a winning streak, leading to radical increases in ticket prices. Under the rocket and feather model, the ticket prices go up swiftly but return to the previous levels slowly even well after the team is no longer performing well. Naturally, when a team is winning games, demand for tickets increases, and ticket prices go up. This is because fans are willing to pay a premium to see a winning team play, and the team and the venue want to capitalise on this increased demand by charging higher prices for tickets. Conversely, when a team is performing poorly, demand for tickets falls, but prices fall slowly, as the team and the venue are hesitant to lower prices too quickly and risk undervaluing their product. The same phenomenon occurs with the price of sporting merchandise too, not to mention in-venue food and beverages. A word of caution is warranted in the intentional use of rocket and feather pricing, as it has the potential to introduce ethical concerns such as price discrimination, where some fans are excluded because they can no longer afford to buy tickets or other products that have suddenly become much more expensive. The approach might also be seen by regular fans as a form of price gouging and lead to resentment and dissatisfaction.

Table 7.1 provides a summary of pricing tactics.

> *Chapter tool 7.5 Select pricing tactics*: A pricing strategy should be related to the positioning strategy that an organisation selects for its product. There are at least 15 types of pricing strategies that sport organisations might employ: prestige pricing, status quo pricing, price skimming, penetration pricing, cost-plus pricing, break-even pricing, competition pricing, market demand pricing, discount pricing, seasonal pricing, off-peak pricing, price bundling, discriminatory pricing, exchange pricing, and rocket and feather pricing.

TABLE 7.1 Summary of pricing tactics

Tactic	*Summary*
1 Prestige (psychological)	Setting a high price for a product that has a high perceived value. Pricing where quality is more important than price because of 'special' circumstances.
2 Status quo	Keeping the price the way it is, or following competitors' prices.
3 Skimming	Setting the highest price possible that consumers will pay.
4 Penetration	Setting a low, introductory price for a product. The opposite of skimming is to introduce the product at such a low price that it will attract a large market share.
5 Cost plus	Pricing calculated by adding the costs of delivering the product, then adding a flat fee or percentage (e.g., cost + 10 per cent).
6 Break even	Pricing products at 'cost'.
7 Competition	Pricing copies competitors.
8 Market demand	Setting pricing according to market demand at the time, taking into account elasticity and growth/shrinkage rates.
9 Discount	Decreasing the price of a service or a product in special circumstances.
10 Seasonal	Pricing according to seasonal demand. Useful for extra stock or downturns due to the season (e.g., winter competitions).
11 Off-peak	Pricing according to daily demand. Useful for maintaining turnover during normally lower daily usage times.
12 Bundling	Offering additional products, services, or benefits at the same price.
13 Discriminatory	Prices change according to categories of customers (differential).
14 Exchange	Reciprocal trade where exchanges are made.
15 Rocket and feather	Prices rise fast but fall slow.

CASE 7.6

YouTube

YouTube is the most popular online video-sharing platform having popularised the activity by providing users with an immense library of video content, including a significant volume of sport-related material. In fact, as the platform has exploded in scope and impact, it has delivered a source of revenue for sport organisations, media, commentators, and broadcasters to monetise their content. YouTube uses several pricing strategies for its sport content where they are influenced by factors such as audience size, exclusivity, and sponsorship deals.

One pivotal pricing model relevant to sport content is revenue sharing. Since revenue accompanies advertising, and advertisers seek out high demand content, sport is particularly well suited to not only high viewership, but also regular repeat viewership as the content turns over so regularly. Sport content owners posting to YouTube can therefore share their advertising revenues with the platform. A watershed arrangement in 2012 saw the International Olympic Committee partnering with YouTube to live stream parts of the London Games based on an advertising revenue splitting deal. It is now commonplace for sport content providers to seek a global audience through such an arrangement.

A second common pricing model offered by YouTube is its subscription-based access fees where users pay a set fee to access premium content offered by a sport organisation. The fee might be ongoing where the content is continually updated, or it might be paid on a pay-per-view basis specifically for a single event or game. In sport more broadly, this type of pricing model has become common for boxing and for the Ultimate Fighting Championship, the latter using a subscription service giving users access to frequent events, exclusive content, and even past fights. For sport, the opportunity to monetise content from past games and events has proven to be an enormous new revenue source.

A third pricing approach relevant to sport employs sponsorship deals where sponsors provide branded content and advertising during live sport broadcasts. This triumvirate arrangement combines the unique and usually live sporting content with sponsor branded content, and the platform's immense reach. In effect the model switches paid advertising for customised sponsor's communications.

QUESTIONS

Undertake some online investigation to answer the following:

1. How does YouTube determine the pricing for sport content on its platform?
2. Does YouTube offer different pricing models for different types of sport content, such as live events versus highlights?
3. Does YouTube ensure that its pricing for sport content is competitive with other platforms offering similar content?
4. How does YouTube work with sport leagues and organisations to determine pricing for their content?
5. What steps does YouTube take to ensure that pricing for sport content is transparent and fair to both consumers and content providers?
6. How might YouTube develop its pricing models for sport content in the future, given the changing landscape of the media industry?

Price point

The final step of the pricing process is to set the final price point for each product. A price point is a deliberately selected level of price that reflects the positioning approach underpinning the product's marketing strategy. In general, it is advisable to select a final price point that makes positioning as clear as possible. For example, if the positioning strategy calls for differentiation from a competitor's product, then it is critical to set a price that is distinctly different from that of competitors. If one were to study the price points of most major sport products, it would become clear that pricing tends to operate at different levels. An obvious example is that it is easy to find tennis racquets and cricket bats at around $150, $250, and $400 for each of the dominant brands. Consumers will tend to select between products that cost approximately the same. This is not the end of the work, however, as pricing strategies need to be reviewed and their success evaluated. Like all stages of the Sport Marketing Framework, pricing requires research and should be managed and controlled over time.

> *Chapter tool 7.6 Select price point*: A price point is a deliberately selected level of price that reflects the positioning approach underpinning the product's marketing strategy.

CASE 7.7

New Technologies

New technologies such as AI, social media, wearables, and apps are exerting a significant impact on sport pricing. Although dynamic pricing is already commonly used to manipulate ticket prices based on real-time market demand, the use of AI can enable far more sophisticated analyses of data and customer behaviour patterns, including making accurate predictions about forthcoming behaviour. For example, AI algorithms can analyse data on weather patterns, player injuries, and social media sentiment to help teams and event organisers set optimal ticket prices.

Social media sentiment offers tremendous insight into the preferences and opinions of fans and consumers, which can be directed towards offering personalised pricing strategies associated with customised product bundles. In fact, social media has transformed sport pricing strategies by enabling teams and leagues to monitor real-time data, market directly to fans, offer more personalised experiences, and reach previously inaccessible global audiences. Added to these insights are data collected from wearable technologies like fitness trackers and smartwatches. One interesting example can be found in the insurance industry where companies provide discounts to prospective consumers prepared to use health monitoring devices. The same data can be employed by sport enterprises to assess the physical impacts of their products, whether in the form of an exciting match or a new surfboard. Virtual and augmented reality technologies can affect pricing too. As these interfaces give fans new ways of experiencing sport, both real and virtual, new pricing models are being conceived to go along with it. For example, attending a match via a virtual headset might seem quite real but still be priced lower than attending at the venue.

Another key transition in sport pricing has accompanied the common use of 'apps' for sport-related and recreational products, from gamified fitness apps for health to in-venue apps to help patrons find food or merchandise. There are at least five standard pricing models used for apps, the first being 'free', where the app is available at no cost to download and the content owner seeks to generate interest in another product like a team or event, advertising revenue, or by capturing and on-selling users' data. Most big leagues use free apps as do media and broadcasters like ESPN. The second pricing model is called 'freemium' where a basic set of features come for free but premium features and content requires payment. This is a typical model used by fitness apps and games. A third pricing model is 'paid'. Users must pay an upfront fee to access the app and its content, and is mostly associated with more sophisticated apps that provide high value content that comes as a full software package like games or a diet app. The fourth model is 'subscription' requiring users to pay an upfront, recurring fee to access content like a sport streaming app. Fifth, in-app purchases allow users to buy specific and virtual products or services as they are needed, usually to access different or new levels of content like pay-per-view events or new release levels in an esport game.

QUESTIONS

Choose a sport-related app and reflect on how it should have determined its pricing model considering the following prompts:

1. **Value proposition:** Consider the unique features and benefits of the app in comparison to other competing apps and products in the market. Determine the value that the app provides to users and how that should be reflected in its price.
2. **Target audience:** Consider the demographics and purchasing power of the target audience. Determine whether the app is priced affordably for most of the target audience while still generating sufficient revenue to cover costs and achieve profitability.
3. **Competition:** Conduct a competitive analysis of similar apps and products in the market. Determine how the app's pricing compares with the competition and whether it is competitive or overpriced.
4. **Market demand:** Consider the level of demand for the app in the market. Determine whether the app is priced appropriately to meet the level of demand and whether any adjustments are needed to maximise sales.
5. **Pricing strategy:** What pricing strategy would you have chosen for the app based on its unique value proposition and target market?

Trends in sport pricing

The sport industry is constantly evolving when it comes to pricing strategies. As noted in this chapter, dynamic ticket pricing, subscription-based models, pay-what-you-can pricing, and revenue-sharing models are just a few examples. Accompanying the rise of digital platforms, sport enterprises have shifted from traditional models to digital platforms, which offer new opportunities to reach more fans and generate alternative revenue streams. This has led to new pricing models, such as pay-per-view and subscription-based access to live games or exclusive content. In addition, the accumulation and analysis of huge quantities of user data has enabled sport enterprises to develop an intricate understanding of fan behaviours and predict their likely future preferences. Moreover, pricing models are increasingly designed to enhance fan experiences and encourage loyalty, often incorporating customised offerings and content, sometimes delivering discounts from sponsors and advertisers as well. If there is any general lesson in sport pricing, it is that dynamic models have become essential.

PRINCIPLES SUMMARY

- Chapter principle 7.1: Pricing communicates an important symbolic positioning message to consumers about a sport product.
- Chapter principle 7.2: The value of a sport product is the relationship between its price and the benefits a consumer believes they will receive from it.
- Chapter principle 7.3: The price of a product is the amount of money a consumer must give up in exchange for a good or service. However, price is not the same as value, since value is the difference between price and the anticipated benefit. Although price is usually viewed in monetary terms, it may also include other consumer sacrifices in order to acquire a sport product, such as time or social cost. Additionally, in some instances the value secured from a sport product can be well in excess of its purchase price. This is a good position for a product to be in, since the expectation of getting more value for money will be an incentive to purchase the product.
- Chapter principle 7.4: *Revenue* is the price that consumers pay for a product, multiplied by the number of units sold. *Profit* is revenue minus the costs of producing and selling the product.
- Chapter principle 7.5: The strategic pricing process provides a structure for setting price. The process involves: (1) setting a pricing goal, (2) determining price sensitivity, (3) conducting a break-even analysis, (4) assessing pricing variables, (5) selecting pricing tactics, and (6) setting a price point.

TOOLS SUMMARY

- Chapter tool 7.1 Pricing goals
- Chapter tool 7.2 Price sensitivity analysis
- Chapter tool 7.3 Break-even analysis

- Chapter tool 7.4 Assess pricing variables
- Chapter tool 7.5 Select pricing tactics
- Chapter tool 7.6 Select price point

REVIEW QUESTIONS

1. What effect does pricing have on positioning? Provide an example of how price can influence a consumer's perception of a product.
2. What is the difference between value and price?
3. Outline the steps of the strategic pricing process.
4. Using examples to illustrate, describe some conditions that make sport consumers more price sensitive.
5. Why is price bundling so popular? Why do you think it works for both consumers and sport marketers?
6. Why has dynamic pricing become the standard?
7. Explain what a price point is and why it is so important to think of pricing in levels.

RELEVANT WEBSITES

FC United of Manchester (www.fc-utd.co.uk)
FIFA World Cup (www.fifa.com/fifaplus/en/tournaments/mens/worldcup/canadamexicousa2026)
HoverGlide (www.hoverglidepacks.com)
Peloton (www.onepeloton.com)
YouTube (www.youtube.com)

FURTHER READING

Fullerton, S. (2021). *Sports Marketing*. Chicago: SAGE Publications.
Kingsnorth, S. (2022). *Digital Marketing Strategy: An Integrated Approach to Online Marketing*. London: Kogan Page Publishers.
Parent, M. M., & Ruetsch, A. (2020). *Managing Major Sports Events: Theory and Practice*. Oxford: Routledge.
Phillips, R. L. (2021). *Pricing and Revenue Optimization*. Stanford, CA: Stanford University Press.
Stewart, B. (2014). *Sport Funding and Finance* (2nd ed.). London: Routledge.

CHAPTER 8

Sport distribution

LEARNING OUTCOMES

At the end of this chapter, readers should be able to:

- understand the importance of distribution to successful sport marketing.
- discuss the basic concepts of sport distribution.
- identify the different types of sport distribution channels.
- specify the importance of the sport facility as 'place'.
- explain the main issues in ticket distribution.

OVERVIEW

The purpose of this chapter is to explore the third of the six elements considered fundamental to the sport marketing mix, which is somewhat simplistically referred to as place. The place can be described more accurately as distribution, which focuses on the ways in which products might be best delivered to customers to facilitate the exchange that is material to marketing. This chapter begins by introducing the basic concepts underpinning sport distribution, and then moves on to examine three central issues. They are first, the different types of distribution channels, second, the sport facility as a 'place' for distributing sport products, and finally the ticket distribution process.

INTRODUCTION

Distribution is a crucially important, but often overlooked, part of the marketing mix. However, before proceeding, it is essential to clarify the concept further, since it is often interchanged with the term 'place'. When the term 'place' is employed in marketing, it can have multiple meanings. It might, for example, refer to the location where goods and services are exchanged for the customer's money payment. Attending a dental surgery for

DOI: 10.4324/9781003391319-8

an annual check-up service is a case in point. It can also refer to a method for distributing products along a specific pathway or channel. In this instance, it might refer to the process by which motor vehicle parts are produced, the vehicles are assembled, the vehicles are shipped to dealers, and the vehicles are sold to customers via the dealer's showrooms and sales staff. Similarly, distribution means transporting products from the producers to the final consumers. Either way, the sale takes place and the good or service is delivered in a designated space. In a product marketing context, this space is identified as the 'place'. To avoid any confusion over definitions and nomenclature, for the purposes of this chapter, the words *distribution* and *place* should be considered interchangeable. The concept of distribution/place, and where it fits within the Sport Marketing Framework, is illustrated in Figure 8.1.

THE SPORT DISTRIBUTION PROBLEM

In sport, like any other industry, decisions must be made about how to get products to customers. Sport distribution concerns how and where consumers access sport products in order to use them. There is little use in having a great product available for a value-for-money price if consumers cannot easily acquire it.

There are several quite different ways in which sport products are distributed in the sport industry, largely due to its fragmented structure and the diverse array of products it supplies to various markets. The first point to note is that the sport industry not only produces highly tangible goods, but also produces many highly intangible services. And, it is easy to see that sporting goods are distributed differently to sporting services.

The transportation of sporting goods from producers to consumers can involve several stages. For example, golf equipment – including clubs, balls, bags, and for the wealthy and physically disabled, motorised golf carts – is, in the first instance, made by a range of manufacturers. These manufacturers will not normally sell direct to the final users – the golf players – but will instead distribute their golf equipment to wholesalers, who will store their products in warehouses together with other golf equipment brands. The wholesalers will then forward these different brands to retailers who will display and advertise them with a view to attracting customers. Sales are made in these retail outlets. This series of connections and transactions reflects the conventional way of getting products to customers efficiently. First, it means that manufacturers do not have to bear the cost of warehousing, and second, customers have the convenience of comparing competing golf brands in the same place under the same roof.

In contrast, sport services tend to be distributed through entirely different methods. For example, a professional sporting match could be 'produced' by two competing teams, filmed by a television network, broadcast live to viewers via television or a streaming service, and deposited in modified form on the internet for later consumption. For a spectator watching the game live at the sport venue after purchasing a ticket at an entry point, the stadium itself provides the 'place' where the sport product is both created and distributed. For the person watching on a screen at home, the venue may impact their enjoyment of the match even though it is consumed from their couch and purchased via an online subscription. Both consumers, despite very different distribution experiences, are ostensibly

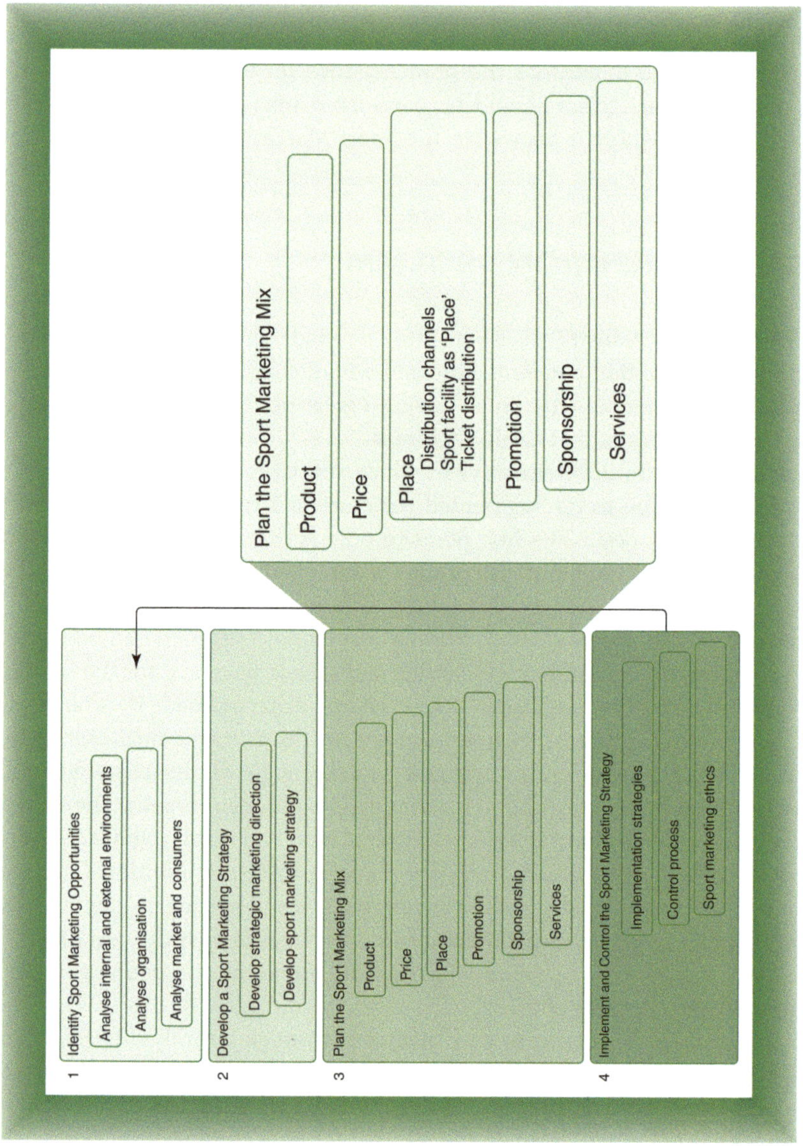

FIGURE 8.1 The sport marketing framework

experiencing the same event, albeit in very different ways. One final example is a sports masseuse running their own business, who produces the service and delivers it directly to the customer; there are no people or organisations in the middle at all.

As can be seen from these simple examples, there are many different means and methods through which sport products are distributed. This chapter will introduce the variety of places pivotal to the distribution of sport products. First, some of the important concepts used in distribution will be introduced, at the core of which is the notion of a distribution channel. Second, the centrality of the sport facility or venue as a place where consumers buy and experience sport products will be considered, followed finally by a review of sport ticket distribution.

DISTRIBUTION CHANNELS

As noted earlier, sporting goods or products can undergo numerous steps in their distribution from the producer to the sport consumer. Take, for instance, the case of basketballs. To begin with, there is the manufacturer who physically makes the ball, but who usually does not sell it directly to the public. Often manufacturers sell their goods to a wholesaler, who in turn sells it to a retailer. Finally, the retailer who may be operating out of a store in a shopping mall, or via an online site, sells the balls to sport consumers. In some instances, the consumer will physically collect the ball from the store, in other cases it will be sent to them, involving further steps in the distribution process involving couriers or postal agents. In other words, there is a chain of businesses that are involved in getting the basketball to the consumer; it gets passed from one to the next down a path or a channel.

The sequence described is all well and good, but what if the sport product comes in the form of a professional basketball game on a streaming service, and what if a sport consumer watches in a bar with friends on the other side of the world? There is no 'manufacturer' or 'retailer' in the same way as there is for basketballs. Rather, two competing teams produce the product. They sell this product (via the league they compete in) to a broadcaster, who may then on-sell the digital distribution rights to a streaming platform which puts the contest online in parts of the world the original broadcaster may not service. In this example, the bar accesses the streaming services and shows it to the consumers present. This is another example of a distribution channel because the product has been moved from the producer of the product (the two professional basketball teams) to the consumers of the product (the people watching the game) via various intermediaries.

When considering the two examples of distribution channels just described, it is obvious that they both involve the circulation of a product from the producer to the consumer through a sequence of operational steps. This sequence of operational steps is known as a distribution channel.

> *Chapter principle 8.1*: A sport distribution channel is an organised series of organisations, suppliers and individuals that move products from the producer to the final consumer.

Distribution systems

Two different kinds of sport distribution channels have been used as examples. They both described the movement of products from producers to consumers, but they do it in different ways, or with different *sport distribution systems*. A distribution *system* is the way that a distribution channel is organised or arranged. There are different ways of structuring distribution, explained in the following sub-sections.

Types of distribution channels

Distribution channels have different lengths, and consequently they may be characterised as *direct* or *indirect*. A direct distribution channel is short where the producer sells the product directly to the consumer. For example, a sports physiotherapist produces the service and sells it directly to the consumer. Direct distribution also occurs when a sporting good producer sells products on the internet, or by direct marketing services such as telemarketing or social media. Many manufacturers of sport products do this in addition to the use of normal retail stores. For example, many popular sport watches used to keep track of fitness activities can be purchased online direct from the company that makes them as well as via a range of suppliers, including major sport shops and general retailers. The process is illustrated in Figure 8.2.

An indirect distribution channel is longer than the direct approach because there are organisations or people involved along the way. Those in the middle are usually called *intermediaries*, because they mediate between producers and consumers. In theory, each of these intermediaries should be adding some value to the process and thus the price of a product grows as it flows through the channel and value is accrued. When it comes to sporting goods, wholesalers and/or retailers are added into the channel. The following

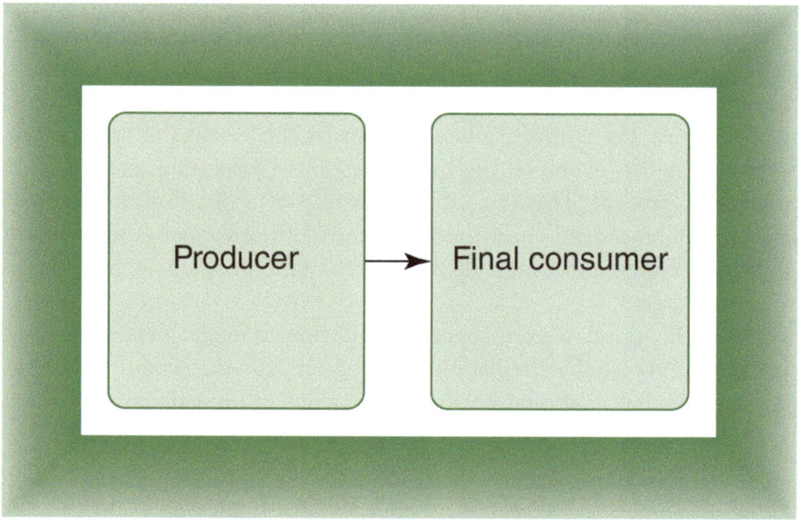

FIGURE 8.2 Direct distribution channel

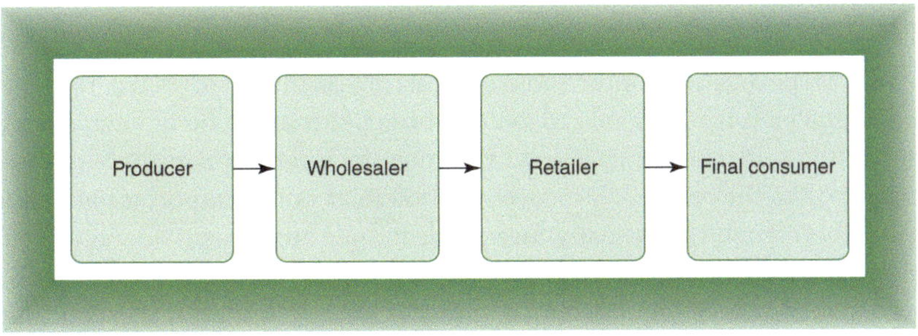

FIGURE 8.3 Indirect distribution channel A

diagrams show two different kinds of indirect distribution channels. Figure 8.3 shows both a retailer and a wholesaler in the channel, while Figure 8.4 excludes the wholesaler step. It is important to keep in mind that even intangible sport services may move through a series of intermediaries like ticketing agencies who handle the sale of tickets in order to maximise supply and demand issues for major events.

> *Chapter principle 8.2*: There are both direct and indirect distribution channels that vary in length. A direct distribution channel is short where the producer sells the product directly to the consumer. An indirect distribution channel is a longer channel where there are a number of intermediaries involved along the way. Each intermediary normally adds some form of value to the distribution process, with the ultimate goal being to connect the final good or service to a consumer.

Channel members

A channel member is any organisation or individual involved as part of a distribution channel. When it comes to sporting goods, in addition to the producers (manufacturers), the most common channel members are wholesalers and retailers.

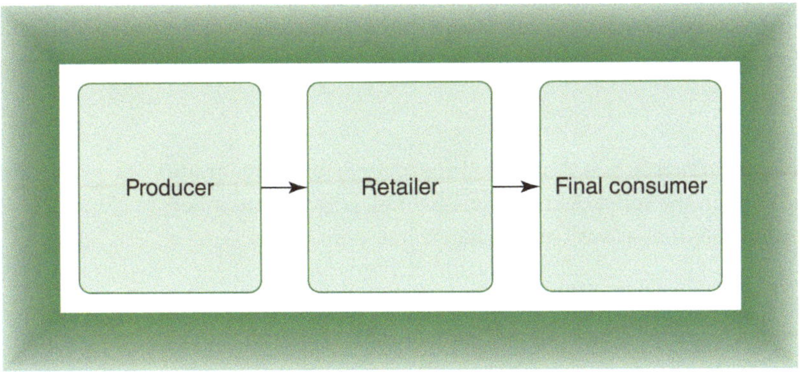

FIGURE 8.4 Indirect distribution channel B

Wholesalers

A wholesaler is an organisation or individual acting as the middle step between a producer and a retailer. It is reasonable to ask what the point might be of having a wholesaler in the distribution channel. Why would the manufacturer not simply pass the sporting goods straight on to the retailer? However, a wholesaler can be important in helping other channel members. First, they usually buy goods in bulk from the manufacturer and then store them. When the retailer is ready to order some goods, the wholesaler transports the sporting goods to them. A wholesaler can also stock a large range of goods from a variety of different manufacturers. As a result, instead of having to contact all of these producers, the retailer only must talk to the one wholesaler to gain access to a range of different sporting goods.

Of course, wholesalers are not always involved in a distribution channel. If a retailer does not want to use a wholesaler (e.g., they may not want to pay extra for the product), then they have to undertake for themselves all the tasks performed by the wholesaler. They may have to store and transport the sporting goods and may have to keep in contact with a diverse number of producers.

Retailers

Retailers are the organisations and individuals involved in the final sale of a sporting good or service to a consumer. There are many kinds of retailers, and choosing the right retail outlet can be an important decision for a sport marketer as retailers are a brand in themselves, much like the brands of products they stock and sell. Any incongruity between brands in these situations – for example, an expensive up-market brand in a low-cost discount retailer – will confuse consumers. Most importantly, the retail outlet that is selected should be convenient for consumers and suitable for the kind of products being sold. For example, it might seem convenient to be able to buy a tennis racquet from the corner store, but a specialised retail sports outlet would be more appropriate for the range and advice required to make a fitting selection.

There are several different kinds of retail outlets. To begin with, there are physical locations housed in buildings such as department stores and shopping centres. These retailers are sometimes called 'bricks and mortar' retailers. There are also 'virtual' stores such as internet sites, television home shopping, and mail order catalogues. These retailers can be called virtual retailers. Some examples of both are provided in Table 8.1.

> *Chapter principle* 8.3: A channel member is any organisation or individual that is involved in the sport distribution channel. Channel members may include wholesalers and retailers, as well as producers and consumers.

Distribution issues for sport products

Table 8.2 highlights the main distribution issues that different sport products, such as sporting goods, sport-consulting services, and facility-dependent sport services,

TABLE 8.1 Types of sport retailers

Bricks and mortar retailers	*Virtual retailers*
Supermarkets	Television shopping channels
Shopping centres	Mail order catalogues
Speciality sporting shops	Special merchandise during televised sport
Sport clubs	Internet sites and downloads
Recreation and leisure centres	Infomercials
Gymnasiums	Mobile or cellular phone offers, including 'apps'
Factory direct outlets	
Sport stadiums and venues	

are faced with. Sport-consulting services include market researchers, sport management consultants, and even sport psychology experts. Facility-dependent sport services are those that need a sport facility to run, like a community netball competition, a recreation centre, or a professional league. Table 8.2 shows that sport products can have different distribution channel lengths, different kinds of distribution locations,

TABLE 8.2 Distribution issues for sporting products

Distribution variables	*Sporting goods*	*Sport-consulting services*	*Facility-dependent sport services*
Length of distribution channel	Long, often many channel members	Short, often just the producer (service provider) and consumer	Short, often just the producer (service provider) and consumer
Location of distribution	Many locations (potentially unlimited)	Many locations (potentially unlimited)	The sport facility
How customer accesses distribution	Consumer goes to distribution point	Service provider usually goes to consumer	Consumer goes to distribution point
Interaction between producer and customer	Indirect	Direct	Direct
Use of technology	Strong growth	Technology usually used for initial contact (e.g., website and email contact) and research services	Heavy for the sale of tickets

different kinds of consumer interaction, and various levels of dependent technology and consumer access.

Chapter tool 8.1 Distribution issues analysis: Different sport products have different distribution issues to deal with. Sport marketers can employ various distribution channel lengths, kinds of distribution locations, consumer interaction, dependent technology and consumer access. These can be examined against the type of sporting product offered, whether sporting goods, consulting services or facility-dependent sport services.

CASE 8.1

The Changing Face of Retail

The internet has totally transformed the ways in which products are sold and purchased. Sporting goods are no exception. There are now thousands of websites around the world where both new and used sporting goods are put up for sale. However, it is unlikely that online distribution will lead to the demise of speciality sporting goods shops. This is because many sport products need to be customised to fit special needs and satisfy the idiosyncratic requirements of individuals. In many instances, it can never be a case of 'one size fits all'. Two good examples of the critical importance of product–user 'fit' are running shoes and tennis racquets.

In the case of specialist sporting equipment, retailers know that many consumers may still prefer the convenience of online shopping given the ease of ordering, the speed of delivery, and the efforts many online retailers undertake to ensure returns and satisfaction. Most concerning for many retailers is the increasing usage of showrooms to try and test products before consumers turn to the internet to seek the lowest price and end up purchasing online. This has led to retailers responding in several ways.

First, there has been an inevitable acceptance that it is almost impossible to just be a 'bricks and mortar' retailer anymore and that online presence, even for the most established of traditional brands is necessary. By having both an online and storefront presence, sporting goods companies can target multiple audiences and use a variety of strategies to engage a broad range of consumers. Secondly, many sporting goods retailers now have invested heavily in creating instore experiences that cater to the sensory pleasure of striking a golf ball, kicking a penalty with a new pair of soccer boots, or seeing how much topspin a new racquet can generate. For sport participants and fans alike, the allure of a sport store where equipment can be tested cannot be replicated online, allowing the retailer to create an environment that is conducive to foot traffic. Thirdly, in a similar fashion, sporting goods retailers can promote specialist advice in equipment that allows a visitor to feel an extra level of service input that is personalised. Specialist footwear stores do this with an array of treadmills and sensors that can recommend shoes based upon running style, while golf equipment salespeople can analyse a swing and suggest custom fitting of clubs to ensure a balance of hitting distances are available in the golf bag of a player. Overall, the visit to a specialty goods store can now be seen as a sensory feast providing tactile, audio, and visual cues geared towards the emotional and pleasurable aspects of sport.

While sporting goods retailers appear to have a strong future given the nature of purchases, in recent years specialty sport stores have grown in popularity to try and home in further on the personalisation and specific skills that consumers might want. While a general sport goods retailer may try and cover hundreds of sports from archery to zorb football, a specialist store will partake in a depth of knowledge with just one, for example, hockey, cricket, rock climbing, or tennis. When walking into one of these specialist stores, consumers would expect to be dealing with experts who can provide an array of services, from what rubber to use on each side of their table tennis bat, to the advantages and disadvantages of different squash balls. While this specialist advice is often critical to their existence, even these kinds of stores will typically have an online presence to cater for returning customers or for those who prefer to browse online first.

QUESTIONS

1. For giant, multi-national online retail brands such as Amazon, what role, if any, can they play in the distribution of sporting goods and services?
2. Beyond the range of items in stock, detail the key marketing differences between a sporting goods store and a speciality sports shop? Would consumer types vary between these two kinds of retailers?
3. Assuming they had minimal funds for promotion, how would a small speciality store focused on a relatively niche sport such as table tennis go about making sure consumers knew about their services?

SPORT FACILITY AS 'PLACE'

Sporting goods are delivered to consumers in quite conventional ways, and most sales end up occurring in retail stores somewhere along a shopping strip or mall, or arrive on your doorstep after an online purchase. Sport services are something else, since they are both delivered and experienced in a specialist 'sport facility', which in and of itself is a critical component of the distribution of sport and the experience being sought.

A sport facility is a place where sport competitions are delivered as entertainment to sport spectators on one hand, and as an activity to sport participants on the other. Thus, the sport facility is the most important distribution channel for two types of sport products: (1) sport activity services and (2) professional sport events. Sport activity services are those offering participation or a personal service in sport including physical education lessons, coaching, community competitions, health, and rehabilitation consultations, and local or recreational sport practice and events. Professional sport events offer a forum for elite athletes to compete, and entertainment for spectators. They include state, national, or international competitions, covering all sports from football, swimming and motor racing, to gymnastics, surfing and rock-climbing. All these sport activities and events need a sport facility. Without a sport facility, these products cannot be made and there is nothing to market.

Designing a sport facility to fit in with the local area can help to make it an attractive distribution point, which is also useful for media attention. For example, many sport facilities possess a special design element that reflects the character of the city or country. However, marketers often have little control over the design of sport facilities and even less over their composition once built. This part of this chapter therefore focuses on the aspects of the sport place that can be manipulated by facility and event marketers. For sport activity services and professional sport events, the sport facility represents the 'place' dimension of the marketing mix. A fundamental point to remember is that the sport product (the competition or activity) is both produced and consumed at the same location and at the same time. There are a range of sport facility features that a sport marketer must manage, which are considered next.

> *Chapter principle 8.4*: The sport facility is the most important distribution channel for sport activity services and professional sport events.

Features of sport facilities

The features of sport facilities have a powerful influence on a sport consumer's experience of an event. These features include seating, layout, accessibility (how easy it is to get to, and to get around in), the overall 'look' or design of the venue, its cleanliness, and even the technical capabilities of the scoreboard and the other digital screens and assets that might exist, such as stadium Wi-Fi and apps. When consumers perceive that a venue is of high quality, they are more likely to be satisfied and return for a similar experience. The sport facility is most effective as a distribution channel when its features are designed and handled carefully as part of a well-considered marketing plan.

Considerable effort is made to design sport and entertainment facilities that go beyond a simple functional purpose. As sport competes for a share of the entertainment market, the facilities that host sporting events have grown in architectural prominence, multi-purpose usage and redesign, as well as the creature comforts and appeal they can offer to visitors. One example is the 'Sphere' located in Las Vegas that garnered world-wide attention for its incredible lighting and sound systems when opened in 2023. Useful beyond sport, this facility will attract tourists from around the world simply because of its design. Other examples of innovation include Tottenham Hotspur's relatively new stadium in London that allows multiple types of pitches to be deployed and accessed, giving the stadium the ability to transform itself for varying sports, including American football. The SoFi Stadium in California suggests it has re-imagined the fan experience with its indoor–outdoor construction and plays home base to two NFL teams.

Sport stadia and venues that have a good location, an attractive atmosphere, luxury seating, excellent eateries, and other entertainment services such as nightclubs, bars, theatres, and shopping areas attract larger crowds. Consequently, sport marketers are compelled to consider four main areas in which they can maximise the sport consumer experience. These pivotal marketing features of a sport facility are: (1) location and accessibility,

(2) design and layout, (3) facility infrastructure, and (4) customer service. The core characteristics of each feature are provided in Table 8.3 and are discussed in more detail in the following sections of this chapter.

> *Chapter principle* 8.5: Sport marketers must consider four main aspects of sport facilities in which they can maximise the sport consumer experience: (1) location and accessibility, (2) design and layout, (3) facility infrastructure and (4) customer service.

TABLE 8.3 Features and characteristics of sport facilities

Location and accessibility • Attractive location • Convenient to get to • Good signage and directions • Enough parking • Accessible by public transport • Easy to enter and exit facility • Disabled access (ramps, lifts, washroom facilities) • App to guide accessibility points and furnish information
Design and layout • Fits in with local area • Attractive design (size, colour, shape, light, and unique features) • Ambience and atmosphere • Easy to get from one area to another • Good direction signs • Seating arrangements with good viewing • Weather protection • Control of noise levels • Areas for non-drinkers and families • Lighting of playing area • Air circulation • Safety issues (emergency procedures, fire detection, standby power, emergency communication, exits) • Security (surveillance, control room, entrance security) • Spectator control (zones, safe barriers, security, police)
Facility infrastructure • Variety of food and drink outlets, including healthy options • Overall seating quality and comfort • Premium seating available • Corporate boxes and special services • Toilets: number and location for convenient access • Childcare facilities • Concierge services • Scoreboards and personal screens • Message centres and sound systems • Emergency medical services • Retail and merchandise areas • Broadcasting and media requirements • Wi-Fi access and network availability

(Continued)

TABLE 8.3 (Continued)

Customer service
- Queuing and waiting times
- Prominent information stands/booths
- Efficient, friendly, and helpful staff
- Sufficient security and emergency staff
- Entrance staff, ushers
- Services for elderly, disabled, and children
- Enquiry service

CASE 8.2

Tailgating

'Tailgating' is a practice where sport fans gather in large open areas near sport stadiums or venues, and have a party, barbeque, or drinking session usually before, but sometimes after, a big game or event. It is especially popular in North America, although the practice has a rich tradition in Europe and Australia as well, particularly for motor and horse racing enthusiasts.

The term tailgating comes from the rear opening of a vehicle, such as a small truck or SUV, where the rear cargo door (or tailgate) can be swung open to provide easy access to a large compartment area. People open the tailgate, which will contain food and drink supplies, and then socialise around this space. As a result, tailgate parties are most typically undertaken in a sporting venue carpark. Participants often arrive many hours in advance to secure a prime position and unload the food and drink, as well as set up various tents, cooking equipment, paraphernalia, and games to enjoy – with many tailgaters forming communities with those around them as the events unfold across a season. Tailgating certainly adds colour and atmosphere to the build-up of an event and it also helps with traffic management to some extent by ensuring some people arrive very early or stay on later. The tailgate also fosters community spirit, allows fans to extend the sporting experience which may just be for a few hours across the entire day, and bring in audiences who may be more interested in the party rather than the sport.

Tailgating is not for everyone, though. The opportunity to tailgate is constrained by first the space available for car parking or partying, and second the ownership of motor vehicles and equipment that is suitable for tailgating activities. Tailgating is also often problematic for the negative environment it may foster. In some instances, fans overindulge in pregame activities, and as a result there have been mixed feelings about the appropriateness of tailgating given its tendency to encourage excessive alcohol consumption. Some sporting bodies for certain events have banned or curtailed tailgate parties citing safety or security concerns. However, given its popularity, sport marketers have typically found ways of supporting the practice while regulating some of its more anti-social and offensive practices. While tailgating has its critics, it provides a good case study of how sport experiences outside of the venue 'space' can be used as an additional marketing strategy.

QUESTIONS

1 Why would a sport event organiser want to encourage tailgating?
2 Other than the possibility of excessive alcohol consumption, why would a sport event organiser want to discourage tailgating?
3 How could a sport facility reliant mainly on public transport access be reconfigured to make tailgating easier to operate and manage?

Tools for marketing sport facilities

In an ideal sport marketing world, every sport facility would be located in a central location, have quick and easy access to public transport, include the latest design and technology features, provide unimpeded sight lines, have a perfect playing surface, include a retractable roof, have a raft of impeccably appointed dining rooms, provide player-friendly training facilities, contain various safety features, have state of the art surveillance, deliver long-life infrastructure, include the highest quality night-lighting, and have well-trained attendants and security staff, and friendly and efficient catering staff.

There are many constraints on what sport facilities can deliver fans and participants. As a result, sport marketers have limited control over the features, and may be able to do little to enact change because to do so would require substantial expenditure on a venue's infrastructure. While sport marketers are frequently unable to make many changes to a facility's features, they need to be aware of the impact that facility features have on the consumer experience. In some cases, it may be possible to act in one area to compensate for poor features elsewhere that cannot be modified. For example, it may be appropriate to reduce the price of seats with sight line obstructions, and thus minimise the likelihood of receiving additional complaints. Additionally, the lack of easy access to public transport may be alleviated by providing high-speed shuttle bus services to surrounding railway stations.

Smart sport marketers are thus not only aware of the limitations imposed by the location, design, and operation of sport facilities, but also understand that adjustments around the edges are always possible. In the following sections, eight practical marketing tools for managing distribution channels in sport are discussed. Customer service is identified as a crucially important contributor to the quality of the experience but is not discussed in detail here. However, it forms a central part of Chapter 11.

Seating

The most important marketing aspects of seating selection include cost, look, comfort, durability, and ease of maintenance. Their purpose is also relevant, such as whether the seats are to be used for a corporate box or for public access. Some sport facilities include ventilation holes and a full back support to prevent spectators from pushing their feet into the person sitting in front of them. It is also useful in most instances to have seats that can be easily removed, so that damaged seats can be replaced, or new sponsorship logos attached. The most versatile seating options in recent venues are moveable seats that can be relocated in sections to different parts of the venue. This is advantageous because it allows more flexibility in the types of sport that can be played and watched at a venue. Some venues use their seating selection as part of their positioning strategy. For example, most contemporary stadia have employed a material and design that increases the sound of the stomping noise spectators make during games, thereby amplifying the atmosphere for fans. In addition, seats can be used to differentiate the level of consumer spending. Most new venues use some form of personal viewing screen for corporate sections or for special kinds of memberships. From a marketing perspective, this means that there is greater opportunity to enhance consumers' interaction with the sport product, other entertainment options such as gaming, statistics, and alternative camera angles, as well as with all marketing messages. It is worth considering also whether seating is needed at all in some stadium parts. Despite safety concerns with standing areas, there is a tendency to incorporate these in some stadia as it provides a unique environment for fans to congregate and enjoy a traditional experience, much like how many concert venues will include standing areas for fans near the stage.

> *Chapter tool 8.2 Seating*: Seating selection influences sport consumers' experience and can be used to enhance their viewing comfort as well as the marketing messages they are exposed to.

Scoreboards, Screens, and Signage

The scoreboard requirements of a small, recreational basketball venue will obviously be quite different to those demanded by an international multi-purpose stadium, which will need to broadcast video replays and advertisements. However, for all sport facilities, the scoreboard is one of the main spaces to promote sponsors. After all, it is guaranteed that spectators will be looking at the scoreboard at some point. Similarly, even a small facility can use signage to promote sponsors, other events, or even further products that are available. The modern scoreboard is increasingly large and seeks to combat the growth of viewing screens in the home that are also much larger than previous decades and which can feature great clarity in high-resolution. The use of high-definition scoreboards not only brings fans closer to the action, but it also provides an environment that allows them to come earlier and stay longer as other events and different forms of vision and access can be offered. Fans attending a football match for a late afternoon kick-off can arrive early to watch early afternoon games on the screen as part of a group experience. The complexity of managing multiple scoreboards in a large venue now entails a large production team who must ensure that the visual experience of the screen complements what is happening on the field. In many instances, premium seating will, as noted earlier, allow fans to interact directly with portable screens and this display also needs to be coordinated and managed to ensure effective messaging is utilised. A complicating factor to all the above is the propensity for fans to now bring their screens, which are a form of scoreboard, community connection, viewing platform, and navigational device, to the game. While mobile phones are ubiquitous, teams must consider whether tablets and other similar devices are permitted from a safety perspective.

> *Chapter tool 8.3 Scoreboards and signage*: Scoreboards and signage are an essential method of communicating marketing messages irrespective of the size of a venue.

Lighting and Sound System

Strong lighting on a sport field is ideal for both large and modest grounds. In fact, smaller-sized outdoor sport venues can attract larger crowds if they employ flood lighting. For example, local recreational and school sport fields can benefit from installing night-time illumination because they can radically increase participation and crowds by allowing activity after working hours. This approach is extremely successful for outdoor tennis courts and athletics tracks. Lighting is also important in car parking areas for both safety and security. For a limited cost, it is possible for indoor venues to install lighting that will have a significant effect on the atmosphere of the event as well as improving general communication about the activities and opportunities in the venue. A sound system will work in partnership with the lighting to create a vibrant and engaging atmosphere that appeals to fans and encourages enjoyment, which fuels the propensity to return for more events. Sound at a stadium can be used as a motivational cue, to fill in quiet moments, engage supporters, and deliver important information, including marketing messages. Given the rise and sophistication of home audio equipment, including personal devices, sound equipment at venues must be of the highest standard, and be thoroughly tested to ensure it does not annoy fans by being too loud or overused. Like portable screens, the use of headphones at stadia is increasingly an issue that marketers have to contend with as consumers in those situations are unlikely to engage with the messaging being broadcast through the sound system.

> *Chapter tool 8.4 Lighting and sound systems*: Lighting and sound systems can be used to attract sport consumers at attractive times and can also improve the atmosphere of a venue and event.

Transport

It is often important for consumers to be able to easily access a sport facility by public transport or by other services offered by the venue. If a facility is easy to get to, then consumers are more likely to make return visits. Public transport is particularly important for large national or international events when many thousands of people need to get to an event. Modest events and venues may consider using buses or minibuses to help move crowds from parking areas to the main doors. It is especially important to provide some transportation services to assist those with restricted mobility. These services may also be branded with marketing signage. They do not necessarily have to be complementary services either.

> *Chapter tool 8.5 Transport*: Transport can be used to assist consumers in accessing a facility and can be marketed as a special customer service.

Technology, Media, and Broadcasting

Fans and spectators attending sporting events in stadia expect connectivity to ensure their personal devices can access both cellular and Wi-Fi networks. Many stadia now have their own specific apps that give patrons directions around the car park and stadium and open up opportunities to make purchases without leaving their seats. These screens can also receive special insights and angles, and accompanying marketing messages, not available to viewers at home – such as views inside the locker rooms of participating teams – to justify the intimacy of attending an event as opposed to consuming from home. Sporting stadiums are somewhat in that the uploads made by fans at events will typically exceed downloads. This is driven by the need of fans to share their experiences with their social media platforms and thus are regularly uploading content. Whether this content creation helps marketing efforts or impinges on copyright is another issue that marketers need to deal with.

Similarly, sport facilities need to consider how they can facilitate media involvement with their sport events given modern broadcast demands will require the latest technology systems in high capacity. Most large sport and entertainment facilities have installed state-of-the-art platforms so that media representatives can use a high-speed connection to both download and upload information. Almost every sport facility can benefit from a dedicated area for sport broadcasting and media commentary. The most recent sport stadia are built as immense television studios with the infrastructure for broadcasting embedded underground.

> *Chapter tool 8.6 Media and broadcasting*: Providing media facilities can encourage broadcasting and general media interest in events that occur in a sport facility.

Childcare Facilities

While a local football ground is unlikely to offer childcare facilities, it has become an increasingly important service for community recreational facilities. Sport facilities, especially where they offer mixed gender activities, need to consider the childcare needs of their staff and patrons. For example, a facility that wants to attract 30- to 40-year-old women to a fitness programme must look at how they can facilitate their potential customers' involvement. It is complex and expensive to set up a childcare centre in a sport facility, but in some cases, it might be possible to work out a deal with a local childcare centre to provide casual care to the children at certain times of the day, or during particular events.

> *Chapter tool 8.7 Childcare facilities*: The provision of childcare facilities can be important in attracting consumers during non-peak periods or to special events.

Merchandising and Food/Beverage

The price of a ticket to a sport competition may not be the only thing that a customer is willing to spend money on at a sport event. In fact, sales from merchandise can be more profitable than gate receipts. Small community facilities can usually accommodate merchandise in the front reception, which takes up less space and staff time. Medium- to larger-sized sport facilities can sell merchandise in several different ways, such as having a temporary sales tent, roaming sales staff, a special merchandise shop, or an online outlet.

> *Chapter tool 8.8 Merchandise*: Selling merchandise in sport facilities is a powerful marketing tool because it provides consumers with a convenient way of spending more money on items that emphasise the sport product's brand image.

The supply of food and beverages is among the most lucrative of all services that can be offered at a sport facility. The type of food and beverages sold should reflect consumer preferences. This means, of course, that some market research is required before food and beverage outlets are planned and built. This is especially important in regard to where the outlets are positioned within a facility. For example, if sport consumers cannot get to a food and beverage outlet within 60 seconds of leaving their seats from anywhere in a stadium, then there are probably too few outlets available. Equally, it is unsatisfying for consumers to have to stand in a queue for lengthy periods. It is critical to examine not only what consumers like to eat and drink but also when, how often, and why they leave their seat to buy food or drinks. Spectators will eat and drink more or less, and at different times, depending on the sport they are watching. It is particularly annoying to spectators when they miss pivotal moments of play because they were standing in a queue. As a result, many venues are beginning to build food and beverage stands facing the field of play so that spectators can continue to watch the action, or adopting an in-seat ordering service that can be accessed via a personal screen either inbuilt to their seat or accessed via a phone app.

> *Chapter tool 8.9 Food and beverages*: The supply of food and beverages is among the most lucrative of all services that can be offered at a sport facility, which means that they demand careful planning.

TICKET DISTRIBUTION

Ticket sales are still one of the most important sources of revenue for sport organisations that conduct competitions or events. It follows then that ticket distribution is an extremely important issue for sport marketers. For large sport organisations, most tickets are purchased from a ticket distributor over the internet, although some sales may still occur in person from a box office or through a telephone call centre. For smaller sport organisations, tickets might be bought directly from a sporting club or event organiser, although even in these circumstances small clubs are turning to apps or specialist online ticketing providers to help capture bookings in an efficient manner. In general, like other sport products, sport tickets get passed down a distribution channel from the producer to the consumer. The ticket distributor is one of the channel members. In this model, ticket distributors do more than just provide tickets, they also show advertisements, offer sales promotions, provide customer service, conduct personal selling, and distribute the tickets to consumers.

When consumers contact a ticket distributor to purchase a ticket for a sport event, they are often looking for more than just a ticket. They want convenience, easy accessibility, and a fast, user-friendly service. Some consumers may want to have questions about the event, or the sport facility answered, and they certainly want a reasonable price that has not been increased too much because the ticket distributor is taking a large percentage. If a consumer becomes unhappy with the service or price they receive from a ticket distributor, they can feel dissatisfied about the sport event or club as well. It is therefore important that the sport organisation carefully discusses the features of a contract with the ticket distributor. Furthermore, sport organisations should maintain communications with the ticket distributor's customer service staff, which should include regular training and information updates. From a sport marketing perspective, it is imperative to be able to access the data that a ticket distributor may amass in selling tickets. Without these data, a sport event promoter may have little idea of the make-up of their audience given all the pertinent information rests inside the systems of the ticket provider.

Tickets to sporting events, particularly major ones, are now almost exclusively distributed online. Ticketmaster in the United States and many other countries is an example of a leading online ticket distributor. Such companies wield significant power given their critical role in the distribution channel process, are specialists at what they do and usually sell tickets for a wide variety of events, including music concerts, comedy, theatre, and sport events. Even though they are not just specialist sport ticket distributors, the general public know that they sell tickets to almost any entertainment event in their city. As a result, it is easy and convenient for consumers to register an account on their website and make purchases, often simply through a couple of clicks on their phone. One of the drawbacks is that consumers are able to easily compare the different entertainment events that are available and could choose another activity. The use of a distribution agent also increases the cost of a ticket as they charge a percentage of the ticket price to manage the booking and distribution process.

> *Chapter principle 8.6*: Ticket sales are one of the most important sources of revenue for sport organisations that conduct competitions or events. The smooth distribution of tickets is essential to the satisfaction of consumers and the maximisation of sales.

CASE 8.3

Fan Zones

In 2006 the FIFA World Cup organisers in Germany instituted an innovative idea for bringing fans together in a physical space away from a stadium. Inspired by the organic gathering of fans in city centres during the 2002 World Cup in Korea and Japan, the German organisers recognised that sport fans, who were unable to get match tickets to support their team, could experience the atmosphere by creating official fan venues. 'Fan zones' or 'live sites' became the place where team supporters congregated to watch the game on big screens, drank the event sponsor product, and embraced the big match atmosphere. For the organisers, it was an opportunity to generate revenue from official partners and other organisations that wanted to feature their brands to a specific target market, as well as harness the energy and excitement that mass viewing events created. It was an innovative idea, and its success started a trend in managing fans at international events that grew to now include almost every major sporting event across the world. Most event organisers now issue formal guidelines for managing such sites, indicating the significance these physical spaces have for marketing an event and seeking to control what brands are allowed to participate to protect the rights of official sponsors. The challenge of marketing 'place' for sport fans is to devise strategies that strengthen the capacity of the fan community to unite, engage, and to sustain a vitality of the space.

In recent times, clubs themselves have worked to create congregation points for their fans that allow them to experience the atmosphere and camaraderie of sport viewership when attendance at a stadium is not possible. One notable example is the fan experience offered by National Hockey League team, the Edmonton Oilers, during the 2023 playoffs. With away games in Los Angeles occurring, the Oilers filled their home rink, Rogers Place, with fans who not only watched the game on the big screen but were also treated to an augmented reality display of the players and puck on the ice-rink in front of them. This real time player and puck tracking added a new technological dimension to the fan experience and fans attended for a small fee of $5 that was donated to charity, thereby amplifying the efforts of the teams branding activities to help unite their community.

Not all fan congregation points need to be physical, however. An online fan zone is all about uniting fans in a virtual space. Online place marketing must have the right mix of 'community' features to encourage a sport's scattered community to come together. Online points of fan congregation are particularly appealing to global sport franchises because their fan base is spread far and wide. Hong Kong Sevens fan zone (www.hksevens.com) creates an opportunity for rugby fans around the world to engage with each other, and at the same time, promote the Rugby Sevens image and services. Online community zones are not exclusive to global franchises. Forums can be created by the fans or for the fans, for events, media, individual players, clubs and associations, and supporter groups such as the 'Barmy Army' who are devoted to the English cricket team.

QUESTIONS

1 Establishing a productive physical or virtual fan space depends on traditional marketing rationale. That is, the basic service provided must satisfy the needs of its fans, other businesses, and visitors in the right place at the right time. If it doesn't have authenticity, it will be worthless to the sport fan. How can sport marketers establish a sense of authenticity in their fan zones? Consider key attributes such as image marketing, site attraction, infrastructure, and people as critical to a successful strategy.

2 Given the rise of technology, including social media, the emergence of unofficial fan zones is increasingly an issue. These zones may be physical or online and bypass the typical marketing arrangements and requirements of official events. Are unofficial events a good or bad thing for a sport marketer? What are the advantages and disadvantages that they bring?

3 How will technology change the zones of the future. Imagine you are organising a FIFA World Cup to be held a decade from today. What will the fan zone experience be like?

PRINCIPLES SUMMARY

- Chapter principle 8.1: A sport distribution channel is an organised series of organisations, suppliers, and individuals that move products from the producer to the final consumer.
- Chapter principle 8.2: There are both direct and indirect distribution channels that vary in length. A direct distribution channel is short where the producer sells the product directly to the consumer. An indirect distribution channel is a longer channel where there are a number of intermediaries involved along the way. Each intermediary normally adds some form of value to the distribution process, with the ultimate goal being to connect the final good or service to a consumer.
- Chapter principle 8.3: A channel member is any organisation or individual that is involved in the sport distribution channel. Channel members may include wholesalers and retailers, as well as producers and consumers.
- Chapter principle 8.4: The sport facility is the most important distribution channel for sport activity services and professional sport events.
- Chapter principle 8.5: Sport marketers must consider four main aspects of sport facilities in which they can maximise the sport consumer experience: (1) location and accessibility, (2) design and layout, (3) facility infrastructure, and (4) customer service.
- Chapter principle 8.6: Ticket sales are one of the most important sources of revenue for sport organisations that conduct competitions or events. The smooth distribution of tickets is essential to the satisfaction of consumers and the maximisation of sales.

TOOLS SUMMARY

- Chapter tool 8.1 Distribution issues analysis
- Chapter tool 8.2 Seating
- Chapter tool 8.3 Scoreboards and signage
- Chapter tool 8.4 Lighting and sound systems
- Chapter tool 8.5 Transport

- Chapter tool 8.6 Media and broadcasting
- Chapter tool 8.7 Childcare facilities
- Chapter tool 8.8 Merchandise
- Chapter tool 8.9 Food and beverages

REVIEW QUESTIONS

1. What is a sport distribution channel? Provide an example.
2. What is the difference between a direct and an indirect distribution channel?
3. What kinds of sport products might pass through wholesaler and retailer intermediaries?
4. Provide five examples of sport activity services and five examples of professional sport events.
5. Of the eight tools for marketing facility features, which three do you think are the most practical for a sport marketer to manipulate?
6. What are the advantages and disadvantages to using a ticket distributor?
7. In what ways is the distribution of sport and its 'place' marketing changing as a consequence of emerging technologies?

RELEVANT WEBSITES

Amazon online retailer (www.amazon.com)
Edmonton Oilers (www.nhl.com/oilers)
FIFA (www.fifa.com)
Hong Kong Sevens (www.hksevens.com)
Las Vegas Sphere (www.thespherevegas.com/)
SoFi Stadium (www.sofistadium.com)
Tottenham Hotspur Stadium (www.tottenhamhotspur.com/the-stadium/)

FURTHER READING

Fried, G., & Kastel, M. (2021). *Managing Sport Facilities*. Human Kinetics.

Schwarz, E. C., Hall, S., & Shibli, S. (2020). *Sport Facility Operations Management: A Global Perspective*. Routledge.

CHAPTER 9

Sport promotion

LEARNING OUTCOMES

At the end of this chapter, readers should be able to:

- define the term promotion.
- outline the elements of the promotions mix.
- describe the strengths and weaknesses of each element of the promotions mix.
- identify the three main goals of promotions.
- explain the steps involved in planning a promotions approach.

OVERVIEW

The purpose of this chapter is to explain the role of the fourth element of the marketing mix – promotion. It begins by examining what promotion means in the context of sport marketing, as well as its range of uses. This chapter also highlights the application of various promotional tools, known collectively as the promotions mix, which includes advertising, personal selling, sales promotions, and public relations. Promotional goals are examined, and the process of promotions planning is outlined.

FROM ADVERTISING TO PROMOTIONS

It is common for people to think of promotion as being nothing but advertising in the form of commercials on broadcast media, online platforms, or in various forms of print media. However, other common applications of promotional activities include personal selling to directly achieve sales, sales promotions to motivate and enthuse consumers and channel members, as well as an array of public relations and publicity to engender positive associations and favourable outcomes. The first step is therefore to clearly define the scope of promotion in sport marketing. Its position in the Sport Marketing Framework is shown in Figure 9.1.

DOI: 10.4324/9781003391319-9

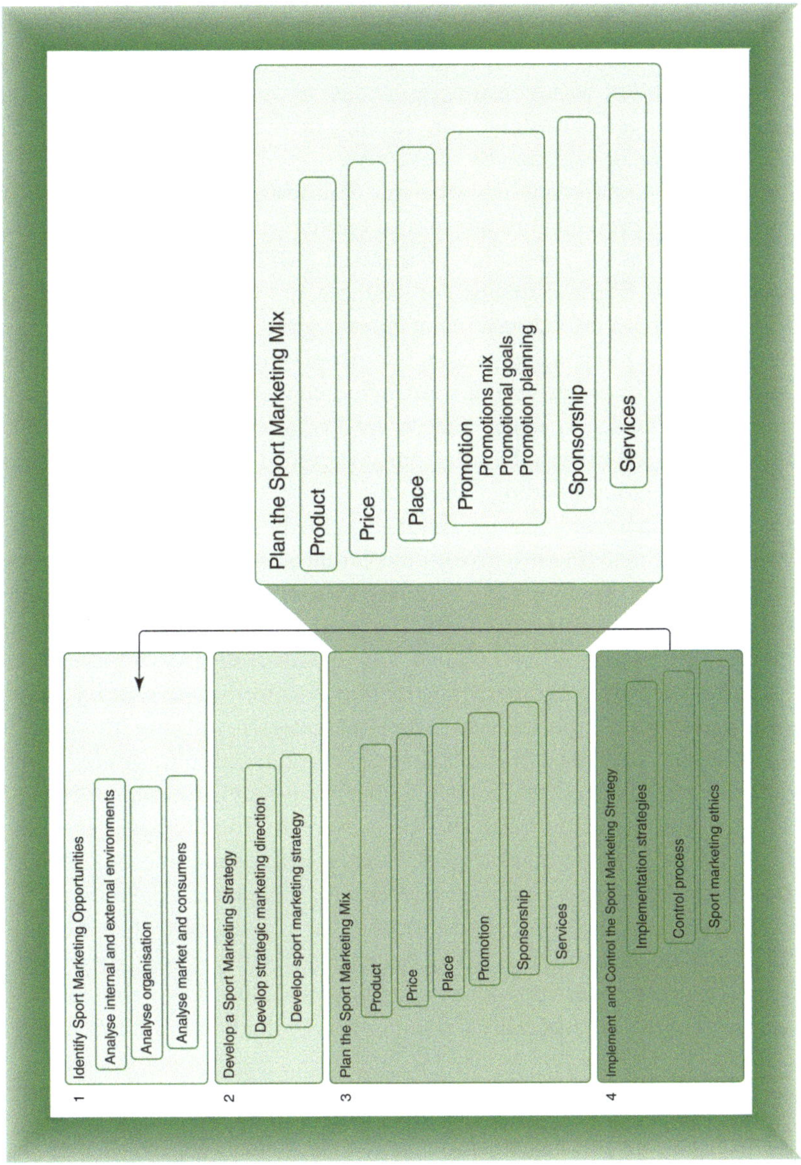

FIGURE 9.1 The sport marketing framework

INTEGRATED PROMOTION

In sport marketing, the word promotion covers a range of interrelated and integrated activities. All these activities are designed to attract attention, stimulate the interest and awareness of consumers, and, of course, encourage them to purchase a sport product. For example, promotion might involve telling potential consumers about a product, reminding them of its benefits, or persuading them that it is worth trying. Promotion involves all forms of communication with consumers, not just advertising. Ideally, such activities should tell one, coherent and consistent, story, keeping in mind that any discrepancies may cause confusion, inaction, or rejection by consumers.

Promotion is about communicating with and educating consumers to move from a path of being aware of a product through to final consumption. Promotion is thus a hierarchical process that relies on a sequence of messaging which can fail at any one point, preventing consumption from occurring. For example, it would be pointless to enthuse and excite consumers about attending a major sport event if tickets were sold out or conversely were prohibitively expensive so that few people purchased one. Fundamentally, every interaction a consumer has with a sport brand conveys some meaning – from the high price of a ticket that might signal scarcity, quality, or elite expectations, through to the look and feel of a well-managed and responsive official social media site that might reflect camaraderie and group bonding behaviours.

It is important to understand that everything a sport brand, or its stakeholders, does, such as uniform design, ticketing price, communication platforms, press conferences, fan events, apps, merchandise, sponsorship, social media posts, and so on is a form of promotion as, whether planned or not, it sends a message to consumers and stakeholders that is pieced together to form shared understanding. Given all these 'puzzle pieces' are going to be amalgamated by consumers in their minds to form a perception (good, bad, or indifferent), it becomes imperative for sport marketers to manage them as best as possible and ensure that they are consistent with the brand positioning desired. For example, the organisers of the Australian Open, a Grand Slam tennis tournament held in the city of Melbourne, work hard to ensure that their event is promoted as accessible to all, featuring an array of advertising that encourages attendance across the two weeks of the tournament, and which includes a number of relatively inexpensive ticketing options. To the international audience, the event is promoted as the crown jewel of Australia's 'summer of tennis', leaning heavily on the relaxed Australian stereotype to suggest Melbourne would be a great place to visit for tourist and sport fan alike. Even the colour of the courts, a sparkling sea blue, is especially chosen to reflect the beach life that the country is renowned for.

Promotion is best seen as the way that sport marketers communicate with consumers to inform, persuade, and remind them about a product. The aim of promotion is to encourage consumers to develop a favourable opinion about a sport product that is aligned to a predetermined positioning strategy, and then to stimulate consumers to try the sport product. While promotion can and should inform and influence people, its goal is that of *selling* the product. It is of little value to have people interested in a product if that interest is not converted to sales, so all promotional plans must feature an emphasis on this aspect. One of the special challenges a sport marketer faces in doing this is uniting all the stakeholders they may have to ensure the promotion messaging undertaken is consistent. In many instances, a sporting brand may rely on its various stakeholders to do much of the promotional work for them in the knowledge that sponsors and media partners are often far better resourced and equipped to achieve such goals.

Chapter principle 9.1: Promotion can be defined as the way that sport marketers communicate with consumers to inform, persuade, and remind them about the features and benefits described by a sport product's positioning.

CASE 9.1

Boxing

Who is the current heavyweight boxing champion of the world? That question, which decades ago was regularly associated with the most famous athlete on the planet, is not always easy to answer.

The sport of boxing is one of the oldest known athletic endeavours, spanning back to various combat sports in ancient times. It featured in the ancient Olympic Games, and in its amateur form remains part of the modern Olympics. It is perhaps best known for its professional side, which was originally known as 'prizefighting' and saw boxers do battle with bare knuckles and few rules in dubious venues where gambling on the outcome was the primary focus. In 1867 the 'Marquess of Queensberry rules' were formulated to help legitimise the sport and protect participants, including mandating the use of gloves and one-minute rest periods between three-minute rounds.

Boxing's golden period was arguably the 1960s and 1970s when Muhammad Ali proclaimed himself 'The Greatest' and captured the world's attention with an extraordinary blend of skill and personality. Ali's marketing brilliance and global appeal highlighted the sport in the heavyweight category, elevating bouts he featured in such as the 'Fight of the Century' (1971) in New York City, 'Rumble in the Jungle' (1974) in Kinshasa, Zaire, and 'Thrilla in Manila' (1975) in Manila, Philippines, to legendary status.

While famous boxers have emerged since the days of Ali, and his legendary compatriots such as Joe Frazier and George Foreman, the sport's positioning in the eyes of world sport has become increasingly disjointed, including safety concerns and fractured governance. Boxing is a brutal sport, and the concept of striking an opponent into physical capitulation is unappealing to many, although the demand for such entertainment is clearly present given the success of mixed-martial art events in recent decades, primarily through the promotional activities of the Ultimate Fighting Championship (UFC).

The UFC was formed in North America in 1993 and overcame numerous struggles, including attempts to have it banned, to rise to prominence in the early part of this century, and become a multi-billion dollar business popular across the world.

Its success is centred on numbered championship events across a series of weight divisions and has included female fighters since 2012. Conducted in an octagonal structure that presents a distinct signature setting for events, the UFC can carefully control its brand positioning and develop promotional ties to broadcasters, as well as its own successful subscription service, to build strong narratives around its fighters. Fans can tune in regularly to follow the progress of the stars and the numbered UFC events now travel the world to capitalise on popularity. The UFC's close and careful control of its mixed-martial arts product gives it the perfect marketing platform from which to promote and build its brand.

By contrast, boxing is lumbered with a series of relatively confusing governing structures, sanctioning bodies, and ranking organisations. The sanctioning bodies are of particular importance as they are the major groups who can offer the professional boxing bouts that capture the widest attention. The oldest of these is the World Boxing Association, formed in 1921. Others include the World Boxing Council (WBC) formed in 1963, the International Boxing Federation (IBF) formed in 1983, and World Boxing Organization (WBO) formed in 1988. Having multiple bodies can mean that each may appoint their own 'champion' in a weight division, and the rankings are further complicated by other platforms, such as 'The Ring' magazine who also offer their own interpretation of ratings and champions.

Boxing bouts, while sanctioned by the bodies noted, are also 'promoted' by companies who have contracts with specific fighters. These promoters become the major marketers of a boxing match, and will negotiate the broadcast deals, sponsorships, and prize money on offer with the hope of creating a positive return on their outlay. Understandably, their priority is with promoting their specific athlete and the event in which they are featuring, not necessarily boxing more broadly.

QUESTIONS

1. Compare the sport of boxing to the UFC product. Outline the features that each has which makes them more or less appealing to consumers.
2. How would you advise the sport of boxing to (re)build its appeal?
3. Who is the current heavyweight champion of the world in boxing? Confirm your answer by visiting the websites of the WBA, WBC, IBF, and WBO.
4. Assuming the various boxing sanctioning bodies could unite with a common approach, what promotion aspects would you recommend they adopt and execute?

The promotions mix

It is common for sport organisations to use several different promotional activities simultaneously, rather than to just focus on one. Because different promotional activities can be combined, they are collectively known as the promotions mix. In other words, it is advantageous to combine numerous promotional activities together into one promotional plan or strategy. A promotional strategy is a plan that aims to use the main elements of the promotions mix for the best results. The promotions mix elements are: (1) advertising, (2) personal selling, (3) sales promotions, and (4) public relations.

> *Chapter principle* 9.2: The promotions mix consists of four marketing tools: (1) advertising, (2) personal selling, (3) sales promotions and (4) public relations.

Advertising

It is easy to think of advertising examples as they surround us in almost every minute of our lives: from online and television commercials, magazine and newspaper advertisements, radio spots, posters, billboards, internet pop-ups, and advertisements on public transport. In all these examples, a sport organisation would pay someone else (such as Google) to present the advertisement. Even though media intermediaries present advertisements, they are always produced from the perspective of the organisation or brand that is paying for it. The media who distribute advertising are all doing the same thing, despite their many apparent differences. That is, they are connecting the message of the brand to what is deemed to be a suitable target audience. Different media platforms will reach different audiences in different ways, and typically the promotion mix will not only need to consider the range of elements it will use, but also how the media will be engaged to ensure the message gets to the right people, in the right way, and enough times to resonate in action. The media platforms that advertising uses are incredibly complex, with the permutations of audiences, timing, and cost seemingly endless. The rise of digital platforms adds to this challenge, with many offering niche opportunities that belie the traditional appeal of advertising in being able to reach large audiences quickly.

A first important point about advertising is that it is one-way communication from marketers to consumers. While social media and digital platforms are changing the interaction between brands and consumers, advertising is traditionally a form of one-way communication where a marketer pays someone else to have a product, brand, or organisation identified. One of the advantages of advertising is that it can, if you choose, reach many people at once. However, it is often an expensive form of promotion that few sport organisations can afford and the direct benefits may be difficult to ascertain. Many sport organisations will rely on their strategic partners, such as major sponsors, to undertake advertising to help generate interest in the event. For example, the International Olympic Committee (IOC) rarely takes out advertisements asking people to watch or attend its events, however, local organisers and media partners will do exactly that, while sponsors will carefully associate their products with the event, building its prestige, impact, and appeal so that their products can reflect in this positive light.

One of the challenges of advertising in the contemporary environment is the ability of consumers to avoid it. While advertising was once embraced by many consumers as a source of information and inspiration, many consumers now feel overwhelmed and avoid it where possible, using adblockers online, diverting their attention to second screens during broadcasts, or using streaming services or approaches that minimise disruption. Advertisers have responded by making their appeals more stimulating and interactive to hold attention and by incorporating advertising directly into content through such tactics as product placement. Interestingly, if we think of the marketing that occurs through sport, the propensity of live sport to attract and hold large audiences means that advertisers tend to remain highly attracted to major events such as the Super Bowl to reach large audiences.

> *Chapter tool 9.1 Advertising*: Advertising is a form of one-way communication where a marketer pays someone else to have a product, brand or organisation identified. Common examples include television commercials, magazine and newspaper advertisements, radio spots, posters, billboards, internet pop-ups and advertisements on public transport.

Personal Selling

Personal selling involves one-to-one communication between a consumer and a salesperson. Personal selling might involve talking to a consumer on the phone or face-to-face, communication through text messaging and email, through a digital platform, or chat function. The aim of personal selling is to build relationships with consumers in order to convince them to accept a point of view about the brand or product in question, and ultimately to convince them to take some action and try the product. Endorsements and sponsorships are two forms of personal selling that are common in the sport industry, each of which will be explained further shortly.

> *Chapter tool 9.2 Personal selling*: Personal selling involves one-to-one communication between a consumer and a salesperson. Common examples include talking to a consumer on the phone, talking face-to-face, communication through text messaging and email, or through a digital platform. Endorsements and sponsorships are two forms of personal selling that are common in the sport industry.

Sponsorship

Sport sponsorship occurs when a sporting organisation or an individual athlete is supported by a separate company (or person). The sponsorship is designed to benefit both parties: the sport organisation (or sponsee) receives money or products, and the sponsor receives the benefits of positive associations with prominent sporting teams or athletes. It can sometimes be unclear what these other benefits are for the sponsor. For this reason, the sporting organisation is nearly always the one approaching a company for a sponsorship. Sport organisations therefore must have a clear idea of what they have to offer or 'sell' to the potential sponsor. Common benefits that are offered to sponsors include:

- naming rights;
- signage;
- media coverage/indirect advertising;
- goodwill (reputation) for being involved with sporting heroes;
- direct advertising opportunities;
- access to a new consumer market;
- opportunity for new sales (e.g., special offers to members);
- demonstration of products (e.g., use of product at a sporting event);
- political benefits.

Because the sporting organisation is nearly always the one asking a company for sponsorship, they must undertake substantial preparatory planning. This involves conducting some research to ensure that they are choosing the right company to approach with a formal proposal. Sponsorship is such an important part of sport marketing that Chapter 10 is exclusively dedicated to it.

CASE 9.2

The Masters

The professional men's golf tour features four 'majors'. These are the most prestigious events that all players covet and comprise the US Open and US PGA Championships, the British Open, and The Masters. Jack Nicklaus holds the record for the most wins across these elite tournaments, with 18, with Tiger Woods in second place with 15 wins.

The Masters is the only one of the four majors to be played at the same venue each year, Augusta National Golf Club. The first of the majors each year, it is an invitational event that has stayed true to its history, building up a reverence and mystique that places it at the summit of most players' ambitions.

The Masters' champion each year receives the coveted 'green jacket', ostensibly a membership jacket of the club given the winner becomes an honorary member. Reigning champions will place the jacket on the following year's winner and host the Champions' dinner which is held in the week of the event and features past winners. The tournament enforces strict protocols around behaviour and dress, including that caddies must wear a uniform of a white one-piece overall. The surname of the player is found on the back of the respective caddie's uniform, along with a number, with the current champion being allocated caddie number 1.

In an era of big business, which professional golf has been particularly good at exploiting, it is perhaps what The Masters doesn't do that feeds most strongly into its legendary status. While tournaments around the world have eagerly latched onto sponsors, television rights, and spectator attendance to fuel revenue, The Masters ostensibly eschews such commercialisation in favour of tradition. The event is broadcast on television, but it was only earlier this century before the host network was allowed to transmit live from each of the 18 holes. Using a year-to-year deal rather than lucrative long-term rights, The Masters only permits its broadcaster to spend four minutes per hour on commercial interruptions, far below the standard 12–15 minutes at other events. Golf fans from around the world who are lucky enough to score a 'badge' (not ticket) to attend the tournament will do so as just one of a small number of patrons (not spectators) lucky enough to have been chosen at random from a long application list to attend. While on the course, they will notice an absence of commercial signage, food and drink prices that are remarkably inexpensive, and an atmosphere that is almost reverential in its tone. Merchandise is only available for sale on-course, and can not be purchased online or in stores. Augusta National Golf Course itself is a beautiful sight to behold, even if you only watch it on television. Each hole is brilliantly manicured, and no expense is spared to ensure that it looks immaculate. This helps reinforce the exclusivity of the event and the essence of it being conducted at a private club.

Despite this inherently conservative and tradition-bound approach, the organisers of The Masters are no slouches when it comes to marketing, whether by accident or design. By creating and fostering scarcity and tradition while other golf events embrace revenue streams and exposure, The Masters has become more and more desirable for its almost anti-marketing, golf first, approach. Notwithstanding this, The Masters has spared no expense to give fans across the world access to its traditions in the most modern way – developing an 'app' that is one of the most elegant, content-rich, and useable across any sport. The app, not surprisingly, is free from corporate clutter, reflecting the values and traditions of the tournament to stay true to its origins.

QUESTIONS

1 Download The Masters app for your phone (available in both the Apple Store and Google Play) and visit The Masters website (www.masters.com). Evaluate the content and features from a promotional perspective. What does the app and website signal to users? Contrast this to the website of any one of the other three majors – US Open (www.usopen.com), US PGA (www.pgachampionship.com), and The Open Championship (www.theopen.com).

2 In an age of increasing digitisation and competition in sport entertainment, how can The Masters continue to balance its traditional, conservative approach with the demands of modern sport marketing?

3 How does golf, more broadly, go about promoting itself in your local market? What efforts or campaigns, if any, have you noticed? How does a major sport like golf create interest more broadly around the world?

Endorsements

An *endorsement* occurs when a well-known celebrity or athlete uses their fame to help a company sell its products. They may also use their reputation to help enhance the image of the company, its products or brand. A celebrity athlete may appear in an advertisement, post on their social media or appear in another public forum using a product, saying that they endorse it, and recommending its usage. Because sport fans can have a strong psychological connection to celebrity sport stars, endorsements can be an effective method of persuading fans to buy products. If the sports star is seen as trustworthy and credible, this can help fans to believe that the product is reliable. This is why superstars such as Stephen Curry in the National Basketball Association in the United States can be so effective when they endorse a product. Sport stars, presuming they manage their own brand well enough, remain highly valuable endorsers even when their playing careers are over or in decline. Roger Federer, Tiger Woods, David Beckham, Floyd Mayweather, Serena Williams, Simone Biles, and Usain Bolt are just some examples of athletes whose fame will likely continue to provide fortune for many years after their retirement.

Sales Promotions

A sales promotion is usually a short-term programme that aims to stimulate an increase in sales. The goal of a sales promotion is primarily to accelerate the purchase process by providing an incentive – usually a form of a monetary saving – to buy now, or buy more now, rather than wait until later. Examples of sales promotions include 'two-for-one' offers, prize give-aways, competitions, discounts, and trials or samples. Sales promotions can be useful supplements to other promotional activities, as they tend to draw attention thereby providing the other activities with more exposure. Sales promotions must be used with care however. If they become too frequent, they start to lose their appeal as the promotion effectively becomes expected and is factored into the price of a product.

A sport organisation may target a sales promotion towards the public or sometimes to wholesalers and retailers. One of the advantages of sales promotions is that it is relatively easy to keep track of how many consumers were enticed to use a product because of a special deal. For example, if a 'two-for-one' coupon is part of the sales promotion, it is possible to count the number redeemed. Sales promotions can help to achieve a variety of promotional goals, such as encouraging loyal customers to buy more often, encouraging consumers to change when they buy a particular product or persuading consumers to switch to the brand being offered. Sales promotions can even be useful as a defensive weapon in marketing by undercutting the pricing of a new competitor in the marketplace, or even matching the sales promotions that other firms use.

> *Chapter tool 9.3 Sales promotions*: A sales promotion is a short-term programme that aims to stimulate an increase in sales. They offer consumers an *incentive* (or a bonus) to buy the sport product. Common examples include 'two-for-one' offers, prize give-aways, competitions, and free trials or samples.

Public Relations

Public relations is concerned with building a good 'image' for sport organisations and is generally connected to the concept of publicity. It is important for sport organisations to have a good relationship with different groups and stakeholders in the community, including the media, government sport departments, local councils, and even fan clubs. To have a good relationship with these groups, sport organisations need to communicate with them on a regular basis. It is therefore essential that sport organisations identify what sort of information about their products public groups will be interested in. Once determined, it is a matter of working out how to communicate this information in a way that will enhance the sport organisation's reputation and cultivate improved relationships. Part of this also involves setting up opportunities to hear back from these groups to ensure there is ongoing dialogue as public relations will require balancing the needs of, and responding to concerns and inputs, of multiple groups. For example, local resident groups might be concerned with noise from a motorsport event, a local council may want to be involved in issuing permits for access to local sporting facilities, and larger governments may be direct investors in procuring and promoting major sporting events and want to be sure they themselves receive positive recognition for this.

Public relations is different to other forms of promotion in that it is often a lower cost to a sport organisation than other forms of promotion, especially advertising. While public relations require planning, organisation, and materials, the expense of purchasing space in media to distribute a direct message is avoided, and thus if executed well can be a great way for a sport brand to have a large impact at low cost. This usually happens by getting some information into the mass media as a newsworthy item. For this reason, *public relations* is often called, or linked to, *publicity*. For example, a surfing manufacturer might provide a 'press release' about an innovative new product in the hope that the media will want to make a story out of it. The likelihood of this occurring is amplified if the surf brand can provide media materials such as professional footage for use, create an exciting event that the media will want to attend, and develop some kind of unique angle (e.g., the surfboard repels sharks) that will provide novelty. Another example could be a junior sport club that demonstrates its connection to a former player that has gone on to become an international star. In these examples, the sport organisation does not have to pay to have their information presented as they would with advertising. However, one problem is that they do not have control over how their organisation or product is presented; it is possible to get bad publicity as it is to get good publicity. Indeed, given the propensity for the media to promote bad news above good news, and the constant spotlight that many sporting brands and athletes are in, the public relations departments of major sporting organisations will often spend large amounts of time trying to mitigate against negative publicity.

> *Chapter tool 9.4 Public relations*: Public relations is concerned with building a good 'image' for a sport organisation. Public relations is different to other forms of promotion because it is free. It usually involves getting some information into the mass media as a news item, and for this reason it is often called *publicity*.

Each of the four elements of the promotions mix represents a tool that can be used to promote a sport product. Table 9.1 summarises the key strengths and weaknesses of each of the four promotion tools and provides examples helpful to their application.

> *Chapter principle 9.3*: Promotional elements should be combined in order to complement one another in order to achieve a promotional goal that is consistent with the overall marketing and positioning strategy.

TABLE 9.1 Promotional techniques

Tools	*Advantages*	*Disadvantages*	*Methods*
Advertising	Wide reach	High initial outlay	Online, broadcast media (TV, radio, pay TV), press, outdoor
	Dramatic and emotive images	Impersonal	Television, YouTube
			Magazines
	Reaches consumers fast	Limited feedback from consumers	Direct marketing
			Ticketing agents
			Scoreboard displays
	High exposure	Delayed feedback	Transport posters
			Billboards and posters
		Hard to customise message to individual consumers on some channels	Brochures
			Ticket stubs
			Internet
			Text messages
		Difficult to tell how many consumers buy the product as a result of viewing or hearing the advertisement Adblockers (online) or time-shifting (traditional media)	Multimedia messages
Sales promotion	Attention-grabbing	Minimum reach	In-store promotions/ point of purchase sales
	Informative	Medium cost per exposure	Exhibitions
	Fast in reaching consumers	Usually impersonal	Product give-aways, stickers, shirts, admission give-aways
	Moderate control over the communication	Difficult to customise message to individual consumers	Two-for-one offers
			Free admission with purchase

(Continued)

TABLE 9.1 (Continued)

Tools	*Advantages*	*Disadvantages*	*Methods*
	Relatively easy to track how many consumers buy the product because of the promotion		Prizes tied to tickets
			Frequent purchaser of cards (loyalty cards)
			'Selling' of heroes
			Competitions
			Free trials or samples
			Bonus packs
			Trade deals
Personal selling	Direct communication	Narrow reach	Direct marketing
	Informative	Variable cost per exposure	Endorsements
			Referrals
			Party plans
	Immediate feedback from consumers	Slow to reach target customers	Sponsorship
	High control over message		Face-to-face (or online) discussions
	Able to customise message to individual consumers	Clutter	Email
Public relations	Wide reach	Variable image	Press releases/result lists
	Informative	Very little feedback from consumers	Photographs
			Commentary and reviews
	Low cost per exposure	Delayed feedback	Feature articles
	Fast in reaching consumers	Impersonal	Social media posts

CASE 9.3

When Things Go Bad!

No matter how hard a sporting league, club, or governing body might try, it is almost certain it will face a public relations crisis at some point. When things go wrong and athletes are found to have acted inappropriately, whether on or off the field, they are often given lengthy suspensions and required to abide by comprehensive clauses that don't bring the brands they are associated with into disrepute.

Sponsors and stakeholders across sport more broadly, remain cautious, however, and are increasingly prepared to walk away from relationships where they feel that negative associations to unsavoury incidents outweigh any marketing benefits they may have initially signed up for. How sponsors and other stakeholders make these decisions has been the subject of considerable research and it is apparent that decisions are highly contextualised.

The issue is essentially one of athlete 'transgressions' which occur when a sportsperson oversteps a boundary. In some cases, this is a legal boundary, making the actions of sporting stakeholders easier to determine. After all, a conviction for a serious crime is unlikely to present sporting clubs and sponsors with a difficult decision to make. When the transgression is less clear cut, however, or happens on the field in the moment of battle, things can be harder to determine. Consider an athlete who is exposed for having an extra-marital affair for example. Some stakeholders may view this as a personal matter, distant from any sporting connection, while others may view it as a betrayal of important brand values.

When sponsors decide what to do when transgressions occur, they generally consider the following items as part of a process of assessing the impact of 'degenerative episodes' on the joint benefits they derive from their alliance. That is, unless the matter is particularly severe or clear cut, it can take numerous episodes to erode trust, cooperation, mutual understanding, and cooperation, to the point where a relationship is terminated.

The first factor is the quality of the existing relationship itself, particularly the levels and openness of communication that exist, and the trust and commitment that has been exhibited. When communication channels are strong, and trust and commitment have been established, episodes can be overcome given a strong foundation.

This impact will, however, be greatly impacted by three additional factors – the attribution of blame, the perceived severity of the incident, and the media attention it may attract. Knowing who to blame is not always easy in complex situations involving athletes, and in many cases the athlete may be the subject of unfair scrutiny or pressures. How this manifests in media coverage is important. Naturally the perceived severity will be paramount, with some transgressions unforgiveable, while others can be ascribed to youthful indiscretion, a challenging upbringing, or being out-of-character. The perceived severity of a transgression will also need to consider the sponsor's business category, with some types of companies more susceptible to negative spillovers from certain events. For example, a car company may have a lower level of tolerance to driving offences than a financial institution would.

Finally, sponsors will consider the management of the episode, noting that transparency, a proactive approach, a clear media management strategy, and ongoing communication may well alleviate any long-term concerns. While sponsors would prefer that incidents didn't occur, they can be placated by knowing that processes exist to mitigate damage when they do.

Sponsors ultimately have various options when transgressions occur. They can continue, albeit with some relational adaptation, knowing that each degenerative episode will chip away at the levels of trust. In that sense, the concept of 'nothing changing' is a false assumption. Sponsors can also terminate a relationship, choosing to do so abruptly and demonstratively if there is some marketing benefit in this approach, or do so in a 'disguised' way by stepping away more quietly at the end of the contract period, citing a range of excuses as to why they didn't renew.

QUESTIONS

1. Sponsors of sport need to enter relationships with their eyes wide open as to the dangers of transgressions affecting their relationship. Which sports do you believe are more susceptible to degenerative episodes than others? Why is this the case, and what could sponsors do to mitigate any negative spill over to them in such instances?
2. It is becoming increasingly common for fan groups to pressure sporting brands to exit relationships with certain sponsors, for example, gambling, alcohol, and fast-food companies. Considering these three categories and your favourite sport, rank them in terms of suitability and whether you would recommend they become a sponsor. What factors did you consider reaching your conclusions?
3. What is the difference between on- and off-field transgressions in terms of impact? Consider similar events such as assault on the field and off the field through the lens of the various factors raised in the case study.

Promotional objectives

To review, promotion is the way that sport marketers communicate with potential consumers to inform, persuade, and remind them about a product or brand. The aim of promotion is to encourage consumers to develop a favourable opinion about a product or brand with the intention of stimulating them to try it, and then to keep on repurchasing it. There are four main kinds of promotional activities that marketers use, and these are collectively known as the promotions mix, because the different activities can be effectively combined. Sport marketers must also understand that, whether planned or unplanned, every element communicates to target audiences in some way and ensuring consistency and coherence will be important to ensure confusion is minimised. With this background in place, it is now time to consider the goals of promotion, or what it aims to achieve. There are three main objectives of promotion: (1) to inform, (2) to persuade, and (3) to remind.

> *Chapter principle 9.4*: There are three main objectives of promotion: (1) to inform, (2) to persuade and (3) to remind.

Informing

Until a new product is promoted, consumers are unlikely to be aware that it exists. Naturally, it is important for potential consumers to be aware of a sport product, to understand its benefits, to respond to how it is positioned in the marketplace, and to know how to acquire it. Promotions that aim to *inform* consumers of these aspects of a product are usually done during the early stages of the product life cycle. Informative promotions are also helpful if the product is complex or technical, such as a range of sport equipment with sophisticated electronic components.

Similarly, a sporting team arriving in a new market would need to expend considerable effort informing various groups of their presence. This includes fans who they want to attend and support the team, as well as sponsors they may want to enter a strategic relationship with. As many sport organisations are not well-equipped to run integrated marketing campaigns, they often rely on partners, such as the media, to do the informing work for them. Consider, for example, the elite football leagues of sport who rarely promote their fixtures, with the media undertaking this task.

> *Chapter principle 9.5:* Promotions that inform aim to communicate the product's existence, its benefits, its positioning and how it can be obtained. Promotions that aim to inform consumers are usually undertaken during the early stages of the product life cycle.

Persuading

Once consumers are aware of a product and its benefits, it may be necessary to persuade them to try it. *Persuading* consumers means convincing them, or influencing them, to buy a sport product. To achieve this aim, it is essential to give consumers a good reason to buy the product. It is important that sport marketers do not deceive consumers in order to persuade them to buy it. Aside from being illegal, it is counterproductive, as the product will not reach expectations, leading to consumer dissatisfaction.

Persuasive promotions are more common when a product enters the growth stage of the product life cycle. By this time consumers should have a general awareness of the kind of product that is being offered, as well as the benefits that it can give them. At this point it is unnecessary for sport organisations to utilise promotional activities that inform, but it remains important to convince consumers to purchase the product on offer and not one offered by competition.

Persuasive promotions are used when the aim is to change the ideas that consumers hold about a product. For example, it might be desirable to change consumers' ideas about a product's features, or a brand's image. Persuasion is also a common strategy that sport organisations employ when they want consumers to switch from a competitor's brand to their own. In these instances, brands may use comparative advertising where they indicate the features and benefits that their product has, aligned to that of competitors. Consider, for example, the highly competitive category of fitness watches that feature a range of major international brands such as Apple, Garmin, Fitbit and Polar. All these companies make appealing watches; however, a consumer is only likely to purchase one brand at a time. In making their choice they will inevitably make comparisons. These might mean taking in the carefully created messages that brands put into their promotional programmes but would also feature review sites, YouTube channels, salespeople offering advice, online influencers, and even observing what friends and family may be wearing. Consumers adapt this approach as they understand that getting information from independent third parties add a layer of information that can be persuasive.

Chapter principle 9.6: Persuasive promotions are utilised when trying to give consumers good reasons to buy a sport product. Persuasive promotions are more common when a product enters the growth stage of the product life cycle.

Reminding

Reminder promotions aim to keep a product or brand name prominent in consumers' minds. Once consumers have been informed about a product and have been persuaded to buy it at least once, it is sensible to remind them to continue buying it in the future. Reminder promotions are most common during the maturity stage of the product life cycle. Reminders are a valuable tool in defending market share as carefully timed promotions can keep a consumer coming back to the same product rather than trying those of others. For example, a consumer who buys a sport supplement powder might be reminded to keep purchasing, and offered incentives to do so, if they are able to join a loyalty programme that captures their contact information.

While consumers often make up their minds as to which brands to purchase at point-of-purchase, such as standing in a supermarket aisle, the service experience inherent in many sporting products will mean that consumers will often need to plan well ahead to access an event or product. In these instances, reminders can work well to ensure that these decisions can be made in time. As many sports collect databases of attendees to their events, modern communication methods can make it easy to target promotions as reminders.

Chapter principle 9.7: Reminder promotions aim to keep a product or brand name prominent in consumers' minds. Reminder promotions are most common during the maturity stage of the product life cycle.

The three types of promotional goals are summarised in Table 9.2 along with advice on their best timing and some typical examples.

TABLE 9.2 Promotional goals

Goal of promotion	*Timing*	*Examples*
To inform	Commonly used during the introduction stage of the product life cycle	Make consumers aware of a new brand
		Make consumers aware of new product
		Inform consumers of product features
		Inform consumers of price and where to buy
		Explain how a product works, especially a complex or technical one
		Build a positive image for the organisation
		Suggest new ways to use a product
To persuade	Commonly used during the *growth* stage of the product life cycle	Encourage brand switching
		Convince consumers to buy a product
		Change consumers' ideas about the product
To remind	Used in highly competitive marketplaces	Remind consumers they need a product
		Remind consumers where to buy it
	Commonly used during the *maturity* stage of the product	Keep consumers aware of the product life cycle

Promotion planning

A common theme in excellent sport marketing is careful planning. Designing a promotional strategy is no exception. A promotions mix needs to be supported by market research and a well-structured plan to ensure that it remains aligned with other marketing initiatives and stays on track once it has begun. The promotions planning process is also essential to determining whether the deployed promotional strategy has been effective. Figure 9.2 outlines the stages of the promotion planning process.

> *Chapter principle 9.8*: A promotional strategy is a plan that aims to use the elements of the promotions mix for the best results. The promotions planning process involves five steps: (1) align with marketing objectives, (2) consider target market, (3) set promotional objectives, (4) set promotional budget and (5) develop promotional mix.

FIGURE 9.2 Promotion planning process

Align with Marketing Objectives

The first step in planning a promotional strategy is to use general marketing objectives as a guide to formulate a promotional plan. As a reminder, a marketing objective is a goal to be achieved as the result of a selected marketing strategy. Any choices made for the promotion plan need to align with marketing objectives and further their achievement.

> *Chapter tool 9.5 Align with marketing objectives*: Any choices made for the promotion plan need to align with marketing objectives and further their achievement.

Consider the Target Market

The second step of the promotion planning process is to examine the intended target market. A target market is a desirable group of consumers (or intermediaries) who share some common elements that the promotional mix can be developed to reach. Target markets can be made up of target audiences, that is different groups of people within a market where specific appeals are likely to resonate differently. For example, while a family might be the target market to attend an athletics event, each family member might be motivated by different factors. The promotional strategies selected should be specific to the target market and be adaptable to the audiences within the market. There are two ways of promoting a sport product, depending on whether the target market is the final consumer of the product, or whether it is an intermediary (an 'in-between' company such as a wholesaler). The two types are known as a push strategy and a pull strategy.

Push Strategy

A push strategy involves promoting a sport product to a wholesaler, or other marketing channel intermediary, with the ambition of convincing them to carry the product. If successful, then the wholesaler must also push the product towards a retailer. In turn, the retailer promotes the product to the eventual consumer and may use advertising or other forms of promotion in the process. This is called a push strategy because the sport product gets *pushed*, step-by-step, down the line of distribution to the final consumer. With a push strategy, it is common to rely strongly on personal selling strategies, although other promotional techniques can also be used. A push strategy is appropriate when specific channel members have been identified as the primary target market. Often in these situations, the members carry considerable power and influence in a marketplace, making promotions to them an imperative. For example, if a country is dominated by one major sport store brand, the success (or failure) of a sport consumable is largely dependent upon being stocked and sold by that retailer in both their physical and online stores.

Pull Strategy

A pull strategy involves promoting a sport product directly to the final consumer. A pull strategy requires that demand for the sport product must first be developed. The assumption behind the pull strategy is that as consumers become aware of the product, they will create a demand for retailers to stock it. Retailers will then have to ask wholesalers to sell them the product, and in turn these wholesalers will have to order it from the manufacturer. When using a pull strategy, it is common to use advertising, as well as sales promotion techniques such as sampling, discounts, and coupons. A pull strategy is appropriate when a group of final consumers has been identified as the primary target market.

Since the goals of sport organisations vary considerably, there are different ways in which a push or pull strategy can be used. For example, a large national governing sport organisation might have the objective of winning more medals at the international level. A push strategy would involve bolstering the grassroots levels of the sport to encourage more participation with the intention that a larger participation base will push a higher range and quality of athletes to the elite level. In contrast, a pull strategy would involve offering more support directly to the elite level through coaching or training academies in order to pull the best athletes through to the highest level. It is important to realise that it is unusual for sport organisations to exclusively use a push strategy or a pull strategy. Rather, most use a combination. For example, sporting equipment and apparel manufacturers work hard to convince wholesalers and retailers to stock their brand (push), while also marketing heavily to consumers about the value of the brand itself (pull).

> *Chapter tool 9.6 Consider the target market*: Promotional strategies should be selected with the target market in mind. There are two strategies behind promotion depending on whether the target market is the final consumer of the product or an intermediary. The two are a push strategy and a pull strategy.

CASE 9.4

Melbourne Cup Carnival

Horse racing has positioned and promoted itself as the 'sport of kings', connecting the owning and training of horses to nobility and royalty. It remains a hugely popular sport in many parts of the world, although the primary reason for its sustained success is its underpinning gambling.

There are numerous famous horse races around the world, including the legendary Triple Crown of the Kentucky Derby, Preakness, and Belmont Stakes in the United States, the Prix de l'Arc de Triomphe in France which is Europe's richest race, the Epsom Derby and Ascot Gold Cup in England, the Dubai World Cup in the United Arab Emirates, and the Melbourne Cup in Australia. Some of these events have been run for hundreds of years, with the Epsom Derby commencing in 1780.

With large racecourses having the ability to attract enormous crowds, and able to operate across carnival periods with multiple days of racing, the marketing of horse racing events has become big business. The Ascot Gold Cup, for example, occurs in the middle of five consecutive days of racing and can attract crowds exceeding 300,000 across the week with visitors coming to the events from all over the world.

Melbourne in Australia has its own version of a horse racing carnival, known as the Spring Racing Carnival (SRC). It consists of 24 race days between September and December each year across a variety of metropolitan and regional racetracks. The feature component of the SRC is the Melbourne Cup carnival, which is spread across four days in a week – a Saturday, Tuesday, Thursday, and Saturday again. The Melbourne Cup itself occurs on the first Tuesday in November, a public holiday in the state of Victoria, and is a 3200-metre handicap race that has run uninterrupted since 1861. The Melbourne Cup carnival is a major part of the city's major events calendar, attracting visitors from across the world drawn by the fashion, food, and fun generated by events across the city. This view of horse racing as a vehicle for wider platforms of entertainment was the mainstay of public relations efforts at the turn of the century to broaden attendance at the races. Melbourne race organisers across the Melbourne Cup carnival were able to instil a passionate sense of 'being seen' to attendance, with many racegoers eschewing watching the horses in favour of picnics on the lawn, and general merriment across the vast expanses the racetracks offered. Using fashion as a mainstay propelled the local fashion industry as attendees dressed up in the latest designer outfits, and almost everyone young and old placed a bet on the 'race that stops a nation' as the Melbourne Cup has been dubbed, despite community misgivings about normalising gambling behaviour more broadly.

The success of the Melbourne Cup carnival was instructive about how big sporting events can become less about the sport and more about the culture of the event, and the Australian Grand Prix Corporation has used the same festival philosophy to attract huge crowds to its four days of racing at its Formula One event. The success of the Melbourne Cup carnival cannot be taken for granted, however, and since 2016 crowds have declined. Where they once topped 100,000 at the Melbourne Cup (e.g., there were 121,000 fans at the 2003 running) only 85,000 fans attended in 2023. Television viewing figures have tumbled as well, suggesting some fans are losing interest. In 2002 over 2.5 million viewers were recorded in metropolitan (Australia's five largest cities) regions, but this was just over 1.1 million in 2023. The claim of the 'race that stops the nation' is becoming harder to justify.

QUESTIONS

1. If the Melbourne Cup Carnival is in decline, as the viewing and attendance figures may suggest, what promotional tactics, particularly centred on public relations can you suggest to turn its fortunes around?
2. How would a sport like horse racing attract younger audiences going forward given it has a strong connection to gambling?
3. Given horse racing can have broad appeal, what mix of promotional mediums (i.e., media) would you suggest to attract visitors to a carnival event like the one at Ascot or in Melbourne?

Set Promotional Objectives

The third step in the promotion planning process is to set promotional objectives. The three main goals of promotion – to inform, persuade, and remind – have already been introduced. These represent the broad objectives of promotion. It is therefore important to pinpoint which of these goals will be the focus of the promotion plan. However, when setting promotional objectives, it is possible to be even more specific. The ultimate promotional objective is to stimulate consumers to act. For example, it may be desirable for consumers to buy the product, volunteer their time, donate money to fundraising or just attend an event. It is easy to understand how to inform, persuade, or remind consumers, but it is more difficult to get them to take action. Sport marketers can encourage consumers to act by guiding them through a series of steps known as *a hierarchy of effects*. The word *hierarchy* means that there are stepped levels, and that one step builds on another to reach a goal. The hierarchy of effects is displayed in Figure 9.3.

The idea behind the hierarchy of effects is that all consumers must pass through each stage (starting at the bottom) before they consume a product. Consumers are unaware, aware, informed, attracted, inclined, and convinced before they consume. It is worth remembering that there are some common situations where consumers might not pass through every stage of the hierarchy. For example, when someone makes a split-second decision to buy a product (called an impulse purchase), they may not know much about the product benefits. Also, sometimes consumers purchase a product for someone else as a gift and may not even like it themselves.

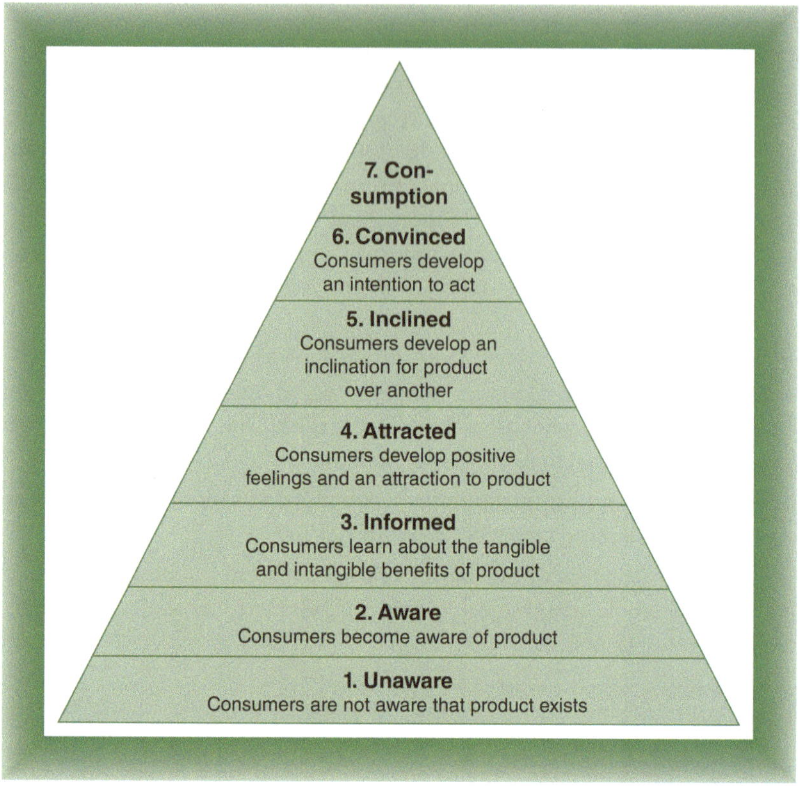

FIGURE 9.3 The hierarchy of effects

Even though the hierarchy of effects is not useful in every situation, sport marketers may employ it to give them a general guide for developing promotional goals. If a group of consumers can be located on the hierarchy, then it is easier to select a matching promotional objective.

The hierarchy of effects starts at the bottom of the pyramid when consumers are *unaware* that a product exists. At this stage, the promotional objective is to make consumers *aware* of the product. When consumers are aware of the product, they know it exists but may not know much else about it. Thus, consumers need to be educated about the product's tangible and intangible benefits. At this stage, the central promotional objective is to give consumers product information so that they become *informed*. Just because a consumer is aware of a product and knows about its benefits does not mean that they will necessarily like it. The main promotional objective at this stage is to encourage consumers to be *attracted* to the product, and to create positive feelings towards it. Once consumers are attracted to the product, it is important to convince them to prefer it or become *inclined* towards it over all alternatives. The corresponding promotional objective is to establish that the product on offer is the best available for the target market. With consumers' interest in the product, they must next become *convinced* that the product is right for them, leading to a definitive intention to make a purchase. Therefore, the main promotional objective at this stage is to create a strong desire to act. Desire does not automatically mean that a consumer will act, as they may not have enough money or time, or new and superior alternatives may become available instead. However, desire is a powerful precursor to *consumption*. There are circumstances where consumers have become convinced about a product and do genuinely intend to purchase it, but still do not act. Dealing with this problem requires a good understanding of what is stopping consumers from buying a product when they desire it. In some cases, the obstacle might simply be price. A Ferrari automobile is desired by many but purchased by few. In the case of sport services, availability might be an issue, such as with tickets to hallmark events or the finals series of a league.

Aside from providing scaffolding to build a promotional mix around, the hierarchy of effects also provides a way of measuring how a brand is progressing with their objectives. It is possible, given the hierarchy is essentially a series of steps, to measure each component to assess how effective a promotional campaign is going. If consumers are aware of a product, and become informed about its attributes, but find it unattractive, then a marketer has a clear understanding of where their messaging needs to be adjusted. Just as a racing car navigates a series of corners to reach a finish line, a marketing manager must complete the hierarchy of effects to get some proportion of its target market to purchase.

> *Chapter tool 9.7 Set promotional objectives*: The hierarchy of effects shows how consumers may pass through a number of stages before they actually consume, and represents a tool for connecting promotional objectives with the promotions mix. The stages of the hierarchy of effects are: (1) unaware, (2) aware, (3) informed, (4) attracted, (5) inclined, (6) convinced and (7) consumption. These stages illustrate how consumers first become aware of a product (from unaware to aware), learn about its benefits (informed), (3) become interested in it (attracted), (4) develop a preference for one product or brand over others (inclined), (5) experience a desire to do something about it (convinced) and (6) then act (consumption).

Set a Promotional Budget

The next step in a promotional plan involves setting a promotional budget. For some planners, the budget might be the first step in the promotion process given access to funding is an imperative to determining what objectives might be attainable and which target markets can be reached. One can think of budget, market, and objectives as being intertwined. In this chapter, however, we have assumed that the budget can be separated from the earlier steps when it adopts a logical approach based on funding what is desired. This budgeting approach considers marketing an investment, rather than an expense. In effect, the money expended will ensure the objectives and target market are reached, as opposed to making them a limitation of what might be available.

A budget determines how much money will be spent on promotion and must be considered in the light of objectives and audiences. In the simplest of terms, a budget is an investment in future sales in that what is expended should come back with a premium. It would not make sense to invest $1 and get back 99 cents (or less), although there may be instances where this occurs in a situation where a brand is clinging to vital market share or is seeking to disrupt a competitor and is willing to cut revenues in doing so. While getting more than $1 back for each $1 invested is the goal, at some point returns will plateau and decline, so budgeting is concerned with mapping this scenario and in ensuring that money is being expended in the right way. As budgets are inevitably out of date the minute an environmental factor changes, they are notoriously complex and sport organisations often have limited abilities to deal with these circumstances.

Not only do sport organisations typically have limited resources available to spend on promotion, but it is also possible for them to choose different methods for deciding on how much is appropriate. Some of the common methods used for deciding on a budget include: (1) arbitrary allocation (effectively what is available), (2) competitive parity (matching competitors), (3) competitive disparity (being deliberately different to competitors), (4) percentage of sales, and (5) the objective and task method (the amount is determined by promotional objectives and tasks). Each is overviewed next. Irrespective of which approach is favoured, it is important to remember that multiple methods can be used to give firms a more grounded sense of what the right number is. For example, while we recommend the objective and task approach given its rationality, adding in a competitor analysis to ensure that their spend is taken into consideration would also make good sense in a highly competitive market.

Arbitrary Allocation

If an amount to spend on promotion is determined *arbitrarily*, then it is done subjectively, or without an obvious reason. Often this means that the sport organisation will allocate as much money as it can afford, or available, to promotion (after all the other business costs are considered). If a sport marketer chooses this method, then they are not paying any attention to what their competitors are doing, what the economic climate is, or how effective their promotional budget was last year. In other words, this is not a very sensible or well thought out way to allocate a budget. While financial realities might mean this option is used in some instances, it is not recommended given the disconnect it has with the other planning components.

Competitive Parity

Competitive parity (or equality) means deciding to spend a similar amount to that of competitors. Competitive parity is more common in highly competitive marketplaces, where a number of businesses are trying to attract the attention of consumers. However, this may be a difficult (and even impossible) method for some organisations if they do not have the same revenue to spend. Despite first appearances, there is some logic to a competitive parity approach in that it presumes the collective wisdom of the marketplace is suggesting a certain amount of investment is appropriate. Sport brands can invest in promotion knowing that the amount is anchored to something measurable, even though the objectives and markets of competitor brands might not be well aligned. In some situations, a competitive parity method might make a good starting point for developing a budget.

Competitive Disparity

It is also possible to estimate what competitors are spending on promotion, and deliberately decide to spend a different amount. This is known as competitive disparity. Disparity means difference or inequality. It can be a way of standing apart from competitors and differentiating the product or brand. Competitive disparity is also common with sporting goods that are designed with a low cost in mind and that are successful when sold in large volumes with few costs allocated to promotions. The logic to a disparity approach is similar to that of a parity approach in that an anchor point is established and a brand then chooses to go below or above this amount. In markets that are highly responsive to marketing messages, spending more than the competition might make sense given the return on the investment will likely make it worthwhile.

Percentage of Sales

It is possible to calculate a promotional budget as a percentage of total sales. To do this, it is first essential to determine a standard, or suitable, percentage of sales that will be allocated to promotions. Sometimes organisations will choose a percentage based on what their competitors are doing, while at other times it may be an arbitrary choice. Once the standard percentage has been determined, the previous year's sales figure is used as a guide to next year's sales. From here, it is possible to calculate a percentage of the predicted amount of sales. For example, if 5% of sales is set as a guideline, and five million dollars in sales is expected in the forthcoming year, then the promotional budget is $250,000 (5% of five million).

There are several significant limitations to the percentage of sales approach. First, it may be difficult to calculate what level of standard percentage should be used in the first place. Second, it may not be accurate to use last year's sales as a guide to estimate the forthcoming year. Thirdly, if sales are declining, it may be more important to spend additional money on promotion rather than less given declining sales will reduce subsequent budgets. Finally, and perhaps most importantly, the percentage of sales approach is not recommended given it effectively reverses the main purpose of a promotion budget in that it is an investment in future sales. The percentage of sales method makes past sales the arbiter of future budgets, which is illogical. Despite this, many firms use this approach as one of their budgeting approaches given the percentage approach provides some reference point.

Objective and Task Method

The final method discussed here is the recommended approach of the objective and task method. This approach demands that the promotional *objectives* that have been set, and the promotional *tasks* needed to carry out those objectives, should guide the budget that is allocated. In essence what is needed to be done, and how, is used to calculate the cost of doing so. It is then a matter of calculating what it will cost to carry out the tasks and assuring that the return is both suitable and appropriate.

This method is logical, but it can run into difficulty if the promotional objectives and tasks that were planned were inappropriate, leading to substantial spending on a promotional plan that is not going to be effective. Some marketers are also uncomfortable with this approach in that their budget is effectively starting at zero each year and must be built up by deciding the objectives and associated tasks required to reach them. While rational, some marketers may prefer to simply be given a sum anchored to some other point (percentage of sales, competitors levels, or what is available) and proceed from there.

> *Chapter tool 9.8 Set promotional budget*: Setting a promotional budget means deciding how much money to spend on promotion. Some of the common methods used for deciding on a budget are: (1) arbitrary allocation (subjectively choosing an amount), (2) competitive parity (matching competitors), (3) competitive disparity (being deliberately different to competitors), (4) percentage of sales and (5) the objective and task method (the amount is determined by promotional objectives and tasks).

Develop a Promotional Mix

The final step of the promotion planning process is to develop a promotions mix. To recap, the elements of the promotions mix are: (1) advertising, (2) personal selling, (3) sales promotions, and (4) public relations. These elements are called a *mix* because they are combined. Sport organisations do not just use one promotions element but rather use a mixture of some or all of them in their promotional strategy. It is important to realise that if a number of promotional elements are used, they should be designed to complement one another. In the end, a promotions strategy should be created so that the different elements of the promotions mix are combined to work towards the promotional goals that have been set.

The promotions mix used will be highly dependent upon all the previous factors and the context within which a brand finds themselves. Often, and particularly with sport organisations, it makes good sense to get outside help in developing the promotional mix given the enormous range of factors that need to be melded to form a coherent approach. Many brands, for example, will use research companies, advertising agencies, digital experts, and consulting firms to navigate the complexities of promotion.

> *Chapter tool 9.9 Develop promotions mix*: In developing a promotions mix, sport marketers must choose which elements of the promotions mix will reach the desired promotional objectives and be achievable within the budget that has been set.

PRINCIPLES SUMMARY

- Chapter principle 9.1: Promotion can be defined as the way that sport marketers communicate with consumers to inform, persuade, and remind them about the features and benefits described by a sport product's positioning.
- Chapter principle 9.2: The promotions mix consists of four marketing tools: (1) advertising, (2) personal selling, (3) sales promotions, and (4) public relations.

- Chapter principle 9.3: Promotional elements should be combined in order to complement one another in order to achieve a promotional goal that is consistent with the overall marketing and positioning strategy.
- Chapter principle 9.4: There are three main objectives of promotion: (1) to inform, (2) to persuade, and (3) to remind.
- Chapter principle 9.5: Promotions that *inform* aim to communicate the product's existence, its benefits, its positioning, and how it can be obtained. Promotions that aim to inform consumers are usually undertaken during the early stages of the product life cycle.
- Chapter principle 9.6: Persuasive promotions are utilised when trying to give consumers good reasons to buy a sport product. Persuasive promotions are more common when a product enters the growth stage of the product life cycle.
- Chapter principle 9.7: Reminder promotions aim to keep a product or brand name prominent in consumers' minds. Reminder promotions are most common during the maturity stage of the product life cycle.
- Chapter principle 9.8: A promotional strategy is a plan that aims to use the elements of the promotions mix for the best results. The promotions planning process involves five steps: (1) align with marketing objectives, (2) consider target market, (3) set promotional objectives, (4) set promotional budget, and (5) develop promotional mix.

TOOLS SUMMARY

- Chapter tool 9.1 Advertising
- Chapter tool 9.2 Personal selling
- Chapter tool 9.3 Sales promotions
- Chapter tool 9.4 Public relations
- Chapter tool 9.5 Align with marketing objectives
- Chapter tool 9.6 Consider the target market
- Chapter tool 9.7 Set promotional objectives
- Chapter tool 9.8 Set promotional budget
- Chapter tool 9.9 Develop promotions mix

REVIEW QUESTIONS

1. In what ways are promotions more than just advertising?
2. What are the four tools of the promotions mix? Provide an example of each.
3. Why is public relations such a useful tool for sport organisations with constrained marketing resources?
4. Describe how a sport brand such as Adidas uses push and pull strategies simultaneously.
5. Provide some examples illustrating when the hierarchy of effects is not an accurate description of a consumer's decision-making process.
6. Explain why the promotions mix should be integrated for best results.

RELEVANT WEBSITES

Australian Open Tennis Championships (https://ausopen.com/)
International Boxing Federation (www.ibf-usba-boxing.com)
The Ring Magazine (www.ringtv.com/
Royal Ascot (www.ascot.com/)
Ultimate Fighting Championship (www.ufc.com)
Victoria Racing Club (www.vrc.com.au/)
World Boxing Association (www.wbaboxing.com/)
World Boxing Council (www.wbcboxing.com/en/)
World Boxing Organization (www.wboboxing.com)

FURTHER READING

Dees, W., Walsh, P., McEvoy, C. D., McKelvey, S., Mullin, B. J., Hardy, S. & Sutton, W. A. (2021). *Sport Marketing*. Human Kinetics.

Pedersen, P. M., Laucella, P. C., Kian, E. M., & Geurin, A. N. (2021). *Strategic Sport Communication*. Human-Kinetics.

Stoldt, G. C., Dittmore, S. W., Ross, M., & Branvold, S. E. (2020). *Sport Public Relations*. Human Kinetics Publishers.

Westberg, K., Stavros, C., & Wilson, B. (2011). The impact of degenerative episodes on the sponsorship B2B relationship: Implications for brand management. *Industrial Marketing Management*, *40*(4), 603–611.

CHAPTER 10

Sport sponsorship

LEARNING OUTCOMES

At the end of this chapter, readers should be able to:

- define the term sport sponsorship.
- identify potential sponsorship objectives and associated market segments.
- highlight the key elements of sponsorship targeting.
- outline the sections of a sponsorship proposal.
- specify how sponsorship may be augmented through leveraging.
- highlight the main principles of sponsorship evaluation.
- explain what is meant by ambush marketing.
- identify the five main tactics in preventing ambush marketing.

OVERVIEW

This chapter describes the use of sponsorship in sport marketing and explains the major principles and tools of its deployment. Although sponsorship is usually considered a sub-section of promotions, it has become so pivotal to sport marketing that it is being treated here as the fifth element of the sport marketing mix. This chapter outlines five essential aspects of sport sponsorship: (1) sponsorship objectives, (2) sponsorship targeting, (3) sponsorship leveraging, (4) sponsorship evaluation, and (5) ambush marketing.

SPONSORSHIP IN THE MIX

Chapter 9 examined promotions as the fourth element of the sport marketing mix. It also introduced the concept of sport sponsorship as a kind of promotional activity. Conventionally in marketing, sponsorship is viewed as a sub-category of personal selling

DOI: 10.4324/9781003391319-10

because it involves personal contact between an organisation and a sponsor. Given that sponsorship has not traditionally been a dominant form of promotion for most non-sport organisations (although that is beginning to change), textbooks have typically treated it as part of personal selling. However, the prominence of sponsorship in sport marketing demands that it be treated as a variable to be managed. As an example of sponsorship's prominence in the sport industry, the global sport sponsorship market was estimated to be worth US$110 billion in 2023. Sport sponsorship is treated here as an equal part of the marketing mix. The chief components of sport sponsorship are highlighted in Figure 10.1, which locates sponsorship within the Sport Marketing Framework.

WHAT IS SPORT SPONSORSHIP?

Sport sponsorship has increased dramatically over the past two decades. For many large non-sport corporations such as Coca-Cola, McDonald's, Toyota, and Vodafone, sponsoring sport organisations and athletes is an important part of their marketing strategies. Several types of sport organisations and individuals may be sponsored, including individual athletes, clubs and teams, events, leagues, unions, federations, competitions, venues, and special causes.

Sport sponsorship occurs when a sporting organisation, club, league, venue, cause, or athlete is supported by a separate company (or person). In England's Women's Super League (WSL), for example, British multi-national bank Barclays is the major sponsor, paying £30 million over a three-year period. The recipient of the sponsorship (the WSL in this example) is known as the *sponsorship property* or the *sport property*. These legal-sounding terms are indicative of the fact that sponsorship is a business agreement between two parties. A non-legal term for the sponsorship recipient is the 'sponsee'.

> *Chapter principle 10.1*: The term sport property refers to the recipient of the sponsorship. This could be an athlete, team, event, venue, association, cause or competition.

Sponsorships are supposed to benefit both parties, which is why they are now sometimes referred to as 'partnerships' or 'alliances', implying that the relationship is both reciprocal and symbiotic. Usually the sport property receives cash, goods, services, or expert advice, and the sponsor receives benefits such as promotional rights and the marketing advantages of being associated with a particular sport property. Sponsors hope that by investing in a sport property, they will increase consumers' awareness of their brand, and consequently build brand equity. It is important to realise, however, that sponsorship can be a high-risk investment. This is mainly because the outcome of the agreement can be unpredictable. For example, there is no guarantee that a sponsor will achieve the increased sales, improved brand image, or changed consumer perceptions that they are seeking. The risk of sponsorship may be particularly high if individuals are sponsored. Like any investment, risk decreases with diversification. Because any individual athlete can easily fall prey to ill-health, injury, poor performance, or even personal circumstances that are unfavourably

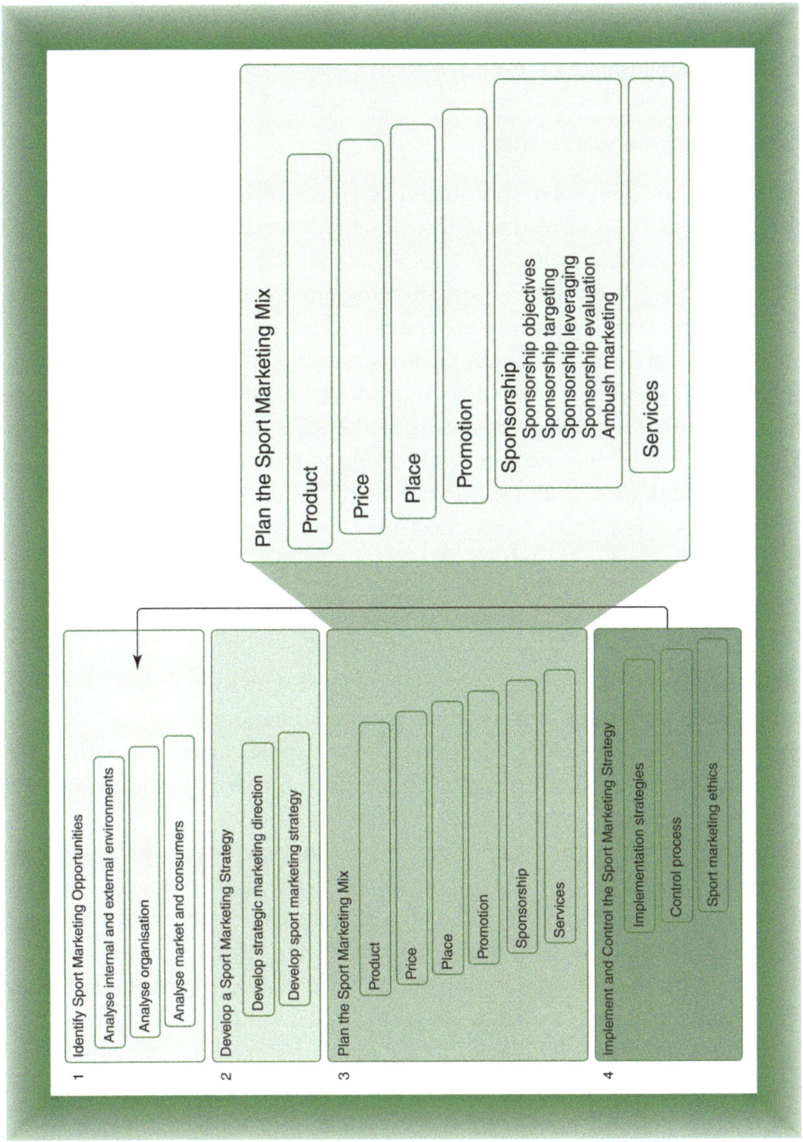

FIGURE 10.1 The sport marketing framework

interpreted in the media, it is more likely that a sponsor can lose its investment. On the other hand, the right prominent athlete can be a sponsor's dream.

> *Chapter principle 10.2*: Sport sponsorship is a business agreement where one organisation provides financial or in-kind assistance to a sport property in exchange for the right to associate itself with the sport property. The sponsor does this to achieve corporate objectives (such as enhancing corporate image) or marketing objectives (such as increasing brand awareness).

Sponsorship and advertising

To really understand the benefits of sponsorship, it is useful to consider the ways in which it can be distinguished from advertising. Consumers generally see advertising, or a paid form of non-personal communication, as a selfish activity; they believe that the company or brand being advertised is out to promote their own interests. Consumers may even suspect that the company is trying to pressure them into buying the product. This can make consumers sceptical and suspicious about advertisements, and they may deliberately resist by ignoring or wilfully disliking the advertised product. On the other hand, consumers are more likely to think that a sponsorship has some benefits beyond those for the sponsor. Although they may realise that the sponsor is trying to persuade them about something, the approach is more disguised and subtle than advertising, and consumers may be less defensive about responding to it. Consumers may therefore react to sport sponsorship communications with a general goodwill.

Sponsorship and goodwill

Goodwill offers an important principle to help understand why sport sponsorships are effective. There are several important dimensions of goodwill. First, more goodwill is created for sponsorship of social causes such as community-based sport organisations than for large profit-seeking sport events and competitions. This opportunity has led some corporations to use sport sponsorship as a form of corporate social responsibility. Second, goodwill is usually greatest when the consumer is personally involved in the sport activity being sponsored. In fact, the more that a consumer is personally involved in the sport property, the higher the level of goodwill generated. Third, the time at which a sponsor becomes involved with a sport property can influence the level of goodwill associated with it. Sponsors who become involved later might be seen to be 'jumping on the bandwagon' compared with those perceived to be instrumental in the formation of a strong relationship with a sport property early in its life, or during a downturn. This leads to the fourth observation, as there can be some risk of a sponsor losing goodwill when it decides to discontinue an agreement. Consumers might conclude that the sponsor was only involved to exploit a temporary opportunity.

> *Chapter principle 10.3*: Sport sponsorship generates goodwill among consumers. The amount of goodwill generated can vary depending on the kind of sport property sponsored, the degree of involvement that consumers have with the sport property, the time at which the sponsor becomes involved, and when and how the sponsor ceases the sponsorship.

Fan involvement

One important implication leading from the previous section is that a sponsor will generate more goodwill among consumers who are personally involved with the sport property compared with those who are more casually involved. The idea of fan involvement was introduced in Chapter 3, and is a term that describes the degree to which fans personally identify with a particular sport, competition or athlete, or the level of personal affiliation and engagement they possess about the sport property.

Fan involvement is an important consideration in sponsorship because a sport consumer's response to a sponsorship is driven by their level of involvement in the sport property. For example, strongly involved sport consumers show higher levels of sponsorship awareness, a more substantial sense of goodwill towards the sponsor, a greater brand preference for the sponsor, and a stronger intention to purchase a sponsor's products. Consumers are also more likely to change brands because of sponsorship, and because they are knowledgeable about the sport property, they are better able to judge whether there is a logical connection or congruence between the sport property and the sponsor.

Positive responses from highly involved sport consumers are more likely to occur in certain situations. In general, sport consumers tend to be more personally involved in events, teams, or individual athletes, and will respond better to the sponsors of these kinds of sport properties, compared with the sponsorship of competitions, venues, or a sporting broadcast. In addition, involved fans are more likely to respond positively when there is one clear sponsor of an activity instead of several sponsors competing for attention. Sport properties must attempt to balance this, as they often rely on multiple sponsors to cover the organisation's costs and to maximise sponsorship revenues. All these points teach us that fan involvement is an important element to consider when looking at sponsorship.

> *Chapter principle 10.4*: Fan involvement is an important consideration in sponsorship because a consumer's response to a sponsorship is driven by the level of involvement that they have with the sport property.

CASE 10.1

Airbnb

Sponsorship through sport is a reciprocal relationship. Companies persistently use sponsorship to leverage their brand value, but not necessarily through the traditional 'tell and sell' method. Sport is ideal for engaging consumers to participate with the sponsor's product or service. One such example is Airbnb, a global company specialising in long- and short-term homestays and experiences. Airbnb became a worldwide Olympic partner in 2020 with a sponsorship deal that spans five Olympic Games and lasts until at least 2028. The Airbnb website describes the sponsorship as one that is, 'designed to create a new standard for hosting that will be a win for host cities, a win for spectators and fans, and a win for athletes'.

One of the reasons the IOC wanted to partner with Airbnb was to reduce the number of hotel rooms needed at Olympic Games, thus increasing the sustainability of the Games by utilising homes that already existed for sport consumers who attend the Olympics. The IOC also said it hopes to give residents of Olympic host cities the opportunity to earn extra income during the Games by providing additional accommodation options for attendees. A study commissioned by Airbnb found that over 130,000 people planned to list their homes on the site during the Paris 2024 Olympic and Paralympic Games, demonstrating that the IOC's goal seems poised to come to fruition. The sponsorship also provides opportunities for Olympic athletes to host 'experiences' on the site, from which they earn revenue, such as the opportunity to train with an Olympian for a day or the chance to take a tour of a city with an Olympian. One example of this was British skateboarder Sky Brown, who hosted an interactive question and answer session with fans prior to the Tokyo Olympics in 2021. Another example was two-time Olympic gold medallist basketball player Scottie Pippen, who hosted three one-night stays for up to four people at his own home via Airbnb. The package not only included accommodation, but also access to Pippen's home indoor basketball court, his personal home movie theatre to watch the Olympic Games, and exclusive access to view Pippen's Olympic memorabilia inside the home. Through its sponsorship of the IOC, Airbnb has developed highly creative ways to engage Olympic fans, create new revenue opportunities for athletes and local residents, and helped develop a more sustainable mode of accommodation during the Olympic Games.

QUESTIONS

1. Do you believe that Airbnb's sponsorship of the Olympics will be more successful engaging highly identified Olympic fans, or more successful in engaging low-to-medium engaged fans? Why?
2. Imagine that you work for Airbnb. Think about the Olympic athletes from your country who are currently most popular with Olympic fans. What type of Airbnb athlete experience would you create in partnership with one of those athletes?
3. Thinking back to your answer the last question, why do you think this experience would be successful in drawing in fans to engage with it?

SPONSORSHIP OBJECTIVES

The sponsors and sport property will have different objectives they want to achieve from of a successful sponsorship. In the previous case, the IOC wanted to achieve more sustainable accommodation options for fans at the Olympic Games, while also giving athletes and residents opportunities to generate income through experiences and hosting guests in their homes. Airbnb likely wanted to increase brand awareness as well as bring in more business from global Olympic consumers. The two most common objectives for sponsors are enhancing brand image and increasing brand awareness. For the sport property, the most common objective is to attract financial support, which in turn helps to meet other administrative and developmental goals. While these may be the most common, the objectives of sponsorship can vary greatly, depending on the size of the partners, the nature of the sponsorship relationship, and the type of sport property being supported. For this reason, it is essential that both the owner of the sport property and the sponsor have a clear understanding of the objectives behind a sponsorship agreement. By understanding the benefits a sponsor seeks, the sport property is in a better position to 'sell' the idea of the sponsorship, and to ensure that they can provide what the sponsor needs. In the next section, possible sponsorship objectives from the perspective of the sponsor, and from the perspective of the sport property, are reviewed.

Sponsor objectives

Although there are some non-marketing goals that will be mentioned shortly, for a sponsor, the objectives of a sport sponsorship programme align to general marketing goals. This means that most sponsorship objectives can be related to a specific market segment (or segments) that a sponsor aims to reach with the sponsorship programme. Some potential objectives are outlined in Table 10.1 where each has been related to a market segment. The table highlights the fact that sponsorship is a versatile promotional tool because it can reach many different market segments and help to achieve a range of promotional objectives relevant to the sponsor.

At first glance, it might appear that the sponsorship objectives highlighted in Table 10.1 are exclusive to the sponsor. After all, one of the main objectives for the sport property is to attract financial or in-kind support, which the owner organisation might employ in a variety of administrative, promotional, or developmental projects. However, the association between the sponsor and the sport property can yield significant branding benefits to both parties. By attracting the 'right' sponsor, the owner of a sport property can influence the way that their target market thinks about their brand (known as 'brand image'). A corporate sponsor can add substantial credibility to this image, in turn enhancing the sport property's brand equity, brand loyalty, and even ticket or product sales. Those employed by the sport property might even feel satisfied and proud to know that their organisation has the reputation to attract powerful or important sponsors. In fact, many of the objectives (either directly or indirectly) may be considered relevant to both the sport property owners as well as the sponsor.

> *Chapter principle 10.5*: The objectives of sponsorship can vary greatly, depending on the size of the partners, the type of sponsorship and the type of sport property being supported. Some common objectives for the sponsor are to enhance sales, to promote the public image of its brand, to increase consumer awareness, to modify its brand image, and to build business relationships.

TABLE 10.1 Major sponsorship objectives for sponsors

Market segment	*Objective*
General public	To promote the public image of the organisation
	To increase mass media exposure and public relations
	To increase general public awareness of organisation and/or product
	To generate goodwill
	To form a general brand perception
	To create a favourable community perception through social or cause-related sponsorship
Target market	To increase consumer awareness of a product/service/brand
	To increase sales/market share of a specific product
	To establish a brand association between the sport property and sponsor
	To create an 'image transfer', where values are transferred from the sport product or type of sponsorship to the sponsor
	To develop brand equity (the added value a product has because of the brand name)
	To develop, manage, and/or change brand image (what values and ideas consumers associate with the brand)
	To promote brand loyalty (e.g., repeat purchasing)
Distribution channel members	To increase sales to channel members (e.g., wholesalers) To promote discounts and deals from channel members (e.g., suppliers)
	To develop new relationships/new distribution channels (e.g., pouring rights at an event)
Internal stakeholders	To improve staff morale and relations To increase staff satisfaction (e.g., through a sense of pride in the association or through corporate hospitality/entertainment)
	To promote satisfaction of shareholders (e.g., due to pride in association, improved brand equity/sales/market share)
	To promote positive communications with the media (e.g., through corporate hospitality, corporate social responsibility)

Sport property objectives

Table 10.2 outlines the major sponsorship objectives of sport organisations as owners of sport properties. Unlike the previous table detailing sponsor objectives, each of the following objectives is not associated with a market segment. This is because several of the objectives relate to non-marketing areas such as corporate and operational development.

> *Chapter principle 10.6*: The objectives of sponsorship for the sport property will vary. In addition to attracting financial support, objectives include increasing credibility, increasing awareness, and managing brand image.

TABLE 10.2 Major sponsorship objectives for sport properties

Activity area	*Objective*
Corporate objectives	To promote the public image of the sport property through a credible association and brand match up
	To increase mass media exposure and public relations (PR) (directly using new funds, or indirectly through PR undertaken by the sponsor)
	To increase public awareness of the property and/or product (directly and indirectly)
Marketing objectives	To increase consumer awareness of a product/service/brand (directly using sponsor funds/resources, and indirectly through the PR undertaken by the sponsor)
	To increase credibility among consumers (via credibility of sponsor)
	To establish a brand association between the sport organisation and sponsor to create an 'image transfer' from the sport product
	To position or re-position the sport brand in the minds of consumers
	To develop, manage, and/or change brand image (what values and ideas consumers associate with the brand)
	To promote discounts and deals from channel members (e.g., from suppliers at an event through offering sponsorship rights)
	To develop new relationships/new distribution channels (e.g., granting exclusive pouring rights at an event)
Operational objectives	To obtain funding, resources, and/or services to support operation and development
	To increase staff satisfaction (e.g., pride/credibility in the association/free goods and merchandise)
	To promote credibility with stakeholders (e.g., politicians, regulators, shareholders, and the media)
	To promote satisfaction of shareholders (e.g., due to pride/credibility in association)

SPONSORSHIP TARGETING

It is more common for the sport property to be the one that introduces the idea of sponsorship to a sponsor rather than the reverse. This is partly because the benefits for the sport property are easier to measure (such as the amount of money received) compared with those for the sponsor. It is difficult, for example, for a sponsor to know how much its sales have increased because of the sponsorship compared with how much they have increased because of other promotions and marketing. Therefore, when a sport property approaches a potential sponsor, it is important that they have a clear idea of what they have to offer or 'sell'. Usually, the sport property would approach a sponsor with a written sponsorship proposal designed to highlight the potential benefits of the relationship. There are two central elements to this process: the first is choosing the right potential sponsor, and the second is writing an appropriate proposal.

Choosing the right sponsor: sponsorship affinity

Attracting the 'right' sponsor for a sport property is not just a matter of locating one willing to hand over some cash. Sponsorship relationships are more successful, and more likely to be renewed, when there is the right match between partners. Sponsorship in motor racing provides a good example. Motor racing teams need large sums of money to maintain their competitiveness in an expensive sport. In other words, they need sponsors. The sport consumers who watch motor racing are usually people interested in buying and maintaining their own cars. It stands to reason that companies such as BMW and Shell want to reach these consumers to influence their buying decisions. Motor racing teams need money from sponsors, and sponsors want to promote their products to the people who watch the motor racing teams.

When companies consider sponsoring a sport property, they focus on two priorities. First, they look for an affinity between the sponsor and the sport property. It is important for the sport property and sponsor's values to be aligned and for both parties to feel they can work well together and communicate effectively. Second, they look for an affinity between the target markets of the sponsor and those of the sport property. The brand positioning strategies of both parties should match, and the target market the sport property reaches should be the same (or partially the same) as the target market the sponsor is trying to reach. Figure 10.2 shows these two vital components for ensuring a good match between sponsorship partners.

> *Chapter principle 10.7*: Sponsorship affinity refers to whether there is a good fit or match between the sponsor and the sport property. Two factors are particularly important for ensuring a good match: (1) an overlap of target markets and (2) a match-up of brand positioning strategies.

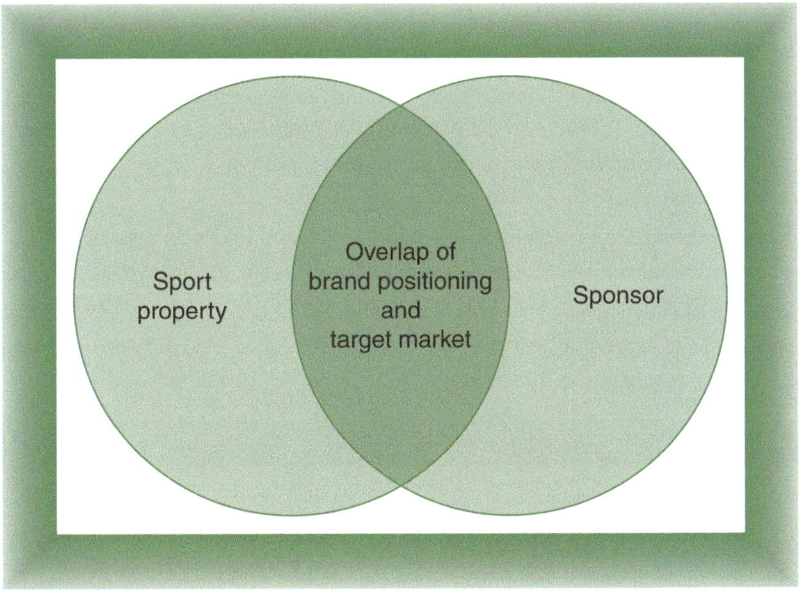

FIGURE 10.2 Sponsorship affinity

CASE 10.2

Women's World Cup Sponsorship

FIFA is undoubtedly one of the most well-known sport brands in the world. As the international federation for football (soccer), FIFA is the ultimate administrator of the world's most popular sport. During the planning stages of the 2023 FIFA Women's World Cup in Australia and New Zealand, it was reported that FIFA was pursuing a sponsorship deal with Visit Saudi, the state tourism authority of Saudi Arabia. The news brought criticism to FIFA given the Women's World Cup tends to involve activism from athletes and fans using their voices to demand equality in terms of women's and LGBTQ+ rights. The national governing body of football in Australia, Football Australia, was vocal in its opposition to the proposed sponsorship, saying in a statement that there was, 'overwhelming consensus that this partnership does not align with our collective vision for the tournament and falls short of our expectations'. FIFA President Gianni Infantino was quick to point out that Australia conducts over $1.5 billion in trade with Saudi Arabia each year, but the public outcry over the potential deal persisted. FIFA ultimately did not finalise the sponsorship, with Infantino calling the situation, 'a storm in a teacup'. Instead of Visit Saudi, the major sponsors of the tournament were Adidas, Coca-Cola, Wanda (a Chinese property conglomerate), Visa, and Xero (a New Zealand accounting software firm).

QUESTIONS

1 Keeping the idea of sponsor affinity in mind, why was the FIFA–Visit Saudi partnership not considered an ideal match? You may want to do some additional research beyond the case to learn more about Women's World Cup fans as well as the nation of Saudi Arabia to answer this question.
2 If FIFA wanted to include a tourism sponsor for a future Women's World Cup, what organisation would you recommend as a better fit, and why?
3 Looking at the brands that sponsored the 2023 Women's World Cup, which one seems to have the best sponsor affinity with FIFA? You may want to do some additional research on these brands to answer this question.

Match-up of brand positioning

To recap, brand positioning or market positioning refers to how a sport organisation would like its consumers to think and feel about its brand when compared to competitors. It is the image or perception of the sport brand that consumers carry in their minds. Positioning considers the fact that consumers will compare a given sport brand with others in the market. When a company sponsors a sport property, the way that consumers think and feel about the sponsor and its brand(s) will be influenced by the way they think and feel about the sport property. Equally, the way that consumers think and feel about the sport property will be influenced by the way they think and feel about the sponsor. The key implication is that there must be a match between the brand positioning strategies of both parties. For example, Nike positions many of its athletic shoes and equipment as being highly innovative and performance-enhancing. This matches the high-performance image of the professional sport leagues, teams, and athletes Nike sponsors. As a result, there is a strong identification overlap between Nike and athletes such as Spanish tennis player Rafael Nadal or English footballer Fran Kirby.

CASE 10.3

Athleta

Athleta is a women's activewear company founded in 1998 and later acquired by fashion brand Gap Inc. It was one of the first of its kind, as it offers apparel that can be worn both for workouts and for everyday life activities, such as running errands or meeting friends for a social occasion. Athleta's website lists its values as being people and planet, inclusive community, and women for women. Largely considered to be an 'athleisure' company like competitors Lululemon and Fabletics, as recently as 2018 Athleta held 21% of the market share in the global athleisure market, second only to Lululemon. Athleta was not traditionally viewed as a competitor to larger sportswear brands such as Nike, Adidas, or Under Armour.

In 2019, however, Athleta gained global media attention when it was announced that would serve as the primary apparel sponsor for six-time Olympic gold medallist Allyson Felix, an American sprinter. Soon after, the most decorated gymnast in the history of the sport, American Simone Biles, followed suit. Both Felix and Biles had been Nike-sponsored athletes before trading in their Swoosh-adorned gear for clothing bearing the Athleta brand mark. Many sport marketing experts questioned why such successful high-profile athletes would leave a more established sport brand to partner with Athleta. For Felix, the answer was that she felt Athleta supported her lifestyle, telling the New York Times, 'I felt like I had more value as a person, and that was something I hadn't experienced before'. Similarly, Biles told the Wall Street Journal that her decision to switch to Athleta was because the brand did not solely value her achievements, but 'it's what I stood for and how they were going to help me use my voice and also be a voice for females and kids'. When Biles experienced mental health difficulties at the 2020 Tokyo Olympics and had to make the decision to not compete in four of the individual events for which she qualified, Athleta issued a statement of support, saying that they stood by her and supported her well-being both as an athlete and off the field of play. Athleta's Chief Brand Officer, Kyle Andrew, said, 'Being the best also means knowing how to take care of yourself. We are inspired by her leadership today and are behind her every step of the way'.

Many female athletes expressed to media outlets and on their own social media accounts that they had not always felt supported and valued by their sponsors in the way that Athleta supported its athletes. The strong match between the brand's values and those of the athletes it sponsored led to positive relationships between the brand and its athletes, as well as positive impressions of the brand among the sponsored athletes' fans and followers, many of whom had not heard of Athleta previously.

QUESTIONS

1 Conduct some background research on Allyson Felix, Simone Biles, and the brand Athleta. Based on the case as well as what you can find in your searches, what values do you believe these athletes have and how do they align with Athleta's stated values?

2 How do you believe Athleta benefits from partnering with successful women athletes such as Felix and Biles?

3 Based on what you know about Athleta, do you believe there are any sporting events or sport teams that would be a strong match for this brand to sponsor? Which ones and why?

SPONSORSHIP PROPOSALS

The sponsorship proposal should be a specific document that is targeted towards a specific sponsor. Writing a general proposal and sending it to several potential sponsors is ineffective because it will be obvious to the sponsors that their brand positioning and target market have not been considered. The proposal should consider the market position as well as the resources of a potential sponsor and should describe the return a sponsor could reasonably expect from their investment. A sponsorship proposal should generally address several key areas including an overview of the sport property, a description of the target audience of the sport property, the goals of the sponsorship programme, the type and period of association, sponsorship benefits and rights, the investment required, the ambush prevention strategy, and an evaluation strategy. A detailed outline of the key sections of the sponsorship proposal is provided in Table 10.3.

TABLE 10.3 Key sections of sponsorship proposal

Covering letter • Maximum one page • Addressed to an appropriate staff member working with the potential sponsor. Usually a marketing manager, but could be a sponsorship manager in a large company.
Cover page • Clear, professional, and attractive presentation • Identify the potential sponsor and the sport property
Executive summary • An overview/summary of the proposal
Overview of the sport property and its owner sport property • History, context, and social/community significance • List of current and past sponsors (if applicable) • References or endorsements from past sponsors (if applicable) • Media attention (frequency and type, include brief examples) • Social media channels (including follower numbers/profile and engagement numbers) • Programmes and events organised by the owner sport property (target groups, participation numbers, audience demographics, promotional activities)
Target market • Identify consumer targets reached by the sport property • Demonstration of how this consumer audience matches and/or expands the target market of the proposed sponsor • Consider internal and external audiences (e.g., existing consumers, potential consumers, local community, public, suppliers, wholesalers, distributors, government, shareholders)
Brand affinity • Identify the brand positioning of the sport property • Demonstrate how this positioning matches or complements the brand positioning of proposed sponsor

(Continued)

TABLE 10.3 (Continued)

Goals of the sponsorship programme • What can be realistically achieved for the sponsor (e.g., brand awareness among a target group, media exposure, increased sales/market share, community involvement/social responsibility, building goodwill, public awareness, staff relations)
Sponsorship type • Event, team/individual, competition, venue
Period of association • Duration of agreement
Sponsorship benefits and rights • Detail the rights of the sponsorship agreement • Note whether these sponsorship rights are exclusive or shared with other partners • Note other benefits for the sponsor (e.g., special seating, client entertainment at events, cross-promotional activities, networking opportunities, image enhancement) • Outline different 'packages' available (if applicable) • Demonstrate how the sponsorship benefits relate to the sponsor's mission/vision and business objectives
Investment • Costs (include varying cost options if appropriate) • Could include an upfront fee and performance-based incentives • In-kind investments • Term/duration of agreement
Exclusivity • Ambush prevention strategy • Outline exclusivity of sponsor rights and how their exclusivity will be protected
Evaluation strategy • Performance measures and targets • How these measures and targets will be assessed

Few of the key areas described in Table 10.3 have already been discussed in this chapter, such as the goals of sponsorship and the issue of brand/target market affinity. The remaining areas are examined in detail in the forthcoming sections of this chapter, including evaluating sponsorships and ambush prevention strategies.

A sponsorship proposal should generally address several key areas including an overview of the sport property, a description of the target audience of the sport property, the goals of the sponsorship programme, the type and period of association, sponsorship benefits and rights, the investment required/cost, the ambush prevention strategy, and an evaluation strategy.

> *Chapter tool 10.1 Sponsorship proposal*: A sponsorship proposal should be researched and written for a specific sponsor (rather than writing a general proposal that is sent out to various potential sponsors). This way the proposal can take into account the market position and resources of the potential sponsor, and it can address issues of sponsorship affinity between the two parties.

SPORT SPONSORSHIP RIGHTS

The rights that are given through a sponsorship are sometimes called *entitlements* or *sponsorship assets*. There is a vast array of rights that can be delivered through a sponsorship beyond the obvious ones such as naming rights and signage. Table 10.4 provides a detailed inventory of the kinds of sponsorship rights that a sport property might offer a sponsor during a negotiation.

> *Chapter tool 10.2 Sport sponsorship rights*: Sport properties can offer a range of sponsorship rights that can be negotiated with potential sponsors into a customised package of benefits. The inventory of sponsorship rights provides the starting point for a suite of rights to be considered.

TABLE 10.4 Sport sponsorship rights

General sponsorship rights
Naming rights to an event, competition, or club
On-site signage rights
On-site sales rights
On-site product sampling/trials
Corporate entertainment and hospitality
VIP tickets
Merchandising and promotional give-aways
Use of venue for sponsor functions
Athlete/celebrity appearances for sponsor
Right of first refusal to new sponsorship opportunities
Use of event volunteers
Additional advertising opportunities
Product placement – use of sponsor branded equipment/product at event Access to mailing lists/databases
Trademark/logo display on equipment, clothing, media promotions Public-speaking opportunities Product category exclusivity

(Continued)

TABLE 10.4 (Continued)

Interactive areas, for example, message boards, polls, quizzes, game-zones
Consumer promotion exclusivity
Non-profit/cause overlay/social responsibility option
Large-screen/scoreboard signage
Other digital screens
Phone content
Radio (buys or event broadcast)
Video-on-demand content
Media rights
Media rights, including photography and footage rights Press releases, announcements, and press kits Public service announcements Internet content/links
Newspaper (buys or special event coverage)
Preevent and postevent promotional activities Print media presence (programmes, guides, etc.) Webcast (live stream or on-demand)

SPONSORSHIP LEVERAGING

Leveraging sponsorships means getting additional value out of an already existing sponsorship investment. It is concerned with getting the maximum benefit and advantage from the sponsorship through careful integration with other marketing activities. Leveraging also helps to combat ambush marketing, which will be explained later in this chapter. In fact, one of the keys to a successful sponsorship for both parties is leveraging activities. Leveraging helps to build a more positive and long-lasting relationship between the partners because it involves investing time and resources in one another and seeing the relationship as a strategic alignment.

For a sponsor to make the most of a sponsorship, it needs to invest resources over and above the costs of the sponsorship itself. By paying the sponsorship fee, a sponsor is only buying the right to associate themselves with the sport property; they must invest more money to make the most of this right by communicating the affiliation to their target market. Many sport marketing experts believe that a sponsor will need to invest up to three times more money than the cost of the sponsorship itself to leverage successfully. The aim of leveraging is to promote the association between the two brands from every angle possible, and not just leave it up to the sport property. An example can be seen in the case of American Express, which sponsors the Wimbledon tennis tournament. Along with the right to associate with the event, American Express leverages its sponsorship in a variety of different ways throughout the two-week tournament, including hosting a 'Fan Experience' village on-site at the tournament where fans can take part in virtual challenges against tennis stars, practice what it would be like to be a ball boy or ball girl at the tournament, and can pick up free American Express branded items such as sunglasses cleaner. American Express cardmembers can also visit the Cardmember Lounge on-site with up to two guests. This space offers guests 10% off all food and beverage purchases along with exclusive merchandise opportunities, and clearly encourages attendees to sign up for an American Express card so they can experience the benefits of the member lounge.

Sponsorship is only one promotional tool. To leverage the value of this tool, it is recommended that sponsors also use the other elements of the promotions mix to complement and draw attention to the sponsorship. For example, advertising, public relations, and sales promotion activities could all be used in conjunction with the sponsorship to strengthen the effect. Corporate hospitality and an online presence could tie in with sales promotions to maximise the impact of the sponsorship. In fact, all four of the traditional promotions mix elements should be used to properly leverage a sponsorship, that is advertising, public relations, sales promotions, and personal selling. Sponsors need to advertise, publicise, promote, and personally sell their sponsorship association to consumers to create greater impact. Using a suite of promotional elements in addition to the sponsorship can create a kind of synergy, where the whole of the marketing programme is greater than the sum of the individual elements of the promotions mix. This is, of course, the whole point of using a strategic framework as the basis of a sport marketing approach. Thus, it is not enough to just use the other elements of the promotions mix to leverage a sponsorship, but the four elements of the general marketing mix should also form part of an integrated sponsorship leveraging plan. For example, a sponsor may introduce a new product for the duration of the sponsorship or use special packaging relating to the event. The price of the sponsor's goods or services may be discounted during the event, or a percentage may be donated to a prominent or related cause. Distribution channels (place) may be expanded so that the sponsor's product can be bought exclusively at the event.

It is not only important to consider how to leverage a sponsorship, but also to whom the leveraging efforts should be directed. One good recommendation is that sponsorships should be leveraged towards a choice of three different groups of stakeholders: consumers, employees, and corporate stakeholders including distribution channel members. These three possibilities are outlined in the following sub-sections.

Leveraging sponsorship towards consumers

Many of the promotional activities that were mentioned in relation to leveraging can be aimed directly at a sponsor's target market. Advertising to promote the connection with the sport property, sales promotions that coincide with the event, and public relations through high-profile media outlets can all reinforce the sponsorship relationship to consumers. The sponsorship may also give the sponsor access to content about the sport property that its consumers may be interested in. This tactic works particularly well with technology or communications category sponsors who can use their sponsorship of sport properties to provide extra content to their customers.

Leveraging sponsorship towards employees

In the earlier section on sponsorship objectives, it was highlighted that a sponsorship may help to meet internal marketing goals by improving staff morale, increasing staff satisfaction, and creating a sense of staff pride in the organisation. If a sponsor's employees have an emotional connection to the sport property being sponsored, then the sponsorship may help them to develop emotional connections to the workplace. As a result, some leveraging can be usefully directed towards the sponsor's employees, offering them the opportunity to attend games or events and receive corporate hospitality. This can create a positive brand experience and enhance loyalty among employees, which in turn is more likely to lead to quality interactions with customers.

Leveraging sponsorship towards corporate stakeholders

A sponsorship can improve the goodwill and business relationships that a sponsor has with its stakeholders. This might include distribution channel members, shareholders, the media, and politicians. For example, corporate hospitality is one concrete way in which sponsors can build positive relationships with their suppliers and other distribution channel members.

> *Chapter tool 10.3 Sponsorship leveraging*: Leveraging sponsorships means getting value out of the sponsorship investment. It is concerned with getting the maximum amount of benefit and advantage from the sponsorship through careful integration with other elements of the promotions and marketing mix. For a sponsor to make the most of a sponsorship, it is recommended that it invest resources over and above the costs of the sponsorship itself.

To leverage a sponsorship, a sponsor should use all four elements of the marketing mix, including all the promotions mix activities.

Leveraging activities should be directed towards three different groups of stakeholders: (1) consumers, (2) employees, and (3) corporate stakeholders (including distribution channel members, suppliers, shareholders, the media, and politicians).

CORPORATE SOCIAL RESPONSIBILITY AND CAUSE-RELATED SPORT MARKETING

Sometimes corporations or other commercial enterprises seek a beneficial brand association with a specific charitable or non-profit cause. It is common in these arrangements for sport organisations to partner with corporations to provide a high-profile cause. The characteristics of sport tend to make it an attractive partner for social engagement. For example, sport generally enjoys a good media profile, is associated with fun and entertainment, is healthy, and encourages social interaction. As a result, sport presents a powerful vehicle for corporations to demonstrate that they are meeting their social and community obligations. Cause-related sport marketing, or its more recent successor sport corporate social responsibility, is effective in heightening the brand awareness of sponsors and tends to connect their brand with a more trusting and caring image. Sport marketers should remain aware of the ways in which sport brands can be employed as platforms for corporate social activity.

SPONSORSHIP EVALUATION

Some sport marketers believe that the true effects of a sponsorship are impossible to evaluate. For example, sponsorship usually occurs in conjunction with other promotional strategies, which makes isolating its effects difficult. It is also possible that the interaction of several promotional strategies is what helps to make a sponsorship work, rather than any one strategy on its own. In other words, different strategies rely on one another to be successful. Sponsorships are more successful at increasing consumer awareness when they are combined with advertising and other leveraging that reinforces and highlights the sponsorship association. The problem is that this interdependence can make it difficult to evaluate sponsorship on its own.

While it is true that measuring the effect of a sponsorship independent of all other marketing activities is extremely difficult, there are ways in which the success of a sponsorship can be judged. A careful evaluation strategy is important because sponsors expect to receive some objective feedback about the effect of the money they have invested in a sponsorship. Without a clear return on their investment, it is unlikely that a sponsor will continue an association. Even small businesses that sponsor on a more modest level (such as local community clubs) need evidence that the money they commit to a sponsorship will yield benefits. After all, small businesses have far less money to spend and will tend to be discerning about such investments. To be able to demonstrate that sponsorship has a positive outcome for sponsors is the best way to legitimise it as a marketing technique, and to attract and retain sponsors.

> *Chapter principle 10.8*: To be able to demonstrate that sponsorship has a positive outcome for corporations is the best way to legitimise it as a marketing technique, and to attract and retain sponsors.

The sponsorship evaluation process is a systematic tool for sport marketers to apply to sponsorship evaluation. The sponsorship evaluation sequence is presented in Figure 10.3, followed by guidance about each stage of the evaluation process.

Review sponsorship objectives

To evaluate the success of a sponsorship programme, there must be a clear understanding of what it was aiming to achieve in the first place. Potential objectives of a sponsorship agreement were highlighted at the beginning of this chapter. They are worth revisiting now because they provide the basis for the next step of establishing performance measures.

Establish performance measures

To evaluate whether objectives have been achieved, it is useful to attach a *performance measure* to each objective. A performance measure is a guide for determining whether the sponsorship

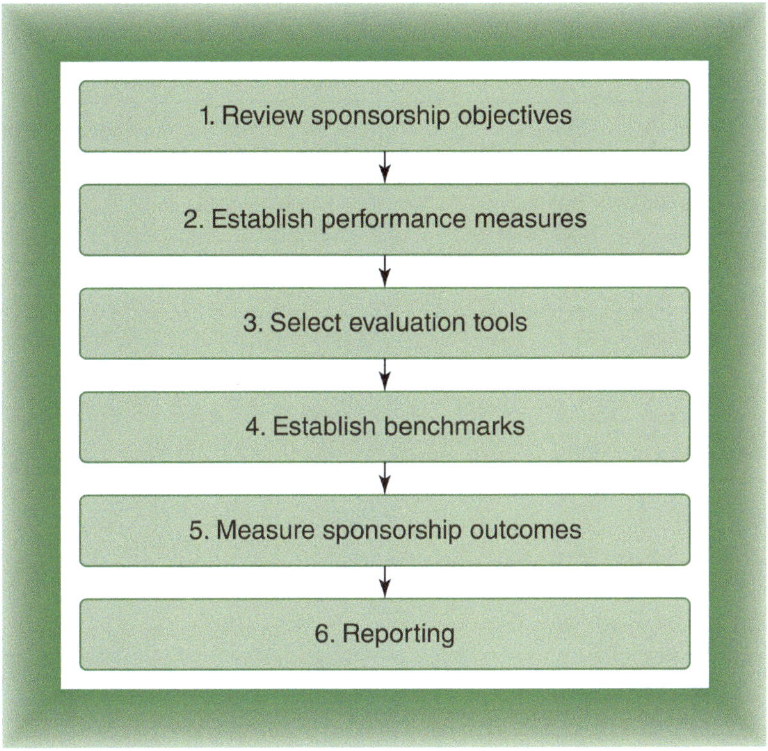

FIGURE 10.3 Sponsorship evaluation

objective has been achieved. The word *measure* means a way of estimating, calculating, or assessing whether a goal has been achieved. It usually involves finding a way to *quantify* or put a number to the objective. Some important basic examples appear in Table 10.5.

Select evaluation tools

Once marketing objectives have been set, and corresponding performance measures allocated, it is possible to choose the evaluation tools that will be used. Each performance measure will be suited to a particular kind of evaluation tool. The key message here is that sponsorship evaluation is best conducted using a range of evaluation tools. Choosing from a 'suite' of evaluation tools helps to overcome the limitations of each method on its own; a number or a group of tools are most useful in providing a breadth of information. Table 10.6 outlines the suite of potential evaluation tools.

Table 10.6 has two important lessons. First, the tools selected to evaluate a sponsorship programme should be directly related to its objectives and performance measures. Second, five main kinds of evaluation are used: (1) exposure, (2) consumer awareness, (3) consumer attitudes, (4) sales effects, and (5) satisfaction. The most effective and informative sponsorship evaluation programme will use tools from many, if not all, of these five areas. Each is expanded and explained in the following sub-sections.

TABLE 10.5 Examples of performance measures

Sponsorship objective	*Possible performance measures*
To increase mass media exposure	Number of times the sponsor logo/name is seen on the live streaming broadcast per game
To increase the number of people who use the product/service because of the sponsorship association	Number of customers who use our service as measured on a postpurchase questionnaire
To increase staff satisfaction levels through corporate hospitality	Satisfaction levels as rated by staff survey, which asks questions about the importance of corporate hospitality
To increase customer awareness of the product	Number of people who have heard of the product in a geographical area as measured by a postevent online survey to all attendees
To increase sales	Sales during the sponsored event, compared with sales at the same event last year

TABLE 10.6 Evaluation tools

Objective area	*Type of evaluation*	*Aim in evaluation*	*Types of tools*
Public image	Consumer attitude	Determine what consumers in the public think and believe about the brand/product/sport	Surveys and focus groups
Media exposure	Media exposure analysis	Determine the type, frequency, and/or duration of exposure	Exposure audit
		Determine readership/viewer statistics and demographics	Numerical estimations of exposure value
Awareness (of general public or a target group)	Consumer awareness	Determine whether consumers can recognise and recall the brands involved in the sponsorship (brand awareness), and the association/link between the partners (sponsorship awareness)	Recall and recognition tests through surveys and focus groups

(Continued)

TABLE 10.6 (Continued)

Objective area	*Type of evaluation*	*Aim in evaluation*	*Types of tools*
Sales rates or market share	Sales effects	Estimate sales made directly and indirectly because of the sponsorship	Tracking of actual sales Consumer self-report survey (claimed sales) Coupons and 'bounce-backs' (sales by proxy) Comparison with competitors' sales to determine market share
Brand association	Consumer attitude Consumer awareness	Determine whether there is a link made between the sponsor and the sport property	Surveys and focus groups
Brand equity	Consumer attitude	Determine what consumers think about the brand. What do they associate with it?	Surveys and focus groups
Brand image management	Consumer attitude	Determine the values and ideas consumers associate with the sponsor/sport property	Surveys and focus groups
		Determine how consumers 'position' the brands/products compared to competitors	
Brand loyalty	Consumer attitude Sales effects	Establish whether the sponsorship affects long-term associations with a brand	Tracking of purchases Loyalty programmes Focus groups and consumer surveys
Satisfaction and positive relationships (consumer, channel member, staff, stakeholder)	Satisfaction	Determine the levels of satisfaction that are generated through the sponsorship agreement	Surveys and focus groups

Exposure

Media exposure monitoring is currently the most widely used form of sponsorship evaluation, mainly because it is one of the easiest methods to use. At its most simple, exposure can be measured by documenting the type, frequency, and duration of sponsor name and logo appearances in television, radio, press, print, online sources (such as number of page views or hits), and social media (e.g., number of impressions for a social media post).

For example, how many times a brand name or logo is observable in print media, or how many seconds it appears on television, may be measured. This can be a simple measure, although it can also become time-consuming if significant volumes of media need to be audited. For larger corporations with sufficient resources, there are software programmes that can help with storing and analysing this kind of data. One of the traditional limitations of collecting information about the type, frequency, and duration of exposure is that it does not provide any indication of how many people, or what types of consumers were exposed. Some social media outlets, however, offer more information on exposure such as the number of people who saw a post, the number who interacted with it, and depending on the platform, the amount of time consumers spent looking at the post. For traditional media, it is useful to gather information about the readership of the publication, the viewer statistics, and the demographic profile of viewers/readers.

Most sport marketers agree that this information is still insufficient on its own, and that it is necessary to put a monetary value on the media exposure that has been obtained. For example, some sponsors may calculate how much it would cost them to pay for advertising of the same frequency and duration as the sponsorship exposure. This usually involves a mathematical calculation, which considers the duration and time of exposure, estimated audience levels, television ratings, the size/location of the exposure as well as the standard cost for advertising at that time. Other methods apply different kinds of advertising rates together with weighting systems that try to put a value on the different kinds of exposure, and even the 'favourability' of the exposure. There are also statistical models that try to estimate the proportion of the target population that was exposed to the media coverage in question.

There are two main problems with these methods of 'valuing' exposure. The first is that they equate sponsorship exposure with advertising, while the second is that they are based on estimations that may not be valid. The assumption that sponsorship exposure and advertising have the same impact on consumers is unproven and questionable. When compared to sponsorship exposure, an advertisement is a targeted communication that is designed to convey a specific message to the consumer. The message that is conveyed to a consumer through a sponsorship alliance is more subtle and complex, requiring an understanding of consumers' attitudes and beliefs about the two brands, both separately and together. Furthermore, it is also unreasonable to assume that all consumers pay complete or even partial attention to a sponsor's logo while exciting sporting action is occurring. This does not mean that the sponsorship alliance is worthless, but it does imply that sponsorship exposure is not the same as advertising. The value of sponsorship is ultimately not found in the value of airtime, but in the way that a match-up of brand images can influence consumer attitudes and purchase behaviour.

To make the approach even more dubious, mathematical methods for putting a 'value' on exposure may be invalid. They may not accurately measure what they say they are measuring. What these formulas try to deliver is a 'best guess' based on assumptions and estimations. There is significant variability in the methods, rates, and weighting systems that different approaches use, so it remains impossible to compare the results of one with another. There is also the tendency towards inflating the advertising rates against which sponsorship exposure is compared, making sponsorship appear better value than it really is. However, to make a business case for the commencement or maintenance of a

TABLE 10.7 Measuring media exposure

Measuring media exposure
At its most simple, media exposure can be measured by documenting the type, frequency, and duration of media exposure, as well as readership/viewer statistics, and their demographic profile. There are many methods that try to put a monetary value on media exposure; these provide a 'best guess' based on assumptions and estimations, and their validity is therefore questionable (although it may still be persuasive)
Media exposure can be one important element of sponsorship evaluation, particularly if it is combined with other methods

sponsorship agreement, these kinds of calculations may be persuasive and have a role to play in evaluation. They are most useful if used on a continuing basis where results can be directly compared from one year to the next. Using the same method consistently can help establish whether there has been a change in exposure. There are specialised sponsorship evaluation consultancies that conduct media exposure measurement for a fee.

In concluding this discussion about measuring media exposure, it is important to remember that media exposure does not in itself reveal anything about consumer intentions. If a logo was seen on television for a total of 45 seconds, there is no information about the impact it had on the people watching it. For example, did it change or strengthen their awareness or attitudes towards the sponsor's brand? While it might be important that consumers are exposed to a sponsor's product or brand, this may not be sufficient to change their attitudes or buying habits. However, if these limitations are considered, measuring media exposure can still be one important element of sponsorship evaluation, particularly if it is combined with other forms of evaluation. It can also be an important tool for small sporting organisations that may not have sufficient money to spend on more complex evaluations. The key points to remember about measuring media exposure are summarised in Table 10.7.

Consumer Awareness

One of the common objectives of a sponsorship agreement is to increase the awareness consumers possess about a sponsor's product or brand. The most common method used to test consumers' awareness of a brand, or a product is based on the ideas of recognition and recall. Testing recognition usually involves showing consumers a list of sponsors' names or logos, and asking which ones they recognise. Sometimes false companies may be added to the list (i.e., companies that are not sponsors) to test the degree to which consumers mistakenly associate brands with a sponsorship just because they are on a list. Testing recall is different because it involves asking consumers to recall sponsor brands spontaneously, without any cues. For example, a consumer may be asked to list the companies or sponsorships that they associate with a sport event, without receiving any prompting. Recalling a brand name without any prompting is obviously more difficult, so this is considered a better test of awareness than recognising a brand on a list once prompted.

When using recognition and recall tests, it is possible to test consumers' awareness of two different aspects of the sponsorship: (1) the individual brands (or products) of the sponsor and the sport property, and (2) the link or association between the sponsor and sport property. In other words, it is possible to look at evaluating brand awareness as well as sponsorship awareness. Surveys looking at the link between the sponsor and sport property are called association measures.

There are several factors that may affect whether a consumer recalls a brand's sponsorship association. These include how long consumers have been exposed to the sponsorship, how strongly they associated previous sponsors with the sport property, how the sponsorship message is delivered, how interested and involved the consumers are with the sport property, the role of other promotional strategies used (such as advertising) to reinforce the sponsorship, and the size of the sponsor. It is also important to realise that recall of a sponsorship can change over time. For example, it may increase just before and during a big sport event but may die away a few weeks after it has finished.

The ability of consumers to recognise and recall sponsorship partners is typically tested during phone surveys and face-to-face surveys, although it is also possible to incorporate them into a focus group analysis. One of the important things to consider when designing a survey or focus group is how consumers will be selected to take part. This will be influenced by the objectives set for the sponsorship agreement. For example, if the aim is to increase awareness amongst the public, then this would be best tested with a large, random sample, which, of course, can be an expensive and difficult undertaking. However, if the aim were to increase awareness within a more specific target group, then an alternative method for selecting participants such as purposeful sampling (e.g., approaching people at an event, or from a membership list) would be appropriate. Measuring consumer awareness is summarised in Table 10.8.

Consumer Attitudes/Image Effects

While media exposure and consumer awareness evaluations are popular ways to assess the success of a sponsorship, they do not uncover anything about the impact of sponsorship on consumer attitudes. Finding out what consumers really think about a product, brand, or sponsorship is not an easy task. It is easier to find out whether consumers can recognise and recall a brand, compared with finding out what beliefs they have about the brand,

TABLE 10.8 Measuring consumer awareness

Measuring consumer awareness
Consumer awareness is most commonly measured by testing recognition and recall of a brand, product, or sponsorship alliance
Recognition is when a consumer can identify the brand/product/alliance from a list. This means that he/she has been prompted to remember it
Recall is when a consumer remembers the brand/product/alliance without prompting or recognising from a list
Recognition and recall tests can measure brand awareness (of the individual partners in the sponsorship) as well as sponsorship awareness (the alliance between the partners)

TABLE 10.9 Measuring consumer attitudes

Measuring consumer attitudes
Consumer attitudes are the beliefs that a consumer has about a product or brand. There are a number of different types of consumer attitudes that are commonly evaluated including: (1) perceptions about positioning, (2) the fit between the sponsor and sport property, (3) the perceived sincerity of the sponsor, (4) purchase intentions, and (5) affinity measures
Consumer attitudes are often measured on surveys with Likert scales using 'agree' and 'disagree' items, and short-answer questionnaires

and what values they associate it with. However, discovering what consumers think can be extremely valuable. For example, consumers' attitudes are more likely to give an indication of their likely buying behaviour than awareness measures alone, although the link between attitudes and behaviour is not direct or causal.

Consumer attitudes are often measured through surveys with so-called Likert scales ('agree' and 'disagree' items), and with short-answer questions that ask consumers to give an unprompted response. There are several different aspects of consumer attitudes that can be evaluated including (1) perceptions about positioning, (2) the fit between the sponsor and sport property, (3) the perceived sincerity of the sponsor, (4) purchase intentions, and (5) affinity measures. Each is discussed in the following sub-sections and summarised in Table 10.9.

Positioning Perceptions

One important kind of consumer attitude evaluation involves trying to understand how consumers conceptualise a sponsor's brand compared to others. In order to uncover such complex issues, surveys and short-answer questionnaires ask consumers to indicate what they associate with the brand, such as values, features, or symbols. For example, do they associate the brand with prestige, reliability, or family values? A questionnaire may also ask how consumers compare the sponsor's brand to others. For example, do they see it as better value or more dependable than other brands? Obviously, before it is possible to design and implement a consumer attitude survey seeking to evaluate consumer beliefs about positioning, it is vital that there is clear information about how a sponsor sought to position its brand in the first place. The key questions are: What values, features, and images do consumers associate with a sponsor's brand; and how do consumers compare a sponsor's brand to others?

Sponsor and Sport Property Fit/Sponsorship Congruence

A sponsorship will be more effective if there is a strong fit or match-up between the sponsor's brand and the sport property. The level of fit, or congruence, that consumers perceive relates to the degree to which they think that there is a logical connection between the two. For example, there is an obvious congruence between a sport event such as a major golf tournament and a sponsor that manufactures golf products. To explore whether consumers perceive a good fit between the sponsor and sport property, survey questions may be posed to determine the characteristics they associate with each, or what consumers think each symbolises or stands for. The researchers can then assess the similarity.

Sincerity of the Sponsor

Consumers are more likely to think favourably about a sponsor if they believe that the sponsor is motivated by a sense of community and philanthropy rather than just financial gain.

Purchase Intentions

It is often difficult to accurately measure sales that have resulted directly from a sponsorship. One of the ways around this problem is to find out whether consumers intend or plan to purchase the sponsor's product. Purchase intentions are therefore a proxy for actual sales, in that they represent a substitute, or a stand-in measure. Purchase intentions can also be considered a proxy for actual behaviour; that is, for buying and consuming a product. It is obvious, however, that planned behaviour and actual behaviour can be quite different.

Affinity Measures

The word 'affinity' in the context of sponsorship evaluation refers to whether consumers feel an attraction to a sponsor's product or brand. More specifically, it refers to the degree to which consumers feel that a sponsor's product or brand is 'their kind of brand'. For example, does it give the consumer the sense of identity that they are seeking? Or, do consumers think that it suits other people that they would like to be similar to? Questions of this kind have a relationship to product and brand positioning because they are designed to find out whether the way that consumers think about a sponsor's product/brand reinforces the way that they would like to think about themselves.

Sales Effects

Linking any promotional activity, including sponsorship, to an increase in sales is problematic. One of the main reasons is that a sponsor will usually implement a whole range of different promotional strategies, making it difficult to separate out which strategies have led to which sales. However, in some instances, it can be easier to track sales effects that have been stimulated by sponsorship, compared with other promotions. For example, food or beverage rights at a sport event give the sponsor exclusive or preferential sales rights to consumers at the event. It is a simple task to calculate the sales that have been made at the sponsored event.

It is more difficult, however, to determine whether there is an indirect increase in sales because of the event. For example, did more consumers choose to use a sponsored product after the event because of its affiliation with the sponsored property? These kinds of sales are sometimes called claimed sales because consumers may 'claim' that they bought a product as a result of being exposed to it in a certain way. Claimed sales can be measured through surveys asking consumers to indicate their awareness of the sponsorship, their

TABLE 10.10 Measuring sales effects

Measuring sales effects
It can be difficult to directly attribute sales to the impact of a sponsorship agreement. Sometimes it may be possible to calculate actual sales, such as when a food or beverage company sponsors an event and makes sales at that event
If it is not possible to measure actual sales, it may be feasible to estimate claimed sales, by surveying consumers about why they purchased a product
Finally, sales can be measured by proxy, which involves estimating sales by using a 'stand-in' such as a QR code that is scanned or redeemed at the point of sale

exposure to the sponsor and their reasoning for purchase. Sometimes brief surveys may even be done at the point of sale to find out what has led the consumer to their decision.

It is also possible to estimate sales by proxy. This means trying to estimate sales by using a 'stand-in', such as a QR code that is scanned at the point of sale. For example, if the QR code has been distributed at a sport event via the consumer's printed or electronic ticket and the consumer uses it at the point of sale, then the sale can be associated with the sponsorship. One of the complicating factors of this method is that QR codes or other electronic tracking methods often include an incentive for people to redeem them, like offering a discount. This makes it difficult to determine whether the sale was made as a result of the sponsorship or the discount promotion. However, while this may make it difficult to accurately estimate sales by proxy, it can be an effective way of leveraging a sponsorship programme. Table 10.10 summarises the important issues associated with measuring sales effects.

To review, three different types of *sales measures* are used in sponsorship evaluation. They are (1) actual sales, (2) claimed sales, and (3) sales by proxy. Sales effects measures can contribute to a sponsorship evaluation, but they do have two major limitations. First, they do not accurately reflect the effect on sales flowing from a sponsorship. Second, the major benefit of sponsorship may be less related to sales and more relevant to the positive effects on consumer attitudes and therefore brand equity.

Satisfaction

The final area for evaluating sponsorships is related to satisfaction. A sponsor may aim to increase customer, staff, or even shareholder satisfaction through the sponsorship. For example, the sponsor may offer staff corporate hospitality at a sporting event with the aim of improving staff morale and loyalty. It logically follows that if this is an objective, then measures using a satisfaction rating of some kind are required.

Establish benchmarks

Once a suite of evaluation tools has been selected to evaluate the sponsorship, it is important to establish a benchmark. Benchmarks are used to determine the 'status quo' before the sponsorship promotions commence. This is essential to find out whether an objective has been achieved over and above the original levels prior to the commencement of the sponsorship relationship. For example, if the objective is to increase brand awareness among a specific target market, then there must be evidence of what the awareness levels were before the sponsorship agreement began. A benchmark therefore works as a point of reference in the evaluation strategy.

Measure sponsorship outcomes and report

The final two stages of the evaluation process are to measure the outcomes of the sponsorship programme and then report these formally to the sponsor. Measuring the outcomes of a sponsorship means using the suite of evaluation tools again after a set duration during which the sponsorship has been in place. These results should be considered against the benchmarks obtained from the previous step to assess whether the desired goals have been realised. The results of the evaluation should be formally reported to the sponsor, along with any recommendations about improvements that can be made or ways in which the sponsorship can be leveraged for even better results in the future.

> *Chapter tool 10.4 Sport sponsorship evaluation*: A step-by-step process of sponsorship evaluation should include: (1) review sponsorship objectives, (2) establish performance measures, (3) select evaluation tools, (4) establish benchmarks, (5) measure sponsorship outcomes and (6) reporting.

The tools that are chosen to evaluate the sponsorship programme should be directly related to the sponsorship objectives and performance measures originally set.

There are five main kinds of sponsorship evaluation to select from: (1) exposure, (2) consumer awareness, (3) consumer attitudes, (4) sales effects, and (5) satisfaction. The most effective and informative sponsorship evaluation programme will use tools from many, if not all, of these five areas.

AMBUSH MARKETING

The word 'ambush' refers to a trap or a surprise attack on a competitor. In the sponsorship world, *ambush marketing* is a term used when a company creates the impression that it is associated with a sport property, whereas they have no affiliation at all. Ambush marketing is planned to establish an artificial association with an event in order to obtain some of the benefits and recognition of an official sponsorship without having to invest any money. Typically, ambush marketing involves an intrusion on the physical space of a sport property or sport event, making use of a particular diversion or grab for attention to wrestle the association away from the actual sponsor.

Ambush marketing occurs most often with large sporting events, where the ambushing company deflects attention away from the official sponsors and onto themselves, without having made the appropriate investment into the sport property. Ambush marketing is sometimes called 'parasitic' marketing because a company is 'free-loading', like a parasite, on the back of the official sponsor. In these situations, consumers can become confused and even believe that the ambushing company is an actual sponsor. Before more stringent legislation was introduced, the earliest attempts at ambush marketing were quite clumsy. For example, the ambush company would park a hot-air balloon with their logo on it above a competing brand's sponsored event or would hand out free memorabilia at the event. Ambush marketing was popularised by the bitter rivalries of companies fighting for the same market, such as Coke and Pepsi, and Fujifilm and Kodak. A further infamous example is Nike and Adidas at the Boston Marathon, which has been sponsored by Adidas since 1989. Nike is notorious for finding creative ways to ambush Adidas, such as when they encouraged fans along the racecourse to wear temporary tattoos of the Nike Swoosh logo on their faces, or when they launched advertising campaigns along the course, in Boston-area hotels, and in Boston newspapers during the marathon weekend.

Ambush marketing attempts to undermine the brand equity of official sponsors at the same time as it aims to increase the brand equity of the ambusher. Ambush strategies can be effective. In terms of the recall and recognition of consumers, non-sponsors can often be perceived as genuine and official sponsors, and they may even become more memorable than the official sponsors because they have employed particularly unusual devices and tactics for stealing the attention of consumers.

> *Chapter principle 10.9*: Ambush marketing refers to a strategy where a company (other than an official sponsor, and often a competitor to the official sponsor) creates the impression that it is associated with the sport property. This is achieved by attracting attention and by giving the impression of a relationship with the sport property.

There are many ways in which ambush marketing can be undertaken. The most obvious is by the illegal use of official logos or merchandise, or by making false claims about being an official sponsor. Because there are clear laws in most countries that prohibit this kind of behaviour, legal action can be undertaken in response to it. However, some aggressive companies continue to mount ambushing campaigns in ways that may not cause a clearcut breach in law, and even in ways that may be completely legal. There are five main ambush marketing strategies that companies may legally use, often with several approaches used at the same time. The five include the ambushing of advertising, broadcast, sub-categories, athletes, or promotions. Each is described in detail in the following sub-sections.

Advertising ambush: buying advertising time around an event

An advertising ambush can occur when a non-official sponsor implements an advertising campaign that coincides with the sport event. This could simply involve buying normal advertising time and space, and the ambusher may argue that it is well within its rights to promote its brand by purchasing legitimate airtime during sporting events. However, the official sponsor is more likely to believe that it has been ambushed. More aggressive advertising ambushes can even imply that there is a link between the ambusher and the event.

An advertising ambush can use any of the forms of advertising that have been detailed in Chapter 9. Some examples include television commercials, magazine and newspaper advertisements, radio spots, posters, billboards, internet pop-ups, social media advertisements, and advertisements on buses and bus stops. Virtual billboards at sporting events offer another avenue through which companies can attempt to ambush.

Broadcast ambush: sponsoring the broadcast of an event

By sponsoring the broadcast of a sport event, a company can create the impression that it is associated with the sport property. It has, in fact, paid for the right to be associated with the broadcast itself, but the awareness that this generates can spill over onto the sport event as well. Interestingly, a broadcast sponsor can associate itself with the sport to a much larger television audience than the event sponsor, who may only be reaching those people in attendance.

Sub-category ambush: sponsoring a sub-category of a sport event

It is common for sport events to offer different categories of sponsorship. In addition to an overall sponsorship of the event, they may also offer sponsorships of smaller categories in the event. An ambusher can invest less money by sponsoring a small element of the event, and then aggressively promote its association. This can even convince the public that the sub-category sponsor is a major event sponsor. As noted earlier, the key to success in this form of ambushing is effective sponsorship leveraging. With this tactic, the best approach is to invest only small amounts in the sponsorship itself, and support it with substantial investments in leveraging, giving the impression of a major event sponsorship. When this approach works, it is far less expensive than paying for a major sponsorship.

Athlete ambush: sponsoring an athlete or team

Sponsors may also support an individual athlete or a team who is usually allowed to seek his or her own endorsements. Some teams, leagues, or events may have rules that prohibit athletes from wearing logos of brands that compete with official sponsors on the sidelines of the event, so it is important for athletes to be aware of any such rules. This is addressed in greater depth later in this chapter.

Promotions ambush: using non-sponsorship promotion

An ambushing company can also use non-sponsorship promotional strategies that coincide with a sport event to create an association. Other strategies can include giving away branded T-shirts or temporary tattoos for spectators to wear, which will be seen on the television broadcast. There are limitless examples of promotional ambush strategies, so the list could go on: conducting competitions, giving away official merchandise as prizes without permission, unauthorised websites, live screenings, phone content, social media posts, unofficial corporate hospitality, unofficial merchandise, unauthorised publications, virtual advertising, advertisements that wish athletes good fortune or congratulate them, and promotions that show famous sporting landmarks in the background.

Chapter tool 10.5 Ambush marketing methods:

- Buy advertising time during the event (advertising ambush)
- Sponsor the broadcast of an event, not the event itself (broadcast ambush)
- Sponsor sub-categories of the event (sub-category ambush)
- Sponsor a team or athlete (athlete ambush)
- Use imaginative, non-sponsorship promotions during the event (promotions ambush)

Ambush prevention

The idea of ambush marketing probably appears unfair to most people. Whether or not it is illegal, however, often depends on the details of the ambushing campaign. Even if an ambushing campaign is clearly illegal, the time and costs of settling a dispute through the courts may be considered excessive, unreasonable, and counterproductive. Some commentators have claimed that even when it is not illegal, ambush marketing constitutes an immoral practice, although this is a controversial position. Putting aside the legal and ethical issues of the practice, the fact remains that ambush marketing is a problem for both the official sponsors and the sport property, and it is vitally important to consider what strategies can be implemented to avoid the problem occurring in the first place. Thus, the professional sport marketer must know how to use forms of ambush marketing at some times and defend against it at others.

Clearly ambush marketing has a detrimental impact on official sponsors. It can limit their ability to recoup their investment because it reduces positive impact on consumer awareness and attitudes. Ambush marketing can also negatively affect the sport property itself. This is because it can damage the relationship with the official sponsor and make it more difficult to secure future sponsorships. It is therefore important to understand when ambush marketing is most likely to occur, and what strategies can be implemented to prevent it. It is generally considered to be more effective to block out ambushers than to instigate legal action because of the significant cost and difficulty in establishing that something illegal has occurred.

There are five major elements of an ambush prevention strategy: (1) control of intellectual property, (2) control of the event environment and locality, (3) control of the event partners, (4) design of the sponsorship programme, and (5) leveraging official sponsorships. Each is described next.

Control of Intellectual Property

The intellectual property relating to a sport event can include names, logos, mascots, and merchandise. Controlling the use of these properties is only possible through legal avenues, such as contracts, copyright law, trademark registration, and other specialised legislation. Logos and emblems are usually protected by copyright legislation as an original work of art. It is important with these works to negotiate with the designer to have the copyright transferred to the sport property. Names and logos can be protected legally in a given country if they are registered as a trademark. Different legislation and registration systems operate in different locations, so it can be difficult to track and protect these rights. In the case of large sport properties, such as the Olympics or the World Cup, governments in the hosting country may enact specific legislation to protect logos, names, and slogans that are related to the event.

For the sport property, controlling intellectual property means ensuring that trademarks are registered in the relevant region and copyright ownership is clarified in contracts. Usually, the sport property will also indicate that a trademark or copyright exists, such as using the letters (tm) or (c) wherever the word or logo appears. However, while copyright, trademark, and other legislation may deter ambushers from using a logo or other forms of intellectual property, it does not guarantee that they will not. It may be effective in some cases to use legal teams to put further pressure on ambushers to stop their use of a proprietary logo or name. Although it can be costly and difficult, the sport property may choose to settle the matter in court.

Control of the Event Environment and Locality

To prevent an ambush at a sport event, the organisers need to plan for what is called a 'clean' venue. This means that no signage, promotions, or advertising appear within the grounds that promote competitors of the official sponsors. This includes the stadium itself, bars and eating areas, toilets, buildings that are visible to the spectators or television cameras, or even the airspace above the stadium. In practice, there must be teams of workers monitoring the event and removing any ambushing material. The terms and conditions of admission can reserve the right for event organisers to refuse entry or eject patrons if they are seen to be participating in an ambush strategy.

The environment surrounding the event should also be controlled where possible, although the extent to which this can be achieved depends upon the available budget and cooperation of local authorities and media. For example, it may be feasible to prohibit promotions by competitors occurring at the event entry, or in nearby streets. Sport events that make use of a wide geographical area, such as marathons and other long-distance events, can pose significant problems.

Control of the Event Partners

In addition to the obvious partners of a sport event (athletes, teams, sponsors, suppliers, and merchandisers), other partners can include licensed broadcasters, media, and local authorities. Some of these partners will have a contract with the sport event (athletes, sponsors, broadcasters, suppliers, and merchandisers), which should bind them to comply with anti-ambush strategies. The other parties such as local councils, police, and local media are not necessarily obliged to support the anti-ambush strategies, but efforts should be made to inform and negotiate with them to play a role.

Controlling Broadcasters

When a sport event organiser negotiates a contract with an event broadcaster, it is essential for it to consider the protection of its sponsors. For example, broadcasters can be contractually bound to give the event sponsors the first opportunity to purchase broadcasting rights as well as advertising time in and around the event. Broadcasters can also be contractually obligated to give the official event sponsors the right to veto their competitors from becoming broadcast sponsors, programme sponsors, and/or buying advertising time during the event. It is common for event organisers to reduce the cost of a broadcast sponsorship in exchange for more control over whom the broadcasters subsequently sell advertising time to.

Controlling Sponsors, Suppliers, and Merchandisers

Sponsors, suppliers, and merchandisers for a sport property or event could deliberately or inadvertently help an ambush to occur. For example, official merchandise could be provided to an ambusher who plans to use the goods as prize give-aways without permission. Similarly, official sponsors could facilitate an ambush by participating in joint promotions with non-sponsors. The contracts that are signed with these parties should therefore prohibit behaviour that may lead to ambushing. For example, sponsors can be prohibited from undertaking joint promotions related to the event, unless the organisation they intend to partner with is also an official sponsor. Sponsors can also be prohibited from sharing their sponsorship rights or from sub-licensing them to another, non-official sponsor. All promotional materials can be subject to prior approval by the event organisers.

The contracts that are signed between the sponsors and sport organisers can give the sponsors certain rights to protect their interests. For example, it can give them the right to approve the promotional material of other licensees and sponsors before it is distributed. Sometimes it can ensure them the first opportunity to advertise in official publications. These rights are often called 'rights of first refusal' because they give the sponsor the first opportunity to be involved, or to refuse if they so wish.

Controlling athletes, teams, and sport associations

Ambushing can occur through the sponsorship of a team or athlete. On the one hand, this is a legitimate agreement, and the athletes/clubs have the right to seek support and endorsement. However, problems can arise if this sponsorship clashes with the overall sponsorship of an event or property. The ability to control this problem will vary from event to event depending on variables such as the relative bargaining power of the event compared with the athletes/clubs, and the regulations of the event itself. However, as mentioned earlier, there are restrictions that may be considered as part of the contractual agreement. Some examples include that (1) athletes may be restricted from wearing branded clothing or footwear; (2) all promotions related to the event may be subject to the event organiser's approval; (3) participants may be required to use specific products or services (those of a sponsor) at the event; and (4) there may be restrictions on participants filming or documenting events.

Design of the Sponsorship Programme

The way that a sponsorship programme is designed may have an impact on whether ambush marketing campaigns will occur. This is because ambush marketing is most likely to happen under certain circumstances. These situations can include when there is a wide variety of sponsorship categories and many sponsors per category, a high cost of official sponsorship, a strictly limited number of sponsors allowed into the event, or side events that are happening outside the main event. For example, if there are a broad variety of sponsorship categories, and/or there are many sponsors per category, it is harder for consumers to identify the official sponsors. This 'clutter' can lead to confusion about who is and who is not involved. It becomes easier for ambushers to take advantage of this confusion, and lead sport consumers to believe that they are officially involved in the event. However, it is also possible that the sponsorship agreement has strict exclusivity rules that limit the opportunity for companies to become legitimately involved, potentially leading them to unofficially try to grab some attention.

Leverage Official Sponsorships

Leveraging official sponsorships means getting the maximum amount of benefit and advantage from the agreement through planning additional and integrated marketing activities. If the official sponsors themselves are not promoting their involvement well enough, this may provide the opportunity for an unofficial sponsor to step in and fill the gap. Sponsors who make the most of their agreement can also minimise the impact of an ambush if it does occur. As outlined in the earlier section on leveraging sponsorships, sponsors and sport properties may use other elements of the promotions mix to complement and boost the sponsorship, as well as use the other elements of the marketing mix.

> *Chapter tool 10.6 - Sport sponsorship evaluation*: There are five major elements of an ambush prevention strategy: (1) control of intellectual property, (2) control of the event environment and locality, (3) control of the event partners, (4) design of the sponsorship programme and (5) leverage official sponsorships.

PRINCIPLES SUMMARY

- Chapter principle 10.1: The term sport property refers to the recipient of the sponsorship. This could be an athlete, team, event, venue, association, cause, or competition.
- Chapter principle 10.2: Sport sponsorship is a business agreement where one organisation provides financial or in-kind assistance to a sport property in exchange for the right to associate itself with the sport property. The sponsor does this in order to achieve corporate objectives (such as enhancing corporate image) or marketing objectives (such as increasing brand awareness).
- Chapter principle 10.3: Sport sponsorship generates goodwill among consumers. The amount of goodwill generated can vary depending on the kind of sport property

being sponsored, the degree of involvement that consumers have with the sport property, the time at which the sponsor becomes involved, and when and how the sponsor ceases the sponsorship.

- Chapter principle 10.4: Fan involvement is an important consideration in sponsorship because a consumer's response to a sponsorship is driven by the level of involvement that they have with the sport property.
- Chapter principle 10.5: The objectives of sponsorship can vary greatly, depending on the size of the partners, the type of sponsorship, and the type of sport property being supported. Some common objectives for the sponsor are to enhance sales, to promote the public image of its brand, to increase consumer awareness, to modify its brand image, and to build business relationships.
- Chapter principle 10.6: The objectives of sponsorship for the sport property will vary. In addition to attracting financial support, objectives include increasing credibility, increasing awareness, and managing brand image.
- Chapter principle 10.7: Sponsorship affinity refers to whether there is a good fit or match between the sponsor and the sport property. Two factors are particularly important for ensuring a good match: (1) an overlap of target markets and (2) a match-up of brand positioning strategies.
- Chapter principle 10.8: To be able to demonstrate that sponsorship has a positive outcome for corporations is the best way to legitimise it as a marketing technique, and to attract and retain sponsors.
- Chapter principle 10.9: Ambush marketing refers to a strategy where a company (other than an official sponsor, and often a competitor to the official sponsor) creates the impression that it is associated with the sport property. This is achieved by attracting attention and by giving the impression of a relationship with the sport property.

TOOLS SUMMARY

- Chapter tool 10.1 Sponsorship proposal
- Chapter tool 10.2 Sport sponsorship rights
- Chapter tool 10.3 Sponsorship leveraging
- Chapter tool 10.4 Sport sponsorship evaluation
- Chapter tool 10.5 Ambush marketing methods
- Chapter tool 10.6 Sport sponsorship evaluation

REVIEW QUESTIONS

1. Identify all kinds of sport properties that can be sponsored.
2. What are the major reasons sport properties and sponsors decide to enter sponsorship agreements?
3. What are the variables that affect consumer goodwill about a sponsorship?

4 Provide a good example of a sponsor and sport property relationship that enjoys a high level of affinity.
5 Describe the process of sponsorship evaluation.
6 Explain why sponsorship leveraging is so pivotal to successful associations.
7 Outline the legal approaches to employing ambush marketing in sponsorship.

RELEVANT WEBSITES

Airbnb and Olympic sponsorship (www.olympics.com/ioc/partners/airbnb)
Athleta (www.athleta.gap.com/browse/info.do?cid=1074427#)
FIFA Women's World Cup (www.fifa.com/fifaplus/)

FURTHER READING

Cornwell, T. B. (2020). *Sponsorship in Marketing: Effective Partnerships in Sports, Arts and Events*. Routledge.
O'Reilly, N., Abeza, G., & Harrison, M. (2022). *Sport Sponsorship Insights*. Routledge.

CHAPTER 11

Sport services

LEARNING OUTCOMES

At the end of this chapter, readers should be able to:

- define the term services marketing.
- outline the differences between sporting goods and sporting services.
- explain the term 'the service experience'.
- identify the three elements of the services marketing mix.
- discuss the key variables of quality service.
- explain the difference between outcome and process quality.
- discuss approaches for measuring service quality.
- define the term customer satisfaction.
- explain the concepts of 'delighting the customer' and 'moments of truth' and examine their strategic implications.
- outline the six-step process of customer relationship marketing.

OVERVIEW

This chapter introduces readers to sport services marketing. It highlights the principles and tools for delivering first, quality service and second, establishing customer satisfaction. This chapter also explains the importance of developing strong relationships with sport customers in their roles as spectators, fans, players, participants, volunteer officials, and citizens in general. Finally, the services marketing mix is outlined, and its applicability to the delivery of services is explained.

SPORT SERVICES

This text has already introduced the four traditional elements of the sport marketing mix, which are product, price, place, and promotion. It has also discussed the concepts

DOI: 10.4324/9781003391319-11

of sponsorship and product endorsement as an extension of the promotional aspect of marketing. We are now in the position to add the idea of 'service' as a way of differentiating products. This chapter begins with a review of the characteristics of sport services before explaining the sport services mix, and considering the concepts of service quality, customer satisfaction, and relationship marketing. Figure 11.1 shows the elements of sport services within the Sport Marketing Framework.

Defining a sport service

Although sport is regularly packaged into tangible goods such as sport equipment, sport apparel, merchandise, and memorabilia, most sport is experienced as a service. People attending an athletics meet are being delivered a service, and so too are people involved in exercise to music classes. Attending a coaching seminar, visiting a sport museum, or having a rock-climbing lesson are also examples of service experiences. It may be useful at this point to review the differences between sport goods and services. Chapter 6 presented four ways in which sport goods and services can be differentiated. They are tangibility, consistency, perishability, and separability. Each point of differentiation is explained in more detail in the following sections.

Tangibility

When a sport product is tangible, it is a physical thing that can be touched, seen, felt, and sometimes even smelt. Sporting goods such as a baseball bat or badminton racquet are tangible because they are physical and are often objects that can be taken away – that is, transportable – such as a football or a team scarf. Some sport services are also intangible because unlike a tube of toothpaste, they cannot be seen, touched, or stored away for later use. They do not exist beyond the memory of their experience. Sport services are like a performance, where a team of players or an individual athlete do two interconnected things. First, they participate – or perform – in a physical contest. Second, this performance delivers fans and spectators – the consumers – an experience. The experience can be memorable, or it can be totally forgettable. Additionally, sport consumers do not actually own the service, and they cannot take it home to keep on a shelf, unless of course, they recorded some of the event on their phone. For the most part they will just experience it for a certain amount of time, and subsequently place it in their personal memory bank for later recall in moments of nostalgic reflection.

Most sport goods and services are a mixture of tangible and intangible elements. This is because many physical sport products have a service or emotional element contained in them. For example, a canoe bought by a consumer is clearly a tangible good. However, whenever it is used on a stretch of water it delivers the participant a benefit, be it a good physical workout, a sense of achievement, or just a vague feeling of happiness. These benefits are, of course, intangible in nature. In addition, many sport services are sold together with something tangible. A season ticket to a football club may come with a subscription package including club stickers, badges, regular newsletters, and discount vouchers for use at selected retail outlets. Sport consumption can thus involve a mixture of goods, services, benefits, and experiences.

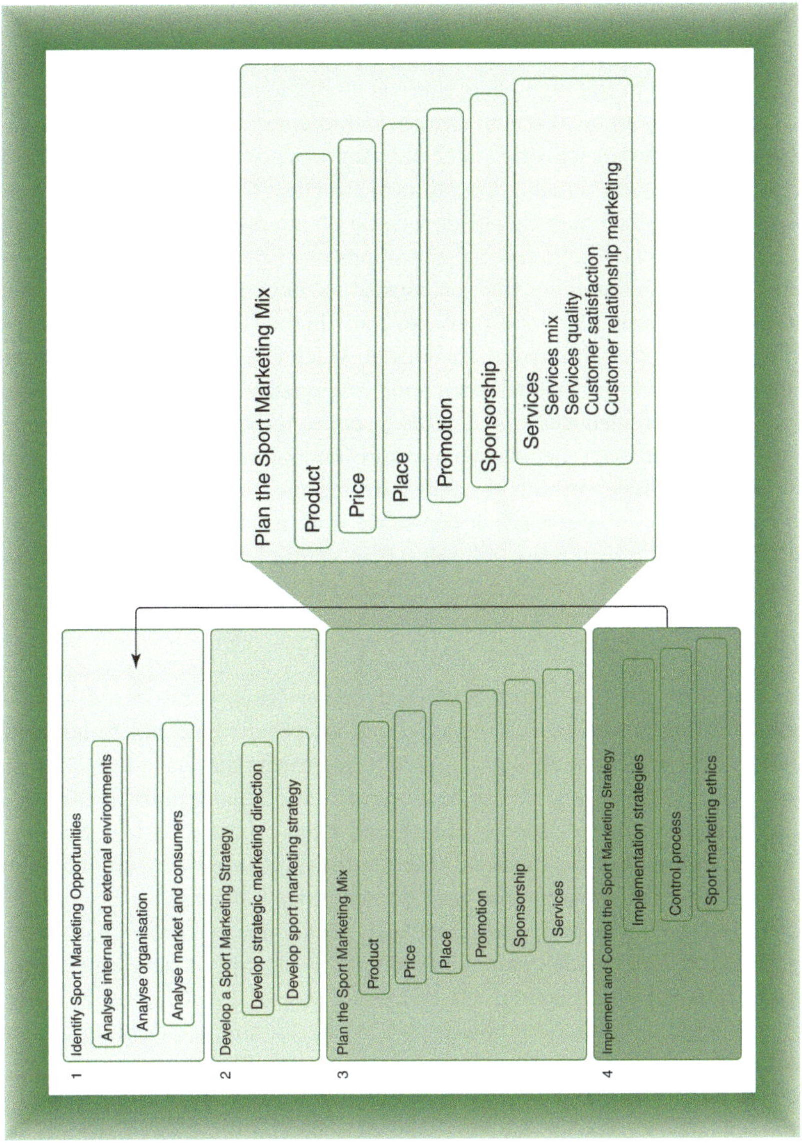

FIGURE 11.1 Sport services and the Sport Marketing Framework

Consistency

Consistency is a second way in which sport goods and services can be separated. Consistency refers to the uniformity of quality from one time that a sport product or service is delivered to the next. Sporting goods usually have a high degree of consistency and manufacturers will typically view this as highly desirable because it is a signal of quality that allows consumers to purchase with confidence knowing what they will get. For example, there is not much change in the quality of one sporting shoe compared with another of the same brand and style from one purchase to the next. And, there is no difference at all between two digital recordings of the same sport content. On the other hand, sport services usually have far more variable quality and marketers will often latch onto this as a positive element in that anything can happen in sport, thus encouraging spectators to attend or watch for the unexpected. The quality of a sport experience may change depending on a range of factors including who is providing the service as well as the special conditions of its offering. For instance, a change in the weather can have a dramatic effect on consumers' experiences. So too can the performance of athletes and teams. Many sport services come in the form of a sporting competition set within the confines of an infrastructure, both of which can vary enormously from week to week. For example, in professional team sport the quality of the spectator experience will be shaped by the refereeing, the field, pitch or court, the catering service provided, the seating arrangements, and even the behaviour of surrounding spectators. And, to top it all off, there is always going to be enormous variability around the contest itself. It could be close, exciting, and spectacular, on one hand, or one-sided, dull, and banal on the other. Similarly, one Crossfit session may prove more enjoyable than another, for no other reason than the instructor, nature of the 'workout of the day', and who else turns up to participate.

Perishability

Perishability refers to whether a sport product or service can be stored and used at another time. Sporting goods such as clothing and equipment tend not to be perishable, although there are exceptions such as nutritional supplements that have a specific life span. Basketballs, cricket bats, and bicycles can be stored and used many times over during their operating life. They can also be traded in the second-hand product markets. Sport services cannot be stored and reused. For example, there is no way to store any unsold tickets to a sport event to sell them at another time. Additionally, once the game has been played, any seats that were not filled are lost forever. Similarly, if only five customers have arrived for an aerobics class in a leisure facility at a given time, the vacant positions represent unsold potential that can never be reclaimed. Of course, as observed in Chapter 6, many sport services are combined with sport products to make up for the perishability of sport services. An example is the content placed online for fans to replay. Since the game or event has been converted to a digital file it can be viewed many times over. This overcomes the perishability problem in sport services that can only be run once by offering something tangible at a low production cost.

Separability

Separability, or more precisely inseparability in the case of services, is a term that is used to describe the extent to which a product or service is consumed at the same time and at the same place it is manufactured. Canned groceries are often consumed months after they are manufactured, and their consumption can take place thousands of kilometres away from the place of manufacture. Sporting goods have the same features. For example, a hockey stick is made in a manufacturing plant, it is delivered to a wholesaler who then supplies it to a retailer. The retailer places the hockey stick on the hockey equipment shelf, and it is hopefully purchased by a consumer at some time in the future. This could be months or even years after its initial production. Another way of looking at this is that the quality of the hockey stick is separated from the quality of service at the sport store where it is bought. It is possible to separate the item from the person selling it, although as we will note later, sometimes one can affect the other.

Sport services, on the other hand, are usually made and consumed at the same time and in the same place. At a live sport event, the competition is both manufactured and supplied in the same space, that is, the production and consumption are inseparable. Anyone who wants to experience the event in real time and real space will have to attend the same stadium at which it is being supplied. Otherwise, they will not be a spectator, but instead will be a media consumer watching on a screen, or just casual fans who might follow the game via regular updates on their phone. Similarly, if people want to participate in a swim carnival, then they must attend the nominated venue at the designated time or else they will 'swim alone', and the communal experience they were seeking will not be realised.

> *Chapter principle 11.1*: There are four characteristics that illustrate the difference between sport goods and services: tangibility, consistency, perishability, and separability. Sport services are intangible because they exist only as an experience. Sport services tend to be inconsistent because they are affected by variables that are difficult to control. Sport services are perishable because they can only be offered and experienced once at any point in time. Sport services are inseparable because they are consumed at the same time as they are produced.

CASE 11.1

Sport Museums

Services may be intangible, but they deliver something of value. They deliver an experience. This experience can be brief, routine, and banal but it can also be prolonged, intense, and memorable. Some people find that church attendance or a music concert can go beyond the intense and the prolonged and enter the transcendental. In sport these prolonged, intense, and memorable experiences can take many forms. They can arise from playing a sport, but they can also come from watching someone else play a sport.

Sporting teams are now seeking to extend these experiences for fans and curious visitors alike by moving beyond matches at stadiums where opportunities to attend are fleeting and results are hard to predict, by creating museum experiences. These museums are often located at the stadium where a team plays, and offer a chance to see the inner workings of a sport facility, as well as get up close with trophies and other paraphernalia.

One of the most well-known sporting museums belongs to Spanish football giants FC Barcelona, whose close community ties are reflected in the club's motto of 'Més que un club' (More than a club). The FC Barcelona Museum, which is one of the most visited museums of any kind across Europe, opened in 1984 and attracts well over 1 million people each year. It allows visitors who book ahead to participate in a range of activities including tours of the stadiums' media facility and a goal-shooting challenge. Fans from all around the world are attracted to this experience when visiting Barcelona, generating a strong source of extra revenue for the club, while also allowing it to deliver clear messaging about its ambitions and accomplishments.

Museums and similar venues are a staple of most teams and are used to bolster understanding and appreciation of sport and to formally recognise the athletes who have participated. One of the most famous of these is the Pro Football Hall of Fame located in Canton, Ohio, which reflects the history of American Football including the National Football League (NFL). The Hall of Fame opened in 1963, choosing Canton in recognition of where the NFL first began. Revamped many times since, the currently facility is over 11,000 square metres in size and is most famous for housing the bronze busts of hall of fame inductees who are chosen each year by a specialist panel for their contribution to the sport.

Other notable sport museums that attract significant numbers of visitors each year include the National Baseball Hall of Fame and Museum in Cooperstown, New York, the Olympic Museum in Lausanne, Switzerland, and the Wimbledon Lawn Tennis Museum in London, UK. All these museums are well-established and resonate with history, catering to both ardent fans and casual visitors. In recent years cities and countries seeking to bolster their sporting connections have also sought to create outstanding sport experiences, including museums that signal their appreciation of sporting history. One example is the 3-2-1 Qatar Olympic and Sports Museum which opened in 2022 and houses an eclectic array of sporting memorabilia from across the world, including a skateboard from Tony Hawk, a cricket bat from Sachin Tendulkar, and a boxing glove from Muhammad Ali.

QUESTIONS

1 How would a sport museum, such as the one at Barcelona FC go about catering for the wide diversity of interest in sport from attendees? Imagine if different attendees are not very interested in football (soccer), somewhat interested, and very interested. How would the experience need to be adjusted for each of these three groups?

2 Sport museums are determined to provide 'experiences' rather than just a collection of exhibits. Pick your favourite sporting team or league and explain what 'experiences' you'd like to encounter at their museum.
3 Aside from a physical sport museum what other digital or online experiences can sporting organisations offer their fans that provide opportunities to boost their engagement and connection to history?

SERVICES MIX

The special nature of sport services when compared with sport goods means that the marketing of services can be substantially different. This has led some commentators to argue that there is a need to augment the conventional sport marketing mix, which was originally devised with goods in mind. Although many supplementary ideas have been suggested to help marketers work directly with services, one approach has become popular. It involves the use of three additional 'Ps', which are (1) people or participants (staff and customers), (2) physical evidence (tangible elements of the service) and (3) processes (the system of service delivery). These additional 'Ps' are not just the concern of sport marketers but are also influenced by the administration and human resources staff, therefore demanding an integrated approach from everyone in a sport organisation. In this respect, the three service mix 'Ps' can be seen as complementary equivalents to the four conventional marketing 'Ps' that are described in Chapters 6–9. As such they provide many useful clues as to how best to market sport services. The three Ps of the sport services mix are described next.

People or participants

Because a sport service is consumed at the same time as it is produced, both staff and other consumers can influence perceptions of service quality. This is particularly true for 'high contact' services such as fitness centres and sporting competitions. In fact, the 'staff' in these examples are part of the service. For example, a sport masseur is part of the massage service, just as athletes are part of a sporting match. The quality and management of employees (and athletes) is therefore an important part of sport services marketing. Furthermore, in sport events other consumers are especially important elements to the service as they have a powerful impact on atmosphere. This means that for sport organisations, the ways in which they allow consumers to interact with one another is a fundamental consideration of the service structure. For some sport spectators, attendance at an event can be strongly driven by the other people who may attend. In effect some people attend sport because other people attend sport, creating the perception of an experience or event that cannot be missed.

Physical evidence

The physical evidence of a sport service includes the environment in which it is delivered, and any other visual or tangible elements. For example, the physical environment of a tennis competition includes the stadium, the food and beverage facilities, the seating, and the scoreboard. Other tangible elements could include the design of tickets, programmes, and merchandise. Not only are these characteristics important components of the service, but they are also significant because consumers use physical evidence as clues to the service quality. In fact, the more intangible a service, the more important it is to include physical elements to reinforce service quality. Consumers are generally attuned to readily understand tangible cues than those that are intangible and carry with them expectations around physical evidence. For example, the modern sport consumer expects stadiums to have reasonably comfortable individual seats, sight lines to a high-definition scoreboard, and food stalls where they can purchase an array of items to consume.

Processes

Processes in sport services marketing refer to the steps that a consumer progresses through to receive a service, as well as those in which a service provider must perform to deliver the sport service. For example, to attend a rugby match, a sport fan may have to buy a ticket online, travel on public transport, wait in queues to enter the ground, submit to a security screening, find the right seat, locate some food and beverages, use the restrooms, and eventually exit. It is therefore important that consumers are educated to understand and anticipate what processes they have to experience to receive a service. It is also important for these processes to be conducted in an appropriate way so that they do not take away from customers' perceptions of the quality of the service. These process moments can be thought of as blueprints of the service experience or reflect what are known as 'moments of truth' where consumers will form an opinion of the service experience. We explore these concepts shortly.

> *Chapter principle 11.2*: The sport services mix is made up of people or participants, physical evidence, and processes. Participants are those who are involved in delivering and receiving a sport service. Physical evidence is the tangible or visual elements of a service such as a sport stadium. Processes represent the steps involved in delivering a sport service.

SPORT SERVICES MARKETING AND THE SERVICE MIX

Although the three services mix elements were originally developed for services marketing in general, they are relevant to the marketing of sport services as well. Chapter 6 showed that most sport products contain intangible elements, and that most sport services include tangible elements. This means that almost all sport marketing involves making decisions about both product and service elements. For example, although sport equipment, memorabilia, and merchandise are tangible products, they are sold to consumers through service outlets that can have an influence over consumer perceptions of the product. This fact can be troublesome for manufacturers who do not have control over the sales-related service of their goods.

In addition, it is obvious that the three elements of the services mix interact in ways that make their independent management difficult. For example, those who deliver a sport service are constrained by the physical environment (evidence) that houses their services and by the processes they employ. As a result, it is difficult to develop tactics for the services mix (participants, physical evidence, and processes) in a sport marketing plan in the same way as it is done for product, price, place, and promotions (and sponsorship as a major part of promotions). In fact, sport services are really just a prominent part of a sport product strategy and should therefore remain consistent with overarching product strategy. The challenge for sport marketers is to determine where to invest their limited resources to create the best service outcomes for consumers.

One way to approach this challenge is for sport marketers to decide *what* is to be done across the services mix that will lead to a better *quality* of service, stronger *relationships* with consumers and higher levels of their *satisfaction*. The remainder of this chapter explains how service quality, customer relationship building, and customer satisfaction are the critical success areas behind the successful marketing of sport services.

> *Chapter principle 11.3*: There are three key principles behind the successful marketing of sport services: service quality, customer relationship building and customer satisfaction.

SERVICE QUALITY

Chapter 6 indicated that product quality is one of the central factors influencing the development of brand equity (brand equity is the added value that a product has because of its brand name). This is also true for service quality. Consumers are more likely to be loyal to a service (leading to greater brand equity) if they perceive that it is of high quality.

> *Chapter principle 11.4*: Sport consumers are more likely to be loyal to a service if they perceive it to be of high quality.

Because of the relative characteristics of sport goods and services, there are different aspects to their quality management. Chapter 6 introduced the elements of product quality, noting that they can be measured relatively easily in terms of whether the product conforms to specifications, how long it lasts and how quickly it is fixed when there are problems. Service quality, on the other hand, is more complex to define because it involves the assessment of an individual consumer's experience, which includes prior expectations that can be formed from a range of actions, including how a sport is itself promoted. Typically, five dimensions of service quality can be specified, as summarised in Table 11.1.

Service quality can be seen as a consumer's general judgement about the value, superiority, or excellence of a service. However, it is difficult to measure this judgement because each consumer will have a unique idea about what value, excellent, or superior service involves. For example, one consumer might believe that the key quality feature of a service is staff courtesy, whereas another might think it more important that the service is delivered on time. To get around this problem, a useful way to understand service quality is to consider the degree to which a service meets the needs and expectations of consumers. When a consumer's expectations are not met, they are likely to perceive that

TABLE 11.1 Five elements of sport service quality

Quality element	*Explanation*	*Examples*
Reliability	The ability to provide a service in a consistent and dependable way. Whether customer expectations will be met every time	Is the service performed right the first time? If a service is promised within a certain time, is it delivered? Is the service the same quality regardless of the time of day or staff member who delivers it? Are reports or statements free of errors?
Responsiveness	The willingness to help customers, and to provide them with the service on time	Does the sport organisation respond to problems quickly? Are employees willing to answer customer questions? Are times for delivery/completion of service given to the customer?
Assurance	The level of confidence and trust that a customer holds in the service	Do employees appear to know what they are doing? Are employees able to use equipment and technology skilfully and quickly? Are the materials provided up-to-date?
Empathy	The ability to get to know customers and their needs, and to deliver a personalised service	Do employees try to get to know the needs of the customer? Is the organisation flexible enough to accommodate the customer's schedule? Do employees recognise regular clients and address them by name?
Tangibles	Physical features of the service (e.g., information booklets, equipment, appearance of staff, facilities, sport venue)	Are the facilities attractive? Does the equipment look modern? Are employees dressed appropriately? Are written documents attractive and easy to understand?

the service quality is low. When a consumer's expectations are met or exceeded, they are likely to perceive that the service quality is high. There are some obvious connections between service quality and customer satisfaction that are explored later in this chapter.

> *Chapter principle 11.5*: Service quality can be seen as the degree to which a service meets the needs and expectations of consumers.

Outcome and process quality

When service quality is defined in terms of customer expectations it means that quality is determined by customers and not sport organisations. It is whether the service conforms to customers' specifications rather than those of the sport organisation that will determine whether service quality exists. Customers will make a judgement about whether a service is meeting their expectations at two points in time: first, they will evaluate what the service delivered after it has been consumed (outcome quality); and second, they will evaluate how the service is delivered during consumption (process quality). A customer's judgement about service quality does not therefore rely just on the outcome of a service, but also on judgements about how a service is delivered. In some instances, it may be difficult for customers to judge the outcome quality of a service. For example, assessing the immediate results of a fitness or health consultation with a personal trainer or a sports medicine practitioner would be impossible without specific knowledge, or time to see whether the advice led to good results. As a result, when customers have difficulties interpreting outcome quality, they tend to rely on how the service was delivered (process quality) to make their judgements.

> *Chapter principle 11.6*: Customers will make a judgement about whether a service is meeting their expectations at two points in time: first, they will evaluate what the service delivered after it has been consumed (outcome quality); and second, they will evaluate how the service is delivered during consumption (process quality).

Process quality (how a service is delivered) relates to how the service is delivered to the customer. For example, whether employees are willing to answer questions, whether they recognise customers, and whether they appear to use equipment quickly and skilfully, are features of how the service is being delivered to the customer. Service quality is more strongly related to outcomes. The physical quality of facilities, equipment, documents, and staff appearance is not primarily associated with how a service is delivered but is part of what is delivered. Furthermore, customers will usually make judgements about how reliable a service is after it has been delivered (such as whether a service is performed right the first time, on time, regardless of who is delivering it, see Figure 11.2).

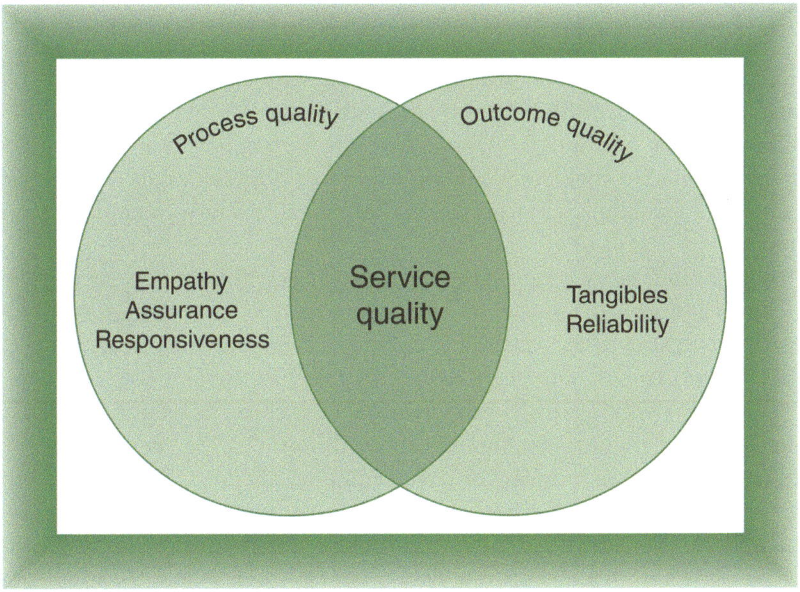

FIGURE 11.2 Sport service quality

CASE 11.2

Stadium Experiences

When sport aficionados draw up a bucket list of sporting experiences a key driver is the excitement and atmosphere that many events generate, ensuring a memorable experience no matter the outcome. While high-profile events – FIFA World Cup finals, the Super Bowl and Olympic 100 metre finals – have appeal, for many fans keen on some 'sport tourism' it is great rivalries that are magnetic.

Fierce rivalries typically have long historical roots, often with teams from the same city competing for bragging rights. In the North of Italy, A.C. Milan and Internazionale share a stadium and a rivalry that began in 1908, while in Rio de Janeiro fierce cross-town rivals Flamengo and Fluminense do battle and attracted a world record attendance of over 194,000 fans to a match in 1963. In other sports, Michigan and Ohio State cast an enormous shadow over college football in the USA, first meeting in 1897. They now meet annually in what locals simply refer to as 'The Game'. Other notable rivalries in the world of team sport include the New York Yankees and Boston Red Sox in baseball, the Los Angeles Lakers and Boston Celtics in basketball, Celtic and Rangers in Scottish football, FC Barcelona and Real Madrid in Spanish football, and the Montreal Canadiens and Toronto Maple Leafs in ice hockey.

All these contests create an electric atmosphere that few other entertainment options can emulate. That passion and energy can spill over however, potentially imperilling the safety of fans. As numerous sporting events have demonstrated, riots, stampedes, overcrowding, and fires can eventuate, leaving fans trapped and vulnerable. One of the most significant sporting tragedies occurred at the Hillsborough Stadium in Sheffield, England during an FA Cup Semi Final between Liverpool and Nottingham Forest in 1989. Overcrowding led to a crush of fans in standing areas and ultimately the deaths of 97 people. The Hillsborough disaster led to a re-design of sport stadiums for football, including a move to fully seated facilities to remove the dangers of standing areas where crowd numbers and movement is not as easily controlled.

Visiting a modern sporting stadium is now a very different experience, with fan safety and comfort a priority. Fans are likely to have public transport – typically free with their game ticket – nearby, and a range of entrances and queuing practices will be in place to ease any chance of danger. For example, many stadiums have outer perimeters where crowds can enter and pass through security checks before stepping into the stadium confines. Tickets will normally be pre-purchased, minimising the risk of large numbers of fans turning up at the stadium in the hopes of entry. Once inside fans will have apps that can guide them to their seats, or order food, and they will readily find ushers who are stationed throughout the facility and who have gone through customer service training programmes. Because game day experiences, often fuelled by sponsor activations, now run for hours before and after an event, peak arrival and departure times are stretched out. Toilets, long the bane of sport fans, are better designed in modern stadiums, including more facilities for women, and change areas for parents of babies. While these features are welcome from a comfort perspective, there is some discontent from fans that facilities are becoming sterile, robbing events of the very atmosphere that attracted fans in the first place. Somewhat ironically, as more and more sport tourists go to big events to experience the atmosphere, their neutrality also serves to dilute the atmosphere, making some big events where ticket allocations are skewed toward sponsors and other corporate guests, rather than season-ticket holders, a poorer experience.

QUESTIONS

1. Imagine you are visiting a sport stadium to watch a rivalry match in the year 2050. What do you expect (or hope) to see and experience?
2. Now imagine you are watching a rivalry match in the year 2050 from the comfort of your living room. What do you expect (or hope) to see and experience from this perspective?
3. The concept of 'sport tourism' is increasingly being factored in by sport marketers who may wish to engage this audience. How does a 'sport tourist' need to be marketed to for a big event, as opposed to a local fan of a team or sport?
4. What one sporting event would be at the top of your list to visit if money and time were no barrier? Explain what appeals to you for this event in terms of the tangible and intangible elements it may offer.

BUILDING RELATIONSHIPS WITH SPORT CONSUMERS

The idea of relationship marketing was first discussed in the 1980s and 1990s. Definitions of relationship marketing typically include statements about attracting, maintaining and improving customer relationships. The word relationship is used because two parties are involved (most obviously a supplier and a customer) who interact with one another. Relationship marketing recognises the importance of keeping current customers, as well as attracting new ones, and emphasises that the relationship with customers' needs to be managed well to encourage loyalty. It also recognises that organisations rely on networks, and interaction between many different people, not just consumers, to deliver a service and/or product. For example, relationships between suppliers and market intermediaries are also important.

Relationship marketing focuses on the one-to-one relationships between parties, often the buyer and seller, or sport fan and sport organisation. It is also concerned with the quality and long-term potential of this connection, and the fact that both parties can derive a benefit from it. The idea of relationship marketing has more recently been instrumental in the development of customer relationship management (CRM).

CUSTOMER RELATIONSHIP MANAGEMENT

Relationship marketing has made way for the concept of CRM. CRM involves using information technology to better manage customer relationships. More specifically, it involves using information technology to collect information about sport consumers to keep track of their consumption activities, and to create long-term relationships with them.

> *Chapter principle 11.7*: CRM involves the use of information technology to create and maintain ongoing, long-term relationships with sport consumers, leading to high levels of loyalty, and improved sales.

Like relationship marketing, the aim of CRM is to create stronger connections between sport consumers and sport organisations. It involves acquiring relevant information about current and potential sport customers, such as their buying patterns, preferences, consumption habits, motivations and purchasing triggers. Much of this information can be collected at the point of sale and is later used to stimulate communication with customers.

Shopping on Amazon provides a simple example. If a consumer were to search for this text, the Amazon CRM software will subsequently suggest that other consumers who bought this book also purchased others, which are listed, and will likely be associated with sport or marketing in some way. This example shows that CRM involves communicating with consumers on a one-to-one basis, in a way that is quite different to mass marketing. It helps an organisation to anticipate the behaviour of their consumers to improve sales and customer loyalty. In a sport context, most professional clubs and teams use CRM systems to enhance their contact with customers. A standard CRM system can be used to collect data relevant to creating new opportunities for contact with consumers. For example, the software can generate an automatic message to the parents of a junior member of a club a few weeks before their birthday. The message might offer to sell the latest club merchandise at a 'birthday' discount. In general, the software can analyse thousands of sales, looking for patterns that might help sport marketers to anticipate the needs of their customers. Among the most helpful information, the software can provide guidance on customer preferences, which customers purchase the most, patterns in demand at different times of the year and which products are the most successful.

Sporting organisations around the world now invest heavily in technology to allow them to better understand and segment their customers. This provides opportunities to monetise relationships in sport that may not have once been possible. Consider for example the Manchester United fan living in South Africa who may never get to experience a match at Old Trafford, the home of the team. Through relationship marketing that fan may subscribe to social media platforms, purchase merchandise, access streaming of platforms like MUFCTV, all while feeling an enhanced and intimate connection to a club that is literally thousands of kilometres away.

Not only will technology play a driving role in sport, but its management as a tool for connecting fans with sport products will become instrumental to success, creating a proliferation of new jobs in sport around relationship marketing and data analysis. Any sport organisation without a sophisticated CRM system will be left behind.

Where CRM was initially just a technical name for a customer database filled with names, addresses and contact details, it now encompasses far more including intricate details on fan preferences, expenditures on merchandise, browsing histories, game attendances, downloads, and social media contributions, and even such nuances such as meal choices. In fact, any activity that can be logged and recorded can also be studied using CRM systems. It is now becoming the standard to use CRM systems to generate creative interaction with fans too. Some common options sport enterprises utilise include online and social media communities, new and customised entertainment alternatives, add-ons such as games, music, statistics and athlete forums, and rewards schemes offering loyalty-based and highly customised returns to fans committed to engagement. CRM systems can also integrate with personalised applications downloaded to smart devices and tablets. As a result, data can be collected about every detail of fan engagement leading to new offerings that are personalised to the point of successfully predicting what an individual fan will want in the future.

CRM involves a six-step process to form the steps identified in Figure 11.3. It should be observed that the process has similarities to the overall Sport Marketing Framework that guides this text because it involves the basic processes of collecting information, segmenting consumers, and developing and implementing a strategy. Each is outlined next.

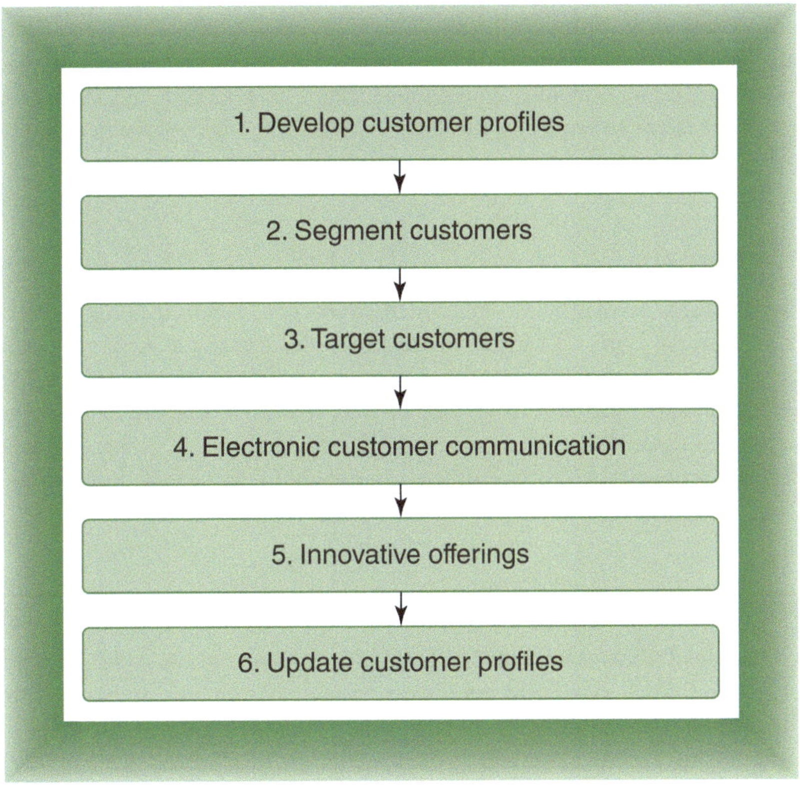

FIGURE 11.3 Six-step process of CRM

Develop customer profiles

Sport organisations gather a wide range of data for CRM including the buying patterns, online and application habits, browsing preferences, shopping and spending, motivations and purchasing triggers for both current and potential customers. Typically, such information is collected at the point of sale and is added to a consumer history 'file', which gives a picture of needs, values, and behavioural patterns over time. It is also important to collect sales revenue information so that it can be linked with customer histories. This way it is possible to link specific customer profiles to specific consumption behaviour. It is also possible to keep track of what follow-up and support is requested by a customer after their purchase, as this can help sport marketers to calculate more accurately what it has cost to make the sale to that customer. It is important for sport organisations who use ticket sellers on their behalf as part of the distribution channel to ensure that they can access the data to build accurate customer profiles. Having data sitting on the server of a ticketing company is of little use to a sporting organisation.

Segment customers

CRM software provides additional information that can be used in segmentation. This information can lead to sophisticated patterns of consumption that can provide the basis for specific segmentation categories. For example, consumers can be segmented according to their attendances, merchandise purchases, social club activities and their online presence. Sport marketers can employ CRM data to help them make decisions about the most appropriate deployment of their marketing resources.

Target customers

Targeting customers involves choosing which sport consumers are going to be the focus of marketing efforts. With CRM, this process includes making a number of estimations about the sport organisation's relationship with the customer such as (1) the likely costs of delivering the sport product or service to that customer, (2) the likely revenue that will be generated through their purchases and (3) the likely value of that customer to the sport organisation over the lifetime of the relationship (this is called customer lifetime value, CLV).

Electronic customer communication

The basic vehicle of CRM is information technology, which of course develops with technological progress. Currently, CRM mainly makes use of database software, websites, apps, mobile or cellular phones and call centres to get messages to consumers. For example, sport consumers may receive messaging, or related apps, on their mobile (cellular) phones offering them live sport, scores, replays, tickets, or discounted merchandise. However, the technology being employed by sport marketers to communicate with consumers is changing all the time. So important is the application and advancement of digital and social media that Chapter 12 is dedicated to it.

Innovative offerings

The key to this step is that sport consumers should be offered opportunities based on their demonstrated needs and buying habits. If the information collected in step one about customer preferences and habits is accurate, it should provide a guide as to what to offer customers next. This personalisation is critical to ensuring strong bonds are formed between an organisation and a consumer and that the correct offers are being made. Consider for example a season-ticket holder who has held the same seats for 25 years. This long-term commitment requires a completely different set of innovative offerings than a casual fan who only attends once every few years.

Update customer profile

Throughout the process of offering sport customers' new products and services, it is important to continue to keep track of how they respond. Over time sport marketers can learn more about consumer habits and preferences, and any changes that occur can lead to an appropriate response. Detailed software now provides simplified ways to manage all such data points.

> *Chapter tool 11.1 Customer relationship marketing process*: The six-step process of CRM is briefly as follows:

1. **Develop customer profiles:** Information could include buying patterns, preferences, shopping habits, motivations for both current and potential customers, and revenue information. This gives a picture of customer needs, values and behavioural patterns over time.
2. **Segment customers:** Segmentation is usually based on buying habits, shopping patterns, preferences etc.
3. **Target customers:** Choose which customers are going to be the focus of marketing efforts. This usually involves estimating (1) the likely costs of delivering the sport product or service to those customers, (2) the likely revenue that will be generated through customer purchases and (3) the likely value of those customers to the sport organisation over the lifetime of the relationship.
4. **Electronic customer communication:** CRM uses information technology such as database software, websites, apps, mobile and cellular phones, and call centres to get messages to customers.
5. **Innovative offerings:** Sport customers should be offered opportunities based on their demonstrated needs and buying habits.
6. **Update customer profiles:** Keep track of customer responses, and learn more about their habits and preferences over time.

CUSTOMER SATISFACTION

There are a wide range of emotional and psychological experiences associated with a sport service that are relevant to satisfaction. In fact, it is reasonable to identify at least five different states of satisfaction: satisfaction as contentment, pleasure, relief, novelty, and surprise. These states are described in Table 11.2.

Whether a customer experiences one of the states of satisfaction recorded in the table depends on what they are expecting out of the service in the first place. A customer will evaluate how a service has performed after they have used it and compare it with the expectations they had prior to consumption. If the customer judges that there is a difference or discrepancy between what they expected and what they received, they will experience a strong reaction to the service. The reaction may be positive or negative, depending on whether the service fell short or exceeded expectations. In other words, there are degrees of satisfaction and dissatisfaction.

> *Chapter principle 11.8*: Since service delivery can stimulate a diverse range of emotional responses, sport marketers must understand how each of their programmes yields different satisfaction outcomes for different consumers. Customer satisfaction can take numerous forms including satisfaction as contentment, pleasure, relief, novelty and surprise. A thorough knowledge of this range, and the service delivery measures to generate them, remains essential in securing satisfaction for as many sport consumers as possible.

TABLE 11.2 Five states of satisfaction

Satisfaction as...	*Characterised by...*	*Example*
Contentment	Habit/continual consumption, low arousal	A leisure facility continues to offer a clean pool as part of their services
Pleasure or relief	Increased pleasure or decreased unpleasant emotions/perceptions (relief)	A sport physiotherapist may help to decrease pain and distress (relief). A close match where a consumer's team wins may stimulate positive emotions (pleasure)
Novelty	New performance/experience	A consumer's local fitness centre installs state-of-the-art equipment
Surprise	When the unexpected happens, or the expected does not	Spectators witness an unexpected, record-breaking performance. When returning a pair of used, faulty running shoes a consumer expects the staff to decline to assist, but they are helpful instead

Satisfaction and quality

Satisfaction and service quality are strongly linked as they represent different sides of the same coin. Both ideas are concerned with what a customer expects from a service. It is important to realise, however, that although these concepts are connected, they are not the same thing. One of the main ways in which they are different is that satisfaction relates to a specific experience (or series of experiences) of consuming a product or service, whereas a customer's perceptions about the quality of a service are not linked to one specific experience. Furthermore, it is also possible for a customer to believe that a service is high quality, even if they have never consumed it. For example, many sport fans would believe that the Wimbledon tennis event offers a high-quality service, although most would never have attended, just as many people consider a Ferrari the pinnacle of a vehicle given its legendary motor-racing history, even though they have never driven one. It is also possible to feel satisfied by a service while still feeling that it is not a high quality. A good example of this may be a customer who is satisfied by a service because it was inexpensive, even if it was of low quality, such as cheap tickets to a sport event that are a long way from the action. Customers can be satisfied by a service that is low in quality if it meets their needs.

Service quality is also different from satisfaction in that customers usually judge quality based on service attributes, and their ideas of what an excellent service should entail. On the other hand, customer satisfaction is affected by many things (other than the service attributes), which are out of the control of the service producer, such as the weather, and parking availability. From this perspective it is likely that customer satisfaction, rather than customer perceptions of service quality, gives a better indication of the sport organisations that perform better in the marketplace.

If a customer experiences satisfaction repeatedly from a sport service, this can lead to a belief that the service is of a high quality. In addition, as service quality increases, satisfaction also tends to increase. In fact, satisfaction can be affected by a customer's perceptions of service quality. Even though satisfaction and quality are two different ideas, they influence each other.

> *Chapter principle 11.9*: Focusing on customer satisfaction ensures that sport marketers make the needs and perceptions of their customers a priority, which in turn leads to stronger loyalty to the sport organisation and its products.

Critical incidents and satisfaction

Satisfaction is also a function of the number of times an incident associated with a sporting service is reported to be negative. Sequential incident techniques (SIT) are often used to capture 'customer experiences'. Within the assumptions of this model customers and fans are asked to identify favourable and unfavourable experiences for specific episodes and incidents that occur in the process of experiencing a sport performance. Episodes and incidents are incorporated into a customer experiential pathway (CEP). Take, for example, the sequence of events involved in attending a motorsport meeting. The first thing to do is identify this experiential pathway that begins from leaving home, travelling to the event, attending the race, going through the race debrief, and returning home. This may involve the following multi-step process:

Step 1: Purchase ticket through online agency
Step 2: Use ticket to access specific public transport to event
Step 3: Arrival and move to venue
Step 4: Entry point to venue and admission
Step 5: Movement to seat
Step 6: Seating and viewing
Step 7: Event quality
Step 8: Purchasing and consuming food and drink
Step 9: Using restrooms
Step 10: Other fans and spectators (behaviour and contribution to atmosphere)
Step 11: Exit from venue
Step 12: Return home on public transport

All negative and positive incidents are compiled, and the most frequently cited incidents are then highlighted and interrogated. When all the data have been complied, and evaluated, action is then taken to remedy the problem incidents, and thus improve the levels of satisfaction for consumers next time round. These remedies and recommendations can then be fed into the planning process for subsequent events.

This approach can be thought of as a 'blueprint' of the service process. Much in the same way a blueprint of a building details its various components and their interaction, a service blueprint does the same tracking consumers through their experience, allowing a marketer to identify good and not so good interactions. In the aforementioned example, imagine if viewing the race was problematic because electronic screens were not well placed, making it impossible for fans to see where cars where on the track. Despite everything else going well, this experience is likely to impact satisfaction to the point where a fan may not return. Similarly, if you consider action away from the event it may also have a significant impact. For example, imagine the fan who thoroughly enjoyed the event and its components but found public transport access to and from the event was long and arduous. This may mean a fan does not return in the future, preferring to watch the race on television instead to avoid the headaches of transport.

Related to blueprints is the concept of identifying and managing 'moments-of-truth', a concept brought to the attention of marketers by airline executive Jan Carlzon, and which identifies the succession of interactions consumers have with frontline service staff as being critical in the process of managing expectations and creating satisfaction. Sport can readily identify these important moments by blueprinting the consumer journey and seeking to delight (or at least meet expectations) at each interaction point. For sport marketers this is especially critical as control of the core product offering is typically outside of their control. Thus, while a marketer may have some influence on how a stadium looks and feels in terms of creating a pleasurable viewing experience, they are unlikely to have any influence as to what happens on the field given the special nature of sport.

CUSTOMER SATISFACTION AND SPORT MARKETING

Customer satisfaction is an important concept for sport marketers to understand for two reasons. First, it encourages sport marketing efforts to remain focused on the needs of customers, making these needs and associated perceptions of sport products a priority. As Chapter 1 stressed, the most basic idea in sport marketing is that of meeting the needs of consumers. Second, customer satisfaction can influence not only a customer's intention to purchase, but also their repeat purchasing over time. Simply put, a satisfied customer is more likely to be loyal than an unsatisfied one.

> *Chapter principle 11.10:* Customer satisfaction is a judgement that customers make after they have experienced a sport service where they compare what they expected from it with what they believe they actually received. When expectations are met or exceeded, customers are satisfied, and when expectations are not met, customers are dissatisfied.

Delighting the customer

An idea related to customer satisfaction is that of delighting the customer. It occurs when a customer's expectations are exceeded to a surprising degree, resulting in an extremely positive emotional state. In these circumstances, the customer is more than just satisfied. They may feel excited, exhilarated or other positive emotions that have a strong physiological element.

The importance of the concept of delight is best understood in the context of satisfaction. As the previous section established, customers compare what they expect from a service with how it actually performs. If the service performs worse than they expected they are likely to feel dissatisfied, but if it meets or exceeds their expectations, they are likely to feel satisfied. It is the degree to which the service exceeds expectations that determines whether a customer experiences satisfaction or delight. If the service exceeds expectations within a normal range or zone of tolerance, a customer may simply feel satisfied. For example, if a parent receives a free coffee when waiting to pick up their child from a karate class at a leisure centre, then they might experience satisfaction slightly above the normal expectations. However, if a service performs to a surprisingly positive degree, then a customer might experience delight. The key here is that delight comes about when the service has performed to a level that the customer could not have reasonably expected. For example, if a sport fan's seat was upgraded at a sport event as the result of a loyalty programme, then they might experience delight. The difficulty for sport marketers is that eliciting delight can only occur if the service performs to a surprisingly high level, and this means that the sport organisation must put in substantial extra effort and resources. There is also the danger of resetting expectations to a higher and unsustainable level. There are three types of delight that are useful for sport marketers to manipulate. Before covering these, it is important to also note that consumers whose expectations are not met also carry a zone of tolerance in their perceptions and may not necessarily act negatively if they accept that some things may from time to time fall just below expectations.

For example, poor weather may influence a sporting contest, but not influence future purchasing behaviour if the consumer has accepted a zone of tolerance that some events will be better than others for a range of reasons.

> *Chapter principle 11.11*: Customer delight occurs when a customer's expectations are exceeded to a surprising degree, resulting in an extremely positive emotional state. Delight transpires when the customer is more than just satisfied. This can happen when a service exceeds a customer's expectations of what they think is normal or reasonable from that particular sport service.

Assimilated, re-enacted and transitory delight

A general principle is that when customers are delighted, they are more likely to be loyal to a sport service than if they were merely satisfied. However, it is also true that delight can increase customer expectations, which will make customer satisfaction much more difficult in the future. How then can a sport organisation know whether it is beneficial to try to delight their customers? Three different types of delight – assimilated, re-enacted, and transitory – help to answer this question as each has a different effect on customer experiences and expectations.

Assimilated Delight

Feelings of delight do not stay permanently with a customer; they will not continue to feel the physical intensity of delight (such as excitement or exhilaration) indefinitely, although they are likely to remember the experience. If, for example, fitness centre customers remember being delighted the last time they used a service, their expectations may be raised well above normal. This may be termed assimilated delight, because the customer has incorporated the things that delighted them into their expectations of what is normal. The customer may even tell others about the features of the service, and as a result others may also come to expect a high level of performance as normal. Worse, competing organisations may hear about what is being offered and duplicate it themselves, which of course will mean that there is nothing unique about the original service. As a result, sport organisations must carefully consider whether the cost of providing a delighting feature is worth it.

Re-enacted Delight

Re-enacted delight occurs when a customer savours the memory of being delighted. A good example is a French football fan who experiences delight when attending an exhilarating match where Kylian Mbappe delivers one of his sublime performances. The delight doesn't stop there since they then enjoy remembering and re-living the experience repeatedly. They may watch replays, post their thoughts on social media, chat about it online, or attend other matches at the same venue or between the same teams to recreate the original feelings. It is as if they re-experience the original delight even though subsequent performances may be inferior.

Re-enacted delight can happen when customers realise that the delighting experience is unique and cannot be easily recreated. They accept that they cannot reasonably expect it to happen on a regular basis. This is often true of experiences of sport participation and spectating. This has marketing implications since a sport organisation may encourage re-enacted delight by creating one-off or once-per-season special events that customers will remember fondly in the future. The organisation can also help customers and participants to develop strong memories through recreations, ceremonies and memorabilia related to the delightful event, as well as recordings or online content.

Transitory Delight

The final type of delight, transitory delight, occurs when customers forget that they had once been delighted. This means that they will not expect the delighting features to be present when they use the service again in the future; they may be delighted all over again as if it is the first time! For example, if a customer attributes the delightful experience to pure chance or fate, they may decide that it is unlikely to happen again. They may also attribute good service to one particular staff member, not the organisation, and therefore not expect the same service again in the future. It is possible, in these scenarios that a customer's reaction to the experience is fleeting, and they forget about what delighted them after some time has passed.

Should delighting sport customers be a priority marketing goal?

At first glance it seems obvious that the more we delight customers the more repeat business we will get. But once we dig deeper into this issue, we find that delighting customers will sometimes pay off, but other times may not. For example, with assimilated delight it is possible that customer expectations will be raised to another level, and that this will make it difficult to satisfy customers' desires in the future. Some critics of 'customer delight' theory argue that, although delighting the customer may help profitability in some situations, it is probable that customer dissatisfaction hurts a sport organisation more than delight helps it. This means that it is generally more effective to focus on reducing dissatisfaction and complaints (therefore increasing overall satisfaction), rather than focusing on trying to achieve the next level of 'delight'. The most important point to take away from these comments is that sport marketers must be aware of the situations in which delighting the customer can be profitable, and the times when it may be a counterproductive investment.

> *Chapter principle 11.12*: Providing customer delight in a sport service can lead to higher levels of loyalty, word of mouth promotion and an advantage over competitors. However, it is essential to know how customer satisfaction/delight influences customer behaviour. It is also important to consider how capable competitors are of copying any innovative service features. It is usually better to invest resources in decreasing customer dissatisfaction than in increasing customer delight.

CASE 11.3

LIV Golf

One of the common misconceptions about sporting leagues is that they have the luxury of operating in a monopoly environment. After all, to see the elite of football in the UK the Premier League stands alone, while baseball in the USA is commanded by Major League Baseball and top-level rugby league in Australia is the domain of the National Rugby League competition. While the barriers to entry are significant, any competitor could emerge and disrupt those markets if they had the will, strategic insight, and a large amount of cash to lure the big teams and players to their competition. This has happened many times across the sporting world, with rival leagues seeking to poach the best of entrenched competitions to serve up a new product. Almost always as these products appear, they are centred on giving fans more access, insight, and enjoyment, eschewing some of the established traditions to provide a spectacle that is innovative and fresh and focuses on a new type of fan experience.

One of the most interesting recent examples has been the emergence of LIV Golf, a Saudi backed golf tour that commenced in 2022 and which shook up the world of golf. Male golf players had competed on the lucrative Professional Golf Association (PGA) Tour since the 1920's, and this tour became a succession of lucrative events held in the United States and which attracted the best players from across the world. The PGA Tour events are spread across four days and feature 72 holes of golf. With sponsorship from leading brands and established broadcast partners, earnings on the Tour for even the average performer were high.

LIV Golf shook that seemingly solid foundation adopting 54-hole tournaments (the LIV being the Roman numerals for 54) and luring a bevy of leading players away from the PGA Tour and to their breakaway league. The LIV Golf League, which emerged in 2023 features 48 players across 12 teams, with all players competing across the 14 three-day tournaments that are spread across various parts of the world, including Singapore, Adelaide (Australia), Valderrama (Spain) Chicago (USA), and Jeddah (Saudi Arabia). Using a 'shotgun' start where players begin from each one of the 18 holes on a golf course, as opposed to moving sequentially from holes 1 to 18 as the PGA Tour does, all the players commence at the same time allowing the event to be compressed in time. In terms of the service experience the LIV Golf League is also very different from the PGA Tour. Music is played across the course, the players are encouraged to interact with fans, golfers can wear shorts (which are not permitted on the PGA Tour), 'stadium holes' with seating reminiscent of a sport stadium are used where a raucous atmosphere can develop, and the experience is one targeted to maximise fan involvement and enjoyment.

Not surprisingly, the future of both the PGA and LIV were questionable if they competed against each other over the longer-term. Splitting players and the attention of various lucrative stakeholders like media networks would prove increasingly challenging. Eventually both parties entered talks to merge their operations, thus potentially returning golf back to some equilibrium, although the experience will be altered by the success of fan engagement and new markets that LIV had demonstrated.

QUESTIONS

1. Golf is a sport based upon tradition and practices that have been enshrined over many decades. How do these behaviours work both for and against attracting audiences? Explain your answer by first segmenting the market for golf spectators.
2. If we accept that sport is entertainment, what other sports do you believe need to rethink some of their approaches to better engage with this philosophy? Give examples of what changes you would recommend and why.
3. If you had the power to change one rule in one sport to make the sport more marketable (that is easier to engage the broadest possible audience) what would that change entail, and how would you expect that it would make an impact?

PRINCIPLES SUMMARY

- Chapter principle 11.1: There are four characteristics that illustrate the difference between sport goods and services: tangibility, consistency, perishability, and separability. Sport services are intangible because they exist only as an experience. Sport services tend to be inconsistent because they are affected by variables that are difficult to control. Sport services are perishable because they can only be offered and experienced once at any point in time. Sport services are inseparable because they are consumed at the same time as they are produced.
- Chapter principle 11.2: The sport services mix is made up of (i) people or participants, (ii) physical evidence, and (iii) processes. Participants are those who are involved in delivering and receiving a sport service. Physical evidence is the tangible or visual elements of a service such as a sport stadium. Processes represent the steps involved in delivering a sport service.
- Chapter principle 11.3: There are three key principles behind the successful marketing of sport services: service quality, customer relationship building and customer satisfaction.
- Chapter principle 11.4: Sport consumers are more likely to be loyal to a service if they perceive it to be of high quality.
- Chapter principle 11.5: Service quality can be seen as the degree to which a service meets the needs and expectations of consumers.

- Chapter principle 11.6: Customers will make a judgement about whether a service is meeting their expectations at two points in time: first, they will evaluate what the service delivered after it has been consumed (outcome quality); and second, they will evaluate how the service is delivered during consumption (process quality).
- Chapter principle 11.7: CRM involves the use of information technology to create and maintain ongoing, long-term relationships with sport consumers, leading to high levels of loyalty, and improved sales.
- Chapter principle 11.8: Since service delivery can stimulate a diverse range of emotional responses, sport marketers must understand how each of their programmes yields different satisfaction outcomes for different consumers. Customer satisfaction can take numerous forms including satisfaction as contentment, pleasure, relief, novelty, and surprise. A thorough knowledge of this range, and the service delivery measures to generate them, remains essential in securing satisfaction for as many sport consumers as possible.
- Chapter principle 11.9: Focusing on customer satisfaction ensures that sport marketers make the needs and perceptions of their customers a priority, which in turn leads to stronger loyalty to the sport organisation and its products.
- Chapter principle 11.10: Customer satisfaction is a judgement that customers make after they have experienced a sport service where they compare what they expected from it with what they believe they actually received. When expectations are met or exceeded, customers are satisfied, and when expectations are not met, customers are dissatisfied.
- Chapter principle 11.11: Customer delight occurs when a customer's expectations are exceeded to a surprising degree, resulting in an extremely positive emotional state. Delight transpires when the customer is more than just satisfied. This can happen when a service exceeds a customer's expectations of what they think is normal or reasonable from that particular sport service.
- Chapter principle 11.12: Providing customer delight in a sport service can lead to higher levels of loyalty, word of mouth promotion and an advantage over competitors. However, it is essential to know how customer satisfaction/delight influences customer behaviour. It is also important to consider how capable competitors are of copying any innovative service features. It is usually better to invest resources in decreasing customer dissatisfaction than in increasing customer delight.

TOOLS SUMMARY

- Chapter tool 11.1 Customer relationship marketing process

REVIEW QUESTIONS

1. Identify the elements of the sport services mix. Provide an example of how each is relevant to the marketing of sport services.
2. Explain what sport service quality is and compare it with sport goods quality.

3 Provide an example of each of the five areas of service quality.
4 Explain how customer satisfaction and dissatisfaction come about.
5 What is the relationship between service quality and customer satisfaction?
6 How does CRM lead to opportunities for customer loyalty?
7 Under what circumstances is customer delight worth pursuing?

RELEVANT WEBSITES

Barcelona FC Museum (www.fcbarcelona.com/)
LIV Golf (www.livgolf.com/)
National Baseball Hall of Fame and Museum (www.baseballhall.org/)
Olympics Museum Lausanne (www.olympics.com/museum)
PGA Tour (www.pgatour.com/)
Pro Football Hall of Fame (www.profootballhof.com/)
Qatar Olympic and Sports Museum (www.321qosm.org.qa)
Wimbledon Museum and Tours (www.wimbledon.com)

FURTHER READING

Buswell, J., Williams, C., Donne, K., & Sutton, C. (2016). *Service Quality in Leisure, Events, Tourism and Sport*. CABI.
Piekarz, M. (2020). *Sport Operations Management and Development: An Applied Approach*. Routledge.

CHAPTER 12

Sport digital marketing and social media

LEARNING OUTCOMES

At the end of this chapter, readers should be able to:

- understand the terms digital and social media marketing.
- define the advantages and disadvantages of digital and social media marketing.
- describe how digital and social media marketing relate to the Sport Marketing Framework.
- identify the six key principles of social media marketing.
- describe the six-step process of engaging consumers with social media marketing.
- outline the five broad categories of digital marketing technology.
- differentiate between available social media tools and their appropriate deployment in sport marketing.
- study digital and social media examples by interacting with cutting-edge existing sites and through brief cases.

OVERVIEW

The purpose of this chapter is to explain the application of digital and social media approaches to sport marketing including the new kinds of thinking they require. It explores the kinds of technologies and tools that are available to sport marketers and considers the influence that digital marketing and media have on the sport marketing mindset.

INTRODUCING THE DIGITAL REVOLUTION

It is easy enough to understand digital sport marketing as any form of marketing that utilises technology, which of course means a focus on the internet and all the devices, channels, and media that it implicates. At the same time, this broad definition no longer helps

DOI: 10.4324/9781003391319-12

distinguish digital marketing from other forms in an era when just about every marketing activity involves a digital aspect. Even conventional printed flyers rely on print-on-demand technologies, while even modest sporting events utilise digital ticketing to save money. The simple act of watching sport live cannot escape the digital era either. Although TV remains the prominent way most sport fans consume live content, digital and streaming options are rapidly catching up in terms of preferences. At the same time as the technologies and tools of the digital era have become entrenched in our marketing expectations, sport marketers must come to terms with a new way of looking at their offerings. In short, sport digital marketing and social media demand a new kind of mindset where the conventional distance between sport properties, their marketing representatives, and fans is completely blurred, and where success means constant adaptation. No longer are digital and social media tools just 'add-ons' to the standard marketing methods. Today, a digital world needs a digital message.

Digital marketing is often described as electronic marketing and is usually associated with the internet, computers, and forms of mobile communications. To phrase this more generally, digital marketing refers to communications that are generated and delivered by electronic means through computers, tablets, mobile phones, or other electronic devices. Digital marketing employs technologically sophisticated platforms or vehicles for transmitting and communicating information, and can include online video, paid social media advertisements, and social media posts. In this chapter, we describe how these digital platforms are revolutionising sport marketing and have justifiably become essential tools in the toolkit. By implication of the escalation of digital channels, as a secondary goal of this chapter, we also explain how social media represents a central element in a sport organisation's overall digital media marketing strategy. The term 'social media', like the term 'marketing', can mean different things depending on the context. From a broad perspective social media includes any platform or application that facilitates the communication of information through interactions between networked groups of individuals. It is important to take a broad view like this because technology has provided the sport marketer with so many innovative ways of communicating directly with the public that they no longer must rely only on traditional 'media' organisations. This direct access is facilitated by the two-way mode of communication within digital media.

> *Chapter principle 12.1*: Digital sport marketing refers to communications that are generated by electronic means and delivered through devices such as computers, tablets, and mobile phones. It refers to technologically sophisticated platforms or vehicles for transmitting and communicating information, including social media channels, which utilise the interactions of networked individuals.

Today, digital content is delivered through many devices with consumers able to transfer information seamlessly from one device to another and from one digital format to another (e.g., from a mobile phone to a computer). Another feature of digital media is that data, or information, is accessible in real time. Digital media is especially important in sport marketing because it permeates all aspects of consumers' lives, delivering marketing content through the communication channels they utilise on a daily basis.

> *Chapter principle 12.2*: Digital media is flexible, transferable and can be customised.

Digital media and social media were once seen as the latest technological trends, but now have significant and permanent implications for sport marketing. Digital media is more than the technology and tools employed to communicate to consumers. Effective digital media marketing requires sport marketers to communicate in novel ways with sport consumers, developing relationships and authentic connections with their target markets. It is also important because it creates additional opportunities in sport, such as new assets and revenues (e.g., website and mobile digital rights, as well as new sales channels), and new possibilities in licensing and merchandising (e.g., in-app advertising). Although the types of technologies that are available continue to evolve, the principle remains the same: sport marketers can use advanced technology to communicate with their customers and sell them extra products and services that are associated with sport. Perhaps more importantly, the social media dimension of the digital revolution allows marketers and sport organisations an unprecedented connectivity with their customer and fan base.

The popularity and prevalence of digital and social media technology mean that it provides sport marketers with innovative ways of communicating with consumers. Many of these communication approaches are far more rapid, responsive, and interactive than other marketing strategies. For example, compare the one-way, standardised content delivery of television with the opportunity to rewind a particular play or have statistical information overlayed on your screen while streaming a sport match. Not only are digital media platforms fast and direct, they are also inexpensive compared with traditional techniques of sport marketing. Even more importantly, digital media enables sport organisations to develop messages that are personalised to key target audiences through audience research gathered from online browsing habits.

> *Chapter principle 12.3*: Digital and social media technologies provide sport marketers with new ways of communicating with consumers, and novel approaches to their marketing activities. Many of these approaches are far more rapid, responsive, interactive and inexpensive when compared with other marketing strategies; they are also more easily customised to key target audiences.

CASE 12.1

#WeThe15

One example of a multi-national digital marketing campaign was developed by the International Paralympic Committee (IPC). To increase awareness and promote greater knowledge about the 15% of the world's population with a disability the IPC developed a campaign named 'WeThe15'. The main goal of the campaign focused on facilitating increased understanding of the barriers and everyday discrimination persons with disabilities encounter in society. The lengthy marketing campaign launched in August 2021, running concurrently with the Tokyo Games, and runs through the Los Angeles Games in 2028.

The campaign has six main aims. These involve (1) shaping the global diversity and inclusion agenda to place people with disabilities at the forefront, (2) organise initiatives during the next decade aimed at various stakeholders such as governments, businesses, and the public to realise greater inclusion for individuals with disabilities, (3) address and remove the barriers that deter people with disabilities from achieving their full potential, (4) increase awareness, visibility, and representation of people with disabilities in society, (5) remove misconceptions in society about people with disabilities through education initiatives, and (6) focus on social inclusion through the promotion of the role of assistive technologies as a driving force.

A wide variety of activations were carried out to launch the campaign prior to and during the Paralympic Games in Tokyo in August and September 2021. The first activations to draw attention to the campaign included a 90-second digital film that aired in 60 countries, as well as the lighting up of 125 global landmarks in the campaign's signature purple colour. These landmarks included the Empire State Building in New York City, the Colosseum in Rome, the London Eye in London, the Rainbow Bridge in Tokyo, and the Story Bridge in Brisbane, Australia. Later activations included the development and promotion of a campaign symbol – a circle with a triangle portion of the interior outlined to represent the 15% of those with a disability – as well as social media activation through targeted campaign posts, and the airing of the campaign film at the Opening Ceremonies for the Paralympic Games.

QUESTIONS

Visit the WeThe15 site (https://www.wethe15.org) to help answer the following questions:

1. What @WeThe15 channels were employed to help build awareness of the WeThe15 digital media campaign?
2. Search #WeThe15 on X (formerly Twitter), what types of social media posts were utilised as part of the campaign?
3. Based on the #WeThe15 search on X, how did athletes (both Paralympian and Olympian) incorporate this campaign into their own social media marketing?
4. What areas of improvement regarding their social media campaign would you recommend to the WeThe15 initiative going forward?
5. How would you employ social media marketing to sustain the WeThe15 campaign during upcoming Paralympic and Olympic cycles?

DIGITAL SPORT MARKETING: RETHINKING SPORT MARKETING

At its most simple, digital sport marketing refers to the use of electronic media technologies, tools and channels in marketing programmes. However, digital marketing means more than just using up-to-date technology within a traditional marketing programme. It also refers to a novel marketing approach that recognises the complex social and technological world that sport consumers occupy. To be effective, digital marketing must do more than just use new technology. It also must respond to the changing lifestyles and expectations of sport consumers who assume content will be available to them at all times, on multiple devices. Common terminology now associated with these changes in content delivery and consumer expectations include over-the-top (OTT), which is content delivered on the internet, and out-of-home (OOH) viewing, which is viewing outside the home on an internet-connected device.

Sport consumers are inundated with marketing messages. Despite the technological options, sport marketers must compete with a vast range of entertainment and communication technologies. There is an enormous amount of 'clutter' in the marketing environment, and sport marketers must find ways to cut through it. In this new environment, conventional marketing strategies, such as traditional advertisements or promotions, are becoming less effective. As a result, sport marketers must be aware of the ways in which sport consumers' lives have changed, and the corresponding new expectations they have of sport products and marketing programmes. Sport consumers have limited discretionary leisure time, consume more media from a greater variety of media outlets, belong to numerous social media networks, and are more fragmented as an audience. Marketing initiatives could previously reach large audiences at once, a benefit of mass media broadcasting and traditional over-the-air (OTA) sport viewing that contributed to media effectiveness. Now, digital marketing initiatives must not only identify target audiences but also determine ways to reach these smaller, fragmented segments with meaningful messages. This ties into sport consumers' expectations of individualised, personalised experiences, interactivity, choice and control, the opportunity to multitask (Generation M), and access to user-generated content (UGC).

Digital sport marketing recognises that consumers are exposed to an immense amount of marketing and have a wide range of sport product choices at their fingertips. Consequently, sport consumers are less likely to be convinced by broad sales pitches. In fact, consumers can be resistant to traditional marketing strategies such as advertising campaigns that target wide audiences and prefer customised content. It is important to note that the digital marketing approach does not render the standard principles of marketing obsolete, but it does give the sport marketer new principles to wield that are particularly relevant to the current environment. The presence of new technological tools should therefore sharpen sport marketers' thinking about the pace of marketing and the nature of interaction and communication with consumers.

> *Chapter principle 12.4*: Digital sport marketing demands customised communication with targeted sport consumers, generated by electronic means or through technologically sophisticated platforms that facilitate the transmission of information.

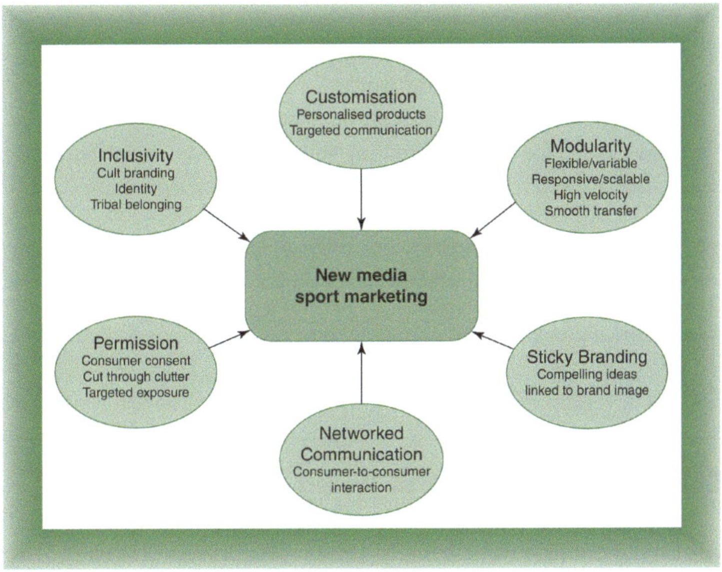

FIGURE 12.1 Digital sport marketing

There are six key dimensions that summarise the thinking that must underpin digital sport marketing that can be employed by sport marketers to engage better with consumers. These are customisation, modularity, sticky branding, networked communication, inclusivity, and permission. The principles are illustrated in Figure 12.1 and are described next.

> *Chapter principle 12.5*: Digital sport marketing involves targeted and personalised interactions based on the principles of customisation, modularity, sticky branding, networked communication and permission.

Customisation

As opposed to a mass marketing approach, digital sport marketing is targeted and customised. New media technology gives marketers specific information about the behaviours and preferences of their consumers, commonly referred to as audience insights. The wide availability of these insights is a direct result of digital content delivery, as it is easier to track consumer behaviour and content consumption online. For example, the Nielsen Company is a global provider of media insights, and measures TV, audio, digital, streaming, and cross-media use. The organisation analyses the data and provides information on audience engagement, which is then used to inform marketing and advertising spending based on the type and amount of content audiences consume. As a result, marketing can become more specialised and nuanced, directed precisely towards the personal needs and choices of customers. Digital options are instrumental in converting scattered mass marketing into surgical direct marketing.

Developing tailored marketing and advertising campaigns through the collection of audience insights is one example of potential customisation. New technology is also changing the way in which sport products can be designed and personalised. For example, most major sport apparel providers such as Nike or Adidas allows customisation of football jerseys. Previously, the process associated with producing replica jerseys prohibited fans from being able to submit custom printing requests. With current capabilities associated with online ordering, consumers can now easily submit custom printing requests to sportswear providers. This in turn enables the production of individualised products, featuring their name or favourite number, reflecting their personal identity.

> *Chapter principle 12.6*: *Customisation*: Digital sport marketing messages should be customised or targeted and adapted to specific consumers and their needs.

CASE 12.2

Mark Cuban Center for Sports Media and Technology

Indicative of the growing emphasis on digital marketing, as well as need to train individuals on the tools to create digital multi-media content within sport, various educational programmes are expanding their offerings to meet this market need. In 2015, it was announced that Mark Cuban, owner of the National Basketball Association's (NBA) Dallas Mavericks, was establishing a revolutionary sport media centre. The Mark Cuban Center for Sports Media and Technology at Indiana University in the United States was made possible by a $5 million USD donation from Cuban, an alumnus of the school. The Cuban Center was designed to partner with the university's Media School, Radio TV Services, School of Informatics, and Advanced Visualization Lab to offer university students the opportunity to work with similar multi-media technologies employed by the Mavericks.

The Cuban Center was incorporated as part of a renovation into an existing college basketball arena. The renovation converted 520 square metres of space into a multi-media studio for university students to produce a variety of content for all 24 sports at Indiana University. Built to facilitate work opportunities, internships, and real-world instruction, students learn to produce high-quality, professional grade sport media content including live event broadcasts, virtual reality videos for fan engagement, promotional videos for recruiting and social media distribution, interactive video board displays that run during games, as well as university team-specific shows. Specific technologies include a virtual reality TV studio with wall-to-wall green screen, a video editing room, a sound editing room, photography studio, and 3-D imaging. This also includes areas for gaming, studio production, gameday video production, motion and broadcast graphics, promotional location production, reporting and play-by-play, and live game casting. All content produced can then be distributed as part of a digital, multi-media strategy across a variety of media channels. This includes online streaming channel HoosiersTV, Indiana University Athletics YouTube channel, as well as the university's Athletics and individual team-specific social media channels on Facebook, Instagram, X (formerly Twitter), and TikTok.

QUESTIONS

Visit the Cuban Center's X (formerly Twitter) feed (www.twitter.com/CubanCenter) to help answer the following questions:

1. Examine the various content distributed on the feed. What are the benefits to students from building a multi-media centre to produce digital media for university sports?
2. What are the various types of digital multi-media (e.g., photos, videos, graphics) displayed on the feed?
3. What does the Cuban Center offer a sport marketer in terms of training to be able to build the digital media skills necessary to transition into full-time employment?

Modularity

A modular object is composed of elements or units that conform to a regular standard and can stand alone in functionality or combine with other modules to provide new functionality. This allows flexibility and variety in the way the elements are used. For example, modular storage cubes can be arranged to fit in a wide variety of spaces of differing size. Digital marketing technology is often structured in a modular fashion, such as sport streaming apps, which allow fans to select specific teams or leagues to follow within a particular sport. Another simple example is SMS or text messaging marketing. It can stand alone as an independent form of communication, or it can be linked into other forms such as social media advertising, email newsletters and promotions, and member discounts.

From a digital sport marketing perspective, modularity means that communication with consumers can be fast, responsive, simple, and flexible. It is important that the marketing message is fast because the more quickly an idea passes from one consumer to another, the larger the number of consumers who will encounter it before it dies out. Velocity is also important in dealing with customer enquiries, orders, and demands. Sport consumers expect services to operate responsively and products to be delivered almost instantaneously.

Digital sport marketing can provide fast and responsive solutions to consumers and allows an unprecedented level of responsiveness to changing demand levels. A modular system can be scaled up and down easily, meaning that it can easily adjust to servicing small or large numbers of people as demand changes. A club's X (formerly Twitter) account, for instance, may need to be monitored more closely during a match, or after a significant win to be able to receive and respond to increased messaging from fans.

Modularity should also enable smoothness of information transfer between consumers. Being able to access and spread ideas through the click of one button is an ideal example. The ideal scenario is to have an idea or product that is so smooth that once someone is exposed to it, they are instantly hooked. Powerful platforms for spreading information quickly are X (formerly Twitter) and Instagram. Examples of functions that make ideas effortless to transfer information on these platforms are the repost and quote function on X, as well as the stories feature on Instagram.

> *Chapter principle 12.7*: *Modularity*: A modular digital marketing programme (including product design) is standardised and automated incorporating flexibility, responsiveness to changes in demand, and ease of transfer.

CASE 12.3

NBA App

Leagues and teams once had to partner with social media platforms to offer additional content or forms of engagement for fans outside of team-specific websites. Today, sport properties can develop individualised apps to offer fans a 'one-stop-shop' for digital content. One league app that has been wildly successful in this area is the NBA App. As part of the NBA's modular, multi-platform digital strategy, the NBA App sits alongside offerings such as the NBA League Pass, all NBA social media accounts, and NBA ID (the league's global membership programme) to deliver tailored content to fans.

Remarkably successful at driving engagement, the NBA App generated more than 1 billion video views during the 2022–2023 season. This was largely due to a reimagined design that incorporated a social media-based vertical scroll of video content to appeal to younger audiences. New original content such as 'Pass The Rock', 'Shaqtin' A Fool', and 'Thinking Basketball', is offered alongside videos of top plays, game recaps, postgame interviews, classic games, as well as live-streamed games. The modular format allowed for video sharing through social media platforms such as Facebook, Instagram, X (formerly Twitter), and YouTube, and offered further engagement by linking to fantasy basketball offerings such as NBA Pick'Em, DraftKings, and the NBA's proprietary betting app, NBABET. Growth was attributed to international fans who represented 50% of the total audience aged 25 years or younger.

Proprietary apps from leagues and teams offer tremendous digital marketing benefits through consumer insights. The more information an organisation can know about their consumers, the more targeted their digital marketing efforts can become. Thus, proprietary sport apps provide a win-win model for organisations to gain valuable insights on their consumers and develop more personalised marketing initiatives, while simultaneously offering fans individualised engagement experiences. For example, the NBA app includes a built-in link to the NBA Store where fans can purchase official jerseys, hats, and footwear, and design customisable apparel. Consumer insights on video views through the NBA app could be tracked to determine favourite players or teams, and then provide a basis for individualised promotional discounts on apparel through the NBA Store. Another example could include tracking video views and consumption patterns through the app, which can then be used to offer targeted additional video content on favourite players or teams that lies behind a subscription feature. The subscription could be offered at a discounted rate for a period of time to entice sign up.

QUESTIONS

Log on to the NBA App here: https://www.nba.com/app or download the app utilising the QR code on the web page. If utilising the webpage, click on the watch tab and scroll through the videos available. After exploring, answer the following questions:

1. What consumer insights can you derive from the video content provided?
2. How would you translate these consumer insights into digital marketing initiatives for fans, building from the examples provided above?
3. What features do you feel are missing from the NBA App that could add additional digital marketing insights for the NBA?

Sticky branding

An idea or product must stand out from the crowd to last or even to be noticed at all. People will respond to an idea if it is compelling or gripping in some way. In the case of sport, what the sport marketer ultimately wants is for an idea to stick that says something about the sport brand. An all-female sport brand, for example, may wish to attach ideas of empowerment and strength when facing adversity to attract more female consumers. Such was the case with Athleta when they signed US athletics star Allyson Felix and incorporated her story as part of their branding to create stickiness in the mind of consumers.

The key point here is that the sport brand must be linked with ideas that are 'sticky' – or that take hold in consumers' minds – and that are consistent with the positioning strategy for the brand image. As consumers may respond to many different kinds of ideas, the key is to identify those that are consistent with the marketing strategy. Some of the more effective 'sticky' ideas are funny, sexualised, thought-provoking, offering financial profit, horrible, shocking, beautiful, hyper-real, attention-grabbing, involving sensory bombardment, unconventional, and unpredictable. A sticky idea may also be one that meets a niche need or fills a market gap. There are many effective digital tools that can be used to propagate sticky content such as social media marketing and streaming advertisements. Following are a number of activities that offer the opportunity to explore and reflect on the marketing potential of these networking hubs. First, consider the essential social networking site, Instagram. It allows consumers to view branded content via posts, stories, and reels, and communicate interactively with sport organisations, athletes, and other fans.

> *Chapter principle 12.8*: *Sticky branding*: Occurs when digital sport marketing content takes hold in consumers' minds in ways that are consistent with the positioning strategy for the brand, and as a result are readily passed on digitally.

Networked communication

The fourth principle of digital marketing is networked communication, which refers to the use of digital platforms and social media to facilitate communication between consumers. It allows a network of communication to develop, rather than just a one-way projection of information to the customer. Put very simply, it means getting consumers to talk to each other. The idea of networked communication is based on the idea that instead of telling consumers about certain products, it is more productive to get consumers to talk to each other about the products, providing authentic viewpoints and recommendations. This is easier than ever before because social media platforms allow an interactive approach where marketers can organise consumers to communicate with one another. For this reason, digital sport marketing tends to be focused on marketing activities that bring consumers together and facilitates communication within online communities formed through various social media platforms, blogs, and podcasts. Digital marketing is not just a set of tools for communication but is also a hub of consumer interaction and commercial activity.

Networked communication provides consumers with a personalised experience and because of this it is sometimes called engagement marketing. It stresses the importance of fostering the interaction between consumers in a way that encourages word of mouth (sometimes called 'word of mouse' when applied to digital forums) communication to facilitate their interest in the sport product. This is based on the premise that consumer-to-consumer (C2C) marketing is more powerful than business-to-consumer (B2C) marketing as occurs with traditional advertising.

Viral marketing is a prominent example of networked communication using digital and social media technologies. A virus is an infectious agent that replicates itself and spreads from one living thing to another. Although it may start out in small numbers, in the right environment a virus will grow exponentially. Viral marketing is a term that describes any marketing message that is designed to be passed on from one consumer to another quickly, utilising this sharing feature to result in exponential message spread. Like a virus, the aim of viral marketing is to encourage rapid communication from one person to another, until thousands, or even millions of people have been 'infected'. Viral marketing is therefore a systematic approach that aims to encourage people to share a marketing message with their personal contact network.

> *Chapter principle 12.9*: *Networked communication*: Networked communication is based on the idea that instead of telling consumers about products, it is more productive to get consumers to talk to each other about them.

Inclusivity

The principle of inclusivity in digital and social media marketing is closely related to the idea of networked marketing. Because digital channels can provide sport consumers with a platform for communication and interaction, it lends itself to offering them something to belong to. Sport consumers are motivated by a psychological need to feel as if they 'belong' to a group. In particular, digital sport marketing can be conducted in such a way that sport consumers feel 'included' in virtual groups.

> *Chapter principle 12.10*: *Inclusivity*: Refers to the use of digital marketing to fulfil the need to 'belong', which in turn fosters the development of identity and a stronger connection to the sport brand.

Permission

The sixth principle of digital marketing is permission. Some traditional approaches to marketing are based on the idea of 'interruption', or marketing at consumers. For example, digital advertisements that play at the beginning of YouTube video content are a form of interruption as they prevent the immediate viewing of desired content. Marketers hope that even though the viewer was not expecting to see their advertisement, the content may influence their brand perceptions and purchase intentions. Another simple example of interruption marketing are the sponsored advertisements that pop up between the Instagram stories of different users. In order to see the next Instagram story in a user's feed, the sponsored advertisement will appear, and individuals will need to actively tap the screen to move forward with the story. These advertisements are typically based on posts that have been viewed or clicked on recently but are still intrusive in the format that they interrupt intended viewing. In both examples, the communication of information is one way: from the marketer to the consumer. Many consumers are resistant to these kinds of advertising campaigns and may not even consciously recognise them. Such advertising strategies are largely ineffective because the market is flooded with them, and consumers have learnt to tune out to their invasive messages.

In contrast to 'interruption' marketing, better digital sport marketing is based on the idea of 'permission', which leads to deeper engagement. This is often referred to as permission marketing and refers to the use of digital content to communicate with sport consumers who have given their permission to receive customised messages by opting-in, usually via email, mobile phones, social media sites and applications, therefore providing consent. Not only can permission-based approaches help to overcome the problem of consumers' inboxes overflowing with spam but they also help marketers to segment and target consumers more accurately and therefore cut through the advertising clutter by sending messages to individuals who are actively interested in the content. This in turn drives engagement and deeper levels of sport brand identification. For example, individuals could opt-in to receive subscription-based SMS or instant messaging from specific teams on match days. Messages to members could inform them about parking or public transportation options, the nearest locations for half-time food and beverage stands and relevant specials, merchandise deals in stadium, and instant video replays.

> *Chapter principle 12.11*: *Permission*: Refers to the effectiveness of communicating with consumers who have consented to receive customised messages, rather than sending random, untargeted and uninvited marketing communications.

Compared with traditional marketing, digital sport marketing can help sport organisations to spread messages quickly to a large but targeted audience at a relatively low cost. However, there are disadvantages as well. First, there is a loss of control over content that is generated through networked communication and interaction. Although moderation policies exist for inflammatory or inappropriate content, sporting properties must accept the possibility of message content spiralling out of control quickly. This exposes sport properties to the risk of negative opinions and public perceptions. In some cases, as we describe in the social media section later in this chapter, sometimes it is athletes and players who generate unwanted attention through inappropriate and occasionally exclusionary content. Second, it is often difficult to control the timing of some aspects of the digital marketing campaign. Technological innovation creates both opportunities and challenges for sport organisations. It is also important to note that digital sport marketing should not replace traditional marketing principles. In fact, digital marketing should be considered a (potentially powerful) marketing strategy that can be used within the Sport Marketing Framework. A summary of the digital sport marketing principles appears in Table 12.1.

TABLE 12.1 Summary of digital sport marketing principles

Principle	*Description*
Customisation	The marketing message, as well as the products themselves, should be targeted and customised to specific consumers and their needs
Modularity	The marketing programme (including product design) should be structured in a standardised and automated way that allows it to be flexible, responsive to changes in demand, and quick and easy to pass from one person to another
Sticky branding	The brand must be linked with ideas that are 'sticky' – or that take hold in people's minds – and that are consistent with the marketing plan for the brand image
Networked communication	Digital content allows a network of communication to develop between consumers, as well as between consumers and the organisation. Networked communication is based on the idea that instead of telling consumers about your products, it is more productive to get consumers to talk to each other about your products
Inclusivity	Through networked communities and user interaction, digital technologies can fulfil the need to 'belong', which in turn fosters the development of identity. Digital marketing can be conducted in such a way that people feel 'included' in virtual groups
Permission	This refers to the fact that it is often more effective to communicate with customers who have given their permission to receive customised messages, rather than to send random, untargeted and uninvited information

THE DIGITAL SPORT MARKETING PROCESS

To review, the six elements of digital sport marketing are *customisation, modularity, sticky branding, networked communication, inclusivity* and *permission*. When these ideas are understood as a package, they suggest that there is a process involved in engaging consumers through digital marketing. First, sport organisations must make *contact* with consumers using compelling ideas to capture their attention and the features of modularity to ensure the contact is fast, flexible, and smooth. Once contacted, consumers may respond to the customised offerings and engage in *conversation* via the networked and interactive capabilities of the platform. Conversation leads consumers to make social *connections* with other users, with whom they can share *content*. Over time this interaction leads to the development of a deeper sense of *community* and belonging to the other users, the platform, and the sport property.

A sport consumer may then become a *convert*: someone convinced of certain beliefs and ideas that are shared through the platform, which, in the best-case scenario, include the sticky ideas that have been attached to the brand image. This process is represented in the diagram in Figure 12.2.

Even though sport consumers may not be receptive to some traditional marketing strategies, they still want to participate in sport-related consumption in both traditional and novel ways. This means that sport marketers must engage the sport consumer and find ways for them to identify and belong to the sport product and organisation. Sport marketers must utilise personalised strategies in their marketing programmes. Fortunately, technology allows sport marketers to develop an unprecedented combination of

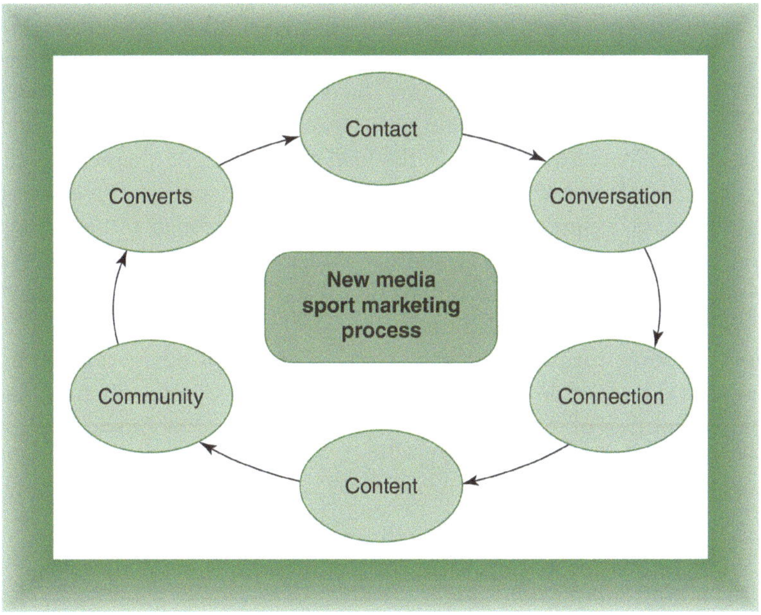

FIGURE 12.2 Digital sport marketing process

consumer interaction and marketing customisation. The tools of digital sport marketing are available to almost all sport organisations and therefore represent an unprecedented level of access to consumers that has conventionally been provided to only the most well-resourced sport organisations.

DIGITAL SPORT MARKETING TOOLS

The digital sport marketing principles outlined in the previous section can be used to help achieve the positioning strategy specified as an outcome of following the Sport Marketing Framework. In this section, some technological tools for implementing digital sport marketing principles are outlined.

The incorporation of digital marketing into the sport marketing realm means that the context of marketing has shifted and that there are more tools for communicating with sport consumers than there have ever been before. In general, the most popular tools of marketing, such as advertising, were only available to those organisations with plenty of resources. However, with the use of new digital tools and their lower costs associated with message delivery, any sport organisation can be seen and heard. Sport organisations may also be able to collect market research data more easily than ever before and therefore understand their customers better. While purchasing audience insights from a major corporation such as Nielsen might be too costly for some, all social media platforms offer analytics to business accounts. These can include information on views, click throughs, shares, and specific words or phrases utilised by individuals in comments. While not as robust as other types of audience insights, this potentially enables sport marketers to monitor engagement, as well as positive, negative, and incorrect information that is being published about them, and to learn about the attitudes and needs of their consumers. These examples exemplify how important it is for sport marketers to understand the different types of digital tools that are at their disposal, and to continue to keep up to date with developments in new technologies, software and applications. In this section, the central, available digital tools are outlined. This leads into the final section of this chapter, which examines social media as the most powerful integrative tool in the digital sport marketing space.

Digital technologies can be classified into five tools, although some overlap between categories is inevitable. They are (1) internet-driven platforms, (2) mobile communications, (3) upgraded conventional technologies, (4) hardware, and (5) software. These categories are illustrated in Figure 12.3.

Following are some further examples of each digital tool. These lists are not exhaustive and, given the pace of development, new devices will continually be added. Despite the inevitable evolution of technological capabilities, these tools provide a useful starting point for thinking about each category.

Internet-driven platforms

Internet-driven platforms include the increasingly sophisticated methods of communicating that the World Wide Web supports. Although the device to access such platforms can vary from person-to-person, examples include blogs, email, web video, podcasts,

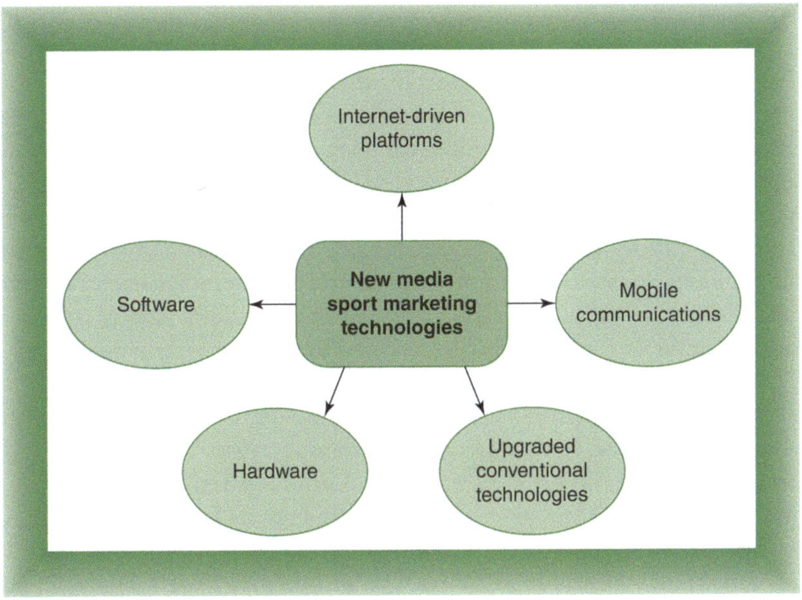

FIGURE 12.3 Digital sport marketing technologies

vodcasts, websites, pop-ups, spam, virtual worlds, wikis, and electronic commerce (such as online and mobile payments), and social media platforms such as Facebook, X (formerly Twitter), Instagram, YouTube and TikTok. The use of YouTube and other similar user-generated video sites or streaming platforms are another popular example of internet-driven technology being used in sport marketing. By broadcasting snippets of compelling content to an audience eager for thrills and entertainment, leagues, clubs, and athletes eager for sponsorship and fame are hoping to reach larger audiences than they have ever been able to access before.

> *Chapter tool 12.1 Internet-driven platforms*: Include methods of communicating that the World Wide Web supports, such as blogs, e-mail, web video, podcasts, vodcasts, websites, pop-ups, spam, virtual worlds, wikis, electronic commerce, and social media platforms such as Facebook, X, Instagram, YouTube and TikTok.

Mobile communications

Mobile communications include the communication tools that are associated with mobile or cellular phones and any wireless communication system. Examples include Bluetooth, wireless, SMS, multi-media messaging service (MMS), and 5G devices, all of which are free from the restrictions of traditional land-based connections. While many of the tools mentioned as internet-driven platforms are accessed via mobile devices, communication is enabled by internet capabilities. Mobile communications such as those mentioned above can be used to distribute information using either a push or pull strategy. A push strategy involves sending unsolicited communications to consumers, such as through a SMS. A pull strategy involves providing free information, such as matchday information, game updates and news headlines that the consumer has given permission to receive, sometimes by downloading a proprietary team app.

The use of in-app marketing is one example of how mobile communications can be used to market goods and services. Individual team apps can do much more than simply house member information or convey matchday statistics. One popular trend is the use of in-app promotions where a barcode or QR code can be provided to a consumer based on past purchase history to encourage spending, and easily scanned at the point of sale. Using this technology, sport leagues, events, and retailers can offer exclusive promotions to consumers who have given permission to receive regular deals through the mobile app. Competitions within the app can also be designed to make use of mobile phone technology, such as competitions for game tickets.

In addition to the potential for messaging information to consumers, mobile communications are now capable of delivering personalised content and streaming broadcasts. Mobile communications can be used to access information, replays, live footage, and historical information about prominent sport events and games from anywhere in the world including from the game venue itself. The utilisation of personal devices facilitates tailored marketing communications sent to consumers, and they can then decide whether they want to purchase something on offer on the spot.

Wireless capabilities within mobile communications allow connectivity between different devices such as smartphones, tablets, and laptops. This integration makes portable real-time sport viewing, referred to previously as OOH viewing, from virtually any location in the world a possibility.

> *Chapter tool 12.2 Mobile communications*: Include the communication tools that are associated with smartphones, tablets, and any wireless communication system. Examples include Bluetooth, smartphones, and tablets, wireless, SMS, multimedia messaging service (MMS), and 5G phones, which are free from the restrictions of traditional land-based connections.

Upgraded conventional technologies

Upgraded conventional technologies refer to the technological advances that have been made with devices such as televisions, video data recorders, video on-demand, and streaming platforms. Examples include internet-connected 'smart' TVs (CTVs) with Web 2.0 features that allow individuals to stream content, combining the features computers, televisions, and digital media players. Digital video recorders are now incorporated into cable or satellite TV set-top boxes, and video-on-demand enables the download and streaming of shows to these boxes. Last, streaming platforms and OTT content are an extension of traditional internet-based video viewing that has been enabled through CTVs or other devices.

In addition to the benefits of interactivity, there are several ways in which digital data can be used to enhance the conventional sport watching experience. First, it can be viewed like ordinary video or television transmissions, and it also offers increased flexibility so that events may be watched over in OTT format via streaming. Wireless connectivity access has improved in quality, cost, and convenience, and thus the option of watching a sporting event through a personal computer, mobile phone, or tablet using OOH viewing is more common. Second, digital can be used to cover specific players or aspects of the sporting event. The viewer can be the director if they choose, selecting camera angles, players, activities, or replays at their discretion. Third, digital can be employed to create new statistics associated with the event. The technology provides more options for measuring and monitoring. These statistics can also be stored for each player or team and revisited later for analysis or even for use in game play as a form of infotainment. Fourth, digital technologies enable real-time interaction such as gaming. As viewers watch the big game, they can link in to play in direct competition through their home gaming console or computer interface. As data are stored historically, game players will be able to create their own teams based on real game performances.

> *Chapter tool 12.3 Upgraded conventional technologies*: Refer to the technological advances that have been made with devices such as televisions, video data recorders, video on-demand, and streaming platforms. Examples include connected smart TVs (CTVs), digital video recorders incorporated into cable or satellite TV set-top boxes, and video-on-demand downloading of content, as well as streaming platforms and OTT.

Hardware

Hardware refers to the physical objects and equipment that make digital technology possible, such as computer systems, mobile devices, portable equipment, and game consoles. New smartphones now contain sufficient processing power to access and replay live sporting content. For most of us, this is nothing spectacular; merely an expectation that comes with owning a smartphone. Another expectation in information technology hardware is the increasing ability for devices to perform multiple tasks and to interact seamlessly with other equipment.

> *Chapter tool 12.4 Hardware*: Refers to the physical objects and equipment that make up new media technology, such as computer systems, mobile devices, portable equipment, and game consoles.

Software

Where hardware refers to the physical equipment involved in digital technology, software enables that equipment to operate. Software includes both the systems software enabling the technology to function (such as the operating system and the utilities), as well as the applications that run the users' programmes. Software (and mobile applications) is therefore the interface that ultimately makes all digital media technologies function. In addition to the proliferation of mobile applications for sport, and for social media engagement that are relevant to sport, augmented and virtual reality software is an example that promises to dramatically change the way spectators view sport in the future. The virtual nature of spectatorship will offer spectacular opportunities for sport enterprises to improve their revenues, particularly if they are a genuinely international property. For example, virtual reality will allow remote users to 'sit' anywhere in the stadium, while augmented reality allows for computer-generated images to be superimposed on video. This could include watching a sport broadcast with stats overlayed on the screen while simultaneously viewing the game in the stadium. Used in combination with social media and through mobile applications, the latest software is bringing sport experiences closer to the consumer all the time.

> *Chapter tool 12.5 Software*: Includes both the systems software that enables the technology to function (such as the operating system and the utilities), and the applications software that runs the users' programmes, including mobile applications.

SOCIAL MEDIA: THE NEW HUB OF DIGITAL SPORT MARKETING

You want to know how your team performed? Forget about the TV or the newspaper, go directly to X (formerly Twitter). For a conversation about the results, you could look at the team's official Facebook page, or browse the team's Instagram account for replays of key moments. All this content is available on your smartphone, tablet, or any other WiFi or mobile device. The use of social media platforms is so pervasive that 32% of the general population uses social media while watching sport, and this figure jumps to 43% when focusing on Generation Z. As we highlight in this section, savvy digital sport marketers know that while data and updates are compelling services for fans, the real power of social media lies in its unprecedented ability to create close, personal engagements between sport properties and their followers. In the end, like all marketing, we aim for better relationships, experiences, feedback, and advocacy. One conclusion is undisputed: the use of social media has become an essential investment rather than an interesting experiment at the periphery of sport marketing.

Few could argue that the contemporary sport consumer has changed radically in just a few, short years. We want sport content at our convenience, and often comes with the expectation of updates from our favourite and most trusted sources on social media. In short, we want to know what is going on, and we want to be able to find out '24/7'. To start with, sport consumers want instant access. Next, that access must be customised, or at least 'customisable', to meet the fickle preferences of each fan. Access must also arrive seamlessly. That means both a smooth download of a preferred app, and an integrated platform where the sport fan can quickly scroll through the content of their choosing. Integration plays a central role in effective digital marketing because consumers are using their mobile devices for internet browsing almost as much as through computers with future growth in mobile use projected to overtake desktop browsing in the next few years. In addition, they check email and social media sites, post photos and comments, listen to voice notes and send messages, consult their calendars, check the weather forecast, and play music and games all using apps. Although it varies depending on the region, research has found that an individual touches their mobile phone on average more than 2,500 times per day. No wonder hardware manufacturers and app developers are so focused on providing an interface that captures the user's demand for intuitive functionality. Because sport consumers are so well educated about sport and technology, they expect more than the garden-variety results delivered via sport apps. Rather, content must be accompanied by novelty, entertainment, and insight. This is driven in part by the growing cost of attending live sporting events, which can be prohibitively expensive leading sport consumers to find alternative ways of engaging with game content as well as looking for new ways of generating the excitement and buzz of the contest. Enter social media.

> *Chapter principle 12.12: Social media*: Can be used as a pivotal tactic in a sport digital marketing campaign for cultivating closer consumer engagement, leading to better relationships, experiences, feedback and advocacy.

CASE 12.4

Over the Top and Streaming

Complementing the digital revolution in sport content consumption on mobile devices are two key contemporary players in content and delivery – OTT content and the streaming technology employed to deliver this content. OTT content providers deliver media exclusively via the internet without the need for traditional cable or satellite providers. Streaming technology is the method that delivers the audio or visual content. Netflix, Amazon Prime, Disney+, and other streaming providers deliver OTT content direct to consumers for subscription fees. OTT and streaming are rapidly catching up with broadcast TV for how sport fans prefer to consume content. This includes matches such as English Premier League football or Grand Slam tennis on Amazon Prime, sport documentaries including F1: Drive to Survive, Cheer, and The Last Dance on Netflix, or sport streaming providers such as DAZN or Twitch.

Research conducted by Amazon on television viewing preferences has found that 74% of individuals between the ages of 18-34 and 64% of individuals between the ages of 35-54 indicated their preference for OTT content delivered via streaming software platforms. This shift to digital content delivery impacts the marketing options available to sport stakeholders. Digital marketing opportunities within OTT, streaming platforms, and social media included OTT advertising airing during live sporting events, as well as sponsorship placements on digital boards that run during games. The benefits of digital marketing within OTT, streaming platforms, and social media include targeted audience reach, as well as increased awareness and audience expansion for sport properties. Audience-level insights can be gathered on individuals' viewing habits and can include personal information, content viewing history, location, and favourite sports, teams, and leagues. Using these audience insights, sport properties can then sell targeted, specific advertising placements that align with viewer demographics, on a local, regional, national, or even global scale.

For example, as live-sporting content is streamed, targeted sponsorships can be sold based on geographic location and demographic analysis. Employing artificial intelligence technology, different sponsorships aligning to viewer characteristics can be overlayed on the screen.

Digital marketing to increase audience awareness and expansion can be achieved through sport documentaries that are designed to educate viewers on a particular sport property, offering dramatic, back-stage access to leagues, teams, and personalities. The Amazon Prime documentary series All or Nothing is an example of educational-based digital marketing designed to attract casual fans. Whether focusing on the National Football League, National Hockey League, or English Premier League, through dramatic storytelling of a sporting season, a previously untapped market of individuals can be converted into fans who not only watched the series, but also then viewed live matches throughout the season. Another example of market expansion through digital marketing is Formula One (F1), which increased their market through partnerships with the OTT platform Twitch. A livestreaming service that includes gaming, entertainment, and sport, Twitch attracts a hard-to-reach younger audience due to its strong videogaming associations. By livestreaming sporting events with popular Twitch personalities, F1 was able to reach and engage with this market.

QUESTIONS

The opportunities for major sporting teams, leagues, and events to incorporate OTT and streaming services into their digital marketing mix is outlined above. Now, think about smaller or niche sporting properties and answer the following questions:

1. How might such smaller organisations utilise a streaming service such as Twitch to target a different audience or increase awareness of their sport?
2. How might such smaller organisations utilise a social media platform such as YouTube to target a different audience or increase awareness of their sport?
3. Should all sport properties incorporate OTT and streaming services into their digital marketing mix? Why or why not?

Social media options

At present, five social media platforms dominate the social media landscape – Facebook, Instagram, X (formerly Twitter), YouTube, and TikTok – although there is always a proliferation of competitors on the rise. One relatively recent platform, TikTok, demonstrates that innovation in social media is always possible. Launched in 2017, the platform has grown exponentially with 627 million app downloads in 2022. Most sport marketers should be using a variety of platforms, as each have their own unique features that promote different types of content. The key lies with using each platform for a different purpose. For example, Facebook, can be a great platform for community building and fan engagement, thus content that promotes fan interactivity works well on this platform. Instagram, which averages more engagements per post than Facebook, YouTube, X, and in some instances, TikTok, focuses on photo and video content. This includes static photos, videos, live video, and stories and reels. Easy sharing features increases UGC, which is content that is produced by fans, and can be utilised by teams and leagues. X established the microblogging trend with a restriction of 280 characters per post. X, although able to post text, photo, and video content, remains most popular for information sharing. In-game updates, team news, and links to news articles also work well on this platform. Although YouTube and TikTok are video-based platforms, YouTube works best for longer-form video content that can include highlight reels, and even full matches. TikTok is designed for short-form video content, with graphical overlays, music, or humour adding to its light, playful tone. Finally, many larger sport organisations develop their own 'television station' (such as Barcelona TV+) and broadcast snippets, highlights, or even live events, as an exclusive OTT and streaming site for all organisational content.

Of course, there is a suite of additional platforms available for sport marketers to experiment with. Some examples include WhatsApp, WeChat, Weibo, Snapchat, Pinterest, Reddit, Discord, and Twitch. WhatsApp is a messaging app, which makes it excellent for marketing communications, and is currently utilised in more than 180 countries. Individuals can utilise WhatsApp to communicate to organisations on their business-specific platform, with customer service a core component. Along similar lines, WeChat is a messaging app that has evolved to include online shopping features and advertisements. It is the most popular social media app in China and presents a good alternative to connect with sport consumers. Taking the place of X (formerly Twitter) and Instagram in China is the social media microblogging app Weibo. Containing a mix of photos, videos, and stories, and trends, individuals can utilise the platform to share content or access news and information.

Snapchat is a platform designed for sharing photos or short videos peer-to-peer, with mobile advertising a part of platform. While similar in functionality to Instagram, users tend to utilise either Snapchat or Instagram, not both. Thus, Snapchat would be a good platform to add to an organisation's social media marketing mix, especially if your sport appeals to a younger audience. Pinterest is a social media platform designed to post photos and is beneficial for discovering new products. It also links well for driving traffic to websites through 'pinned' photos.

Reddit is a news aggregation-based website that builds around topical networked communities. Featuring a dedicated feed for sport, which can be subdivide into teams and leagues around the world, fans can engage in discussion, while sporting properties can advertise to more than 430 million monthly users.

Finally, Discord and Twitch are two platforms designed specifically for gamers and capture the ever-expanding esports market. Discord is a communication platform designed to build communities where consumers can chat or text in real time. Twitch is a live streaming platform where individuals can stream gameplay and interact with audiences watching the livestream. Creators can build large followings or communities through these platforms and subsequently offer advertising, sponsorship, and brand reach opportunities to sporting properties.

Managing all these social media channels within a social media marketing strategy can be time consuming and require significant levels of staffing to create, coordinate, and dissemination content. Feed column platforms such as Hootsuite or Tweetdeck can help manage the clutter of different channels by allocating or redirecting content across a range of outlets automatically. Bringing together a social hub for consumers has become known as social 'curation'. Typically, through the sport enterprise's website, all of its social media accounts can be accessed in a sleek and interactive manner, while also including live event broadcasts.

> *Chapter principle 12.13: Social media platforms*: Encompass a wide variety of sites and applications including the big five, Facebook, Instagram, X (formerly Twitter), YouTube, and TikTok where each plays an essential role in a digital sport marketing strategy.

CASE 12.5

FC Barcelona Social Media

With the ever-expanding options of social media platforms available for fans to utilise, one challenge for sport organisations, teams, and leagues revolves around how to diversify their digital media portfolio of content. Simply cross posting the same content across all social media platforms does not make for a successful digital and social media strategy. Each of the major social media platforms – Facebook, Instagram, X (formerly Twitter), YouTube, and TikTok – offers individual features that make it advantageous to post certain content.

A great example of a sport property that employs a successful digital media strategy across all social platforms is FC Barcelona. With active accounts on Facebook, Instagram, X, YouTube, and TikTok, the team regularly posts content that engages fans across all platforms. The official FC Barcelona Facebook page boasts more than 113 million followers, and averages five posts per day. Content primarily includes static photos and videos and focuses on a mix of historical moments and current team highlights to celebrate the club's success as one of the top teams in the world. Post captions highlight these moments to fans, and result in community engagement through comments celebrating the team.

On Instagram, where the club has 125 million followers, a similar strategy is employed to Facebook, but is applied across different features within Instagram. For example, historical and current in-game moments comprise the photo-based content, while team highlights and behind-the-scenes footage are posted as reels. Utilising Instagram stories, FC Barcelona posts time-sensitive giveaways related to specific matches, capitalising on the limited time frame of Instagram stories. The FC Barcelona X (formerly Twitter) feed has more than 48 million followers and posts a variety of content related to in-game information, but also features news articles about the team that link to the official FC Barcelona website, enabling cross promotion of content and driving fans back to a central site for team information.

The official YouTube page for FC Barcelona was the first sport-based page in the world with more than 15 million subscribers. It contains long-form videos of the team during training, as well as offering an interactive live-stream of matches where pundits watch and comment on the action. In addition, video comments include links to all FC Barcelona social media and Barcelona TV+, a subscription-based television channel where all matches are streamed live for a fee. Last, the FC Barcelona TikTok page currently has 32 million followers, but this number is sure to grow with TikTok's increasing popularity. Keeping with the short-form video format of the platform, video content is under 30 seconds, and contains music video, content overlays, and other features to add a fun, relaxed feel to the feed.

QUESTIONS

Visit the Facebook, Instagram, YouTube, and TikTok pages for FC Barcelona and answer the following questions:

FC Barcelona Facebook (www.facebook.com/fcbarcelona/)
FC Barcelona Instagram (www.instagram.com/fcbarcelona/)
FC Barcelona YouTube (www.youtube.com/@FCBarcelona)
FC Barcelona TikTok (www.tiktok.com/@fcbarcelona)

1. On Facebook, scroll through the feed and note the posts with the highest number of likes, then highest number of comments, then highest number of shares. What do you notice about the posts that get the highest engagement in all three categories?
2. On the FC Barcelona Instagram, scroll through the photos and reels. Is there content you feel FC Barcelona could incorporate to enhance engagement or further differentiate their Instagram feed from their other platforms?
3. On YouTube, what do you think this content offers fans that resulted in the channel reaching 15 million subscribers before any other sports club?
4. How does FC Barcelona incorporate the unique features of TikTok into their feed?

The other screens

Most of modern life is spent within proximity to several screens including the television, computer, tablet, and smartphone. In fact, most of us take at least one device with us everywhere we go, and sport viewing is no exception irrespective of whether it is live or through a broadcast. Sport marketers have grasped the opportunities that go with constant connectivity to draw fans more deeply into the game, its players, and all the intrigue, excitement and hype that occurs via the seemingly personalised communications that smartphones deliver. A sporting experience no longer means just viewing a game or event. Sport fans have at their fingertips a smorgasbord of information, statistics, live feeds, replays, messages, and insider observations with which to engage. It is now common for individuals to engage in 'second screening' while watching sporting events in-person, which consists of streaming games for additional OTT content such as match insights and statistics. This can be achieved as sport organisations and media channels provide customised apps with live feeds and real-time updates to enhance the viewing experience. Additionally, major sporting venues now provide enhanced WiFi to encourage fan use of social media and apps to access content highlights.

Of course, from the sport marketer's viewpoint, there is also unprecedented opportunity to utilise competitions and prizes delivered via social media for augmenting engagement. For example, American football team the Arizona Cardinals held a 'Fan of The Year' contest on Instagram where followers could nominate people they felt were 'extraordinary' fans. Contests and giveaways such as this are a great way to engage fans while offering the chance to win prizes. Other forms of engagement could include 'ask me anything' question and answer sessions with players, managers, or coaches, where they respond to fan questions and the best question wins a prize.

In addition, an increasing number of major sport properties are partnering with social media and broadcasters to channel customised advertising and merchandise to sport fans. 'Twitter Amplify' is a service that pairs brands with content providers, events, or topics that have established audiences. For example, Twitter Amplify Sponsorships allows brands to connect with single, premium publishers to create ideal brand alignments. One notable Twitter Amplify Sponsorship campaign was run by electronics company LG in the United Kingdom. Ads promoting their products, specifically smart TVs, were run during a major football competition to increase awareness. This alignment paired the device utilised to watch sporting events, TVs, with the sporting event itself.

New business models

Social media's impact has not just affected business models around branding, commercialisation, sponsorship, and broadcasting, it has also propelled some athletes further into the spotlight as social networking superstars and immense brands. Even more daunting, some high school players have become the subjects of social media trends to entice college recruiters to post about their nascent talents. This has extended so far that some top-level high school players will hold livestreamed media events on various social media platforms to announce for which collegiate team they will play. For some broadcasters and franchises, social media can be employed to amplify pre-season hype and maintain fan interest during times when sponsor awareness and merchandise sales can flag. This practice of amplifying content during breaks in competition was predominant during the COVID-19 pandemic, as teams and leagues were not allowed to hold regularly scheduled matches. To fill this gap sporting properties developed alternative forms of content. For example, the English Premier League was able to increase its social media engagement by 146% during the first part of 2020 by utilising video content such as highlight clips from classic games on their platforms. We can expect this form of engagement where social media and conventional broadcasting content become integrated through social media, customised apps and leveraged, cross-promotional advertising and sponsorship campaigns. The sky is the limit for new forms of social media marketing.

Fame and followers can happen sharply as well. For example, tennis star Emma Raducanu was ranked 345th in world tennis as an 18-year-old in 2021 with around 2,000 Instagram followers. A strong performance at Wimbledon followed by winning the US Open at Flushing Meadows in New York later that year resulted in an increase to 1.2 million followers. This was so dramatic that Instagram initially blocked her account.

There is, however, a double edge to the social media opportunity. Vast reach brings with it serious brand management consequences when athletes make poor tweeting decisions about personal opinions or activities. An example of this downside is Brooklyn Nets star Kyrie Irving receiving a suspension from his team following from his sharing of a link to an antisemitic movie on social media. As a result, rigid team, league, and event policies around tweeting are commonplace to control brand image, and in some cases, diminish the likelihood of gambling-related information distribution. For example, the NBA has banned posting on social media from 45 minutes before tip-off until after postgame media responsibilities have been completed.

> *Chapter principle 12.14: Social media integration*: Social media and conventional broadcasting content can be integrated through social media, customised apps and leveraged, cross-promotional advertising and sponsorship campaigns.

CASE 12.6

Influencer Marketing

One of the primary features of social media is access to athletes. The insider perspective and behind-the-scenes information that can be obtained by following athletes on social media has proved to be a massive draw for fans around the globe. This interest in athletes' daily lives has resulted in follower numbers that reach into the hundreds of millions for certain athletes. For example, the most followed footballers (soccer) on Instagram in 2023 include Cristiano Ronaldo (615 million), Lionel Messi (495 million), Neymar (217 million), and Kylian Mbappe (110 million). Utilising their follower numbers, these athletes regularly engage in digital marketing partnerships and sponsorships to increase brand awareness, turning athletes into influencers. While these formal sport marketing relationships can sometimes feel inauthentic or forced, seemingly more spontaneous promotions can elicit a more authentic feel, linking products that might otherwise have seemed misaligned.

For example, the Los Angeles Lakers posted a photo to their Instagram feed of Lebron James wearing a Nike sweatshirt or hoodie with the AFC Richmond badge on the front. AFC Richmond is the fictious English Premier League team featured in the popular Apple TV series Ted Lasso. While this may feel like a spontaneous digital marketing choice by the Lakers, there are several links that make this a highly effective and natural sport marketing promotion. First, the timing of the post aligned with both the airing of the third season of Ted Lasso, as well as the NBA Playoffs. The inspirational motto for the show 'Believe' was utilised as the photo caption, connecting the show and the specific moment in the teams' season. Second, both the Lakers and the AFC Richmond apparel are produced by Nike, creating a seamless tie between the branded sportswear. Last, and perhaps less well known is that Lebron James is a football fan and owns a 1% share in the Liverpool FC ownership group Fenway Sports Group. James also collaborated with Liverpool and Nike to create a clothing line that combined fashion with style. In this instance, one photo of Lebron James wearing a Nike AFC Richmond hoodie resulted in increased awareness for three brands simultaneously.

QUESTIONS

The example provided above outlines how the immense reach of certain athletes can be employed as part of a social media-based marketing strategy to leverage increased brand awareness.

1. Utilising this example, how could a smaller organisation or club leverage the popularity of star athletes from their team?
2. What creative ways could a smaller organisation utilise different platforms to leverage on the popularity of superstar athletes? How could you utilise TikTok to complement Instagram content.
3. Do you feel this type of influencer marketing is more, or less authentic than traditional forms of digital advertising?
4. Think of influencers that are not superstar athletes, but who still have huge followings. How could smaller organisations partner with such individuals to capitalise on their social media followings figures?

Social media lessons for digital marketing

Social media works best when marketers focus on creating high-quality, 'native' experiences in the platforms rather than trying to use them to drive traffic elsewhere. Context remains instrumental. Sport fans will go to X (formerly Twitter) to obtain information about matches but might become irritated if they are redirected to a team or league's official account. As a result, sport marketers need to abandon the lingering idea that social media provides a channel for directing consumers towards other content. For the most part, the better tactic involves committing to the quality of each social media platform being employed so that it provides a unique and fulfilling experience with each engagement. One example can be seen through English Premier League club Chelsea FC and their Instagram account. The club has created an engaging mix of content including match-day photos and game-specific posters, fan curated content, original illustrations, short-form video reels, and stories featuring contests and promotional giveaways.

Sport marketers should keep in mind that social media does not magically create new fans, but it does deliver an unprecedented opportunity to connect with them, and to help them connect with each other. In this respect, social media helps cultivate relationships that can lead to stronger affiliation, brand identification, and ultimately, more spending. First comes connection, then comes the commercial realisation of a sporting brand's connection value. Some sport enterprises are even using social media to crowdsource ideas for new marketing collateral. Social media is redefining market research with sport consumers. Some essential starting points could be to:

- promote a hashtag on all marketing collateral and tweet consistently with at least daily updates on events, players, commentaries, media links, giveaways and promotions, or just retweet interesting tweets from high-profile sources in the same sport. Provide match/game updates and live results where possible. Use software platforms (such as RSS) to leverage content between the club website and its X (formerly Twitter) feed;
- set up a Facebook page as a community building and information distribution method. Promote and sell merchandise, tickets and events;
- post video content on a team-specific YouTube channel for the sport or sport organisation;
- post regularly to a photo and video-sharing application such as Instagram and TikTok featuring the team and players; and
- use the official club website or app as a central hub for club information and statements, and link all social media connections.

> *Chapter principle 12.15: Social media native experiences*: Social media works best when marketers focus on creating high-quality, 'native' experiences in the platforms, rather than using them to drive traffic elsewhere.

CASE 12.7

Virtual Paddock Club

While social media marketing does not always result in the creation of new fans, it is remarkably effective at connecting with fans. This was witnessed during the COVID-19 pandemic, when many sporting events were prohibited from having fans in the stadium, and travel was heavily restricted. Thus, sport leagues, teams, and organisations had to develop creative ways to connect with fans remotely.

F1 developed several digital initiatives to engage with fans during this time with great effect, with one specific initiative continuing post-pandemic – the F1 Virtual Paddock Club.

The traditional F1 Paddock Club is part of the VIP hospitality offerings from the elite level of motorsport and allows individuals to observe a race in seats directly above team garages. From these seats action from the garages including every pit stop is visible, offering a behind-the-scenes look at all the intricacies of F1 racing. Additional features include a pit lane walk, observation of interviews with current and former drivers, and a tour of the track in an open-top truck. Hospitality features include access throughout the race weekend to dining experiences created by top chefs featuring local food and wine selections, in addition to live music, race simulators, and other cultural experiences.

Shortly after the COVID-19 pandemic began, and many fans were unable to attend races, the switch to a digital experience was necessary to keep the connection with fans and continue the unique experience offered by the Paddock Club. To accomplish this task, F1 partnered with Zoom to create the Virtual Paddock Club. The feature was so popular that it extended beyond the short-term partnership and is now a long-term feature of F1's hospitality offering at several venues.

Where available, the Virtual Paddock Club offers two days of interactive experiences that include backstage access to events and a virtual tour of the paddock area, track, and podium that is guided by F1 ambassadors and drivers, as well as hosts. Each experience offers tailored features for each location and track, and individuals can go behind-the-scenes of their favourite track or choose to be guided by their favourite ambassadors. Each day consists of scheduled events, with the Saturday events including a 60-minute session pre-qualifying, and the Sunday event including a 90-minute session prior to the race, filled with interactive interviews where fans can pose questions to drivers and ambassadors.

QUESTIONS

You may wish to visit the F1 Virtual Paddock Club website here (https://tickets.formula1.com/en/pcv-virtual-paddock-club) to help answer the questions below:

1. Search for similar events that were conducted remotely during the COVID-19 pandemic. How would you compare their experiences to that of the Virtual Paddock?
2. How would you go about marketing the F1 Virtual Paddock utilising various social media platforms? What key features would you highlight as a sport marketer?
3. How would you position this virtual experience alongside the in-person experience as a sport marketer?
4. Explain some of the novel interactions fans who participate in the virtual club will experience?
5. How could smaller organisations recreate or adapt this virtual experience?

From now to the future of digital and social media sport marketing

Current research highlighted by media research companies such as Nielsen that focus on emerging sport consumption trends carry implications that will impact digital sport marketing for all sport and leisure organisations irrespective of size.

First, there is no such thing as 'appointment' television anymore when it comes to sport. Live, on-demand highlights, replays, streaming video, and tweets are all expected parts of the sport consumption experience. Most sport consumers expect a variety of content to be always available to them, curated and housed in convenient locations such as proprietary league or teams' apps. As the case study on the NBA app highlighted, when done well, a team app can drive large amounts of engagement and interactivity, as well as marketing touchpoints.

Second, the actual event represents only a portion of the available content for sport fans. Viewers can engage through contests, blogs, tablets, smartphones, smart TVs, and social media sites. Sport video content distributed through social media such as Facebook, Instagram, and YouTube are a significant contributor to the growth of sport consumption. Specifically, video views are driving engagement in sporting prosperities, with The UEFA Champions League and Major League Baseball being prime examples. With specialisation comes fragmentation. As highlighted above, the dominant social media platforms continue to expand with additional platforms constantly emerging. TikTok's success and rapid incorporation into most social media marketing plans demonstrate this phenomenon. Each new platform will be highly customised and designed to meet niche market demands.

Third, streaming platforms and OTT content will overtake traditional television broadcasts as the preferred way fans choose to watch live sport. From 2019 to 2021, the percentages of individuals who preferred to view live sport content through satellite or cable TV decreased from 48% to 43%. During this same time, preferences for OTT and streaming live sport increased from 30% to 39%. Thus, this gap is decreasing, with an eventual overtake by OTT platforms almost certain. In fact, when looking at regional trends, individuals in North Asia have already indicated a 51% to 45% preference for OTT and streaming delivery of live sport.

Just as we have seen on a modest scale in the form of YouTube content, there will be more aggressive moves to integrate sport enterprises with broadcasting. As sport enterprises come to terms with their immense, potential global audiences, they will become more reluctant to forge partnerships with existing broadcasters beyond television, instead creating their own bespoke television channels. This is already occurring with sport properties such as FC Barcelona creating Barcelona TV+, a subscription-based OTT streaming platform that was a natural extension of the club's popular YouTube channel. With this unprecedented ownership of novel content, sport enterprises can maximize revenue opportunities from selling online advertising through these channels to fans.

Finally, the convergence of hardware technology, software development and application, digital channels and social media will create new opportunities for mobile devices to become more seamlessly connected to the human senses. Wearable technology has seen immense growth with recent market size projections of more than $300 million USD.

These wearables can include the Apple Watch, the Oura Ring, or wristbands such as WHOOP or Fitbit. Currently, high-profile players and athletes can wear tracking devices such as WHOOP that allow fans to monitor physiological performance live on screen during challenging moments, such as heart rate variability during a putt in golf. In addition, sport fans could also watch their favourite content through virtual technology in their own homes, replicating the feelings of being at the stadium.

There are numerous technologies that are almost certainly going to have an impact on sport marketing in the future. Many of them will diminish the gap between the most powerful and well-resourced sport organisations, and those that have traditionally struggled for exposure. Smaller sports will find that web broadcasting and all its digital opportunities are their best bet for finding a stable niche.

While new media technologies can offer significant advantages for sport marketers, there are also dangers associated with digital and social media marketing. Sport organisations must have the tools to ensure that the relationships they cultivate with fans bridge the gap between commerce and community. In turn this necessitates the careful management of customer input into products and services. Sport enterprises will have to work to ensure experiences are created for sport consumers that are superior to those they might receive through other leisure pursuits. Technology has the sometimes unwelcome potential of converting services or customer experiences into commodities. To fortify the sporting experience, sport organisations must continue to focus on understanding the feelings of belonging in sport supporters.

PRINCIPLES SUMMARY

- Chapter principle 12.1: Digital sport marketing refers to communications that are generated by electronic means and delivered through devices such as computers, tablets, and mobile phones. It refers to technologically sophisticated platforms or vehicles for transmitting and communicating information, including social media channels, which utilise the interactions of networked individuals.
- Chapter principle 12.2: Digital media is flexible, transferable and can be customised.
- Chapter principle 12.3: Digital and social media technologies provide sport marketers with new ways of communicating with consumers, and novel approaches to their marketing activities. Many of these approaches are far more rapid, responsive, interactive and inexpensive when compared with other marketing strategies; they are also more easily customised to key target audiences.
- Chapter principle 12.4: Digital sport marketing demands customised communication with targeted sport consumers, generated by electronic means or through technologically sophisticated platforms that facilitate the transmission of information.
- Chapter principle 12.5: Digital sport marketing involves targeted and personalised interactions based on the principles of customisation, modularity, sticky branding, networked communication and permission.
- Chapter principle 12.6: *Customisation*: Digital sport marketing messages should be customised or targeted and adapted to specific consumers and their needs.

- Chapter principle 12.7: *Modularity*: A modular digital marketing programme (including product design) is standardised and automated incorporating flexibility, responsiveness to changes in demand, and ease of transfer.
- Chapter principle 12.8: *Sticky branding*: Occurs when digital sport marketing content takes hold in consumers' minds in ways that are consistent with the positioning strategy for the brand, and as a result are readily passed on digitally.
- Chapter principle 12.9: *Networked communication*: Networked communication is based on the idea that instead of telling consumers about products, it is more productive to get consumers to talk to each other about them.
- Chapter principle 12.10: *Inclusivity*: Refers to the use of digital marketing to fulfil the need to 'belong', which in turn fosters the development of identity and a stronger connection to the sport brand.
- Chapter principle 12.11: *Permission*: Refers to the effectiveness of communicating with consumers who have consented to receive customised messages, rather than sending random, untargeted and uninvited marketing communications.
- Chapter principle 12.12: *Social media*: Can be used as a pivotal tactic in a sport digital marketing campaign for cultivating closer consumer engagement, leading to better relationships, experiences, feedback and advocacy.
- Chapter principle 12.13: *Social media platforms*: Encompass a wide variety of sites and applications including the big five, Facebook, Instagram, X (formerly Twitter), YouTube, and TikTok where each plays an essential role in a digital sport marketing strategy.
- Chapter principle 12.14: *Social media integration*: Social media and conventional broadcasting content can be integrated through social media, customised apps and leveraged, cross-promotional advertising and sponsorship campaigns.
- Chapter principle 12.15: *Social media native experiences*: Social media works best when marketers focus on creating high-quality, 'native' experiences in the platforms, rather than using them to drive traffic elsewhere.

TOOLS SUMMARY

- Chapter tool 12.1 Internet-driven platforms
- Chapter tool 12.2 Mobile communications
- Chapter tool 12.3 Upgraded conventional technologies
- Chapter tool 12.4 Hardware
- Chapter tool 12.5 Software

REVIEW QUESTIONS

1. Describe the key characteristics of the digital sport marketing approach.
2. Provide a sport example of each of the following principles: customisation, modularity, sticky branding, networked communication, inclusivity, and permission.

3 What implications do digital sport marketing principles have for conventional sport marketing techniques?
4 Provide some examples of how mobile communications might be pivotal to the future of marketing communications within venues.
5 Speculate on the future of sport marketing-related software and applications. Provide an example that you think might be developed in the future.
6 Describe how to employ different social media platforms at the same time for maximum marketing impact.

RELEVANT WEBSITES

Barcelona TV+ (barcatvplus.fcbarcelona.com/en/live)
Cuban Center X (Twitter) (www.twitter.com/CubanCenter)
F1 Virtual Paddock Club (tickets.formula1.com/en/pcv-virtual-paddock-club)
NBA App (https://www.nba.com/app)
We The 15 (www.wethe15.org)

FURTHER READING

Abeza, G., O'Reilly, N., Sanderson, J., & Frederick, E. (2021). *Social Media in Sport: Theory and Practice*. World Scientific.

Seymour, A., & Blakey, P. (2021). *Digital Sport Marketing: Concepts, Cases, and Conversations*. Routledge.

CHAPTER 13

Sport marketing implementation and control

LEARNING OUTCOMES

At the end of this chapter, readers should be able to:

- describe the importance of implementation and control strategies in a sport marketing strategy.
- explain how implementation differs from planning sport marketing strategies.
- identify the key concepts behind successfully transforming a sport marketing strategy into action.
- outline the steps of a control process.
- understand how to link the control process to improved strategic decisions.
- debate the ethical and social responsibilities of sport marketers.
- critically anticipate new developments in sport marketing, especially those associated with new technologies.

INTRODUCTION

This chapter presents the final stage of the Sport Marketing Framework, the process of implementing and controlling the sport marketing strategy. It introduces the strategies available for enhancing the success of the implementation process. This chapter explains how to develop a control process for implementation and shows how its use can help evaluate and improve a sport marketing strategy. It also highlights some of the key variables and trends in sport marketing, including ethical considerations as well as the implications of new technological advances. The final section of this chapter provides a summary of the philosophy, process, principles, and tools of sport marketing highlighted in the text. Before this chapter moves into new territory, some summarising observations will set the scene.

This text started by commenting that sport marketing has come a long way since its inception in the early 20th century. It has grown from kitchen tables and a poorly

DOI: 10.4324/9781003391319-13

understood niche-offshoot of mainstream marketing into a global industry worth billions, and a fully fledged discipline with specialised practitioners and professionalised training. Sport marketing first came to light in the early 1900s when companies began to sponsor sporting events and athletes. In fact, Coca-Cola sponsored the 1900 Olympics in Paris. This sponsorship marked the beginning of a trend that would continue throughout the 20th century propelled by new forms of radio and print media in the 1920s. It was another Parisian Olympics in 1924 that signalled sport's first global marketing when the event was covered by live radio. Although the world's first major league – England's Football Association – had begun in 1863, the 1930s witnessed the birth of the first American major league sports with the formation of the National Football League (NFL) and the National Basketball Association (NBA). In turn, Major League Baseball (MLB) followed, providing in the process the first sport icons like Joe DiMaggio, Jackie Robinson, and Babe Ruth, whose superstar status and household names were also marketing vehicles for major companies. As the television era began in the 1950s, sport became a seductive channel for sport brands and companies wanting to use them and their players as marketing channels. Television opened major sport events to a global audience in the 1960s as the World Cup and Olympic Games made celebrities of players like Pelé. The 1968 Olympic Games in Mexico City saw the first major sponsorship deal between a company and an individual athlete, when Adidas signed a deal with runner Abebe Bikila. But this was just the beginning of serious sport marketing. The 1970s and 1980s foreshadowed the rise of the global sport superstar with athletes such as Muhammad Ali, Michael Jordan, and Pelé becoming major marketing vehicles for companies. Not coincidentally, these decades provided an unprecedented platform for major sports apparel and fashion manufacturers such as Nike, Adidas, and Reebok to leverage their brands.

Then the world of sport marketing transformed again with the invention of the internet in the 1990s. Companies began to create their own websites to connect with fans. The 1996 Olympics in Atlanta offered the first extensive use of the internet to cover the event, signposting a significant milestone in the history of sport marketing. Following on from the internet, the 2000s revealed a smorgasbord of new technologies such as smartphones and tablets, which created remarkable new avenues for sport marketing from apps to social media. The 2012 Olympics in London marked the first comprehensive use of social media to promote and leverage the event, with official sponsoring companies like Nike and Coca-Cola employing platforms such as X (formerly Twitter) and Facebook to connect with fans. Accompanying the ubiquitous and fast mobile connectivity that became standard moving into the second decade of the new millennium, esports surfaced as a new, fast-growing sport marketing platform. Events such as the League of Legends World Championship and The International Dota 2 Championships attract millions of viewers and millions of dollars in sponsorships. At the same time, superstar athletes and players burst into immense personal brands driven by insatiable fans eager to connect not only through sporting performances but also much more intimately through social media accounts. The prodigious reach of these global sporting personalities has also allowed them to use sport marketing to bring attention to social causes like climate change and social justice, LeBron James and Serena Williams being two excellent examples.

As the later sections of this chapter will consider, sport marketing's future will continue to be characterised by technological revolutions and emerging business models.

Among other possibilities, the future will likely feature: social media and networking; greater product and service personalisation based on the analysis of 'big data' and predictive artificial intelligence (AI); improved integration of emerging technologies like wearables, augmented, and virtual reality; the ongoing blurring of social causes and sport brand responsibility; ethical concerns regarding manufacturing, social issues, and the environment; deeper expansion into new geographical territories; and the use of sport to leverage new products and companies from versions of blockchain-driven cryptocurrencies to non-fungible tokens (NFTs).

The success of sport marketing strategies can be measured and evaluated in numerous ways. Of course, as the strategic framework outlined in this text emphasises, it all depends on the specific aims and objectives of the strategy that has been planned and implemented. Before getting into the details of the measurement and evaluation process, however, it is worth highlighting some of the common types of measurement categories found in sport marketing.

To begin with, a foundational measure used by sport organisations is ticket sales to games and events, although for professional clubs and teams, even sold-out venues pale in significance compared to the importance of revenues from broadcasting rights and sponsorships as well as the sales of branded merchandise. Increasingly, sport marketers are focusing on social media engagement as insightful measures of strategy success. For example, website traffic, likes, shares, comments, and posts all reveal significant data about fan engagement, as well as their potential to be monetised; that is, sold extended products and services beyond sport consumption.

It is not all about revenue though. At a macro level, all sport organisations are interested in growing their brands as measured through the brand awareness they command among fans and consumers, and which is realised through what marketers refer to as 'brand value'. In sport, brand value is not only manifested in revenues and fan numbers, but also in long-term loyalty. Whatever is being measured, a strong trend in sport marketing involves a data-driven approach, which means that evaluation prioritises objective evidence based on clear and tangible information.

CASE 13.1

National Basketball Association

The NBA is one sport organisation that has taken a data-driven approach to measuring and evaluating the success of its marketing strategy, characterised by the collection of key analytics selected to track the effectiveness of specific aspects of their brand's market performance. To begin with, the NBA considers its social media metrics as decisive indicators of the league's brand profile and performance. The league has established a significant presence on social media platforms such as Facebook, X (formerly Twitter), Instagram, and YouTube, and they use analytics tools to track engagement metrics such as likes, comments, shares, and views. By examining social media data analytics, the NBA can determine the impact of different types of content, identify trends, and adjust their social media strategy based on quantifiable feedback. The league also utilises data analytics in assessing the performance of their other digital platforms, including the official website and mobile app. Similarly, a series of tracking tools are deployed to monitor fan behaviour, including the number of page views, time spent on the site, and conversion rates that calculate how many site and app visitors end up spending money or signing up for products or services. To test the effects of different marketing appeals, the league experiments with different versions of their digital content, tracking the outcomes to compare which performs better.

In addition to social media and digital platforms, the NBA also uses a data-driven approach to evaluate their more traditional sport marketing elements, the most prominent of which are television advertising and corporate sponsorships. The league tracks metrics such as audience reach, frequency and duration of fan television viewing, and return on investment on sponsorships – the effect on sales during a company's sponsorship of the NBA – to determine which marketing campaigns are most effective, and then adjust their strategies accordingly. One example of how the NBA uses data to measure the success of their marketing approach is in their sponsorship with Kia Motors. The NBA tracked the impact of Kia's sponsorship by measuring metrics such as Kia's brand awareness, purchase consideration, and brand preference before and after the sponsorship. They found that the sponsorship had a significant positive impact on these metrics, which led to a renewal of the sponsorship.

QUESTIONS

1 Visit with the NBA website (www.nba.com) and make a list of the kinds of data about users' activities and interactions that might be useful to measure.

2 The NBA has nearly 50 'league-level' sponsors. Locate 10 and highlight the categories they represent. Provide one measure for each sponsor that would represent a good way of evaluating that company's return of their sponsorship investment.

3 What other measures of the NBA's sport marketing would be useful that has not already been noted in the case?

OVERVIEW

The first three stages of the Sport Marketing Framework – (1) identify sport marketing opportunities, (2) develop sport marketing strategy, and (3) plan the sport marketing mix – have been explained. It is now time to outline the final stage of the Framework, which is to *implement and control* the sport marketing strategy. The implementation and control process is shown in Figure 13.1, within the Sport Marketing Framework.

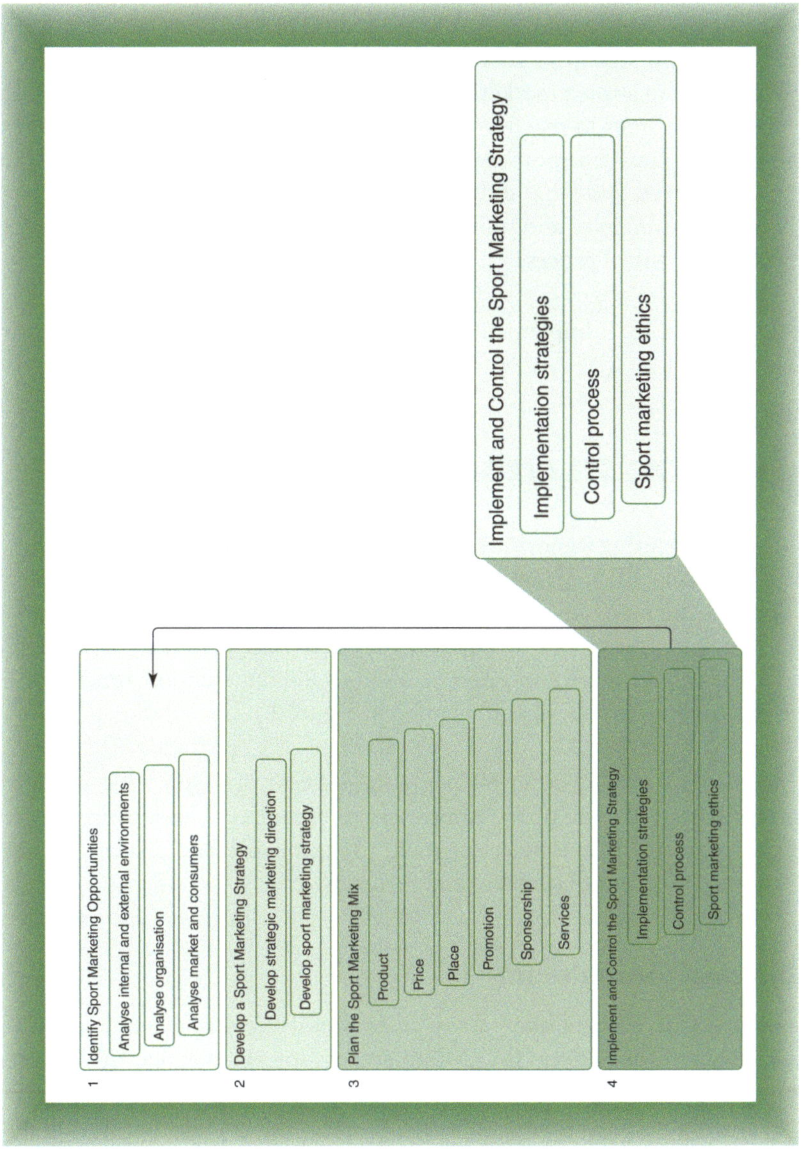

FIGURE 13.1 The sport marketing framework

Implementing a sport marketing strategy means putting the plans that were devised into action. Controlling a sport marketing strategy means keeping the implementation of marketing activities consistent with the plan and the measures that were put in place to indicate success. In practice, control is all about ensuring that a plan's objectives are going to be achieved, and taking action to correct any problems if it looks as though things are not going as they should. As a result, a central function of control is to evaluate implemented marketing activities to see whether they have achieved what they were supposed to. To evaluate a sport marketing plan means to assess it, or to weigh up its positive and negative outcomes to reach a view on its performance. In the end, it is essential to determine how successful a sport marketing strategy has been, or else there is no way of knowing what worked and what did not, and no way of improving in the future. This chapter provides the principles and tools underpinning the successful development of an implementation and control process.

> *Chapter principle 13.1*: Implementing a sport marketing strategy means putting the plans into action.

IMPLEMENTATION STRATEGIES

When it comes to executing a sport marketing plan, it might seem simple enough to follow the plan, but many sport organisations find that it is much harder than it sounds. A marketing plan may be innovative, but if it is not implemented properly it will fail. While it is common for sport marketers to discover that executing a strategy is more difficult than they anticipate, there are five sport marketing implementation tools that greatly increase the probability of success, as illustrated in Figure 13.2.

> *Chapter principle 13.2*: The implementation success of a sport marketing plan is enhanced through the use of five implementation tools: (1) leadership and commitment, (2) communication and delegation, (3) teamwork and projects, (4) rewards and reinforcement and (5) control and feedback.

Leadership and commitment

A sport marketing plan is more likely to be successful if there is a clear leader or group of leaders who take responsibility for its implementation. In practice this ensures that the sport organisation is committed to the plan it has devised. The role of the leader is to coordinate and organise marketing activities, as well as to manage the control process.

There are a number of levels at which leadership or initiative is required in the implementation of a sport marketing plan. Implementation begins with senior management leaders who have to develop and oversee the timeline associated with the marketing plan and every activity within it, along with the allocation of whatever resources are needed to take action. Any marketing plan will need resources to make it a reality. Every activity in a sport marketing plan will have a corresponding cost for implementation such as staff

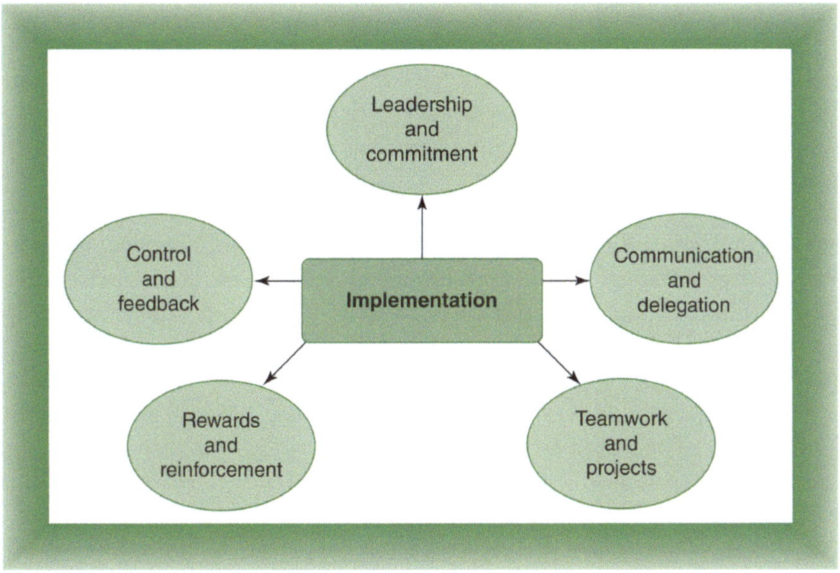

FIGURE 13.2 Sport marketing implementation tools

time and training, the research and development of products and promotions, and even the need to pay for specialist consultants or external contractors if the right expertise is not available internally. It is important not to underestimate the investment in staff time that will be needed. Developing and implementing a marketing plan will not only need the time of marketing staff but also administration staff and management.

> *Chapter tool 13.1 Leadership and commitment*: A sport marketing plan is more likely to be successful if there is a clear leader or group of leaders who take responsibility for its implementation. Leadership and commitment involves the designation of a timeline and the allocation of resources.

Communication and delegation

It is important that all members of the sport marketing team have a good understanding of the marketing plan. Rather than just telling everyone about the plan after it has been developed, it is more effective to involve them along the way. Sport marketing strategies are more likely to be supported by the sport marketing team if all of its members have made a contribution.

Marketing leaders have to make decisions about how marketing activities should be delegated and what information should be provided to those empowered and responsible for tasks. Teams may need to be created, individuals may be given specific assignments and outside contractors may be engaged. The delegation of decision-making authority is delicate for sport marketers. Because of their centrality to the functioning of sport organisations, it is important that volunteers are given sufficient levels of responsibility to challenge and stimulate them. Equally, they should not be given roles that will burden them or cause serious anxiety and stress. Most of all, volunteers should not be given tasks and responsibilities for which they do not have the authority to fulfil or the accountability to answer for. The delegation of decision making for marketing activities is therefore complex. A number of issues should be considered that are strongly connected with effective communication.

There are four preconditions to successful delegation. Delegation of marketing tasks can only work if leaders are: (1) receptive to the ideas of subordinates and volunteers, (2) prepared to let go of tasks, (3) willing to let others make mistakes, and (4) ready to trust subordinates. However, even if marketing leaders are ready to delegate the performance of planned marketing tactics, subordinates, and volunteers may not be ready. Resistance to delegation may arise from: (1) the fear of criticism over possible mistakes, (2) lack of confidence, (3) inadequate resources to do the job properly, (4) lack of an incentive, and (5) already too much to do. If these concerns can be alleviated, then delegation is workable. Since a sport marketing plan cannot be deployed without a significant amount of help from employed staff and volunteers, there is really no choice but to make it work.

Delegation is not just a way of involving more people in the implementation of sport marketing, it is a way of accessing a wider range of skills and abilities from those who want to contribute. Effective delegation will also lead to greater clarity about what needs to be done since the delegation process requires a clear statement of the jobs and responsibilities involved. It will also lead to faster decisions since those actually involved in the activity do not need to seek approval before they take action. Delegation allows staff and volunteers to act responsibly when dealing with fans and consumers to improve customer satisfaction.

All activities within a sport marketing plan should be delegated or allocated to specific staff members or teams. If duties are not delegated, it becomes easy to assume that someone else is doing it. It is best to have a detailed job assignment that is put in writing after the marketing leader and the staff member or volunteer have agreed on the details. A detailed job assignment should address the following issues:

- name: name of the person responsible for the project (job);
- marketing plan: short description of the relevant objective of the marketing strategy;
- project title: short, clear description of the specific project (job) being delegated;
- project description: detailed description of each part of the project;
- methods: statement of *how* the staff member is expected to carry out the project (e.g., processes and techniques they should use);
- reporting systems: who the staff member should report their progress to, how they should communicate it, and how often they should do this;
- performance measures: indicators of performance;
- timeline: timeline for each stage of the project; and
- resources: what resources the staff member is able to use (e.g., money, materials, administration staff time, training).

It is also important to regularly communicate with other people in the organisation who are not in the marketing team. The more the employees and volunteers of a sport organisation support the marketing plan, the more likely it is to succeed. This underpins the relevance of communicating the marketing plan internally within the organisation. Internal promotion and marketing means educating every staff member, volunteer, and stakeholder about the contents of the plan.

> *Chapter tool 13.2 Communication and delegation*: Marketing leaders have to make decisions about how marketing activities should be delegated and what information should be provided to those empowered and responsible for tasks. Delegation of marketing tasks can only work if leaders are: (1) receptive to the ideas of subordinates and volunteers, (2) prepared to let go of tasks, (3) willing to let others make mistakes and (4) ready to trust subordinates. Resistance to delegation may arise from: (1) the fear of criticism over possible mistakes, (2) lack of confidence, (3) inadequate resources to do the job properly, (4) lack of an incentive and (5) already too much to do. A detailed job assignment should be created for every major marketing project or activity within the plan.

Teamwork and projects

The successful implementation of a sport marketing plan requires the involvement of a combination of staff and volunteers who have the right mix of skills, experience, and attitudes. One way of ensuring that implementation is effective is to make project teams responsible for certain projects or groups of activities. Project teams are an indispensable tool for achieving quality service outcomes and sporting clubs in particular can make use of project teams because of the need to conduct events with a combination of paid and volunteer staff. A project team structure also has a fixed life and involves delegation, and is therefore a useful device for the organisation of special one-off functions at both the local level and for larger, more complex events. For example, if a marketing plan includes a promotional barbeque, marketing leaders may decide to establish a special project team to conduct the event. The project team operates as long as it takes to organise, conduct, and evaluate the event, after which time it disbands.

Not all marketing teams will produce high-quality outcomes in implementing their set projects and activities. However, the chances of a project team fulfilling its potential are dramatically increased when the following are in place:

- agreement that the project is vitally important to the success of the marketing strategy;
- the project team has a guaranteed and appropriate lifespan;
- the team has a shared purpose;
- realistic and concrete goals are agreed upon by the team;
- a common understanding on exactly what has to be done;
- agreement that the rewards and accolades for successful completion will be shared;
- unimpeded flows of communication, both within the team, and with marketing leaders; and
- strong working relationship with other related teams.

TABLE 13.1 Team knowledge and skills

Knowledge of	*Skills in*
The sport industry and marketplace	Communicating with staff, consumers, and other groups
Marketing principles and concepts	Talking with the media
General business and management principles	Public speaking and hosting events
The target consumers and sport consumers in general	Generating and developing ideas
The range of goods and/or services being offered	Problem-solving and negotiation
Specialist areas (e.g., contacts, sponsorship, event management and budgeting, risk management, facility development)	Organisation, time management and project coordination
	Personally promoting the value of the product and organisation
	Understanding market research and statistics

Part of building a team is choosing the right members who provide a mix of skills and abilities so that a team can tackle different kinds of marketing tasks. A mix of the knowledge and skills as shown in Table 13.1 is a good start for most marketing implementation teams.

> *Chapter tool 13.3 teamwork and projects*: The successful implementation of a sport marketing plan requires the involvement of a combination of staff and volunteers who have the right mix of skills, experience and attitudes. Implementation teams work best when: (1) there is agreement that the project is vitally important to the success of the marketing strategy, (2) the project team has a guaranteed and appropriate lifespan, (3) the team has a shared purpose, (4) realistic and concrete goals are agreed upon by the team, (5) there is a common understanding on exactly what has to be done, (6) agreement that the rewards and accolades for successful completion will be shared, (7) there is an unimpeded flow of communication, both within the team, and with marketing leaders, and (8) a strong working relationship with other related teams exists.

Rewards and reinforcement

Whether the implementation of marketing strategy will be successful depends on the individual and team efforts of staff and volunteers. It can be helpful to put rewards into place for those who do a good job with implementing the strategy. Rewards can include positive feedback (e.g., praise, recognition), money (e.g., commissions, bonuses, raises), or other rewards such as stock options or promotions and special assignments. It can be useful to offer smaller rewards along the way, as well as bigger rewards when major targets are achieved. Irrespective of their composition, the purpose behind all rewards is to reinforce the kinds of behaviours and actions that are conducive to effective plan implementation.

> *Chapter tool 13.4 Rewards and reinforcement*: It can be helpful to put rewards into place to reinforce the kinds of behaviours and actions that are conducive to effective plan implementation. Rewards can include positive feedback (e.g. praise, recognition), money (e.g. commissions, bonuses, raises) or other rewards such as promotions, days off and special assignments.

Control and feedback

The final part of implementing a marketing strategy is to review and evaluate its outcomes on a regular basis. It is vital to keep track of how well the plan is going, and to make changes if things are not going as intended. This is such an important part of implementation that the next topic, the control process, is dedicated to it.

> *Chapter tool 13.5 Control and feedback*: Regular evaluation of the performance of a marketing plan is necessary in case corrections need to be made. This is achieved through the introduction of a control process.

CONTROL PROCESS

Controlling a sport marketing strategy involves six steps, which are summarised in Figure 13.3.

> *Chapter principle 13.3*: Controlling a sport marketing strategy means keeping it on track, making sure that it is achieving what it set out to, and making changes to correct variations and problems. The control process involves six steps: (1) set performance measures, (2) define critical success factors, (3) measure performance, (4) compare results, (5) identify variations and (6) make corrections.

Set performance measures

Setting performance measures is the first step of the control process. Because setting performance measures is part of the strategic process, they should have already been determined in stage two of the Sport Marketing Framework. It might be advisable to re-read the section on setting performance measures in Chapter 5.

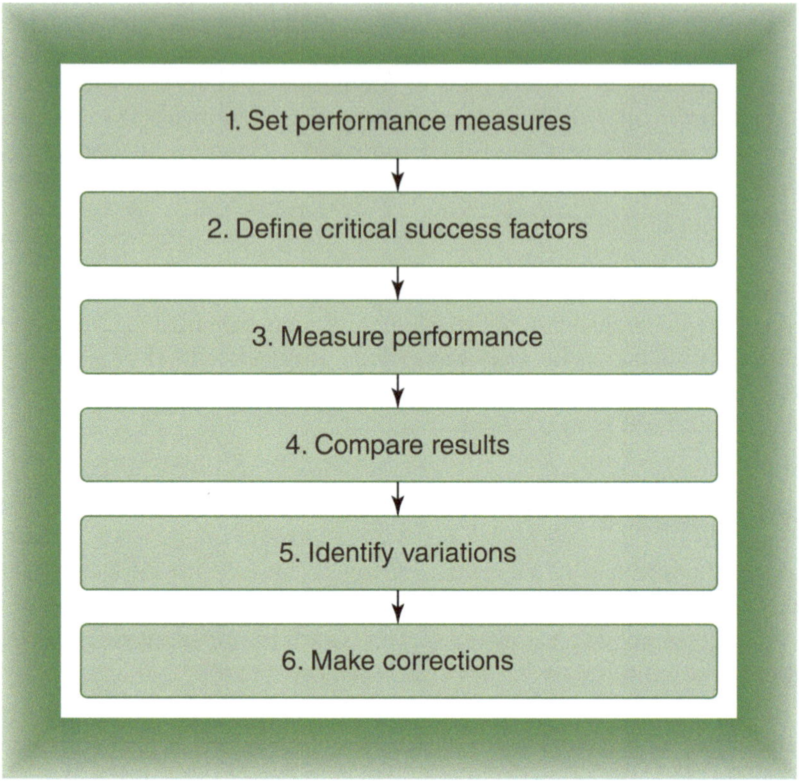

FIGURE 13.3 The control process

Define critical success factors

Critical success factors (CSFs) represent those marketing projects and activities most influential to the successful implementation of a marketing plan. CSFs are the critical actions in marketing that when appropriately implemented have the most impact on the success of the plan. CSFs are determined by asking the question, 'what must go right for the marketing plan to be successfully implemented?' The key to using CSFs is to prioritise them, thereby showing which areas demand the greatest implementation attention. For example, after some prioritisation it might become clear that the most important CSF is a new sponsorship deal. If this is the case, resources can be allocated towards the development of a proposal and the staff to personally sell it.

Measure performance

The next step is to put the performance measures identified in step one into action. How performance is measured will depend on the nature of the measures that were set. For example, if a performance measure was to increase membership numbers by 10% in one year, then information on membership rates needs to be collected. If a performance measure was to increase merchandise revenue to $120,000 by June 2026, then the relevant

TABLE 13.2 Performance measures and required information

Examples of performance measures	*Examples of required information*
To increase membership from 70 to 100 members by January 2026	Membership numbers
To increase the number of people who use our service to 50 customers per month by July 2025	Numbers of people who use the service
To increase spectator levels to an average of 25,000 spectators per game, by December 2026, as measured by ticket sales	Spectator numbers (e.g., ticket sales)
To increase customer satisfaction levels to 7/10 as rated by them on a customer satisfaction survey	Customer satisfaction levels (in this example a customer satisfaction survey is used)
To increase profit to $120,000, calculated at the end of the 2026 financial year	Profit figures
To increase the number of people who have heard of our club in this area to 1,000, as measured by a phone survey	Survey responses of who has heard of the club

financial information needs to be acquired. With the before and after measures it is a simple task to determine the success of the marketing plan and its implementation in the next step. Obviously, an outcome of step two is to focus on the measurement of CSFs. Some further examples of performance measures and the corresponding information needed are given in Table 13.2.

Compare results

Comparing results means examining the outcomes of performance measurement *before* the marketing strategy was implemented and *after* it was implemented. For example, if the performance measure of 'increasing profit by 10% by the end of the financial year' was set, then the level of profit prior to the implementation of the marketing strategy (the previous year's profit level) should be considered against the measurements made at the end of the financial year in which the strategy was deployed.

Identify variations

To ensure that the objectives of the marketing plan are being achieved, it is necessary to find out whether there are any variations between what was planned and what actually happened. Sport marketers usually call this *variance*. Sometimes the variance is positive because something beneficial occurred that was not planned. For example, it is common in sport to sell more merchandise if a team performs unexpectedly well during a season. On the other hand, at other times the variance may be negative such as the sudden emergence of a scandal involving the behaviour of a prominent athlete. Variance can also been seen in the light of whether something can be done about it or whether it is unavoidable.

Once variation has been determined it can be classified as either acceptable or unavoidable. For example, membership numbers might actually increase to 25% in a year even though the performance measure set was an increase of 10%. Clearly, this is an acceptable variation as it has a positive impact on the achievement of marketing objectives. Other examples of acceptable variations could include good publicity that was not expected, or an offer of sponsorship that was unsolicited.

An example of an unavoidable variation might be a circumstance where membership numbers dropped by 8% because of a particularly bad season. Unavoidable variations are often random or infrequent events that cannot be foreseen or are difficult to plan for. Other examples of unavoidable variations could include negative publicity from misbehaviour by players, or financial mismanagement. Part of the control process is to learn from these experiences and to try to improve them in the future. It is advantageous to measure performance as often as is practical to have time to take corrective action if something is going wrong.

Make corrections

The final step in the control process is to make changes if they are needed. This will depend on the types of variations noted in the previous step. If the variations are within acceptable limits, then no action may be necessary. But, if variations are significant enough, then corrective action will be needed to adjust the original plan to the new circumstances. For example, imagine that a performance measure reflected a goal to increase customer satisfaction ratings to 7/10 on a customer satisfaction survey by the end of June 2026. However, when June 2026 arrives, a new survey reveals that satisfaction actually dropped to 4/10. Naturally, this would constitute an unacceptable variance and it would be essential to immediately study the survey results to determine exactly what customers are unhappy about in order to take remedial action.

CASE 13.2

Nike and Under Armour

Nike and Under Armour, as sport apparel, fashion, and sport marketing companies, use a range of marketing performance measures to evaluate the effectiveness of their marketing campaigns and initiatives. There are numerous commonalities as well as some interesting differences. For example, like many organisations, Nike starts with sales measures in order to reveal how well its marketing is succeeding in sustaining revenue growth. Second, at a broader level, Nike considers its market share, or the percentage of all sales in the product categories it competes in as a way of evaluating its performance against rivals. To that end, the company tracks its share of the overall athletic footwear and apparel market, as well as its share of specific product categories, such as running shoes or basketball apparel. This allows Nike to understand its marketing success in specific segments and against close competitors. Third, Nike seeks to measure its marketing outcomes as a function of customer engagement, or the ways in which its campaigns effect customer loyalty, repeat purchasing behaviours, after-sales satisfaction, and advocacy for the products. These include measures of social media engagement, customer feedback, satisfaction, and referral rates. In addition, fourth, Nike considers the brand awareness it commands among consumers as measured by surveys of brand recognition, brand recall, and brand perceptions. The variety of brand awareness measures help to reveal how well the company's marketing resonates with consumers and influences their opinions. Finally, Nike pays careful attention to the return on investment it yields from different types of marketing, especially the sponsorships it holds with leagues, teams, and athletes.

Under Armour, like Nike, uses a range of marketing performance measures to evaluate the effectiveness of its marketing campaigns and initiatives. Similar to Nike, Under Armour tracks its sales data to determine how well its marketing efforts are driving revenue growth, as well as its market share in product segments and across the industry. Also like Nike, Under Armour measures brand perception among its target audience including brand recognition, brand loyalty, and consumer sentiment to evaluate the effectiveness of its marketing campaigns. However, Under Armour also considers customer acquisition costs (CAC) to determine how much it is spending to acquire new customers through marketing efforts. For example, the company looks at the costs associated with each of its marketing initiatives such as sponsorship, advertising, promotions, and social media marketing activities to determine how much it is spending to attract every new customer. Another more bespoke measure Under Armour uses is customer lifetime value, which is a way of assessing the long-term value of each customer to the company. For example, the company collects metrics such as average order value, purchase frequency, and customer retention rates, employing these to predict how much money each customer is likely to spend on Under Armour products over the long term.

QUESTIONS

1 Under Armour places more emphasis on metrics related to customer acquisition and lifetime value, while Nike focuses more on customer engagement and ROI. Can you explain the difference in emphasis?

2 On the surface, sales are the most direct measure of success. Why do you think the companies measure so many other marketing metrics as well?

3 Both companies are heavy sport sponsors. Where would measures of sponsorship performance and return on investment fit in to the measures mentioned in the case?

SPORT MARKETING ETHICS

One aspect of sport marketing that has gained importance reflects the ethical implications of initiatives and campaigns and can have a significant impact on the decisions about measurement and evaluation. This section introduces some of these critical ethical dilemmas as well as the responsibilities sport marketers should uphold. Increasingly, sport marketing has faced critical scrutiny about its ethical impact, particularly because sport businesses may aim to maximise profits at the expense of athlete welfare, health promotion, consumer and fan preferences, social justice, and community values.

Several ethical issues have become prominent in sport marketing that practitioners need to consider as they formulate strategies and respond to measurement feedback. First, since many sport marketing campaigns – especially sponsorships – are designed to maximally exploit the notoriety, reach, and influence of athletes, practitioners need to be sensitive to the potential for inappropriately exploiting them for commercial gain. For example, this might include using athletes' names, images, and likenesses to promote products and services without providing fair compensation or treating them as commodities to be manipulated.

A second, and associated, criticism of sport marketing is that it excessively pursues the commercialisation of sport for profit overshadowing sport's early ideals of intrinsic value, community, and character. Some even suggest that the commercial development of sport because of its relentless marketing has detracted from its authenticity and meaning.

Third, sport marketers are sometimes disparaged for dishonest or misleading advertising. Most of the time, sport marketers act appropriately, but do periodically take advantage of fans' powerful emotional responses to their teams to sell them extras like merchandise. A common complaint among fans is the excessive cost of game tickets when they are priced to maximise profit rather than with the intention of giving as many fans as possible a chance to attend. Some products associated with sport have particularly poor track records of honest and transparent advertising, especially concerning claims about product attributes or effects. The sport supplement industry is one example where exaggerated claims about product performance might be promoted without evidence.

The rise of gambling, gaming, and betting has created not only new marketing opportunities for sport but also signals a fourth major ethical concern. Sportsbooks and betting companies commonly sponsor sport teams, leagues, and other associated products, using social media and digital platforms to promote their services. While digital gambling has launched a new stream of sport marketing channels, it can lead to the unwelcome situation where sport organisations promote anti-social behaviours including addiction. In addition, the use of sport to promote gambling or wagering on sport outcomes can encourage criminal activities such as match-fixing and corruption.

A relatively new but immensely problematic issue associated with ethics offers a fifth trend that sport marketers need to respond to. This ethical concern revolves around privacy as the collection of consumer and fan personal information is often done without their knowledge or consent. Sport marketers need to be transparent about the data they collect and how it will be employed, including how the personal details of consumers will be safeguarded. In addition, consumer data can be manipulated by AI, which can also initiate autonomous action manipulating choices that could infringe upon users' rights.

A final potential ethical minefield for sport marketers concerns a lack of diversity and inclusivity in marketing campaigns, which can perpetuate stereotypes and even reinforce inequalities. The most common examples can be seen in advertisements containing marketing imagery exclusively of male athletes, or of one race or background. Able-bodied athletes are almost always the only ones presented, while unhealthy and unrealistic body images also feature prominently. Sport marketers must therefore consider the implications of their campaign content to avoid excluding or marginalising groups and contributing to discrimination, prejudice, and stereotypes. In addition, stewards of global sporting brands need to remain aware that every culture and location is likely to possess unique social dynamics. Campaigns do not necessarily translate well. Major variables include language, religion, political climate, socio-demographic profile, legal structures, regulatory environment, and of course, history of sport preferences.

CASE 13.3

FIFA

The Fédération Internationale de Football Association, more commonly known as FIFA, is the international governing body of association football, beach soccer, and futsal. The body provides an example of one of the world's largest and most powerful sport organisations that has grappled with ethical controversies and the marketing and branding implications accompanying them. Going back to the mid-2010s, FIFA faced several ethical issues, including allegations of corruption and bribery within the organisation, as well as concerns about labour practices and human rights abuses associated with the construction of World Cup stadiums in Qatar for the World Cup in 2022.

In response to these concerns, FIFA implemented reforms aimed at improving the transparency and accountability within the organisation. For example, the appointment of a new president, Gianni Infantino, in 2016, was intended to give the body a fresh start to clean up the organisation and restore public trust. Under Infantino's leadership, FIFA revised its Code of Ethics, making it more comprehensive and better aligned with international legal standards. It now includes stronger provisions against bribery and corruption, conflicts of interest, and the protection of whistle-blowers who reveal unethical conduct. In part, the Code led to a strengthening of FIFA's compliance and governance systems, which now include an independent Ethics Committee to investigate and adjudicate potential violations of the Code. Similarly, a new internal compliance division oversees compliance with the Code and ethical standards throughout the organisation. Although still controversial, FIFA attempted to reform labour practices associated with venues built for its tournaments, most notably with the construction of World Cup stadiums in Qatar. Accordingly, the Qatari government developed and implemented a labour reform programme designed to improve worker living conditions, enhance labour protections surrounding health and welfare, and address issues such as worker exploitations, retention, and recruitment. Despite these measures, FIFA received significant negative publicity during the World Cup concerning the labour conditions of the migrant workers who had built Qatar's World Cup stadia. Finally, FIFA introduced greater transparency around its operations, with a particular emphasis on openness about its decision-making processes and financial transactions. It now publishes information on its website about its finances, governance structure, and decision-making procedures.

QUESTIONS

1. Do you think that FIFA has satisfactorily addressed its ethical issues? What else could it do?
2. What impact do you think ethical issues have on a sport brand's value? With reference to FIFA, has it adversely affected the sport?
3. How can a sport organisation like FIFA use marketing to improve fans' perceptions of their sport and brand?

While the implementation of a sport marketing plan should align with an organisation's objectives, it should also fit within the broader boundaries of ethical behaviour. Ethics in sport marketing typically refers to whether the traditional four Ps of the marketing mix are deployed within a moral and professional code. Mostly these include issues associated with unsafe or poor-quality products, deceptive or predatory pricing, misleading or dishonest promotions, and exploitative or collusive distribution. In the sporting world, other major marketing issues are concerned with publicising the private lives of athletes, exploiting passionate fans and children who idolise sport stars through athlete endorsements of commercial products, the use of venues with unsafe facilities, unrealistic promises associated with health, fitness, and weight loss products, and the overpricing of high-profile matches and special sport events.

One helpful view of marketing ethics proposes that there should be three basic tenets against which behaviour must be matched: (1) the buyer and seller must both be fully informed as to what is being purchased and what is being paid in exchange, (2) neither the buyer nor the seller is compelled or coerced in their choices, and (3) both buyer and seller are capable of making a rational decision concerning the transaction. In short, informed, autonomous decisions based on the faithful representation of the product features and its price lie at the core of responsible sport marketing.

> *Chapter principle 13.4*: There are three basic tenets against which sport marketing behaviour must be matched: (1) the buyer and seller must both be fully informed as to what is being purchased and what is being paid in exchange, (2) neither the buyer nor seller is compelled or coerced in their choices and (3) both buyer and seller are capable of making a rational decision concerning the transaction.

TABLE 13.3 Professional code of conduct for sport marketers

1	Products and services should be safe. Sporting venues and their facilities should meet all health and safety legislation requirements
2	All marketing communications honestly represent the products offered
3	The product-price exchange should represent fair value
4	Prices are transparent and clearly associated with products
5	Product features are clearly demonstrated and honestly represented
6	Sport marketers should not engage in price fixing or collusion outside of regulated practices
7	Marketing communications should not be coercive or manipulative
8	Athletes' and participants' private lives should not be used for marketing advantages without permission
9	Minors should not be exploited for marketing messages
10	Supply of sporting products should not be manipulated to influence pricing

Sport marketers and organisations might elect to follow a professional code of ethics, which can be employed as a guideline for dealing with uncertain situations. In general, professional codes contain rules about norms of behaviour, ethical values and core principles such as honesty, responsibility, and fairness. Table 13.3 provides a set of common professional guidelines for sport marketers.

SPORT AND SOCIAL RESPONSIBILITY

Sport brands such as Nike, Patagonia, and Asics have incorporated a 'green' lens in their branding strategies in response to a growing concern about the environmental damage caused by sport and as a way of augmenting their brand images. Environmental sustainability is not only making sporting events more marketable but is attracting corporate sponsors who are keen to gain public approval to enhance their corporate reputations. As a result of innovative branding techniques such as corporate/non-profit partnerships, social awareness is playing an increasingly important role in consumers' brand perceptions, prompting questions about the best ways for 'green branding' to be married with marketing and issues of social responsibility.

The result is that sport organisations are faced with the challenge of communicating their social branding messages to consumers in an attempt to positively influence perceptions about the brand and its associated causes without stimulating a cynical consumer backlash.

In order to reap the benefits of social branding from both the organisation and cause perspectives, a sport enterprise needs to increase its social exposure while still connecting with its fans and consumers. This is easier said than done, as there is a fine line between exposing and over-exposing a social message to consumers. An obvious risk is that sport brands run the risk of undermining their images through what is seen as gratuitous social promotion. At the other end of the continuum, some sport organisations have begun incorporating CSR into their branding outlooks, yet are relatively silent about their engagement. For example, in the surf-fashion context, an increase in the popularity of surfing, along with technological advances in equipment, has seen the emergence of a profitable global surf industry. Numerous parochial surf brands have developed into multinational corporations selling surfwear and sporting equipment to consumers globally, sponsoring professional surfers and staging international competitions.

Increasingly, sport organisations are applying a 'green' lens together with a drive towards sustainability in their branding approaches in response to growing consumer awareness about sport's impact on the environment. Social awareness is therefore a relevant variable in the way consumers' brand perceptions are forged, suggesting that sport brand managers need to understand how environmental or social messages can be embedded in branding without creating cynicism. Some entrepreneurial sport brands are seeking innovative ways to differentiate themselves beyond more traditional sport sponsorships through the use of social, green or other cause-related marketing. In fact, an increasing number of sport organisations have been proactive and entrepreneurial in their approach to branding, incorporating social messages into their mission, vision and value statements, and engaging in innovative branding techniques such as partnering with non-profit organisations in order to secure a competitive edge.

CASE 13.4

International Wheelchair Basketball Federation

The International Wheelchair Basketball Federation (IWBF) is the governing body for wheelchair basketball worldwide. In 2019, when many much better resourced sport governing bodies were floundering about a decisive position and policy on sustainability, the IWBF launched its sustainability strategy. It outlined its commitment to reducing environmental impact, promoting social responsibility, and promoting good governance. The IWBF's sustainability strategy includes several key initiatives that are worthy of further comment.

First, the IWBF's sustainability strategy contains a carbon offsetting policy, a remarkable development considering few nations let alone individual sport organisations have managed to put one in place. Partnering with ClimateCare, a carbon offsetting company, the policy orchestrates ways that the IWBF can offset the carbon emissions generated by its events and other activities. For example, they offset the emissions generated by air travel, hotel stays, and emissions connected to other activities associated with hosting international tournaments such as lighting and power. A second pillar of the strategy pursues waste reduction. Here, for example, the IWBF has implemented waste reduction programmes at its events, including recycling and composting initiatives. In addition, the governing body has taken measures to reduce the use of single-use plastics while prioritising sustainable transportation options. The third element of the strategy revolves around a commitment to social responsibility, which includes ensuring that all events are inclusive and accessible with a careful custodianship of local communities, social issues, and diverse groups. Finally, the IWBF has initiated a sweeping series of governance reforms aimed at ensuring transparency, equity, fairness, accountability, integrity, and ethics. According to the IWBF, the sustainability strategy has yielded numerous benefits already such as a 90% reduction in waste generated by their major events.

QUESTIONS

1. How has the IWBF promoted sustainability in wheelchair basketball?
2. What is the IWBF's sustainability strategy, and what are its key initiatives?
3. How can other sports organisations learn from the IWBF's approach to sustainability?
4. What are the challenges and opportunities associated with promoting sustainability in disability sports?

Like many terms in business and marketing, social responsibility has been variously interpreted. However, a consensus has emerged suggesting that sport organisations are accountable not only to shareholders (when in a profit-making business model such as a franchise) in the form of economic returns but also to stakeholders and fans in the form of greater responsibility for social and environmental footprints. Nevertheless, irrespective of whether social responsibility is a thinly veiled attempt to convince consumers that companies care about them beyond the contents of their wallets, is a sophisticated version of philanthropy, or part of a larger agenda towards brand image, managing consumer perceptions remains the central issue.

In considering the dimensions associated with social responsibility in sport, it should be acknowledged that we seek those characteristics that are distinguished in sport. In other words, if we are to use sport as a means to deal with social issues, it is up to sport organisations to clearly identify and communicate what they perceive their social responsibilities to be. This does not mean that the generic elements of social responsibility for organisations should be overlooked. For example, relevant issues include internal (e.g., policies on non-discrimination in the workplace), external (e.g., policy on labour standards of suppliers), accountability (e.g., commitment to reporting on social activities), and citizenship (e.g., educational programmes for the promotion of social initiatives) elements guided by sources such as the UN Declaration of Human Rights, the UNESCO Project on Technical and Vocational Education, the UN Global Compact, the International Labour Standards Convention, and the International Programme on the Elimination of Child Labour. There are, of course, social issues that are exacerbated by elite and/or professional sports people and organisations and hence are of direct relevance to the conduct of sport. These issues involve, but are not limited to, performance enhancing drug taking, crowd violence, racial vilification, gender inequality, sex and alcohol offences, anti-competition legislation regarding the structure of sporting competitions, and general role modelling. Not only are all of these issues pertinent in terms of sport's social responsibilities but they also offer a unique and powerful angle for sport branding and health promotion.

> *Chapter principle 13.5*: Social awareness and social responsibility are variables in the way consumers' brand perceptions are forged, suggesting that sport brand managers need to understand how environmental or social messages can be embedded in their activities to achieve social outcomes, and into their branding without creating cynicism.

CASE 13.5

International Olympic Committee

Despite the positive glow surrounding the Olympic Games, the International Olympic Committee (IOC) has not been immune from negative brand implications in the past related to its perceived performance on ethical matters. This included how it managed the host city selection process for the Olympic Games, while human rights commentators have criticised the body for failures concerning the displacement of local residents, environmental damage caused by venue construction, and human rights abuses in countries with poor records on civil liberties.

To address these accusations, the IOC has moved to transfer its marketing messaging to emphasise a commitment to sustainability and human rights. Underpinning their public relations efforts, the IOC developed a sustainability strategy they called 'The Olympic Agenda 2020+5', which outlines a range of measures to reduce the environmental impact of the Olympic Games and promote sustainable development. It also created guidelines for selecting host cities that incorporated the prioritisation of environmental and social sustainability. Included are requirements for the protection of human rights, the engagement of local communities, transparency of decision-making, and the use of sustainable materials and construction practices. Finally, the IOC launched a major marketing initiative designed to promote gender equality and diversity in sport, including the creation of a Women in Sport Commission and the adoption of a policy requiring gender balance in all areas of Olympic governance.

QUESTIONS

1. Visit the IOC's Human Rights webpage (www.olympics.com/ioc/human-rights). Do you think that the page successfully communicates its human rights commitments? Explain why or why not.
2. Now consider the IOC's sustainability profile (www.olympics.com/ioc/sustainability). How has the organisation used their sustainability commitments in their branding and marketing?
3. What are some of the other ethical issues and domains that the IOC is facing? Explain how the body has responded.

FUTURE CONNECTIONS

As noted, sport marketing has been constantly changing, adapting to new technologies, changing consumer behaviours, and shifts in global reach. One thing is certain: sport organisations will continue to find new and innovative marketing approaches to engage with fans and to generate revenue. Building on the future connections already highlighted, this section expands some of these further while introducing some additional trends that are shaping the way sport marketing is being practiced now, as well as how it will likely be deployed in the future.

The future of sport marketing will be determined by the impact of numerous powerful platforms and media distribution channels that are converging to forge a new level of technological integration. Sport spectators will wield unprecedented freedom of choice as well as new levels of interaction and engagement, in the process becoming sport participants. However, sport spectators and participants will also become more fragmented as the interactive, participative aspects of technologically driven sport offer customised possibilities that reimagine fandom. With this 'new' form of virtual (and/or online) participation comes significant competition for the traditional meeting place of the amateur sport participant, the sporting club. It can be argued that significant social changes are occurring as fans connect 'virtually' rather than in a face-to-face environment.

Technological convergence refers to the merging of computing characterised by a combination of connectedness and ease of access. In practice it means that computing technology with different functionality is capable of integration so that it can work together seamlessly and with unprecedented levels of customisation. For example, wireless networks, roaming connectivity between different portable and permanent technologies such as phones, laptops, handheld computers and the internet, are instrumental in allowing sport to be viewed on demand from almost anywhere and with a range of different devices. Not only does convergence make portable real-time and recorded sport viewing from virtually any location in the world an inexpensive possibility, it opens the door to a suite of new sport products packaged for instant experience. A central pillar in this process comes about in consequence of the availability of digital transmissions through free to air and fee or pay television.

There are several ways in which digital data are being used to diversify the sport watching experience. First, it can be viewed like ordinary video or television transmissions, but is more flexible and easily manipulated so that content may be streamed over portable devices via the internet or smartphones. The implication here is that more sport will be packaged in modular forms for on-sale; niche sporting content will be available where it has never been before and popular sport content will increasingly be subject to a fee for service access. The demand for convenience will drive commercial offerings. As a result, watching sport through a personal computer, phone, or tablet is becoming quite common. In fact, technological convergence means that a single portable device can serve all computing, entertainment, and communications needs. Second, digital can be used to cover specific aspects of a sporting event. A viewer can act as a director if they choose, selecting camera angles, players, activities, or replays at their discretion. Third, digital can be employed to create new statistics associated with sport content, allowing for enthusiasts to have more options to interact with and participate in online sport. Finally, digital convergence allows sport fans to connect easily with each other through forums and social media, often augmented by, or facilitated through, sport brands.

The relevance of data has been observed repeatedly throughout this text, the most recent trend associated with the use of data analytics in sport marketing. As data collection and analysis become more sophisticated, commonplace, and automated, sport organisations will be able to use the information to better understand their target audiences and make more precisely informed decisions about their marketing strategies. For example, personal data of consumers and fans are used to analyse their behaviours and preferences, like attendance and spending habits, thereby creating more personalised and resonant marketing campaigns. In addition, we can expect to see the widespread use of AI and machine learning algorithms to help companies create more effective marketing campaigns by anticipating or predicting the preferences of consumers and fans. AI is revolutionising the way that sport businesses connect with fans, anticipate their needs, and personalise their experiences because it can analyse vast amounts of data in real time, from social media trends to ticket sales and merchandise purchases, leading to the targeting of fans with personalised ads or promotions based on their past behaviour. Similarly, predictive analytics are being used to forecast demand for specific games or merchandise, or to identify which fans are most likely to upgrade their ticket packages or purchase premium experiences. Chatbots and virtual assistants powered by AI are already being used by many sport businesses to provide 24/7 customer service and support. They help fans find information about upcoming games, purchase tickets and merchandise, and get answers to common questions, all without the need for human services. Furthermore, as AI continues to improve, chatbots and virtual assistants are likely to become even more like real humans and be able to provide fully personalised and authentic interactions with fans.

At the same time, the rise of esports and digital platforms like immersive online worlds will provide new opportunities for sport organisations to reach and engage with fans. Perhaps the most radical possibilities for sport experiences will accompany content that employs sport as a theme rather than in its original form. The separation between spectator and participant is diminishing as a consequence of virtual sport experiences. The real power of virtual technologies is their increasing ability to intersect with the real world and blur the distinction between virtual reality and enhanced reality. A good example can be found in online virtual worlds where consumers' virtual participants – avatars – live, play, work, and engage in commercial transactions that have value in the real world. Virtual sporting worlds are readily available, with many new applications devised with sporting brand affiliations.

CASE 13.6

Twitch

Twitch delivers a live streaming platform for gamers, esports, and other entertainment events that have transformed aspects of sport marketing. To begin with, Twitch invented a new way of promoting esports events through live streaming.

Before Twitch, esports events were often streamed on smaller, more niche platforms with limited audiences. Twitch's platform has a much larger user base, which has allowed esports events to reach new audiences and gain more exposure. Twitch also uses influencer marketing, partnering with popular streamers and esports teams to promote events and drive viewership. In addition, Twitch has disrupted the traditional distribution model for sport events by providing a free, accessible platform for live streaming. This has made esports events more widely available to audiences, regardless of their location or ability to pay. The platform's reach has led to innovative ways for brands to sponsor and advertise during esports events. For example, brands can sponsor individual streamers, who will then promote their products and services to their followers. Brands can also advertise during esports events, with Twitch offering a range of advertising formats, such as pre-roll and mid-roll ads.

Fans engage with esports events by creating a more participatory viewing experience. Twitch's platform also allows viewers to interact with each other and the event in real-time through chats, adding an additional layer of engagement to the viewing experience, as well as engage with streamers and esports teams through social media. This has created a more immersive and engaging experience for fans, leading to increased loyalty and advocacy for esports.

QUESTIONS

1. What types of sport content are most popular on Twitch, and how does Twitch curate and promote this content?
2. What role do esports play in Twitch's sports marketing strategy?
3. What metrics does Twitch use to measure the success of its sport marketing initiatives, and how does it use this data to inform future strategies?
4. What ethical considerations are involved in Twitch's sport marketing, such as the use of sponsored content or data collection from users?
5. How does Twitch's sport marketing strategy compare to traditional marketing approaches, and what are the advantages and disadvantages of each approach?

Not only can sport be experienced in virtual worlds through avatars but also through first person, physical, virtual reality. Already, for example, leading labs have designed interactive, three-dimensional virtual environments where users can physically participate in sport simulations. Virtual reality programmes seek to create realistic but usually fictional environments using sophisticated software in real time and with responsiveness to the actions of a user. An inevitable combination of virtual reality and technological convergence will be the opportunity to engage in virtual sporting environments through the internet from almost anywhere with portable devices. Temporarily the interaction will be physically superficial. For example, numerous game consoles employ controllers with positioning systems that detect spatial orientation, allowing a correspondence between the physical actions of the user and their gaming activity. Add to this the opportunity to personalise the appearance of the characters in line with the user's image, as well as the introduction of AI in the software, and the cyber athlete becomes an evolving, unique character. Shortly, entertainment-based sport games will become even more real as wireless connections and digital screens are replaced by goggles, contact lenses, sensor-detection feedback suits, and images projected directly onto the retina. Online cybersport is already so popular that it is developing a professional circuit where real leagues and teams are reproduced in a cyber world, complete with genuine prize money, sponsorships, and real-time audiences.

The traditional spectator is no longer a passive viewer, but a player in their own right. In fact, sport itself is changing sport marketing along with it. How many recreational sport enthusiasts would play from their own consoles if they could get their exercise and fun in front of immense virtual crowds in replications of the most famous stadia in the world? There is no reason why the same group of Sunday players could not link up in the virtual world and play in the virtual game of their choice, followed by a collective trip to a virtual bar of their choice. Virtual sporting clubs may well become a realistic alternative to the 'real' thing. For the more leisure-minded, hours on the keyboard interacting with players and other fans is time well spent.

In the future, virtual spectators may be 'placeless'; the distribution of sport entertainment through conventional stadia and venues less important as a result of digitally changeable environments. As a result, future sport consumption will move away from the geographic focus of a city or region, instead revolving around the construction of artificial hubs through which supporters can become attached in vast networks. Virtual sporting clans will determine their own preferred virtual environments for sport watching and will create their own virtual geographic replacement. In a way, professional sport will best be described as media content, deliverable through a range of distribution services, but probably available via any multifunctional portable device. This will also encourage the further fragmentation of fans whose tribal affiliations will differ depending upon their method of access and interaction. In other words, sophisticated technological options will offer sport marketers access to bigger markets and it will offer the sport consumer more variety, more access flexibility (on demand), and more and richer information. It will also create new 'places' where sport enthusiasts view, perform, meet, congregate, and participate in sport experiences. New virtual communities may well harness the potential to create meeting places, togetherness, and social cohesion analogous to traditional meeting places such as the sporting club. All of these developments will be augmented by sport brands and their marketing teams. The progress of media technology will encourage increased fan engagement and integration with sport.

Next, the massive proliferation of social media will only increase in prominence within sport marketing. Social media platforms like X (formerly Twitter), TikTok,

Facebook, and Instagram have already become essential tools for sport marketers, allowing them to connect with fans, build brand awareness, and engage with audiences in real-time. In the future, we can expect to see even more innovative uses of social media in sport marketing, such as the incorporation of virtual reality and augmented reality technologies to create immersive experiences for fans. Platforms such as YouTube might become subject to competition from new sites and apps that allow users to experience what they watch.

A relentless thirst for new revenue streams has fuelled ethical concerns about the rise of sport gambling, betting, and gaming. For example, in 2021, the US NFL announced a partnership with four sports betting companies, which is estimated to be worth billions of dollars in revenue. What is more, gambling opportunities have permeated sport marketing as a form of engagement where fans are more likely than ever to watch games, follow teams, and interact with sport content online when they have money riding on the outcome. For example, during the 2022 World Cup, more than USD$30 billion was wagered on the tournament with bets placed on the eventual winner, individual game outcomes, and the top scorer.

Another over-the-horizon possibility is known as 'The Metaverse', which refers to a virtual shared space that is created by the convergence of virtual reality, augmented reality, and the internet. In the metaverse, sport marketing could take on entirely new dimensions. For example, sport organisations could create immersive virtual environments that allow fans to experience a game as if they were actually there by using VR technology. These virtual experiences could include the ability to move around the stadium, interact with other fans, and even participate in the game itself. In addition to immersive virtual experiences, the metaverse could also create new revenue streams such as selling virtual merchandise like jerseys or other branded items, that fans could use to customise their metaverse avatars. Similarly, they could also sell virtual tickets to games or events, allowing fans to attend even if they are unable to physically travel to the event.

Since athletes will probably employ advanced wearable technology that will allow them to monitor their body in real-time, detecting, for example, heart rate, respiration, and brain activity, all this feedback can be incorporated into the metaverse's radical new sporting experiences.

There will also be new advancements in human enhancement technologies, such as implants that can improve vision or hearing, or even exoskeletons that can augment an athlete's physical abilities. This could lead to new categories of sport, such as 'cyborg' or 'augmented' sports. Of course, with virtual reality technology, it is likely that sport will no longer be confined to physical locations. Virtual reality sport will allow athletes to compete against each other from anywhere in the world, and athletes will be able to compete in virtual stadiums that can perfectly accommodate their preferences. Finally, another potential development in the metaverse is the use of NFTs. These are unique digital assets that can be bought and sold, where in the metaverse, they could be used to represent ownership of virtual sport assets such as exclusive virtual experiences or even ownership of virtual teams.

CASE 13.7

YouTube and Artificial Intelligence

YouTube is a major platform for sport content and uses AI-powered tools to review user data and deliver customised content that anticipates consumer preferences. Several elements are noteworthy.

First, the site provides users with content recommendations, which arrive because YouTube's 'recommendation algorithm' employs AI to suggest videos to viewers based on their viewing history and preferences. For example, if a viewer watches a lot of football videos, YouTube's AI algorithm will recommend more football-related content to that viewer. This helps to personalise the viewing experience for each user and keeps them engaged with the platform. Since the AI-engine becomes more accurate as a user engages with more content and makes choices about earlier recommendations, most YouTubers find that the automated suggestions are increasingly satisfying over time. Second, although less attractive to users, YouTube's AI-powered ad targeting system uses machine learning to identify the most relevant ads for each viewer. It evaluates factors such as the viewer's demographics if they had created an account with personal information and their apparent interests based on browsing behaviour. As a result, the system serves up ads that are more likely to be of interest to the viewer, which of course is less annoying to the YouTuber while also yielding a much higher level of ad effectiveness for the company and its advertising clients. Third, YouTube offers an AI-driven content creation video editing tool called 'YouTube Director' that helps creators to produce and curate videos quickly and with little skill or experience. The tool uses AI algorithms to analyse video footage provided by the users, helping them by automatically selecting the best clips and sequences, adding music and sound effects, and ultimately allowing them to produce a professional outcome, which means more engaging sport content and more viewers. A fourth and final AI-governed tool delivers summarised analytics to content creators. These metrics are constructed by YouTube's AI engine by crunching viewer data about preferences and behaviours. A YouTuber's analytics 'dashboard' displays the number of views per video and highlights more specific data about viewer demographics, engagement levels like 'watch time', and even estimated revenues.

QUESTIONS

Visit YouTube's site starting here –www.youtube.com/intl/ALL_uk/howyoutubeworks/our-commitments/protecting-user-data/

Attempt to locate the answers to the following:

1 How does YouTube ensure that sponsored content and advertising are clearly disclosed to viewers?

2 What is YouTube's policy on user data collection, and how are these data used?

3 How does YouTube ensure that sport content on its platform is appropriate for all viewers, including children?
4 How does YouTube promote diversity and inclusion in its sport content, both in terms of the athletes and sports featured and the demographics of viewers?
5 How does YouTube balance its commitment to free speech with its responsibility to prevent harm and maintain a safe and respectful environment for all users of the platform, including athletes, sport organisations, and fans?

CONCLUSION

This text has explored sport marketing over four levels. The most fundamental level describes the philosophy of sport marketing: to satisfy the needs of sport consumers. One of the features that makes sport marketing unique is the range and diversity of sport consumers' needs. Not only can sport products be offered in the form of goods and services, but sport itself can be both the target of marketing and a vehicle for marketing. Furthermore, sport consumers may be involved personally in the delivery of sport products, such as with sporting competitions, or may be passive recipients of an experience, such as spectators at a sporting contest.

At the next level – the process of sport marketing – this text has reviewed and explained the four stages of the Sport Marketing Framework. Stage one requires the identification of sport marketing opportunities. This is achieved through the assessment of the internal and external environment, the sport organisation, and the sport market and its consumers. After this information has been collected and analysed, it is possible to undertake stage two of the Sport Marketing Framework and develop a sport marketing strategy. To construct a sport marketing strategy, sport marketers must make a series of decisions about the direction of the marketing programme, culminating in the formulation of marketing objectives and performance measures. Stage two also involves deciding on the core of the marketing strategy. This involves deciding exactly what products and services will be marketed to consumers (segmentation), and how the brand will be positioned in the marketplace against competitors. With a target market and a positioning strategy in place, stage three of the Sport Marketing Framework, planning the sport marketing mix, can begin. Here, tactics for marketing the sport product, price, distribution (place), promotion, sponsorship, and sport services are established. It is imperative that these tactics are integrated and consistent with the chosen positioning strategy. Finally, stage four can be introduced, which requires the implementation and control of the sport marketing strategy. This means that plans are put into action using implementation strategies and kept on track through a control process. Part of the control process re-engages the objectives and performance measures set in stage two, to see whether the targets set were achieved. In this final stage of the process it becomes transparent which parts of the marketing plan have been successful, and which parts require remedial action.

At the third and fourth levels of sport marketing are principles and tools, respectively. The principles of sport marketing represent the general rules and guidelines of good practice, while the tools of sport marketing are techniques that can be used to execute the principles. The combination of the philosophy, process, principles, and tools articulated in this text forge the relationship a sport brand enjoys with sport consumers.

PRINCIPLES SUMMARY

- Chapter principle 13.1: Implementing a sport marketing strategy means putting the plans into action.
- Chapter principle 13.2: The implementation success of a sport marketing plan is enhanced through the use of five implementation tools: (1) leadership and commitment, (2) communication and delegation, (3) teamwork and projects, (4) rewards and reinforcement and (5) control and feedback.
- Chapter principle 13.3: Controlling a sport marketing strategy means keeping it on track, making sure that it is achieving what it set out to, and making changes to correct variations and problems. The control process involves six steps: (1) set performance measures, (2) define CSFs, (3) measure performance, (4) compare results, (5) identify variations and (6) make corrections.
- Chapter principle 13.4: There are three basic tenets against which sport marketing behaviour must be matched: (1) the buyer and seller must both be fully informed as to what is being purchased and what is being paid in exchange, (2) neither the buyer nor seller is compelled or coerced in their choices and (3) both buyer and seller are capable of making a rational decision concerning the transaction.
- Chapter principle 13.5: Social awareness and social responsibility are variables in the way consumers' brand perceptions are forged, suggesting that sport brand managers need to understand how environmental or social messages can be embedded in their activities to achieve social outcomes, and into their branding without creating cynicism.

TOOLS SUMMARY

- Chapter tool 13.1: Leadership and commitment
- Chapter tool 13.2: Communication and delegation
- Chapter tool 13.3: Teamwork and projects
- Chapter tool 13.4: Rewards and reinforcement
- Chapter tool 13.5: Control and feedback

REVIEW QUESTIONS

1 What is the difference between implementation and control?
2 Provide an example for each of the five implementation tools.

3 Outline the steps of the control process.
4 How can CSFs be used to enhance the success of a control strategy?
5 Do you think there are any aspects of sport marketing that make the development of a code of professional marketing ethics different to mainstream marketing? If so, what are they and how should they be incorporated into a code?

RELEVANT WEBSITES

The Fédération Internationale de Football Association (FIFA) (www.fifa.com)
International Olympic Committee (www.olympics.com/ioc)
The International Wheelchair Basketball Federation (IWBF) (www.iwbf.org)
NBA (www.nba.com)
Nike (www.nike.com)
Twitch (www.twitch.tv)
Under Armour (www.underarmour.com)
YouTube (www.youtube.com)

FURTHER READING

Dingle, G., & Mallen, C. (2020). Sport and Environmental Sustainability. Routledge.

Hums, M. A., Kluch, Y., Schmidt, S. H., & MacLean, J. C. (2023). *Governance and Policy in Sport Organizations*. Taylor & Francis.

Lough, N., & Geurin, A. N. (Eds.). (2019). *Routledge Handbook of the Business of Women's Sport*. Routledge.

Millington, R., & Darnell, S. C. (Eds.). (2019). *Sport, Development and Environmental Sustainability*. Routledge.

Ratten, V. (2019). *Sports Technology and Innovation*. Springer Books.

Triantafyllidis, S., & Mallen, C. (Eds.). (2022). *Sport and Sustainable Development: An Introduction*. Routledge.

Winand, M., & Anagnostopoulos, C. (Eds.). (2019). *Research Handbook on Sport Governance*. Edward Elgar Publishing.

Appendix

OUTLINE OF CASES

Case #	*Name*	*Page*	*Overview*	*Learning Focus and Key Concepts*
1.1	World Wrestling Entertainment (WWE)	4	Introduces the WWE and its curated entertainment package with an emphasis on the types of audiences it attracts.	Review of WWE website. Fan interests. Social media and fan engagement. Motivations by demographic and psychographic segments. Rise of an entertainment brand. Fan motivations and characteristics. Balance of orchestrated event versus sporting uncertainty.
1.2	Drone Racing League	10	Provides an illustrative case of an entirely new sport and its premier competition, which has successfully transformed a hobby into an entertainment arena.	First impressions of a new sport. Engagement with interactive app. Comparisons to existing sports and differences/similarities. Chance to explore 'what is sport'? New sport development. Technology. Audience appeal. Fan engagement. Market growth.
1.3	Major League Eating	14	Explores a novel sport league that has expanded immensely over recent years, particularly with the rise of social media and the curiosity factor associated with sharing remarkable eating achievements.	Sport strategy decisions. Appeal of sport to certain audiences. The broad range of entertainment opportunities that exist. What constitutes an athlete or athletic endeavour? Stakeholder involvement. Revenue streams in sport. Consumer impressions. Sport strategy.

(Continued)

Case #	*Name*	*Page*	*Overview*	*Learning Focus and Key Concepts*
1.4	Serena Williams	18	Presents Serena Williams from a sport marketing viewpoint, where she is not just an athlete but a brand, whose assets have been carefully managed over the course of her career.	Women and underrepresented groups in sport. Development of an individual brand persona and strategic alliance to commercial brands Athlete endorsement and branding. Rise of Serena Williams as a tennis and marketing star. Use of name, image, and representation to build branding. Brand authenticity.
1.5	Chinese Super League	21	Outlines the preeminent professional football (soccer) league in China in terms of its expansion efforts and subsequent challenges.	How sport markets and leagues need adjustment for environmental factors. Factors sport brands are reliant on for success. Challenges in a global market. Chinese perspective on sport investment. Rise and decline of the CSL. Marketing strategy. Sport planning. COVID-19 impacts. Product innovation.
1.6	Super Bowl	24	Explores the championship game of one of the world's most professionalised competitions, the US National Football League and offers a remarkable example where the marketing of and through sport can be seen in a gigantic commercial collision.	The power of sport to unite communities. Major events and key stakeholders. Engaging traditional and digital media audiences. Investing through sport. Impact, scale and size of a major event. Changing landscape of broadcasting, Advertising. Investment, costs. National Football League.
1.7	Tokyo Summer Olympic Games 2020	28	Considers whether the Tokyo 2020 (2021) Summer Olympic Games was worth the investment given a significant COVID-19 delay, and subsequent impact on attendances.	Major event benefits and risks. Impact of uncertainty on sport planning. How investments in and via sport can be leveraged. Economic and reputational impact. Economic legacy. Destination marketing. Sporting legacy. Sport tourism. Major event challenges. Role of sport in society. City and nation branding. COVID-19 impacts.

(Continued)

Case #	*Name*	*Page*	*Overview*	*Learning Focus and Key Concepts*
2.1	Clearinghouse for Sport	36	Presents an Australian government sport information repository storing a wide range of information that can be used by all sectors, including interested individuals.	Challenges in accessing and evaluating sport information. Consideration of the size and components of sport markets. Sport data. General market information. Sport contribution. Volunteers.
2.2	Forbes World's Most Valuable Sport Teams	42	Building valuable sport brands is challenging, so to gain an insight into which brands are leading the pack, *Forbes* provides a regular update of the world's major sport brands.	What is brand value? Comparing markets around the world. Competition and cooperation in sport. How sporting teams build value. Differing marketing approaches. Accessing and utilising sport data.
2.3	Parkrun	53	Run by volunteers, Parkrun is now considered the largest mass-participation sporting event on the planet, capturing the interest of over a quarter of a million runners each Saturday morning, and introducing many of these people to the simple pursuit of running.	Creation of sporting opportunities. Engaging communities. Social and cultural aspects of sport participation and fandom. Product development. Fandom. Participation. Running.
3.1	Nielsen's Sports Consumption Evolution Report	59	Highlights key aspects from Nielsen's 'Year in Review: Sports Consumption Evolution' report presenting consumption data on changing habits from various media markets on events and leagues	Changing media landscape. Increased OTT consumption. Digital viewing. Diversity of sporting content. Content delivery strategies. Streaming platforms. Changing consumer habits. Generation Z. COVID-19 impact on broadcasting.
3.2	Hope United	66	Provides an example of an initiative to call attention to online abuse of athletes.	Managing athlete relationships with fans. Negative fan sentiment – when fandom crosses the line. Self-concept and socio-cultural motivations. Online abuse. Sponsor initiatives.

(Continued)

Case #	*Name*	*Page*	*Overview*	*Learning Focus and Key Concepts*
3.3	Chase Center San Francisco	72	Presents the state-of-the-art Chase Center in San Francisco, detailing how venues can be used to successfully market sport events and draw fans into games.	Stadium design. Fan interaction with facilities. Changing consumer behaviour. Facilities and impacts upon fan behaviours. Appeal of new arenas and required offerings.
3.4	Barmy Army	75	Chronicles the 'Barmy Army' entourage which comprises a colourful ensemble of fanatical cricket supporters who liven up the game with their songs, merchandise, and banter in support of their team.	Group affiliation development. Fan behaviour. Ancillary sport products. How supporter groups add to the sport experience. How fan engagement can be generated. Associations that extend beyond sport. Cricket.
4.1	Youth Olympic Games	81	An introduction to the International Olympic Committee's Youth Olympic Games from the perspective of conducting a SWOT analysis.	New products. Marketing to different audiences. Social causes. Strategic planning. Major events. Use of a SWOT analysis to aid in developing marketing strategy. How new sport offerings are designed to appeal to audiences and adapt as they grow.
4.2	Lawn Bowls	84	Review of Lawn Bowls as a sport product and how it needs to adapt to engage with new audiences.	Market expansion. Audience segmentation. Product positioning. Product Innovation. Competitor analysis. Audience and target market analysis. New markets. Product expansion possibilities. Lawn Bowls.
4.3	Sport New Zealand	87	Considers the strategy of a government sport development agency.	Marketing objectives. Audience identification. Sport participation. National sporting strategies. Responsibility for sport development agencies. Funding of sport. Investments in sport. Audience alignment.

(Continued)

Case #	*Name*	*Page*	*Overview*	*Learning Focus and Key Concepts*
4.4	Netflix: Drive to Survive	89	Presents the increased interest in Formula One following the success of the Drive to Survive streaming series.	New audiences. New media. Product enhancement. Consumer engagement. Engaging new audiences. Reviving existing audiences. Developing interest through media and character building. New technology. Segmentation. Product enhancement. Motorsport.
4.5	Ski Dubai	91	Describes an indoor ski resort operating in the United Arab Emirates.	Novelty experiences. Destination marketing. Sport tourism. Motivations to harness sporting interest. Understanding of target market. Enhanced product value. Using sport to create tourism appeal and enhance entertainment options. Skiing.
4.6	Under Armour	99	Reviews the mission, vision, and core values of Under Armour and their connections to high-profile athletes.	Corporate planning. Marketing strategy. Athlete and consumer alignment. Application of vision and mission statements. Corporate values and links to marketing. Usage of athletes for endorsement. Sportswear.
4.7	Oiselle	107	Outlines the keys to success and differentiation adopted by a running apparel brand competing in a challenging marketplace.	Porter's Five Forces. New market entry and establishment. Product differentiation. Establishing brand loyalty. New market entry. Product design. Audience understanding. Customer engagement. Usage of social media. Sports clothing.
5.1	Esports	112	Outlines the growth of competitive esports, including comparisons to traditional sports.	Nature of sport products. Building awareness. Strategic marketing planning. Positioning. Product design. Comparisons to other entertainment products. Consumer mindsets. Video games.

(Continued)

Case #	*Name*	*Page*	*Overview*	*Learning Focus and Key Concepts*
5.2	Name, Image, and Likeness	116	Considers the impact of a landmark decision to allow student athletes in the USA the right to market their name, image, and likeness, much like professional athletes are permitted.	Athlete rights. Personal branding. Collegiate sport. Revenue streams. Social and digital marketing. Authentic marketing. Endorsements. Athlete activism.
5.3	Smart Sport Stadiums	118	Captures a popular trend within the sport industry to build or update current stadiums to increase gameday fan experiences	Technological impact. Customer experiences. Customer relationship management. Ticket distribution. Stadium design. Audience segmentation. Artificial intelligence. Fan expectations.
5.4	User-Generated Content	130	High levels of social media utilisation have resulted in sport brands incorporating consumer-generated content into their social media feeds as a form of authentic promotion.	User-generated branding. Integrated marketing communications. Influencer marketing. Digital channels. Social media. Messaging. Fan engagement. Authenticity. Employee promotions. Content creation.
5.5	Angel City FC and Corporate Social Responsibility	133	Angel City FC's mission extends beyond its on-field performance and success, focusing heavily on a community-driven business model with a corporate social responsibility marketing strategy as a key component	Corporate social responsibility. New team positioning. Women's sport. Mission statements. Fan alignment. Consumer engagement. Strategic marketing. Community outreach.
6.1	TikTok	138	TikTok is a popular video-sharing social media platform and a go-to destination for sport fans, athletes, and teams to engage with each other.	Social media. Product augmentation. Fan content creation. Technology in fan engagement. Product development. Artificial intelligence. Augmented reality.

(Continued)

Case #	Name	Page	Overview	Learning Focus and Key Concepts
6.2	Goalball	146	Goalball is a physically demanding and highly competitive Paralympic sport for players with visual impairments.	Product design. Appeal of sport to broad participation. Competitiveness. Modifications for equity. Inclusivity. Product features. Empowerment. Paralympics.
6.3	Women's Professional Bodybuilding	149	Women's professional bodybuilding is a niche sport that has struggled to gain recognition and acceptance in the sport and fitness industry but has made numerous product innovations to address the challenges associated with its negative public perceptions.	Product modification. Gender. Overcoming stereotypes and negative perceptions. Influencer marketing. Technological innovations. Gender portrayal. Product enhancement. Health and wellness. Social media.
6.4	The Hundred	152	Launched in 2021, The Hundred is a professional franchise cricket tournament played in the United Kingdom as a faster-paced and action-packed version of limited overs cricket.	New product development. Innovation in saturated markets. Segmentation analysis. Marketing communications campaigns. Audience appeal. Rule changes. Product modifications. Product portfolio expansion. Branding. Evaluation approaches.
6.5	ESPN	158	ESPN is a market-leading sport media company that has been in operation since 1979 and has cultivated a global reputation for its comprehensive sport coverage, analysis, and entertainment.	Innovative product marketing strategies. Changing media landscape. Multi-platform content. Innovative strategies to enhance media engagement. Changing consumption patterns. Platform diversification.
6.6	Mumbai Indians	161	The Mumbai Indians are a professional cricket team that compete in the Indian Premier League, one of the world's most popular and lucrative Twenty20 cricket leagues.	Brand attributes. Marketing campaigns. Social marketing. Branding strategy and features. Identity. Merchandise.

(Continued)

Case #	*Name*	*Page*	*Overview*	*Learning Focus and Key Concepts*
6.7	City Football Group	166	The UAE's City Football Group owns football clubs around the world and displays how a sport organisation can be used for nation branding.	Nation branding. Philanthropy in sport. Sport tourism. Positioning. Sport in society. Sport partnerships. Club ownership. Manchester City Football Club.
7.1	Peloton	176	Explores the pricing approach used by Peloton, a US-based company within the fitness industry noted for its high-quality equipment and related subscription service.	Setting prices. Premium positioning through pricing. Global pricing. Pricing strategy. Product differentiation. Bundling.
7.2	FIFA World Cup	180	The FIFA Men's World Cup is arguably the world's preeminent sporting event and uses a complex ticketing strategy to balance returns and availability.	Major event pricing. Ticketing strategies. Demand pricing. Balancing revenue and other priorities.
7.3	Dynamic Pricing	186	Dynamic pricing, or what is sometimes called 'surge pricing' features prominently in sport marketing because it involves the adjustment of price in response to changes in supply and demand.	Pricing scarce commodities. Ticketing revenue. Creating pricing opportunities. Dynamic pricing objectives. Equity issues. Transparency and fairness. Advanced analytics.
7.4	HoverGlide	188	The HoverGlide backpack presents an unusual pricing case in the marketing of a recreational product that was developed via a crowdfunding model.	Crowdfunding. Premium pricing. Innovation. Funding sources. Profit margins. Price setting through lifecycles. Production costs. Competitive pricing. Backer rewards.
7.5	Pay What You Can Pricing	192	Explores the phenomenon of sport teams that allow fans to select ticket prices that are matched to their self-assessed means.	Inclusivity. Affordability. Brand reputation. Pricing models. Audience needs. Pricing logistics. Success measurement.

(Continued)

Case #	*Name*	*Page*	*Overview*	*Learning Focus and Key Concepts*
7.6	YouTube	198	YouTube uses several pricing strategies for its sport content where they are influenced by factors such as audience size, exclusivity, and sponsorship deals.	Revenue sources for sport. Revenue sharing. Subscription services. Sponsorship. Content pricing approaches. Pricing models. Pricing transparency. Changing media markets.
7.7	New Technology	200	New technologies such as AI, social media, wearables, and apps are exerting a significant impact on sport pricing.	Data analysis. Consumer behaviour. Algorithms. Market demand. Fan preferences and opinions. Data collection and usage. Pricing models for apps. Value propositions.
8.1	The Changing Face of Retail	212	The Internet has totally transformed the ways in which products are sold and purchased, with sporting goods no exception.	Retailing changes. Types of channel members. Online sales. Instore experiences. Product distribution channels. Specialty stores. Impact of online shopping.
8.2	Tailgating	216	Explores the practice where sport fans gather in large open areas near sport stadiums or venues for pre- or post-match parties.	Fan experiences. Community Spirit. Product augmentation. Socialisation. Sport experiences outside the venue. Safety and security concerns.
8.3	Fan Zones	222	Details the increasingly popular spaces around major events where team supporters can congregate to watch on big screens and partake in a range of experiences.	Broadening the concept of the sport 'place'. Strengthening fan communities. Catering to large audiences. Fan engagement. Technology impact. Physical and online spaces. Authenticity. Crowd management.
9.1	Boxing	229	The sport of boxing is one of the oldest known athletic endeavours, however in recent years it has faced significant marketing challenges including competition from sports like the Ultimate Fighting Championship.	Brand building. Competitive markets. Identity. Market positioning. Market appeal. Athlete branding. Sport governance. Promotional campaigns. Boxing and Ultimate Fighting.

(Continued)

Case #	*Name*	*Page*	*Overview*	*Learning Focus and Key Concepts*
9.2	The Masters	233	Arguably the most prestigious of golf's four 'majors', The Masters is renowned for its enormous appeal that has been built on the back of tradition and scarcity.	Sporting traditions. Major event marketing. Product positioning. Preservation of sporting mystique and scarcity. Product orientation. Integrated communication strategy. Professional golf.
9.3	When Things Go Bad!	239	No matter how hard a sporting league, club or governing body might try, it is almost certain it will face a public relations crisis at some point that will require a carefully coordinated marketing response.	Athlete transgressions. Public relations and publicity. Sponsorship reactions. Degenerative episodes. Relationship building. On- and off-field behaviours. Sponsor expectations. Athlete punishment and expectations.
9.4	Melbourne Cup Carnival	246	Horse racing is a hugely popular sport in many parts of the world and often uses a carnival structure and clever promotion to attract large crowds over multiple days and events.	Sport carnivals and festivals. Public relations and publicity. Major events. Mass attendances. Push and pull strategies. Atmosphere creation. Sporting culture. Horse racing.
10.1	Airbnb	259	Airbnb became a worldwide Olympic partner in 2020 and has developed highly creative ways to engage fans, and create new revenue opportunities to maximise their investment.	Strategic partnerships. Brand objectives. Long-term sponsorships. Fan identification. Activation and leveraging. Fan experiences Sponsorship investment and returns. Olympic Games.
10.2	Women's World Cup Sponsorship	265	Explores a situation prior to the 2023 Women's World Cup where it was reported that FIFA was pursuing a controversial sponsorship deal with Visit Saudi, the state tourism authority of Saudi Arabia.	Sponsorship. Public relations. Brand affinity. Sponsor fit. Promotional objectives. Sport activism. FIFA.

(Continued)

Case #	*Name*	*Page*	*Overview*	*Learning Focus and Key Concepts*
10.3	Athleta	266	Athleta is a women's activewear company that has moved into athlete sponsorship using a highly supportive approach.	Sporting values. Apparel sponsorship. Athlete endorsement and engagement. Sponsor fit. Strategic alliances. Brand values. Brand partnerships.
11.1	Sport Museums	297	Sporting organisations are seeking to extend experiences for fans and curious visitors alike by moving beyond matches at stadiums where opportunities to attend are fleeting and results are hard to predict, by creating museum experiences.	Sport experiences. Sport nostalgia. Sport tourism. Visitor and fan engagement. Product augmentation. Memorabilia. FC Barcelona.
11.2	Stadium Experiences	304	Contemporary sport stadiums are purposefully planned to maximise the entertainment experience, safety, and comfort of fans; not just host a match.	Sporting rivalries. Venue facilities. Sporting experiences. Satisfaction. Fan comfort. Safety. Expectations management. Sport tourism.
11.3	LIV Golf	316	LIV Golf, a Saudi-backed golf tour, commenced in 2022 and shook up the world of golf by offering a very different experience to golf fans.	Product experiences. Sporting competition structures. New products. Fan expectations. Product modifications. Professional golf.
12.1	#WeThe15	322	To increase awareness and promote greater knowledge about the 15% of the world's population with a disability the International Paralympic Committee developed a campaign named 'WeThe15'	Digital marketing channels. Social media marketing. Activations. Social marketing. Building awareness. Paralympics.

(Continued)

Case #	*Name*	*Page*	*Overview*	*Learning Focus and Key Concepts*
12.2	Mark Cuban Center for Sports Media and Technology	326	Indicative of the growing emphasis on digital marketing, as well as need to train individuals on the tools to create digital multi-media content within sport, various educational programmes are expanding their offerings to meet this market need.	Sport media. Technology. Multi-media content. Content creation. Training. College sport. Basketball.
12.3	NBA App	328	While leagues and teams once had to partner with social media platforms to offer additional content or forms of engagement for fans outside of team-specific websites, sport properties can now develop individualised apps to offer fans a 'one-stop-shop' for digital content.	Apps. Digital marketing content. Digital modularity. Consumer insights. Fan demographics. Individualisation and personalisation.
12.4	Over the Top and Streaming	339	Complimenting the digital revolution in sport content consumption on mobile devices are two key contemporary players in content and delivery – over-the-top content and the streaming technology employed to deliver this content.	Emerging digital channels. Demographic changes. Audience appeal. Customised content and advertising. Streaming services. Audience expansion.
12.5	FC Barcelona Social Media	342	Provides an example of a sport property that employs a successful digital media strategy across all social platforms.	Media strategy. Digital portfolio. Fan engagement. Social media integration. FC Barcelona.

(Continued)

Case #	*Name*	*Page*	*Overview*	*Learning Focus and Key Concepts*
12.6	Influencer Marketing	345	The insider perspective and behind-the-scenes information that can be obtained by following athletes on social media has proved to be a massive draw for fans around the globe.	Influencers. Digital marketing partnerships and sponsorships. Authenticity. Social media strategies. Product linkages.
12.7	Virtual Paddock Club	347	During the COVID-19 pandemic, sport leagues, teams, and organisations had to develop creative ways to connect with fans remotely.	Fan engagement. Virtual communities. Online marketing. VIP hospitality. COVID-19 impact. Formula One.
13.1	National Basketball Association	355	Presents the NBA as an organisation that has taken a data-driven approach to measuring and evaluating the success of its marketing strategy, characterised by the collection of key analytics selected to track the effectiveness of specific aspects of their brand's market performance.	Data analysis. Measuring and evaluating objectives. Social media. Brand profile. Digital and traditional channels. Sponsorship effectiveness.
13.2	Nike and Under Armour	366	Explores commonalities and differences between two major sport apparel, fashion, and sport marketing companies, who use a range of marketing performance measures to evaluate the effectiveness of their marketing campaigns and initiatives.	Customer lifetime value. Customer acquisition costs. Sales measures. Market share. Customer engagement. Brand awareness. Return on investment.

(Continued)

Case #	*Name*	*Page*	*Overview*	*Learning Focus and Key Concepts*
13.3	FIFA	369	In response to concerns about its ethical practices, FIFA has implemented reforms aimed at improving the transparency and accountability within the organisation.	Ethics. Governance. Transparency and accountability. Brand integrity.
13.4	International Wheelchair Basketball Federation	372	Highlights a governing body who has outlined its commitment to reducing environmental impact, promoting social responsibility, and promoting good governance.	Sustainability. Environmental impact. Waste reduction. Social responsibility Sporting policy and governance. Disability sports.
13.5	International Olympic Committee	374	To address criticisms, the IOC has moved to transfer its marketing messaging to emphasise a commitment to sustainability and human rights.	Human rights. Sustainability strategy. Environmental and social impact. Gender equality and diversity.
13.6	Twitch	376	Twitch is a live streaming platform for gamers and esports events that has transformed aspects of sport marketing.	Live streaming. Participatory viewing experiences. Fan immersion and engagement. Digital platforms. Esport.
13.7	YouTube and Artificial Intelligence (AI)	380	YouTube is a major platform for sport content and uses AI-powered tools to review user data and deliver customised content that anticipates consumer preferences.	AI. Algorithms. Content personalisation. Targeted advertising. Content creation. Digital analytics.

Index

Note: Page references in *italics* denote figures and in **bold** tables.

5G phones 335–336

ABC Sports 16
Abebe Bikila 354
ACE Programme 76
A.C. Milan 304
actual product 145
adidas 9, 130–131, 265, 267, 285, 326, 354
advertising 231–232; ambush 285–286; and promotions 226–227; sponsorship and 258; time 285–286
aesthetic (visual) pleasure 63
affinity measures 281, 282
Airbnb 259–260, 261, 393
Al Hilal FC 175
Ali, Muhammad 229, 298, 354
Ali (Amazon Prime documentary series) 340
'alliances' 256
Amazon 306, 339
Amazon Prime 339, 340
ambush marketing 255, 271, 284–290
ambush prevention 287–289; and broadcasters 289; control of event environment/locality 288; and event partners 288; and intellectual property 287–288; and merchandisers 289; and sponsors 289; and suppliers 289
American Express 271–272
Andrew, Kyle 267
Angel City FC 133–134, 389
Apple 25, 242
Apple Watch 350
arbitrary allocation 250
Arizona Cardinals 344
artificial intelligence (AI) 355, 376, 380–381, 397
Asher-Smith, Dina 9
Asics 107, 371
assimilated delight 314
Athleta 266–267, 394
athletes: ambush 286; controlling 289–290; sponsoring 286
augmented reality (AR) effects 138
Augusta National Golf Course 233–234
Australian Football League (AFL) 119
Australian Grand Prix Corporation 246
Australian Open 187, 228
Australian Sports Commission 36

Back to the Future (movie)16
Barcelona TV+ 341, 343, 349
Barclays (British multi-national bank) 256
bargaining power: of buyers 97; of suppliers 97
Barmy Army 75–76, 223, 387
Beckham, David 235
belonging and group affiliation 65
benchmarks: establishing 283–284; sponsorship evaluation 283–284
Biles, Simone 17, 235, 267
BMW 10, 264
Bolt, Usain 235
Borg, Bjorn 16
Borussia Dortmund 174
Bowerman, Bill 16
boxing 229–230, 392

Brady, Tom 100
brand awareness 160
brand equity 162–163
brand image 161
branding 157–158, 160–164; brand equity 162–163; brand loyalty 163–164; building sport 160–164; develop/manage brand image 161; establish brand awareness 160; and licensing 164; nation 165–166
brand loyalty 50–51, 163–164
brand mark (logo) 159–160
brand name 159–160; building 160–164; suggestions for 160
brand positioning 266
break-even analysis 189–191
break-even pricing 195
'bricks and mortar' retailer 210, 212
British Heart Foundation 84
British Open 233
broadcast ambush 286
broadcasters/broadcasting 9; controlling 289; sport facilities 220
bureaucratisation, of sports 6
business: bureaucratisation of sport 6; corporatisation of sport 7; managerialism 7; sport 5–8
business-to-consumer (B2C) marketing 330

Carlzon, Jan 312
cause-related sport marketing 273–274
changing face of retail 212–213, 392
channel members 209–210; retailers 210; wholesalers 210
Chase Center San Francisco 72–73, 387
Cheer 339
childcare facilities 220
China Football Association Super League 21
Chinese Super League (CSL) 21–22, 385
City Football Group (CFG) 166–167, 391
Clearinghouse for Sport (Clearinghouse) 36–37, 386
Club Atlético Huracán 192
Coca-Cola 9, 17, 25, 47, 256, 265, 354
Code of Ethics 369
commitment 358–359
communication 359–361; mobile 335–336; networked 330
competition pricing 195
competitive disparity 251
competitive parity (or equality) 250
competitors: analysis 94, **95**; direct 92–94; indirect 92–94; intensity of rivalry among industry 95–96
complaint analysis 105
connected fitness 176
consistency: sporting goods 141; sporting services 141; sport services 296
consumer attitudes/image effects 280–281
consumer awareness 279–280, **280–281**
consumers: analysis 101–105; becoming *57–58*; in Generation Z 58; leveraging sponsorship towards 272; sport (*see* sport consumers)
consumer- to-consumer (C2C) marketing 330
control process *364*
corporate social responsibility (CSR) 273–274, 389
corporate sponsorship 3, 9
corporate stakeholders 273
corporatisation of sports 7
cost-plus pricing 195
COVID-19 pandemic 22, 59, 344, 347
critical incidents and satisfaction 311–312
critical success factors (CSFs) 364
Cuban, Mark 326
cultural connections 64
Curry, Stephen 100, 235
customer experiential pathway (CEP) 311
customer lifetime value (CLV) 308
customer profile: developing 308; updating 309
customer relationship management (CRM) 305, 306–309; Amazon CRM software 306; develop customer profiles 308; electronic customer communication 308–309; innovative offerings 309; segment customers 308; six-step process of *307*; target customers 308; update customer profile 309
customers: delighting 313–314; segment 308; target 308
customer satisfaction 310–312; assimilated delight 314; critical incidents and satisfaction 311–312; customer, delighting 313–314; re-enacted delight 314–315; satisfaction and quality 311; and sport marketing 313–317; transitory delight 315
customisation 325–327, 333; digital sport marketing 325–327
Cybersmile Foundation 67

Dallas Mavericks 326
database software 309
DAZN 339
delegation 359–361
delight/delighting: assimilated 314; customer 313–314; re-enacted 314–315; sport customers as priority marketing goal 315; transitory 315
demographic segmentation 121–122
design of sponsorship programme 290
digital marketing 16, 320–350; digital revolution 320–323; digital sport marketing process 333–334; digital sport marketing tools 334–338; overview 320; rethinking sport marketing 324–332; social media lessons for 346–348
digital media 321–322
digital revolution 320–323
digital sport marketing *325*; customisation 325–327; defined 321, 324; future of 349–350; inclusivity 330–331; modularity 327–329; networked communication 330; permission 331–332; principles **332**, 334; process *333*, 333–334; rethinking sport marketing 324–332; and social media 338–350; sticky branding 329; technologies *335*
digital sport marketing tools 334–338; hardware 337; Internet-driven platforms 334–335, *335*; mobile communications 335–336; software 337–338; upgraded conventional technologies 336–337
digital video recorders 336
DiMaggio, Joe 354
direct competitors 92–94
direct distribution channel 208, *208*
direct marketing services 208
Discord 341
discount pricing 196
discriminatory pricing 196–197
Disney+ 339
distribution 205; issues for sport products 210–212, **211**; systems 208
distribution channels 207–213; channel members 209–210; distribution issues for sport products 210–212; distribution systems 208; types of 208–209
diversification 106
DraftKings 328
drama/entertainment 63
Drive to Survive 89–90, 339, 388
Drone Racing League (DRL) 10–11, 384
Durant, Kevin 21
dynamic pricing 391

economic benefit, and sport fans 64
economic environment: macroeconomic elements 88; microeconomic elements 88; sport marketing opportunities 88
electronic customer communication 308–309
emotion/passion, and sport 46–47
employee-generated content (EGC) 130
endorsements 8–9, 16–17, 21, 232, 234–235
English Football Association 49
English Premier League football 339–340
entitlements assets 270
escape, and sport fans 63
ESPN 9, 11, 14–15, 158–159, 201, 390
esports 112–113, 376–377, 388
Europe 19–20
evaluation tools 275–283, **276–277**; affinity measures 282; consumer attitudes/image effects 280–281; consumer awareness 279–280; exposure 277–279, **279**; positioning perceptions 281; purchase intentions 282; sales effects 282–283, **283**; satisfaction 283; sincerity of the sponsor 282; sport property fit/sponsorship congruence 281–282
event: advertising time 285–286; environment and locality 288; partners, control of 288; sponsoring the broadcast of 286
exchange pricing 197
exposure as evaluation tools 277–279, **279**
external environment: defined 81; direct and indirect competitors 92–94; sport marketing opportunities 80–82; SWOT analysis 85–87, *86*

Fabletics 267
Facebook 326, 328, 335, 340, 341, 342, 349, 354, 355, 379
facilities 213–214; childcare 220; features of 214–217, **215–216**; lighting and sound system 219; merchandising and food/beverage 220–221; scoreboards, screens, and signage 218–219; seating 217–218; technology, media, and broadcasting 220; tools for marketing 217–221; transport 219

facility-dependent sport services 211–212
FA (Football Association) Cup 3
family and social interaction 63–64
fan involvement 259–260
'Fan of The Year' contest 344
fan zones 222–224, 392
FC Barcelona 19, 174, 298, 304; social media 342–343, 395
FC Barcelona Museum 298
Fédération International de l'Automobile (FIA) 49
Fédération Internationale de Football Association (FIFA) 265, 369–370, 397
Federer, Roger 235
Felix, Allyson 267, 329
female athletes 17–18
FIFA Men's World Cup 180–181, 222, 304, 391
'Fight of the Century' 229
Fitbit 242, 350
Five Forces Analysis 94–95
fixed supply schedule 52–53
focused segmentation 124–125
Forbes 'World's Most Valuable Sport Teams' 42–43, 386
Ford, Henry 12
Foreman, George 229
FORTO Coffee Shots 10
Frazier, Joe 229
Fujifilm 285

Gap Inc. 266
Garmin 242
Gatorade 16, 18
General Sports Authority (GSA) 175
geographic segmentation 123
Goalball 146–147, 390
GoDaddy 17
goodwill and sponsorship 258
Grand Slam tennis tournaments 17, 228, 339
The Greatest 229

Hamm, Mia 18
Hanes 16
hardware 337
Hawk, Tony 298
hierarchy 247; of effects 247, *248*
High Performance Sport New Zealand (HPSNZ) 87
HoosiersTV 326
Hootsuite 342
Hope United 66–67, 386
HoverGlide 391
Hoyt, W. 11
The Hundred 152–153, 390

inclusivity 331, 333; digital sport marketing 330–331
indirect competitors 92–94
indirect distribution channel 208, *209*
Infantino, Gianni 265, 369
influencer marketing 345–346, 396
informing, and promotional objectives 241, **243**
innovation: forms of 148; marketing mix 153–154; new product development 149, *149*; new product opportunities 150–151; new products introduction 154; new products testing 151–152; product composition 153–154; rank and prioritise opportunities 151; rapid prototyping 151–152; smart products 148; sport products 147–154
innovative offerings 309
Instagram 326, 327, 328, 335, 342, 349, 355, 379
intangible sport products 143
integrated promotion 228–252; promotional objectives 240–243; promotion planning 243–252; promotions mix 230–240
Intel 18
intellectual property 287–288
intermediaries 208–209
internal environment: defined 80; sport marketing opportunities 80–82; SWOT analysis 82–83, **84**
International Gymnastics Federation (FIG) 89
International Management Group (IMG) 15, 114
International Olympic Committee (IOC) 3, 9, 81–82, 231, 374, 397
International Paralympic Committee (IPC) 58, 322
International Programme on the Elimination of Child Labour 373
International Wheelchair Basketball Federation (IWBF) 372–373, 397
Internet 208, 212
Internet-driven platforms 334–335, *335*
interviews and focus groups 104–105
Irving, Kyrie 345

James, LeBron 21, 354
Johan Cruyff Arena 119
Jones, Jerry 174
Jordan, Michael 16, 354

King, Billie Jean 17
Kirby, Fran 266
Knievel, Evel 16
Knight, Phil 16
Kodak 285
Korean Esport Association (KeSPA) 112

The Last Dance 339
lawn bowls 84–85, 387
leadership 358–359
League of Legends World Championship 18
legal environment, and sport marketing opportunities 88–89
leveraging sponsorship 290; defined 273; towards consumers 272; towards corporate stakeholders 273; towards employees 273
Lewis, Michael 47
Liberty Media 89
licensing 164, **165**
life cycle 121–122
lifestyle (psychographic) segmentation 122–123
lighting and sound system 219
Liverpool FC 19, 304, 346
live sites 222–224
LIV Golf 316–317, 394
logo *see* brand mark (logo)
Los Angeles Lakers 8
Louis, Spyridon 53
Lululemon Athletica Inc. 58, 61–62, 122, 267

Major League Baseball (MLB) 42, 354; in Japan 3; in United States 17; World Series 25
Major League Eating (MLE) 14–15, 384
managerialism 7
Manchester City Football Club 165
Manchester United Football Club 8, 192
marathons 53–54
Mark Cuban Center for Sports Media and Technology 326–327, 395
market analysis 101–105
market demand pricing 195
market development 106
marketers 217, 221; professional code of conduct for **371**
marketing 226, 320; ambush 284–290; angles/intentions to 23–25; cause-related 273–274; commercialisation of sport 5–8; context 2–5; customer satisfaction and 313–317; emergence of 15–19; ethics 368–371; framework *30*, 78–80; influencer 345–346; multidimensional nature of 23; objectives 113–115, **114**, 244; overview 1–2, 11–12, 13–14; parasitic 285; philosophy of 26–29; process 13; rethinking 324–332; speciality 19–22; sport consumers 70–71; sport industry 8–11; sport services 300–301; structure of *27*
marketing framework 205, 226, **227**, 256, *257*, 294, *295*, 307, 353, 356, *357*, 363, 381
marketing implementation/control: communication and delegation 359–361; control/feedback 363; control process 363–367, *364*; critical success factors 364; future connections 375–381; identify variations 365–366; implementation strategies 358–363; introduction 353–356; leadership and commitment 358–359; making corrections 366; measure performance 364–365, **365**; overview 356–358; results 365; rewards and reinforcement 362–363; set performance measures 363; sport and social responsibility 371–374; sport marketing ethics 368–371; teamwork and projects 361–362
marketing mix 102; composition **132**; innovation 153–154; place 132–133; planning 139–142; price 132; pricing variables 192; product 131–132; promotion 133
marketing opportunities 105–108; analysing market and consumers 101–105; analysing organisation 98–101; internal/external environments 80–82; SWOT analysis 82–98
market penetration 106
market positioning 118–119, 266; and differentiation 128, **129**
market research: applications of *102*; complaint analysis 105; interviews and focus groups 104–105; qualitative research 104; quantitative research 103–104; suggestion boxes 105; types of 103–105

market segmentation 120–127; approaches to using 124–127, *125*; benefits of 124; defined 120; demographic 121–122; examples **123**; geographic segmentation 123; lifestyle segmentation 122–123; market positioning/differentiation 128, **129**; process of 120–121; product behaviour segmentation 123–124; socio-economic segmentation 122; target marketing 127–128; ways of 121–124
market share 181–182
The Masters 233–234, 393
Mayweather, Floyd 235
Mbappe, Kylian 314, 345
McCormack, Mark 15–16
McDonald's 256
media: exposure **279**; social (*see* social media); sport facilities 220
Melbourne Cricket Ground 119
Melbourne Cup Carnival 246–247, 393
Mercedes-Benz Stadium 118–119
merchandisers/merchandising 220–221, 289
Messi, Lionel 345
The Metaverse 379
Middle East: sport for nation branding 165; sport industry in 19
mission statements 98–99
mobile communications 335–336
modularity 328, 333; digital sport marketing 327–329
Monday Night Football 16
Moneyball (Lewis) 47
multi-media messaging service (MMS) 335–336
multiplayer online battle arenas (MOBAs) 112
multiple segmentation 126
Mumbai Indians161–162, 390

Nadal, Rafael 266
Name, Image, and Likeness (NIL) 116–117
Nathan's Hot Dog Eating Contest 14–15
National Basketball Association (NBA) 42, 326, 354, 355–356, 396; in China 3; Finals 25
National Basketball League (NBL) 235
National Collegiate Athletic Association (NCAA) 117
National Football League (NFL) 9, 42–43, 298, 340, 354
National Hockey League (NHL) 97, 223, 340
National League of Professional Baseball Clubs 3
nation branding 165–166
NBA App 328–329, 395
NBABET 328
NBA Pick'Em 328
Netflix 89–90, 339
networked communication 330, 333; digital sport marketing 330
new business models 344–346
new entrants, threat of 96
new products testing 151–152
new technologies 200–201, 392
New York Times 11, 267
New York Yankees 8
Nicklaus, Jack 15, 233
Nielsen Media Company 59–60, 325
Nielsen's Sports Consumption Evolution Report 386
Nike 9, 16, 18, 21, 266, 267, 285, 326, 346, 354, 366–367, 371, 396
non-fungible tokens (NFTs) 355, 379
non-profit or voluntary sport sector 38, 40–41
non-sponsorship promotion 286–287
North America 19
Nothing (Amazon Prime documentary series) 340
Nottingham Forest 304

objective and task method 251–252
official sponsorships 290
off-peak pricing 196
Oiselle 107–108, 388
Olympics 3, 9, 16, 25, 28, 187, 229, 260, 267, 288, 354
Olympic Esports Series (OES) 113
organisational objectives 100–101
organisation analysis 98–101; mission statements 98–99; organisational objectives 100–101; stakeholder analysis 101; vision statements 99
Oura Ring 350
Outside 107
over the top (OTT) content 339–340, 395
ownership models and sport pricing 174–178

Palmer, Arnold 15
Par 3 tournament 233
parasitic marketing 285
Paris Saint-Germain (PSG) 43, 165
parkrun 44, 53–54, 386

'partnerships' 8–10, 21, 42, 87, 147, 256
'Pass The Rock' 328
Patagonia 371
Patrick, Danica 17
pay-per-view prices 175
pay what you can pricing 391
Peloton 176–177, 391
penetration pricing 195
people or participants, services mix 299
PepsiCo 47, 285
perceived value 187–188
percentage of sales 251
performance measures 115–117, **116**, 274–275, **276**; and required information **365**
perishability: sporting goods 141; sporting services 141; sport services 296
permission 331, 333; digital sport marketing 331–332
personal selling 232
persuasive promotions 241–242, **243**
philosophy: defined 26; of sport marketing 26–29
physical environment 301; and sport marketing opportunities 90–91
Pinterest 341
place 132–133, 204–205; sport facility as 213–221
Plank, Kevin 100
Polar 125–126, 242
Porter, Michael 94–95
positioning perceptions 281
premium pricing strategy 176
prestige pricing 194
price: in marketing mix 132; sport consumption 74; of sport-related product 177
price bundling 176, 196
price elasticity 185–186
price point 200–201
price sensitivity 182–188; and demand 182–183; perceived value 187–188; price elasticity 185–186; and supply 183–185
price skimming 194–195
pricing, sport: multifaceted issue 171–174; overview 171; and ownership models 174–178; strategic pricing process 179–202; trends in 202
pricing goals 179–182; profit-based 180, 181; sales-based 180, 181–182
pricing tactics 193–199; break-even pricing 195; competition pricing 195; cost-plus pricing 195; discount pricing 196; discriminatory pricing 196–197; exchange pricing 197; market demand pricing 195; off-peak pricing 196; penetration pricing 195; prestige pricing 194; price bundling 196; price skimming 194–195; rocket and feather pricing 197; seasonal pricing 196; status quo pricing 194; summary of **198**
pricing variables 191–193; competitor pricing 191; legal and technical boundaries 191; marketing mix 192
Principles of Scientific Management (Taylor) 11
prizefighting 229
process, sport marketing as 26
product 131–132; augmentation 144–146; behaviour segmentation 123–124; defined 13; development 106; sport 13
product life cycle 154–155, **156–157**; decline stage 155; growth phase 155; introduction phase 154–155; maturity phase 155
Professional and Amateur Sports Protection Act of 1992 (PASPA) 64
professional/corporate sport sector 38–39, 41–42
Professional Golf Association (PGA) 316
profit 178; -based pricing goals 180, 181; maximisation 181
promotion 133, 229; from advertising to promotions 226–227; ambush 286–287; integrated promotion 228–252; overview 226
promotional budget 249–250
promotional goals **243**
promotional mix 252
promotional objectives 240–243; informing 241, **243**; persuading 241–242, **243**; reminding 242, **243**; setting 247–249
promotional techniques **237–238**
promotion planning 243–252; align with marketing objectives 244; arbitrary allocation 250; competitive disparity 251; competitive parity (or equality) 250; developing promotional mix 252; objective and task method 251–252; percentage of sales 251; process *244*; pull strategy 245; push strategy 245; setting promotional budget 249–250;

setting promotional objectives 247–249; target market 244–245
promotions mix 230–240; advertising 231–232; endorsements 234–235; personal selling 232; public relations 235–239; sales promotions 235; sponsorship 232–233
psychological motives: aesthetic (visual) pleasure 63; drama and entertainment 63; escape 63; sport fans 62–63; stimulation 62
public/government sport sector 37–40
publicity 236
public relations 235–239
pull strategy 245
purchase intentions 282
push strategy 245

Qatar 165
Qatar Olympic 298
qualitative research 104
quantitative research 103–104

rapid prototyping 151–152
Rapinoe, Megan 17
Real Madrid 304
Red Bull 9, 17, 18
Red Bull Air Race 17
Red Bull Flugtag 17
Reddit 341
Reebok 354
re-enacted delight 314–315
reminder promotions 242, **243**
retail/retailers 207, 208–210, 212–213; 'bricks and mortar' 210, 212; sport **211**
revenue 178
right sponsor, choosing 264, *265*
The Ring magazine 230
Robinson, Jackie 354
rocket and feather pricing 197
Rogge, Jacques 82
Ronaldo, Cristiano 9, 345
Rugby League World Cup 9
'Rumble in the Jungle' 229
Ruth, Babe 15, 354

sales-based pricing goals 180, 181–182
sales effects 282–283, **283**; measuring **283**
sales maximisation 182
sales promotions 235
satisfaction: as evaluation tool 283; five states of **310**
satisfactory profit 181
Saudi Arabia 166
Scientific Sales Management (Hoyt) 11
scoreboards 218–219
Scottie Pippen 260
screens 218–219
seasonal pricing 196
seating 217–218
segment customers 308
self-concept motives 68; belonging and group affiliation 65; sport fans 65–66; tribal connections 65; vicarious achievement 65–66
separability: sporting goods 141; sporting services 141; sport services 296–297
sequential incident techniques (SIT) 311
service mix 299–300; people or participants 299; physical evidence 299–300; processes 300; sport services marketing and 300–301
service quality 301–305
'Shaqtin' A Fool' 328
Shell 264
signage 218–219
sincerity of the sponsor 282
Ski Dubai 91, 388
Sky Brown 260
smart sport stadiums 118–119, 389
SMS 335–336
Snapchat 341
social curation 342
social environment and sport marketing opportunities 90
social media 208, 320–350; democratisation of sport through 17; female athletes 17; integration 345; lessons for digital marketing 346–348; native experiences 347; new business models 344–346; new hub of digital sport marketing 338–350; options 340–343; other screens 343–344; platforms 342; sport marketing 349–350; technologies 322
social responsibility and sports 371–374
socio-cultural motives: cultural connections 64; family and social interaction 63–64; sport fans 63–64

socio-economic segmentation 122
software 337–338
spectator behaviour 68–70, **70**; aficionado 69, **70**; champ followers 68–69, **70**; passionate partisans 68, **70**; reclusive partisan 69, **70**; theatregoers 69, **70**
sponsoring: athlete or team 286; broadcast of an event 286; sub-category of a sport event 286
sponsors: controlling 289; major sponsorship objectives for **262**; objectives 261–262; sincerity of 282; and sport property fit/ sponsorship congruence 281–282
sponsorship evaluation 274–284; establish benchmarks 283–284; establish performance measures 274–275, **276**; measure sponsorship outcomes and report 284; review sponsorship objectives 274; select evaluation tools 275–283, **276–277**
sponsorship leveraging 271–273; towards consumers 272; towards corporate stakeholders 273; towards employees 273
sponsorship objectives 260–263; reviewing 274; sponsor objectives 261–262; sport property objectives 263, **263**
sponsorships 3, 9, 232–233, 256–260; and advertising 258; affinity 264, *265*; ambush marketing 284–290; assets 270; cause-related sport marketing 273–274; corporate social responsibility 273–274; evaluation 274–284, *275*; fan involvement 259–260; and goodwill 258; leverage official 290; leveraging 271–273; objectives 260–263; outcomes and report 284; overview 255; programme 290; property 256; proposals **268–269**, 268–270; rights 270–271; and sport marketing 21; targeting 264–267
sponsorship targeting 264–267; brand positioning or market positioning 266; right sponsor 264, *265*
sport 44–45; blind optimism 52; brand loyalty 50–51; as business 46; collaboration and competition 48–49; commercialisation of 5–8; emotion and passion 46–47; fixed supply schedule 52–53; on-field *vs.* off-field success 47; and social responsibility 371–374; variable quality 50
sport associations 289–290
sport commentators 45
sport consumers: building relationships with 305; categories of 60–61; influence on motives 67–68; marketing implications 70–71; motives 61–62; overview 57; sporting goods consumers 60; sport participants and volunteers 60–61; sport services consumers 60; sport supporters, spectators, and fans 61
sport consumption 58–60; alternative activities 74–75; balance and uncertainty 72; external factors influencing 71–76; income levels 74; likelihood of winning 72; price 74; promotional factors 74; special experiences 74; sport type 71; venue 72; weather 73–74
sport distribution 204–225; distribution channels 207–213; introduction 204–205; overview 204; problem 205–207; sport distribution problem 205–207; sport facility as 'place' 213–221; ticket distribution 221–224
sport fans 62–67; economic benefit 64; psychological motives 62–63; self-concept motives 65–66; socio-cultural motives 63–64; spectator behaviour 68–70, **70**
sport industry 8–11, 33–43; environment 92; multi-sector nature of 37–43; value chain 34, *35*
sporting goods 139, 212–213; consistency 141; consumers 60; perishability 141; separability 141; tangibility 141
sporting identification 51
sporting services 139, 141
sport leagues 2, 7–8, 48–49, 51, 191, 196, 266, 336
sport marketing strategy: developing 110, *111*; developing direction 112–113; marketing objectives 113–115, **114**; market segmentation 120–127; overview 110; performance measures 115–117, **116**; sport marketing positioning 118–119
sport museums 297–299, 394
Sport New Zealand (Sport NZ) 87–88, 387
sport organisations 221–222, 235–236, 256, 263, 372
sport participants and volunteers 60–61
sport products 13; augmentation 144–146; brand loyalty 50–51; continuum 142–143; defined 139–141; distribution issues for 210–212; features of 44–54; innovation 147–154; key variables of *144*, 144–146; overview 136–137

sport properties 256, 258; defined 256; major sponsorship objectives for **263**; objectives 263, **263**
sport regulators 49
sport services 205, 293–299, *295*; building relationships with sport consumers 305; consistency 296; consumers 60; customer relationship management 306–309; customer satisfaction 310–312; customer satisfaction and sport marketing 313–317; defining 294–299; marketing 300–301; overview 293; perishability 296; physical evidence of 299–300; processes in 300; separability 296–297; service quality 301–305; services mix 299–300; sport services 293–299; sport services marketing/service mix 300–301; tangibility 294
Spring Racing Carnival (SRC) 246
stadium experiences 304–305, 394
stakeholder analysis 101
status quo pricing 194
sticky branding 329, 333
stimulation 62
strategic pricing process 179–202; break-even analysis 189–191; price point 200–201; price sensitivity 182–188; pricing goals 179–182; pricing tactics 193–199; pricing variables 191–193; trends in sport pricing 202
streaming technology 339–340, 395
substitute products and services 97–98
suggestion boxes 105
Super Bowl 9, 24–25, 385; commercials 25
Surrey County Cricket Club 76
SWOT analysis: external environment 85–87, *86*; internal environment 82–83, **84**

tailgating 216–217, 392
tangibility: sporting goods 141; sporting services 141; sport services 294
tangible sport products 143
target customers 308
target market/marketing 127–128, 244–245
target return on investment 181
Taylor, Frederick Winslow 11
teams: controlling 289–290; knowledge and skills **362**; sponsoring 286
technology: sport facilities 220; and sport marketing opportunities 89; streaming 339–340
Ted Lasso (Apple TV series) 346
telemarketing 208
Tendulkar, Sachin 298
Thinking Basketball 328
'Thrilla in Manila' 229
ticket distribution 221–224
TikTok 138–139, 326, 335, 340, 341, 342, 378, 389
Tokyo 2020 (2021) Summer Olympic Games 28–29, 385
tools for marketing sport facilities 217–221
Tottenham Hotspur Stadium 119
Toyota 256
'transgressions' 239
transitory delight 315
transport 219
tribal connections 65
Tweetdeck 342
Twitch 339, 341, *376–377*, *397*
Twitter 326, 327, 328, 335, 354, 355

UAE 165; City Football Group (CFG) 166–167
Ultimate Fighting Championship (UFC) 229–230
Umbro 9
UN Declaration of Human Rights 373
Under Armour 9, 99–100, 267, 366–367, 388, 396
undifferentiated segmentation 126–127
UNESCO Project on Technical and Vocational Education 373
UN Global Compact 373
Union of European Football Associations (UEFA) 9
upgraded conventional technologies 336–337
US Air Force 10
US Army 10
user-generated branding (UGB) 130
user-generated content (UGC) 130–131, 324, 389
US Open 233
US PGA Championships 233

value: and pricing decisions 177–178; sport memorabilia 178
variable pricing 175
viral marketing 330
Virtual Paddock Club 347–348, 396
virtual reality sports 379
virtual stores 210

Visa 265
vision statements 99
Vodafone 256
Vonn, Lindsey 100

WADA (the World Anti-Doping Agency) 89
Wall Street Journal 267
Wanda 265
WeChat 341
Weibo 341
'WeThe15' 322–323, 394
WhatsApp 341
when things go bad! 239–240, 393
wholesalers 208–210
WHOOP 350
Williams, Serena 17, 18–19, 235, 354, 385
Williams, Venus 18
Wilson 9
Wimbledon 9
Women's Professional Bodybuilding 149–150, 390
Women's Super League (WSL) 93, 256
Women's Tennis Association (WTA) 17
Women's World Cup (FIFA) 17–18
Women's World Cup Sponsorship 265–266, 393
Woods, Tiger 233, 235
World Boxing Association (WBA) 230
World Boxing Council (WBC) 230
World Boxing Organization (WBO) 230
World Wrestling Entertainment (WWE) 4–5, 384

X 342, 355, 378; *see also* Twitter
Xero 265

Youth Olympic Games (YOG) 81–82, 387
YouTube 198–199, 328, 335, 340, 341, 342, 347, 349, 355, 379, 380–381, 392, 397

Zoom 348